Books by Ronald Steel
Pax Americana
The End of Alliance

Imperialists
and Other Heroes

Imperialists and Other Heroes

A Chronicle of the American Empire

Ronald Steel

Random House
New York

ISBN: 0-394-46255-6
Library of Congress Catalog Card Number: 75-140729

Portions of this book first appeared in *The New York Review of Books, Book Week, Commentary, Mademoiselle, The New Leader, Book World, Atlantic Monthly, The Observer, Saturday Review,* and *The New York Times Book Review.*

"Nixon's Mandate" is reprinted from the HEADLINE SERIES #193, entitled *New Directions in U.S. Foreign Policy: A Symposium.* © 1969 by the Foreign Policy Association, Inc.

"No More Vietnams" is reprinted from *Pax Americana* Revised Edition by Ronald Steel, published by The Viking Press, Inc.

Manufactured in the United States of America
The Book Press, Brattleboro, Vt.
98765432

First Edition

To Walter Lippmann

Contents

Preface

When I first started writing about foreign affairs back in the early sixties, the nation was still basking in the euphoria of the Kennedy years, and Vietnam was only a dim smudge on the horizon. That was a time when we worried about NATO, and Berlin, and Cuba, and whether Khrushchev (remember him?) had the proper respect for our young hero-President.

That was a long time ago, and we have come a long way since, although not necessarily on the path we would have liked to travel. The specter of nuclear war has been raised—NATO is irrelevant, Berlin is a matter to be settled among the Germans, and Cuba is forgotten—but we are in deeper trouble than we were during any of those cold war crises. Somewhere along the way we discovered that our motives were not so pure as we thought, that the Free World might be a euphemism for Empire, and that the effort of holding that empire together was tearing our own society apart. Vietnam taught us all that, and a good deal more.

We are learning that the rhetoric of the past quarter-century, the rhetoric so many of us grew up on, was designed to lull us to sleep. It assured us that our motives were pure, our actions noble, our ambitions self-denying.

It told us that our society, while not perfect, was the nearest thing to perfection man had achieved—and that it was getting better every day. It taught us that "liberty and justice for all," meant all, not just for whites and those who could afford a lawyer, or a doctor, or the price of a decent education. It also told us that Americans were being sent out to die so that freedom might live in such places as Korea, Vietnam, Cuba, and the Dominican Republic. But we have learned that another word for that kind of freedom is counter-revolution.

A few years ago, in a book called *Pax Americana,* I tried to show how the United States, under the stimulus of combating Soviet imperialism, developed an empire of its own, an anti-communist empire of acquiescent allies, client states, and wobbling satrapies. The essays in this collection, most of which were written since that book, deal with the formation of the empire, the military strategies it inspired, the alliance with Europe and the imperial war in Vietnam, the arenas of America's struggle to suppress revolution, and the effect of imperial politics upon our own society.

The essays stand as they were originally published, except in a few cases where I have felt it necessary to shorten them slightly or update references. Most of the longer ones first appeared in the *New York Review of Books,* and I am particularly grateful to Robert Silvers for persuading me to explore new areas, for his wise editorial advice, and for offering the space and the encouragement to deal with these issues.

While I am not sure how apparent it will be to the reader, one of the things that struck me in assembling this collection, was the change that these essays indicated in my own thinking. Whereas I started out in the early sixties as a conventional liberal—believing in much of the rhetoric of the anti-communist crusade and the values of white America—I find that I have been pushed, not always willingly, by the force of events, toward skepticism not only about our policies but our motives. I think that this is something that has been happening to a good many conventional liberals as we have been confronted by the truth of imperialism abroad and racism at home.

Where this is going to take us I cannot say, for in truth I do not know. It depends on what happens over the next few years, on whether the society can be turned away from its fascination with empire and toward the democratic resolution of its own grievous internal problems. That, in turn, depends on whether all of us have the courage to face the truth, and to deal with it accordingly.

This book is not so much a call to action as it is an attempt to understand and, perhaps underlying it all, the account of a personal journey.

R. S.

Imperialists
and Other Heroes

A
Cold War
Education

The crusade was over for me before it began. By the time I was old enough to take a serious interest in politics, the Berlin blockade was practically forgotten, the Truman Doctrine a historical document, and the Korean war put to rest with the vow that nothing like that would ever happen again. For people of my generation, those who were in college in the mid-fifties, the cold war was a matter-of-fact condition of everyday life. Although we were taught to hate and fear communism, few of us absorbed this emotionally, and we had reached our own private *détente* long before the official one was declared in the early sixties. We grew up too late for the cold war crusade and too early for the youth rebellion. We were the generation in between, going directly from adolescent conformity to adult skepticism, without ever stopping off for a genuine political passion. We missed the commitment of the true believer, but we were spared his fanaticism too. Maybe we were luckier than we realized.

Like nearly everyone else I know who was at college in the fifties, I was more concerned with football games, weekend dances, and the elusive quest for personal identity than I was with politics. The rise and fall of Senator

Joe McCarthy took place without my ever being very much aware of it, and even the Korean war passed me by because I was lucky enough to have a college deferment. It never occurred to me at the time that this was a class privilege, that in the absence of people like me the war was obviously being fought by the poor and the black. I didn't feel that I was shirking a duty by not getting my head shot off in Korea since I never could understand what we were doing there in the first place. But neither did I see anything evil about the war. So long as it didn't touch me personally, I felt little concern with it.

I was much more interested in trying to find out who I was than in thinking about foreign affairs or domestic politics. Looking at the old photos taken at the time —in front of the fraternity house in a blue blazer and narrow, striped tie surrounded by identical-looking "brothers," in the ballroom of a Chicago hotel wearing a white dinner jacket down to my knees—I cannot relate that person to me as I am today.

While there is no precise point when the pattern began to change, I suppose it happened somewhere near the end of my freshman year, when my fraternity brothers ceased looking like Dick Stovers and began to resemble the dull louts briefly glimpsed in *The Graduate*. When I returned from summer vacation, I moved off campus into a drab little room, which seemed exotic to me at the time because it gave me the privacy I had never had. The rooming house also threw me into contact with people whose existence I had barely been aware of—those who had not been invited to join a fraternity, or, incomprehensibly, had not wanted to.

Gradually I came to appreciate qualities in these people —irony, detachment, independence, even alienation— that I had never noticed among my fraternity brothers. I stopped taking my meals at the fraternity house, skipped most of the parties, dated girls with long hair and dirty Burberrys who didn't belong to any sorority, took to hanging around a bookstore where seedy-looking history and English lit majors played chess all day and argued all night. By my junior year I had formally dropped out of the fraternity, thrown away my white bucks, moved into an "international house" where I had a black roommate, stopped going to football games, took courses in Joyce, Yeats, and the French symbolist poets, scorned the world of commerce and industry, and mused about going to Paris and living in a garret. I had, in the context of the times and by the definition of those around me, become what used to be called a bohemian.

Actually I was quite conventional. I did not go off to Paris and write a book in an attic (at least not until much later). I did not head for Mexico in search of mushrooms. I did not go to California and become a beatnik. In fact, I doubt that I ever heard of people like Jack Kerouac and Gregory Corso until *Life* magazine finally got on to them. I was timid, unimaginative, and confused about what I should do with my life. While I had decided that the academic world was not for me, and while I knew I could never go into my father's business or any other, I couldn't think of a single thing I sincerely wanted to do. More out of inertia than anything else, I let myself be drafted into the U.S. Army.

I can't expect anyone of college age today to understand this. In fact, I don't even know how to explain it to myself. All I can say is that it was peacetime. The Korean war was over, nobody was getting shot, and since I took it for granted that sometime or other I would have to serve in the army, it seemed like a good idea to get it over with before I started on a career. Secretly, I was also relieved at deferring the career decision for two years, and hoped that by the time I got out of the army I would have a better idea of what I wanted to do with my life.

As it turned out, I didn't. But I did learn what I did not want: to shuffle papers, to carry out nonsensical commands, to spend time doing work that was boring or meaningless—which is what most of my time in uniform consisted of. This didn't leave much, as I learned when I got my army discharge and went to New York to look for a job. In fact, my job-hunting experience was so discouraging that I decided that I would either have to go back to school for a degree that would allow me to teach, or else try to find something in the government.

Over this period my interest in politics had sharpened considerably. Through the intercession of a kindly professor I had won a scholarship which allowed me to do graduate work in political science. My army experience in Europe had convinced me that I wanted to deal in some aspect of foreign affairs—preferably through involvement rather than academic contemplation. Diplomacy seemed a logical choice, and I took the exams to enter the Foreign Service.

My second stint on a government payroll can best be described by Marx's comment about history repeating itself first as tragedy, then as farce. Not long after I solemnly swore to defend the Constitution and be the President's faithful emissary, it became obvious to me, if not to my superiors, that the diplomatic life was not for me. The civilian bureaucracy was the army all over again—a different uniform, but the same rules nobody could explain, the same assumption that people are "personnel" and personnel are mentally retarded, and even, as we used to say in the army, the same chicken-shit.

It was not that I was asked to carry out policies that seemed silly or misconceived, although that was often the way I felt about them. Rather, it was that I was no more involved in foreign policy than the elevator operator, and considerably less so than the ambassador's chauffeur. Despite my imposing title of vice-consul, I was a glorified houseboy, entrusted with such delicate tasks as making sure there were enough towels in the washrooms, that the air conditioners worked, and the luggage did not get lost when people were transferred from places like Tegucigulpa to Nicosia.

I knew the insult was not personal. This was, after all, the common lot of junior Foreign Service officers, and my colleagues, many of whom were intelligent and dedicated people, bore their tasks with humor and a saintly grace. I discovered that I had neither their patience nor their dedication. After a stint abroad that was in many ways enlightening, but where my professional duties consisted mostly of filling out requisition forms in sextuplet, I decided to take my leave of the Foreign Service and return to what we then referred to as Stateside. Through a series of trials and errors I got a job writing on foreign affairs for a weekly magazine, and eventually started doing political articles on my own.

I bring all this into my narrative not from an assumption that my career was unique, but rather because in many ways it was typical of the problems faced by many people of my generation—of our efforts to find a job worth doing and to create an identity for ourselves that reflected our own experience of the world. While we never felt that society owed us a living, we were brought up to believe that we could find a decent living within it. We were taught that work was honorable, self-fulfilling, and socially useful. And we believed that fulfillment came from finding whatever niche was best suited for us.

What a shock it was when we discovered, in our own fumbling way and in our own good time, that there was no decent niche worth filling. Those of us lucky enough to get a college education gradually discovered what those who worked in factories knew all along: that within the confines of the System every job was piece-work. You were programmed for a job—either at an assembly line or in an office—you did it, you punched in and out, you kept your nose clean, and you got your weekly paycheck, with deductions, of course. It turned out that we were all in the same boat. Even success turned out to be meaningless in a society where you could make it one day and be nothing the next. What did it mean to be a cog in the world's biggest industrial-bureaucratic machine?

We discovered that the American Dream was unreal. By the evidence of our own lives we were forced to let it go. While we rejected it a lot more quietly than those who followed us, we rejected it nonetheless. In a sense, we paved the way for the others. The price we paid for it was confusion, guilt, and psychoanalysis. We thought there must be something wrong with us because we could not find a niche for ourselves within the System. Now that we have found a niche of one kind or another, we know that it is the System itself that is wrong. It is corrupt and it is also corrupting. Our parents took it for granted, we rebelled against it, and the young have rejected it categorically. For us this rebellion was a deeply troubling experience because we had to work out our own ground rules, often painfully and with little help from anyone. For the young it is a crusade, with the demarcation lines already established.

Because we hacked the way, we do not find the younger generation either incomprehensible or threatening. Confused, intolerant, sanctimonious—yes. But also committed, sympathetic, and vital. Here is where we part company with our elders, many of whom fear and even hate the young. We cannot do this because we are a part of them. We have a foot in both worlds and belong fully to neither. Unable to believe in the old values of self-denial, patriotism, and order, we also cannot fully accept the new values of guiltless permissiveness, pacifism, and moral absolutism. Understanding the language of both sides, we cannot adopt either as our own.

The reason, I think, is that we cannot believe in absolutes. Categorical imperatives are not for us. Our elders talk of patriotism, respect for the law, and defense of the Free World, and we know that these decent words cover shabby actions that can better be described as intimidation, injustice, and exploitation. The young talk of pigs, fascism, and revolution, and we wonder whether they have any idea what fascism really is, or whether the kind of revolutionary society they praise is not more repressive than the one we have. We see all too clearly, and with the help of the young, what is wrong with America—its injustice, its ugliness, its acceptance of poverty amidst plenty, its racism, its imperialism. But we also know that violence on the left breeds repression and counter-violence on the right, and the end of that particular road is the police state.

If the young often seem intolerant and ready to jump at instant solutions, our elders seem mired in the dead past: the Depression, the War, and the competition with

Russia. The Second World War, which most of us are too young to remember except through the movies, was the last war that conceivably could be defined as just. What followed the defeat of Germany and Japan was a series of dynastic struggles between the new super-powers. Korea, like Vietnam, now seems like just another imperial war for spheres of influence, and the cold war itself little more than a power contest between rival empires, both prevented from launching a full-scale war from fear of suffering instant obliteration.

Can there be anybody under forty who sincerely believes in the *morality* of American foreign policy, or that such a word is relevant to any nation's diplomacy? The faith of our fathers was buried for us at Hiroshima and Nagasaki, and its benediction read periodically at places like Guatemala, the Bay of Pigs, Santo Domingo, and Vietnam. We know that what America has done in Asia and the Caribbean is no better than what France or Britain did in their colonies before they were forced to give them up. Unlike the young, however, we cling to the belief that, Vietnam excepted, it is not much worse.

While we wince at people who brandish the flag as though it were a good luck charm to be plastered on windshields, or as a symbol of defiance against those who question the old values of patriotism and obedience, we do not feel any desire to spit on it or burn it. Maybe we find it irrelevant. I don't know anyone of my generation who gets a lump in his throat when "The Star Spangled Banner" is played, or who, like Lyndon Johnson, could declare, "I have seen the sunrise on Mont Blanc, but the most beautiful vision that these eyes ever beheld was the flag of my country in a foreign land." But I also don't know anyone who looks on it as a symbol of evil. For people of my generation, America is neither the "last best hope of earth," nor the leading outpost of fascism. Rather, it is a place of infinite promise and spotty fulfillment, where much has been accomplished but a great deal has gone wrong, and where the conflict between what it is and what it might be has led to a kind of national schizophrenia.

I think the young have a legitimate grievance against our society, and I respect them for their passion and their faith in the trampled ideals of American democracy. Also, I think we should be grateful to them for forcing us to pay something more than lip service to those ideals. They came out against the war without the qualifications that paralyzed so many liberals, and they taught us that much of what passes for mature responsibility is simple hypocrisy. By shouting the truth when nobody wanted to listen, they made us discover that we, too, have a voice.

No longer being in my twenties, I don't take an apocalyptic view of what is happening in this country. I continue to believe that there is a core of essential decency and common sense in Americans that can be tapped by leaders willing to tell the truth. I think that white America has gradually (if grudgingly) come to accept the Negro's right to full equality, and that all Americans would like nothing better than to wash their hands of Vietnam, foreign interventions, and self-assumed "responsibilities of power." I do not believe that our present national leaders are fascists, or that all policemen are pigs, or that any group of people (hard hats, the lower middle class, Birchites) can be written off as beyond redemption and treated as though their anxieties didn't matter.

Like the young, I am worried about a social system that consigns millions of people to misery and ignorance because of the color of their skin or where they happened to be born, about growing militarism in our society, and the ravaging of our landscape and the pollution of our air and water in the name of progress. There is a lot of loose talk about social crisis, but that seems to me where Americans are today in their relations with one another. We were never a unified people, but at least we had a tolerance for individual differences that gave a framework to our diversities. But the dialogue and the sense of tolerance have been broken. The old refuse to listen to the young, the whites to the blacks, the rich to the poor. Two nations are being carved from one, two Americas that have nothing to say to each other, and even if they did, could not communicate for they speak mutually incomprehensible languages.

The chasm is not only between the generations and the races, but also—contradictory though it may be to the American ethic—between classes. The myth of the melting pot has been destroyed, and millions of middle and lower-class Americans are seething with resentment over their inability to find status, security, or respect. Unable to strike out at the real causes of their alienation, even if they understood them, these people feel cheated and seek the most obvious scapegoats—the blacks, the intellectuals, and even their own children. To relieve this alienation is a task of education. This means showing Middle America —with its tinny household gadgets and cars, its polluted air and water, its stultifying jobs, its terror of sinking into a lower class, its hypocrisy about sex and religion—that it is a victim of the very social and economic order it upholds so vehemently. For the young it means toning down a lot of silly talk about revolution, recognizing that getting stoned is no more revolutionary than getting drunk, realizing that random violence against the symbols of authority only plays into the hands of the forces of repression.

Underlying the fear of change is the growing realization that it must take place if the society is not to be torn apart by violence, repression, and even some form of guerrilla warfare. The young and the black have been in the forefront of this movement for social change. But they cannot accomplish it without the support of a majority which has for too long been silent in the face of racial injustice, exploitation, social inequities, and imperial adventurism.

That voice has not yet been aroused, but there are signs that Middle America is becoming aware of what has to be done, and, with a continuing faith in moderation, is seeking a middle way out, somewhere between the equally destructive extremes of revolution and repression. Despite its understandable fear of violence and its incomprehension of much of what is happening in American society today—from the drug culture and commercialized sex to the banning of school prayers—Middle America is still groping for a peaceful solution.

This puts a heavy responsibility on those who advocate change, for it means that in addition to being agitators they must be educators. It is not enough to rail against pollution, racism, and imperialism. There is the higher responsibility of making others aware of what exists, and what can be done about it. Usually what must be done can be accomplished within the framework of the social system—given the will and the ability to educate the public. To some this may lack drama—or guts. It certainly offers no instant solutions. But the real revolutionaries of a society such as ours are those who influence the way that people think about their world, and thereby lead them to do something about changing it. Change begins with education, whether it be the exhortations of Malcolm X or the proddings of Ralph Nader. Malcolm was a great leader because he was a great educator, and when he spoke he was urged on by his listeners with a cry, "teach, brother." We all need to be taught about what is happening to us so that we will be able to act.

The demand for change is everywhere—among young doctors who are in revolt against the shame of medical care in this country, among factory workers who are challenging conservative union leaders, among middle-class parents who do not understand why their children cannot receive an adequate education, and among all Americans at the near-breakdown of essential public services, such as mass transportation, pollution control, and protection from criminal violence. There is even the recognition that foreign policy, which is no longer abstract and remote from people's lives, has escaped popular control and has become bureaucratized, militarized, and elitist.

While discontent is rife at every level of society, there is no assurance that it will lead to structural change. None of those who have been seeking new social structures have as yet been able to organize on a large scale, nor have they developed plausible theories to show how large corporations and government bureaucracies can be brought under control and operated with greater public responsibility. Both kinds of political work reman to be done, and the need is urgent.

The search for new alternatives could be side-tracked and bought off with palliatives. It could well be smothered in the formulas of the old welfare liberalism or the modish imagery that we have come to associate with Kennedyism. The changes that are necessary to reform this society are not going to be accomplished by a single charismatic leader miraculously striking forth to solve our problems. We have wasted too much time waiting for leaders, watching them fail to keep their promises, and then mourning what they might have been once they have disappeared. It is a delusion to put much faith in a leader, and it is an evasion of responsibility. In a society where men are truly free, they need not seek salvation in their leaders. Happy the land, as Brecht once wrote, that needs no hero.

An inveterate optimist, I like to think that America can change and that it will change in ways that will fulfill its promise and its ideals. There is too much that is good about this country, too much that is vital, creative, and decent, to let it fall victim to fear and repression. I happen to believe that American democracy, for all its flaws, is an impressive achievement. Although for many people; particularly the blacks and the poor, it is mostly a sham, it can be made a reality for all, if we want to take the effort and the pain to do it.

It won't be easy and much of it will not be very pleasant. The time is coming when it may be no easier to be a white radical (and I don't mean a revolutionary) in places like Los Angeles or Detroit, than it was to be a freedom rider in Mississippi in the mid-Sixties, or than it is to be a Black Panther today. There will be a lot more cracked heads, a lot more people calling for repression in the name of law and order, the creation of something very much approaching local fascism in some cities, and a growing pressure for all of us—whether we consider ourselves liberals, radicals, pacifists, or even conservatives—to lay ourselves on the line in defense of the values our education as Americans has taught us to believe in. The sidelines are getting narrower all the time.

The search for new alternatives is not a question of liberalism or conservatism or radicalism and it would be self-defeating to fall into the old trap of labels. The liberalism of the 1930s, in its various latter-day incarnations, such as the New Frontier and the Great Society, has become a bankrupt philosophy with few answers for the problems that beset contemporary American society. Often it is barely aware of how serious these problems are. Nor is there any other ideology in which we can put our faith. American conservatism, for all its emphasis on the integrity of the individual, is a formula for social irresponsibility and a rigidified class society. Radicalism, for its part, is not a program, or even a philosophy, but rather a way of perception. As such it is a tool of analysis, not an alternate political system.

What are we left with? No formulas, ideologies, or solutions. But perhaps the realization that there are no answers in conventional labels and rhetoric. Whatever hope there is lies in our ability to see things as they are, to ask the right questions, and to suspect those with ready solutions. Above all it lies in re-examining what we have learned to take for granted. From that point on, nothing is certain. But until that point, nothing is possible.

I. ROMANTIC IMPERIALISTS

Present At the Creation, Acheson's *apologia pro vita sua* is a masterly defense of his roles as Assistant Secretary of State from 1941–45, Under Secretary from 1945–47, and Secretary of State from 1949 53. He does not in this book deal with the earlier years, covered with considerable charm in his memoir *Morning and Noon*. The son of an Episcopal bishop, Acheson attended Groton, Yale, and Harvard Law School, and went to Washington in 1919 as law clerk to Justice Brandeis. There he met the mighty and the rich, joined the influential law firm that is today known as Covington and Burling, briefly served as Under Secretary of the Treasury under Roosevelt, established the contacts and polished the manner that allowed him to circulate in the highest realms of finance and government, and returned to the administration at the outbreak of the war. It is at this point that his present narrative begins.

As is evident from his prose and his public behavior, Acheson is neither cold nor unflappable. Beneath the urbane elegance and the studied arrogance there is an emotional man whose temper has more than once got the better of him and who likes a good fight even if he has to pick it himself. At several points he describes himself as a would-be schoolteacher, trying to inform the ninnies in Congress and elsewhere on the facts of political life. But the more appropriate word is brigadier. Acheson was never interested in education. What he wanted was compliance, acceptance, surrender. People were stupid in so far as they opposed him, and enlightened whenever they agreed.

As chief architect of American foreign policy under Harry Truman, Acheson had a stormy tenure in the State Department—owing, in no small part, to his own contentiousness and belligerence. Although much abused by headline-hunting right-wing politicians such as Nixon and Joseph McCarthy, he also abused others and suffered from his inability to conceive that his might not be the ultimate wisdom on every issue. His career in public life is the story of a man who was too clever for himself,

The foundation stones for the anti-communist empire were laid down shortly after the end of the Second World War. George Kennan's celebrated policy for the "containment" of the Soviet Union in Eastern Europe served as the intellectual scaffolding for those, like Dean Acheson and John Foster Dulles, who wanted to construct an American-designed "Free World" from the North Sea to the Tonkin Gulf. This was the period of the Korean war, the formation of the alphabet alliances, the support for the French in Indochina, and the interventions in Guatemala and Lebanon. Under Kennedy the vocabulary became rather less messianic, and the military strategy was flexibly designed to carry out interventions without setting off nuclear war. The intellectuals of the New Frontier were not fundamentalists like Dulles, and, in fact, continually vaunted their pragmatism. Nor were they, for the most part, ideologues— even though at times they seemed mesmerized by the effort to forge a counter-ideology to the communism they were combatting. Rather, they were convinced imperialists who believed in the political and economic necessity for the American empire, as well as in its moral superiority.

Throughout the cold war the unparalleled military, economic, and political power of the United States has been put at the service of a talented, dedicated corps of imperial managers. In many respects their premises are shared by a whole generation of Americans that came to maturity in a time of economic crisis, fought a war that brought no peace, and were saddled with the burdens of empire in the name of a higher morality. The advocates of America's imperial foreign policy are not, as some purists on the New Left would have it, a small band of conspirators. They are everyone who benefits from the military machine and its offspring: congressmen and generals, contractors and defense plant workers, shipbuilders and scientists on Pentagon research grants.

The managers of the cold war empire come and go. Acheson and Dulles gave way to Dean Rusk and Henry Kissinger, Douglas MacArthur to Maxwell Taylor. But their instruments remain the same: the formal alliances and the military assistance programs, the Voice of America and the CIA, foreign aid and selected coups and interventions. While they formally deny the effort to forge a Pax Americana, their policies have been based on just such an ambition. The Cuban missile crisis was their moment of glory, and Vietnam was supposed to have been their Austerlitz. It turned instead into their Waterloo. What we are now experiencing is the bitter morning after.

●

Commissar of the Cold War

"I hope that Mr. Acheson will write a book explaining how he persuaded himself to believe that a government could be conducted without the support of the people."
—Walter Lippmann

The wish has now been granted. Seventeen years after leaving the State Department, Dean Acheson has finally unveiled his memoirs of those tumultuous days. He was wise to wait. The unhappy Truman Administration, embellished by the passing of time and the fading of memories, has taken on a historical patina. The New Left is too young to remember the China White Paper, the Berlin airlift, or the Korean war, and probably never even heard of John Carter Vincent or Owen Lattimore. Cold war liberals hope that most people have forgotten their role in the Truman Doctrine and the rearmament of Germany—two of the capstones of Acheson's tenure as Secretary of State. And the Right, which once, bizarre as it now seems, accused him of being sympathetic to the communists, has found new virtues in the tart elder statesman who defends the Vietnam war and extols the misunderstood governments of Rhodesia and South Africa.

whose intelligence was often self-destructive, and whose arrogance never allowed him to realize it.

This densely printed volume of nearly 800 pages is a defense of those policies taken when Acheson was a good deal more than merely "present at the creation" of the post-war world. The prose rolls on majestically and inexorably in a mighty tide of recapitulations, explanations, character sketches, put-downs of those who disagreed or displeased, and self-justifications. It is an impressive but not quite convincing achievement. While one does not expect the memoirs of public officials to be dispassionate, it is unfortunate that Acheson is not able to look back on that period with the objectivity gained from hindsight. Acheson not only knows what happened, but orchestrated the cold war empire during its formative years. He is singularly equipped to help put that dark period into an honest historical perspective. But what he has produced, however fascinating, is something less than the whole truth, not so much false as it is selective.

Much that is relevant has either been omitted or summarily dismissed. Invariably these are items that cast doubt on the wisdom of his judgment or the ineluctability of his decisions. "It could not have been otherwise" is the theme that runs through his account of the famous White Paper on China, as well as of policies of such dubious wisdom as the Truman Doctrine, the rearmament of Germany, the Japanese Peace treaty, and the intervention in Korea. That it could, perhaps should, have been otherwise is apparently, from these memoirs, not a judgment that an honorable man could have held at the time.

With customary modesty, Acheson reminds us that he has a reputation for "not suffering fools gladly." What he seems to mean is that he does not suffer critics, for he records few instances of arguments other than his own as having any merit. He is contemptuous of Congress for daring to infringe on what he deems executive prerogatives, such as undeclared acts of war. He upbraids Senator Kenneth Wherry for suggesting that perhaps Truman should have sought Congressional authorization before sending troops to Korea, and chastises what he terms "the kind of sulky opposition that characterized the last two years of relations between the Senate Committee on Foreign Relations and the Johnson Administration"—in other words, the Fulbright Committee's hearings on the Vietnam war and the hastily granted and leisurely repented Tonkin Gulf Resolution.

Among the numerous individuals who crossed his path and made his life more troublesome, there is curiously not a single reference to Richard M. Nixon, who first showed his gift for phrase-making by referring to the then Secretary of State as the "Dean of the Cowardly College of Communist Containment." How curious that this episode seems to have slipped Acheson's otherwise retentive mind.

A broker in power, Acheson was fascinated by its use. Like Truman, for whom he expresses so much admiration, he exercised it with a pleasure bordering on the obscene. He favored the unconditional surrender of Japan and never questioned Truman's decision to use the atomic bomb. When Mossadegh nationalized the British-owned oil wells in Iran, he supported the oil cartel's embargo, cut off American aid, tried to drive the nationalist premier from office, and set the stage for the CIA coup in the summer of 1953 that brought back the Shah and cut the American oil companies a sizeable slice of the formerly British-controlled pie.

Like his disciple Dean Rusk, he was a military-minded Secretary of State: a hawk in Berlin and Korea, a hawk at the Bay of Pigs and during the Cuban missile crisis, and a hawk on Vietnam. In his book of diplomacy, negotiation is a dirty word, the sort of thing a respectable great power ought not to engage in. He felt, as Coral Bell pointed out in her critique of Acheson's diplomacy, *Negotiation from Strength,* you cannot negotiate when you are weak, and when you are strong there is no need to negotiate. He certainly saw no need to negotiate with the Russians ("Soviet authorities are not moved to agreement by negotiation") and instead preferred to create what he called "situations of strength" to gain what he wanted without giving up anything in return.

George Kennan's various proposals for a settlement with the Russians had little appeal for Acheson, who felt that "to seek a *modus vivendi* with Moscow would prove chimerical." He did, however, like certain parts of Kennan's analysis of Soviet behavior contained in the "long telegram" from Moscow of February 1946 (later summarized in the famous "X" article as the "containment doctrine"), particularly statements about the "Kremlin's neurotic view of world affairs," and its methods to "infiltrate, divide and weaken the West." Acheson took what he wanted from Kennan, rejecting as of "no help" his recommendations that we try to understand Russia's view of the world and keep our own house in order. But he found that Kennan's "predictions and warnings could not have been better" for the get-tough policy he was already formulating.

The first testing of the new diplomacy came early in 1947 when the British informed Washington that they could no longer afford the cost of supporting the Greek royalist government against communist insurgents. Acheson, substituting for Secretary Marshall, convinced Truman of the need to preserve the Western sphere of influence in the eastern Mediterranean. Congress was asked to provide $400 million for emergency aid to Greece, with Turkey thrown in for good measure. During the initial briefing, the Congressmen were skeptical about providing help for Britain's client state. Instead of arguing that the balance of power required U.S. intervention, an argument which he evidently assumed his audience would not understand, Acheson chose to scare them with the specter of communism running rampant. "Like the apples in a barrel infected by one rotten one," he told the skeptical legislators,

> the corruption of Greece would infect Iran and all to
> the East. It would also carry infection to Africa through
> Asia Minor and Egypt, and to Europe through Italy
> and France, already threatened by the strongest do-

mestic communist parties in Western Europe. The Soviet Union was playing one of the greatest gambles in
history at minimal cost. It did not need to win all the
possibilities. Even one or two offered immense gains.
We and we alone were in a position to break up the
play. These were the stakes that British withdrawal
from the eastern Mediterranean offered to an eager and
ruthless opponent.

Of course, as Milovan Djilas later pointed out, not only
was Stalin not instigating the communist uprising in
Greece, but was actually trying to discourage it and told
the Yugoslavs to stop supporting it. "What do you think,"
Djilas quotes Stalin as saying in February 1948, "that
Great Britain and the United States—the United States,
the most powerful state in the world—will permit you to
break their line of communication in the Mediterranean?
Nonsense. And we have no navy. The uprising in Greece
must be stopped, and as quickly as possible."

But Acheson was not interested in such subtleties at
the time, nor is he now. His lurid analysis scared the legislators, and the Greek-Turkish aid bill was sent to Congress on March 12, 1947, encapsuled in the message that
came to be known as the Truman Doctrine. In his pride
over the doctrine, Acheson neglects to mention what one
learns from Charles Bohlen's *The Transformation of
American Foreign Policy*—that Secretary of State General
Marshall, who was at the time en route to Moscow with
Bohlen, thought the message unduly severe and asked
Truman to change it:

> When we received the text of the President's message,
> we were somewhat startled to see the extent to which
> the anti-communist element of this speech was stressed.
> Marshall sent back a message to President Truman
> questioning the wisdom of this presentation, saying
> he thought that Truman was overstating the case a
> bit. The reply came back that from all his contacts
> with the Senate, it was clear that this was the only
> way in which the measure could be passed.

In assessing the Truman Doctrine it is important to remember that in the spring of 1947 the discord between

Russia and the West had not yet hardened into the confrontation of the cold war. The division of Europe was not yet completed, and at the time many believed that the Truman Doctrine was hastening it. Particularly troubling was the sentence, which later came to be considered the key part of the Doctrine, in which Truman declared:

> I believe that it must be the policy of the United States to support free peoples who are resisting attempted subjugation by armed minorities or by outside pressures.

In this seemingly innocuous sentence there lay what was later to become a formula for the repression of revolutionary movements. Gradually the American people became convinced, above all by the propaganda of their own government, that they were involved in a life-or-death struggle with an ideology. Communism, whatever its form, became equated with a threat to America's survival.

The fault lies with the cold war liberals such as Acheson. They treated the American people cynically, thinking they could be manipulated, giving them injections of anti-communism in order to get through military appropriations they felt inadequate to explain otherwise. Acheson is not the only offender, but he is among the worst, for he was intelligent enough to know what he was doing. With a distaste for public opinion bordering on contempt, he did not tell the truth to Congress and he did not tell the truth to the people. The wave of anti-communism Acheson helped to unleash proved far too powerful for him to handle, especially after McCarthy appeared on the scene. It paralyzed him as Secretary of State, discredited the office he held, justly drove the Democrats from office, and made it virtually impossible for the nation to follow a rational foreign policy. Treat the people with contempt, and you will be treated contemptuously in return. That is the lesson of Dean Acheson's presence at the creation, and the greater misfortune is that we have all been paying for it ever since.

In selling the Truman Doctrine to a skeptical Congress,

Acheson laid down the basic tenets of American post-war foreign policy: the ideological division of the world, the equation of "freedom" with American strategic and political interests, the belief that every outpost of the empire (the "free world"), however unimportant it might be in itself, must be prevented from falling under communist control lest the entire structure be threatened (collective security). These were Acheson's justifications for Korea, as they are for Vietnam.

As part of his program, as he phrases it, to "shock the country . . . into facing a growing crisis," Acheson followed up the Truman Doctrine with a speech in Mississippi on May 8, 1947, in which he laid down the outlines of what became the Marshall Plan. While he refrains from taking full credit for the European Recovery Program, granting the official parenthood to General Marshall, he describes his speech as a "reveille" which awakened the American people to the "duties of that day of decision."

The Marshall Plan is, of course, considered an unprovocative act of enlightened self-interest that saved Western Europe from falling into the communist orbit. But at the time many Europeans, despite the economic crisis they were facing, feared American assistance presented in a form that might antagonize Moscow. As Louis Halle has observed, in *The Cold War as History*, "When the offer of rescue came at last, in the form of the Marshall Plan, it undoubtedly did contribute to the final fall of Czechoslovakia and its incorporation in the Russian empire." To Stalin's mind the Marshall Plan, coming hot on the heels of the Truman Doctrine, was a design for an anti-communist Western Europe backed up by American military power. This, one recalls, was at a moment when the United States still had an atomic monopoly, and when certain high officials in the government were calling for a "preventive" nuclear strike against the Soviet Union. We cannot know what effect a different American posture would have had on Stalin's plans. But from the record available to us it seems clear that the hardening American attitude reinforced traditional Russian fears of isolation by hostile forces and led the Kremlin to tighten its grip on the territories already under its control. The Russians rejected Washington's call to cooperate in the European Recovery Program and forbade their satellites from participating—just as Washington expected they would. As Charles Bohlen further notes in *Transformation:*

> Kennan and I . . . said we were convinced that the Soviet Union could not accept the plan if it retained its original form, because the basis of self-help and the fact that the United States was to have a voice with the receiving country as to how the aid was used would make it quite impossible for the Soviet Union to accept . . .

Russia's rejection was greeted with relief in Washington and saved the Marshall Plan from almost certain Congressional dismemberment. The breach was widened.

The division of Europe was sealed in the winter of 1948 by the coup in Czechoslovakia and the blockade of Berlin. Today it is assumed that the blockade was an unprovoked act of Soviet aggression to push the Western allies out of Berlin. But it was not that clear-cut. In retrospect, the Russian aim was to prevent the United States, together with Britain and France, from establishing an independent, anti-communist West German state. Nothing that happened during this or any other period can excuse the ruthlessness with which Soviet puppet regimes treated the peoples of Eastern Europe and East Germany. For the most part, however, Russia's diplomatic moves were made in response to Western initiatives, as the sequence of events reveals: In May 1947, the U.S. and Britain fused their occupation zones into an economic union. The next month General Marshall proposed the European Recovery Program in his speech at Harvard, and a month later Washington announced that the German economy was to be self-sustaining. In August, the Germans were allowed to increase production to the 1936 level, and at this point the French agreed to fuse their zone with the other two. "By November," Acheson reports, "the three allies were able to present a solid front to the Russians."

The inability of the Western allies to work together with Russia in governing Germany led to discussions in London in February and March 1948 toward the creation of an independent German state in the Western zones: the so-called "London Program." That same February the Russians gave the go-ahead for the coup in Czechoslovakia, and, upon the allies' signing the Brussels Defense Pact, walked out of the Allied Control Council in Berlin. The U.S., Britain, and France proceeded with the integration of their zones, and in June announced they would proceed to form a West German government with "the minimum requirements of occupation and control." As a first step they set up a separate currency for West Germany.

This, in Acheson's words, "triggered the final break with the Soviet Union in Germany." Five days after the announcement of the Western currency reform, the Russians set up their own currency system for East Germany and all Berlin. The Allies responded by extending the West German currency reform to Berlin (still under four-power control). The next day the Russians imposed a full blockade on Berlin.

For Acheson, this sequence of events, culminating in a separate West German state, was a triumph of U.S. diplomacy. But it solidified the division of Europe. Was it entirely the fault of the Russians, or was Moscow reacting defensively? According to George Kennan, chief of the policy planning staff of the State Department at the time:

> There can be no doubt that, coming as it did on top of the European recovery program and the final elaboration and acceptance of the Atlantic alliance, the move toward establishment of a separate government in Western Germany aroused keen alarm among the Soviet leaders. It was no less than natural that they should do all in their power to frustrate this undertaking and to bring the three Western powers back to the negotiating table in order that Russia might continue to have a voice in all-German affairs.

Kennan feared that the London Program, providing for a separate West German state, would induce the Russians to set up a rival government in the East, and "the fight would be on for fair; the division of Germany, and with it the division of Europe itself, would tend to congeal." Instead of a separate arrangement for Berlin, he favored a settlement for Germany as a whole involving the withdrawal of Russian troops. In November 1948, the Planning Staff presented a package entitled "Plan A," which provided for a new provisional German government under international supervision, withdrawal of allied forces to garrisons on the periphery of Germany, and complete demilitarization of the country. Kennan says the plan was never seriously considered: "Mr. Acheson, if I read his mind correctly in retrospect, regarded it as no more than a curious . . . aberration," while "the London Program . . . was being rushed frantically to completion with the scarcely concealed intention that it should stand as a *fait accompli* before the Big Four Foreign ministers."

Acheson's formula for German reunification, expressed at the foreign ministers' meeting in Paris in May 1949, was "to extend the Bonn constitution to the whole country." This would, of course, not only have eliminated the pro-Soviet regime in the Eastern zone, but have brought a unified Germany into the Western camp. As Acheson was no doubt aware, this possibility was anathema not only to the Russians but to the East (and even West) Europeans who had twice been invaded by Germany in this century and were opposed to reunification under any conditions.

Of course Acheson did not seriously expect the Russians to accept. He wanted to anchor West Germany firmly to NATO and feared that unification through neutrality would lead to European neutrality, if not communization. In his eyes there was nothing to negotiate, other than a Russian withdrawal from Eastern Europe— for which he was willing to give up nothing in return. He believed the United States must stand firm everywhere the status quo was tested, such as Berlin, and later in such places as Korea and Vietnam, lest the Soviets be tempted to make even greater incursions elsewhere.

Like his followers Rusk and Rostow, Acheson saw every situation as a global confrontation. There were no local contests, but only localized testing of America's will to resist Soviet (or Chinese, or simply "communist") aggression. As part of his policy of creating situations of strength, Acheson was engaged in a race against time to build up German and European military power before the participants lost interest, "to achieve the European Defense Community and end the occupation in Germany before ebb tide in Europe and America lowered the level of will too far."

A momentary threat to these plans came in March 1952, when Stalin sought four-power talks on a German peace treaty. Stalin's proposal differed from previous ones in calling for a reunified Germany free of foreign troops, neutralized, demilitarized, and with the boundaries agreed upon at Potsdam. Acheson surmised, quite correctly, that this was designed to prevent the further integration of Germany into the West. It was, in his words, "a spoiling operation." Rather than an unified neutral Germany, Acheson, like Adenauer, wanted a divided Germany with the strongest segment linked to the West. If Stalin were really serious, German unification would have meant abandoning NATO. The price was too high.

Although he knew better, Acheson persisted in equating communism with Soviet imperialism even in cases where it obviously did not apply. This is a legacy he passed on to his protégé, Dean Rusk, whom he later recommended to Kennedy for Secretary of State. As Acheson's Assistant Secretary of State for Far Eastern Affairs, Rusk in 1951, declared that China is "a colonial Russian government—a Slavic Manchukuo on a large scale—it is not the government of China. It does not pass the first test. It is not Chinese." This insistence on a Russian-controlled communist monolith helped Acheson to squeeze foreign and military aid out of a recalcitrant Congress and to justify policies which might otherwise have seemed unjustifiable. "Of course we opposed the spread of communism," he writes of U.S. policy in Asia with the marvelous assurance of one whose hypocrisy has moved on to the higher plane of self-congratulation, "it was the subtle, powerful instrument of Russian imperialism, designed and used to defeat the very interests we shared with the Asian peoples, the interest in their own autonomous development uncontrolled from abroad."

To show our concern for the interests of the Asians, Acheson, in May 1950, called for American military and economic aid to France to help put down Ho Chi Minh's independence movement. This was justified under the catch-all strategy of blocking Soviet imperialism. "The United States government," the official State Department document declared:

> convinced that neither national independence nor democratic evolution can exist in any area dominated by Soviet imperialism, considers the situation to be such as to warrant its according economic aid and military equipment to the Associated States of Indochina and to France in order to assist them in restoring stability and permitting these states to pursue their peaceful and democratic development.

Helping French colonialism caused him no moral pain, although he continually griped about the stubbornness of the French in wanting to run their colony themselves rather than turn it over to American "advisers." His sympathies naturally seem to lie with the colonizers rather than with those being colonized. By the time Acheson left office, the United States was paying nearly half of France's military bill in Indochina. "I could not then or later," he explains of this policy, "think of a better course." After all that has happened there since, he still cannot.

The inability to think of a better course is the dominant motif of Acheson's letter of transmittal accompanying the China White Paper, a thousand-page document released in the summer of 1949, defending U.S. policy toward China. Trying to explain the victory of the communists despite more than $2 billion in American aid to Chiang Kai-shek, Acheson said, in effect, that what happened had to happen because it could not have been otherwise.

> The unfortunate but inescapable fact is that the ominous result of the civil war in China was beyond the

control of the government of the United States. Nothing that this country did or could have done within the reasonable limits of its capabilities could have changed that result; nothing that was left undone by this country has contributed to it. It was the product of internal Chinese forces, forces which this country tried to influence but could not.

Although designed to answer right-wing charges that the administration had allowed Chiang to be defeated, the White Paper failed to satisfy even those who had little sympathy for Chiang. Acheson's statement, Walter Lippmann pointed out at the time, was "tantamount to saying that there was no such thing as a sound or unsound, a right or a wrong, a wise or an unwise policy toward the Chinese civil war." What is crucial is not why Chiang lost, but why the United States persisted in supporting him to the bitter end, long after it became apparent that he could not possibly have won without American intervention. But Acheson evades this question both in his letter of transmittal at the time, and in his current account of the incident.

The heart of the White Paper concerned the long suppressed report by General Wedemeyer which concluded that the Nationalist government, described as "corrupt, reactionary and inefficient," could not win unless the United States took over not only the running of the war, but the government itself. He advised that Manchuria, then under communist control, be abandoned to a five-power guardianship, and that the Chiang regime submit to American "advisers" who would put together and run a new government. Unlike General Stilwell who also reported that Chiang could not withstand the communists, Wedemeyer thought the United States should intervene. To his credit and our good fortune, Marshall rejected Wedemeyer's recommendation. But while the administration refused to take over Chiang's government and fight his war, neither could it bring itself to abandon him to his fate.

Having failed to cut itself loose from Chiang, the administration soon found itself involved in a war on

China's borders. When North Korean troops streamed across the 38th parallel on June 24, 1950, Acheson immediately blamed the Russians and considered it another "testing" of American will. "It seemed close to certain that the attack had been mounted, supplied and instigated by the Soviet Union," he relates, "and that it would not be stopped by anything short of force." Truman saw it as the potential opening shot of World War III. "Every decision made in connection with the Korean war," he wrote in his *Memoirs,* "had this one aim in mind: To prevent a third world war and the terrible destruction it would bring to the civilized world." Acheson apparently never considered the possibility that the causes of the war might have been based to a large extent on local factors —on the weakness of Rhee's repressive government, his threats to march on the north, the belief of the North Koreans that they could unify the country easily, that, as Professor Stephen Ambose of the Naval War College has stated, in regard to I. F. Stone's *The Hidden History of the Korean War,* "the Chinese never wanted the war and did not support the North Koreans until MacArthur forced them to do so." The same was true for the Russians who had no hand in the initial attack. For Acheson the attack was "an open, undistinguished challenge to our internationally accepted position as the protector of South Korea."

> To back away from this challenge, in view of our capacity for meeting it, would be highly destructive of the power and prestige of the United States. By prestige I mean the shadow cast by power, which is of great deterrent importance. Therefore, we could not accept the conquest of this important area by a Soviet puppet under the very guns of our defensive perimeter with no more resistance than words and gestures in the Security Council.

Although Acheson considered American prestige to be involved, prior to the invasion there was no commitment to the defense of Korea. Indeed it had been explicitly omitted from the U.S. defense perimeter by Acheson himself and by the Pentagon. In *War in Peacetime,* General

J. Lawton Collins, Army Chief of Staff during the Korean war, reminds us that in April 1948, President Truman and the Joint Chiefs of Staff approved a policy stating: "The United States should not become so irrevocably involved in the Korean situation that an action taken by any faction in Korea or by any other power in Korea could be considered a 'causus belli' for the United States." The JCS felt that, in the context of a general war, Korea was indefensible and "of little strategic value to the United States." They recommended a complete withdrawal of American troops, which was done by the end of June 1949. They optimistically assumed that the South Koreans could "check and delay any attack by the North Koreans long enough to allow pressure from the United Nations to force a halt." The peripheral value the administration placed on Korea was confirmed by Acheson on January 12, 1950, in a speech drawing a U.S. defense perimeter that "runs along the Aleutians to Japan and then goes to the Ryukyus . . . from the Ryukyus to the Philippine Islands." Both Korea and Formosa were excluded from this perimeter.

The attack was immediately treated as a major provocation of the United States itself, even though the evidence indicates that was not necessarily the intention of the North Koreans or their Russian advisers. Naval and air forces were ordered to support the South Koreans. In addition the President, in a move that has had lasting repercussions, interposed the Seventh Fleet between Formosa and the Chinese mainland. The island had now become strategically important as a base to be kept out of "communist" hands and as a symbol of prestige. Having decided to defend Korea, which it never expected to be attacked, the administration could not afford to lose Formosa, which it had virtually written off to Mao. Thus by a face-saving logic that distorted the real issues, the administration involved the United States directly in the Chinese civil war and became the enemy of the new government in Peking.

Immediately the issue was expanded from the defense of a client state to a struggle against ubiquitous "international communism." "The attack upon Korea," Truman declared in his message to Congress, "makes it plain beyond all doubt that communism has passed beyond the use of subversion to conquer independent nations and will now use armed invasion and war." Of course it proved no such thing. At the most it showed that an imbalance of forces in a divided nation and the absence of a formal guarantee from a powerful protector invite civil war. However, the administration did not choose to interpret it that way. Otherwise it could never have won the popular support it needed to fight the war.

While the invasion caught Washington flat-footed, the immediate assumption was that it was a prelude to a possible Russian move against Western Europe. The last thing that occurred to anyone at the time was that even if the Russians gave their blessing to the North Korean attack, it might have had nothing to do with Soviet ambitions in Europe but rather was a response to U.S. policy in Asia: specifically to the decision to shut Russia out of the proposed treaty with Japan. One of the few who believed this was George Kennan, who told Acheson that the U.S determination to sign a separate peace with Japan and retain military bases on Japanese soil probably had an important bearing on the attack on South Korea. "But," he notes in his memoirs, "official Washington appeared, particularly at that time, impervious to any understanding of the possible effects of its own acts and policies on Soviet behavior beyond the rather primitive question as to whether what we did deterred or did not deter the Soviet government from its assumed desire to launch military attacks in every direction."

Once the decision was made to intervene in Korea, the political goals escalated rapidly. In June our stated purpose was to repel the invasion; by August it was to destroy the North Korean army; and by September to unify all of Korea. In June there was hesitation about sending planes across the 38th parallel; by August the administration was ready to send U.S. ground troops. With the success of MacArthur's armies, what had begun as a defensive war to defend South Korea was transformed into an offensive war to unite all of Korea and destroy the communist regime in the North.

After the North Koreans were turned back by MacArthur's brilliant landing at Inchon, the next decision was whether to penetrate beyond the 38th parallel. Despite opposition from within the State Department by Kennan and others, the administration was intoxicated by the brilliant possibilities then opening up: the destruction of the North Korean army and the unification of the country. On September 27, MacArthur was given new instructions: to cross the parallel and destroy the North Korean army, provided that Soviet or Chinese troops did not enter the war or threaten to do so. General Marshall, then Secretary of Defense, even sent MacArthur a telegram saying, "We want you to feel unhampered tactically and strategically to proceed north of the 38th parallel." The administration submitted a new resolution to the UN, which dutifully approved it on October 7, calling for a "unified, independent and democratic government of Korea," though the resolution did not explicitly authorize crossing the parallel.

As Allied troops approached the parallel, China voiced increasing concern. In mid-September Peking declared that it would stand by the Korean people and criticized the U.S. for supporting Chiang and blocking China's admission to the UN. On September 30, Foreign Minister Chou En-lai stated that the Chinese would not "supinely tolerate seeing their neighbors savagely invaded by the imperialists," and would not stand aside if the parallel were crossed. On October 1, South Korean troops moved across the parallel and MacArthur demanded the unconditional surrender of North Korea. Chou informed the Indian Ambassador that if American troops followed across the parallel, China would enter the war. The message was relayed to Washington on October 3, but scornfully dismissed by Acheson. His weakness for the use of force outweighed his political judgment. Chou's warning was ignored, the Indian diplomat was written off as an alarmist and communist sympathizer, and U.S. troops surged across the parallel.

MacArthur pushed north and on October 24, swept past the restraining line beyond which only South Korean troops were supposedly to be used. Two days later a Korean unit along the Yalu encountered Chinese troops, and for four days engaged in hand-to-hand fighting. Suddenly the Chinese withdrew. Were they protecting their dams and electric plants across the Yalu? Were they giving the U.S. a signal that they would intervene in full force if American troops pushed to the Yalu? Acheson expressed his "bafflement" about their intentions. The stillness was shattered on November 5, when MacArthur received permission to bomb bridges and installations along the Yalu. The war was now on China's border. Four days later a strong Chinese attack broke out all along the line and the Allies were driven back with heavy casualties. "We face an entirely new war," MacArthur informed Washington.

From Acheson's account, flavored with such phrases as MacArthur's "manic tide," and "his own hubris," one would think that he violated clear policy lines laid down by Washington. In fact, MacArthur's instructions were deliberately left vague and he was allowed considerable latitude. To be sure, he used all the authority he had, but he did not—at least until the Chinese intervention—contravene Washington's instructions. It was the National Security Council, with Acheson's and Truman's approval, which permitted him to advance to the Yalu, with instructions to use his discretion. Having abdicated its authority, the administration was hardly in a position to complain when MacArthur's judgment proved faulty. Although everyone feared the Chinese might enter the war, no one had the courage to stop MacArthur's advance before it happened. Acheson passed the buck to the Pentagon, the JCS said it was up to the President to decide, and Truman —in the absence of strong support from his advisers— was too intimidated by MacArthur to change his orders.

The march to the Yalu was a disaster, but it followed from the earlier decision to move north across the 38th parallel and destroy the North Korean regime. The responsibility for that decision rests with Acheson, Marshall, and Truman.

After the Chinese prevented the unification of Korea by force, MacArthur's armies were pushed back below the 38th parallel, the General was dismissed by Truman, and armistice talks dragged on interminably, with continuing casualties on both sides, until the Democrats were finally sent out to pasture by the disgusted voters, and Eisenhower entered with a pledge to "go to Korea." Acheson describes his final two years in office in chapters with such dispiriting titles as, "NATO in Stagnation," "NATO Meets in Rome," "Death of a King," and finally, none too soon, "Last Farewells." By the time they come, the reader is as weary as Acheson himself must have been after four years as Secretary of State.

But he obviously loved every minute of it. Those who congratulate themselves on the sacrifices they make in "public service" are pulling the public's leg. As one always suspected, it is no sacrifice for those doing the "serving," since it gives them positions of power, not to mention ego-gratification, they could never have in their law firms, executive suites, and university offices. They don't even mind selling their stocks—which in any case they put in trust until they return to private law practice, where they represent giant corporations in their dealings with the government. It is not that they love money less, but that they love power more. As Acheson comments on his enforced return to private life in January 1953, when the Republicans took over: "To leave positions of great responsibility and authority is to die a little."

As it turned out, Acheson didn't die very much. After the bucolic Eisenhower years when, for a change, the United States was not involved in any wars, Acheson returned to the White House as a sometime adviser to Presidents, with such pieces of advice as telling Kennedy to bomb the Russian missile sites in Cuba and assuring Johnson that he was defending the Free World in Vietnam. Even Nixon, once the bane of his existence, has invited him to the White House. Now savoring the role of elder statesman, Acheson is neither gone nor forgotten. His influence lives on and the heritage of his years in office is still very much with us.

In the pages of this long memoir lie the intellectual justification for the cold war, the enormous expansion of American military power, and the ignoble interventions that have been carried out with the most noble rhetoric. The world Acheson helped to create is the world we still live in. Although his book tells us what it was like to be "present at the creation" of the postwar world, as we enter the 1970s his pride in that role seems strangely misplaced.

Man Without
a Country

George Kennan's *Memoirs 1925–1950* is the story
of a sensitive, intelligent boy from Milwaukee, Wisconsin
who goes off to Europe, where he gains fame, if not fortune, in the service of his country, and after many trials
and tribulations discovers that nobody ever understood
him. It is a sad tale in which the author suffers mightily
from snubs, rebuffs, frustrations, discomfort, and the
boorishness of his fellow countrymen. Although he deserves a better fate than he meets, he keeps a stiff upper
lip through his adversities, and eventually triumphs over
defeat by finding a better life in the cloisters of Princeton,
New Jersey.

For all its sadness, the story is an inspiring one that
will move many readers to emotions of pity and indignation: pity for a man who was too wise to be listened to by
his superiors; indignation at a system that did not provide
him with even greater rewards and recognition than he
received. It was George Kennan's misfortune to live in a
crass country and in a century where his finest qualities
were not truly appreciated. In this lengthy reminiscence,
gleaned from voluminous diary notes, unread documents,
unpublished poems and travel impressions, thumbnail
sketches of famous and obscure individuals, attempts at

self-analysis, and accounts of crises and decisions in which the author was involved, the reader gains a new impression of a man who has become the nearest thing to a legend that this country's diplomatic service has ever produced. These memoirs are expertly written, often fascinating, and in many ways depressing. In them this hero is transformed before our eyes into a very fallible mortal, and in some ways even into an anti-hero. What the author conceives as an eighteenth-century autobiography turns into a twentieth-century tale of alienation, very modern, very sad, and unintentional.

For all its limitations, this is an important book, both as diplomatic history and as intellectual biography. These memoirs are more than a recollection of a distinguished, if disappointing, career in diplomacy. More than an explanation of how the embassy in Moscow is run, or what the author thought of Averell Harriman and Dean Acheson, or how the Russians took over Eastern Europe. They are about a man as much as about a time: a man of intelligence and integrity whose effectiveness was hobbled by insecurity, intellectual arrogance, and a tendency toward self-pity. A man who counsels the virtues of being, like himself, "a guest of one's time and not a member of its household"; who was "concerned less with what people thought they were striving for than with the manner in which they strove for it"; who recognized "that I stood temperamentally outside the passions of war—and always would"; who watched the Nazi rise to power, the dismemberment of Czechoslovakia, and the devastation of Rotterdam with analytical dispassion, but who was painfully wounded when snubbed at Princeton as an undergraduate, or when his superiors forgot to make a place for him on a special diplomat's train from Rome to Berlin. Forever giving warnings that went unheeded and penning diplomatic dispatches that remained unread, Kennan shows himself in these memoirs as one who struggled to protect the interests of the United States in distant lands, yet who became increasingly estranged from his own compatriots. His book is an effort at self-analysis—a thinly-disguised confessional. What he reveals is not always flattering, but it offers a fascinating insight into a career which fell short of what it might have been, and suggests why this may have been the case.

Kennan is perhaps the most impressive figure ever to have emerged from the shadowy labyrinth of the American diplomatic establishment. His quarter-century in the Foreign Service was marked by loneliness and frustration, by dubious triumphs, and finally by the taste of ashes. These memoirs end with his departure from the Foreign Service, and with his frustration when he felt that he would never be able to translate his views into policy. By 1950 he decided that his usefulness was at an end, and, as he left the State Department to begin his second career as an historian at Princeton, he wondered, speaking of himself and his friend Chip Bohlen, "whether the day had not passed when the government had use for the qualities of persons like ourselves—for the effort at cool and rational analysis in the unfirm substance of the imponderables." Much of his dissatisfaction was due to the nature of the organization in which he spent so many years of his life. But equally responsible were some traits of Kennan's own personality. He was used by the Foreign Service, and sometimes used badly. He became a gadfly intellectual whose views were accepted when others found them convenient, and rejected when they were troublesome or untimely. But he also used the State Department for his own purposes. It provided him with a forum that permitted him to influence policy—although not always in the way he would have preferred.

He is hard on the State Department, and rightly so. Its inability to find a place for perceptive and grating individuals like himself is one of its gravest shortcomings. But in the 1920s the Foreign Service was an entirely appropriate place for the unformed but perceptive and intelligent George Kennan to make his hesitant entry into the world. He chose it, he confesses, because "I feared falling into some sort of occupational rut and I thought that I would be best protected in the Foreign Service from doing so." The decision was a good one, as he himself admits, and if in the years that followed he berated his superiors for their unresponsiveness to his suggestions, he nonetheless cherished the bureaucracy for the protective coloration it offered.

Kennan gave himself to the discipline of the Foreign Service, rose rapidly within its clogged hierarchy, gained more from it than he may yet recognize, and suffered from its virtually unavoidable limitations. The Foreign Service did more than make Kennan famous: it made him what he is. Without it he would no doubt have become a distinguished scholar. Perhaps a professor of history at Harvard or Chicago. But by training him in Russian and German, by taking him away from his parochial preoccupations and exposing him to an international setting, it transformed a self-doubting, neurotic boy from Wisconsin into a world statesman. In so doing, however, it alienated him even further from the country whose interests he sought to protect, but whose manners and whose qualities he came to look upon with a coldness bordering on contempt.

The opening chapter of the memoirs is certainly the most revealing, and in many ways the most interesting part of this book, for it offers a clue to Kennan's puzzling character. Although telling us little about his family, he introduces us to the "grubby military school cadet" who lived "in a world that was peculiarly and intimately my own, scarcely to be shared with others or even made plausible to them." It was a private world filled with monsters and demons, in which he imagined a perfectly ordinary brick building in Milwaukee to be "a house of horror—horror unnamed, unmentionable, not to be imagined." This horror of the unknown remained with him throughout his life, coloring his perceptions and his diplomatic dispatches with a touch of paranoia. Retreating to his private world, he rejected the unpleasantness of the actual one as though it were an aberration that did not concern him personally. He yearned for the tidier world of the eighteenth century and freely confesses "the discomfort I experience in my own status as a contemporary of the twentieth." He liked to think of himself as the child of a happier, more reflective, more aristocratic age, in which his secret qualities would be admired, and in which less worthy figures would tender the respect that was due.

Suffering terribly from feelings of social inadequacy, he unerringly chose to attend the college that would intensify these feelings to the utmost: Princeton. There, unsurprisingly, he found himself "always at the end of every line, always uninitiated, knowing few, known by few." It brought out all his latent masochism and self-pity, filled him with admiration for those he considered to be his social superiors, and intensified his growing sense of isolation. He considered himself "an oddball on campus, not eccentric, not ridiculed or disliked, just imperfectly visible to the naked eye." Although invited to join an undergraduate club, he later resigned and became what he terms one of the "social rejects," most of whom were scarred "by the realization that they had been held to judgment by their fellow students and found wanting." It was a judgment that has haunted Kennan throughout his life, persuaded him to see himself as another Gatsby, infinitely worthy but never fully appreciated, forever on the fringes of the real elite, and although occasionally allowed to enter the mansion and converse with the swells, never to feel a part of it. "The portrayal," he confesses,

> in the hauntingly beautiful epilogue to *The Great Gatsby* of the Midwesterner's reaction to the fashionable East held, to be sure, such familiarity for me that when I first read it, while still in college, I went away and wept unmanly tears.

Rather than curing him of his social insecurity, Princeton intensified it, leaving him with yearnings that could never be fulfilled and anxieties that could never be assuaged. It fed his sense of isolation and contributed to the feelings of martyrdom that color these memoirs. Nobody understood him, nobody wanted him, nobody appreciated him. He chose the Foreign Service because of its "protective paternalism," and perhaps because it provided a certain social cachet, but he resented its slowness to appreciate his merits. It was, in a sense, Princeton all over again. Although he remained in the club for a quarter-century, he never really felt a part of it, nor was he fully accepted by those on top, whom he viewed with mixed resentment and admiration. Ignored for many years, his political-literary dispatches unread or unacted upon, he saw himself as a prophet forever doomed to murmur his warnings in the wilderness.

These feelings were intensified by his experience in Russia, where his personal sense of isolation combined with the real isolation that is the lot of foreign residents. To him the Soviet Union was a nightmare and he could never understand why his sentiments of horror and outrage toward it were not fully shared by his superiors in Washington. There were times when he thought it must be part of some conspiracy, and he periodically detected "the smell of Soviet influence, or strongly pro-Soviet influence, somewhere in the higher reaches of the government." But more often it was simply due to the failure of others to understand him. "There will be no place," he wrote in 1944, when Washington and Moscow were still allies in the struggle against Hitler, "for the American who is really willing to undertake this disturbing task" of understanding Russia. "The best he can look forward to is the lonely pleasure of one who stands at long last on a chilly and inhospitable mountaintop where few have been before, where few can follow, and where few will consent to believe that he has been."

While such remarks reflect the ordeal of a lonely man who feels he has been unjustly ignored, they also reveal the "difficult" side of Kennan's character. Others are continually failing to follow his advice, including the President of the United States. "These various people," he writes of those in Washington who were conducting the rather farcical negotiations with Portugal over the wartime use of the Azores, "were unquestionably wrong. I knew more about Portugal, and about the ins and outs of the situation, than any of them did." What was true of Portugal was also true of most other places, such as Poland. Of the talks on the composition of the postwar

Polish government he writes: "I was probably the only non-Pole present who had enough experience of Eastern Europe to be thoroughly aware of the factors involved." While such observations may well be true, it is not surprising that the attitude they reflected did not endear Kennan to his Washington colleagues, nor improve the chances for his voice to be heard.

For such a sensitive and high-strung man, he often seems oblivious to the sensibilities and weaknesses of others. He was, as he says of himself, given to "pride, oversensitivity, a sullen refusal to be comforted, an insistence on knowing and experiencing the worst in order to be the more deserving of sympathy, at least in my own eyes." Suffering fools with difficulty and unable to understand why his recommendations were not accepted, he saw himself as a victim of ignorance, or envy, or duplicity, or a combination of them all.

He had little sympathy for the political problems of decision-making in a democracy, and no use for Congress, most of whose members he considered ignorant and boorish. He saw no reason why individual Congressmen should be catered to, nor by what justification they could challenge the considered wisdom of the State Department. The function of Congress, apparently, was to approve what had been decided at more elevated levels. "I could not accept the assumption," he writes of Senator Vandenberg's efforts to win approval for the Marshall Plan, "that Senators were all such idiots that they deserved admiring applause every time they could be persuaded by the State Department to do something sensible." Nor did he see why the administration should lobby important congressmen in order to secure the passage of certain bills. "I had never understood," he states with the unconcealed indignation of a man whose dignity has been stepped on, "that part of my profession was to represent the U.S. government vis-à-vis Congress."

Perhaps lobbying is demeaning and boring, but our form of government rests, at least in theory, on congressional assent to major foreign policy desisions—particu-

larly on treaties and on the decision to go to war. Diplomatic professionals, even those as distinguished as
George Kennan, do not always possess the wisdom they
imagine on such crucial issues. If they did, Americans
would probably not be dying today in Vietnam. Diplomats
may like to think of themselves as part of an intellectual
and social elite, but we still live in a democracy, where
public opinion can have an influence on legislators, even
if it cannot on the President and his foreign policy
advisers. Congressional interference is a nuisance to the
State Department, but it is not so presumptuous as
Kennan imagines.

His attitude toward Congress is indicative of his conception of diplomacy, which he seems to view as a private
function to be performed by a specialized elite—something like the sale of municipal bonds or the removal of
tumors. Certain work can be performed only by specialists, and the clients have no business giving advice.
Things were better back in the eighteenth century, although one wonders whether a boy from Milwaukee
would have risen to be ambassador in the court of Louis
XVI or of Frederick the Great. Democracy is a sloppy
system of government, and one cannot help but detect
Kennan's persistent irritation with it.

Combined with this elitism is a snobbery which tran-
scends social class to embrace whole peoples. Just as he
finds the eighteenth century he never knew more congenial than the twentieth century he lives in, so he finds
cultured old Europe more appealing than brash, upstart
America. His admiration for the ways of the Old World
cause him to be embarrassed about the country he is
officially representing. While stationed in Berlin as a
young Foreign Service officer he patronized "a small
Anglo-American eating club for bankers and diplomats,
a club run, fortunately, by the English (who know how
to do that sort of thing) and not by the Americans."
Would the club have been even more desirable had it
excluded Americans (who generally do not appreciate
that sort of thing)?

Years later, returning to Germany shortly after the war, he finds it occupied by American GIs and comes away.

> with a sense of sheer horror at the spectacle of this horde of my compatriots and their dependents camping in luxury amid the ruins of a shattered national community, ignorant of the past, oblivious to the abundant evidences of present tragedy all around them, inhabiting the very same sequestered villas that the Gestapo and SS had just abandoned, and enjoying the same privileges, flaunting their silly supermarket luxuries in the face of a veritable ocean of deprivation, hunger and wretchedness, setting an example of empty materialism and cultural poverty. . . .

What did he expect, one wonders? Should the U.S. Army, which had fought a bloody campaign in which many Americans lost their lives in the struggle against Nazi tyranny, have lived in tents and turned the sequestered villas back to the Gestapo and to the "good Germans" who supported its activities? Whose fault was it that the Germans suffered some of the horrors of a war they inflicted upon others? Who were these Germans, who cheered Hitler for twelve years and repudiated him only in defeat, to give lessons to the Americans on "empty materialism and cultural poverty"? What, one must ask, is Kennan complaining about: that war is nasty, that innocent people suffer, that foot soldiers are not philosophers?

One might sympathize more with Kennan's sensitivities if they extended to the victims of Nazi Germany, rather than merely to those who got back something of what they inflicted on others. When he visits Rotterdam shortly after its destruction by the Luftwaffe, he shows none of the outrage toward its destroyers that he does toward the unfortunate American GIs in the occupation forces. And in 500 pages of text virtually his only comment on the Jews is not regret at the fate they met at the hands of their Nazi executioners, but indignation that some U.S. diplomats were bumped from a ship returning to the U.S. "in order to free space on the exchange vessel for Jewish refugees . . . because individual Congressmen, anxious to please individual constituents, were interested in bringing these refugees to the United States." Kennan's moral outrage is highly selective, though his countrymen often bear the brunt of it.

His alienation from American life is not unique. Many Foreign Service and army officers share it to one degree or another. This is one of the problems Americans encounter when they spend much of their life abroad—particularly in countries they admire. But this alienation is one to which Kennan—with his identification with the "cultured"—is particularly prone. It is reflected in his dyspeptic comment on the GIs, and even more specifically in his account of a visit to Wisconsin in 1936. "I came away from the summer's visit," he writes,

> aware that I was no longer a part of what I had once been a part of—no longer, in fact, a part of anything at all . . . Increasingly now, I would not be a part of my country . . . I would continue to pay it my loyalty. This was a matter of self-respect and of a deeper faith in the values of our civilization. What else, after all, could I be loyal to? But it would be a loyalty *despite*, not a loyalty *because*, a loyalty of principle, not of identification. And whatever reciprocation it evoked could never be one based on a complete understanding.

While one can admire the honesty that allows him to admit such feelings, one cannot help but suspect that this profound estrangement from his own country diminished Kennan's diplomatic effectiveness and contributed to the disappointments of his career. Impatient with America, feeling it was culturally inferior to Europe, unable to consider himself a part of his country, perhaps no longer even wanting to understand it, Kennan became a spiritual exile. His return to the United States during the war did little to change his outlook or his sympathies. This spiritual isolation from his countrymen was intensified by a Calvinist upbringing that was reflected in a weakness toward sanctimony and a refusal to compromise what he believed to be moral principles. This can be considered a mark of his integrity, but it also made it exceedingly difficult for him to engage in the give-and-take that is so much a part of policy formation. Kennan chose to be "right" rather than to be effective. Whether or not this was a conscious choice, it was a real one.

Unfortunately he was not always right, and he was never more effective than when he wrote the famous "X" article in *Foreign Affairs* (regrettably not included in the book) which was executed in a way that undermined much of what he really believed. Even at the height of his success in the early postwar years, when he became Forrestal's fair-haired boy, General Marshall's aide, head of the Policy Planning Staff, and drafter of the economic recovery program that was to become the Marshall Plan, he often felt that he had little real influence on policy. "There were times," he comments on this period, "when I felt like a court jester, expected to enliven discussion, privileged to say the shocking things, valued as an intellectual gadfly on hides of slower colleagues, but not to be taken fully seriously when it came to the final, responsible decisions of policy."

It is a bitter comment, but a fairly accurate one. The nearer Kennan got to the seats of power, the more aware he became of the limitations on his influence. He thought he could use the bureaucracy and operate outside it. He discovered that he was used by it, and could escape its restrictions only by leaving it entirely. Someone less idealistic would not have been so deceived, nor so disillusioned. He despaired of the bureaucracy, just as he despaired of a system that would allow foreign policy to be judged by Congress. In the moments of depression to which he was, apparently, frequently given, he asked "whether a government so constituted should deceive itself into believing that it is capable of conducting a mature, consistent and discriminating foreign policy."

Kennan declared that diplomacy should be divorced from sentiment. He was a firm supporter of the classic doctrines of national interest and spheres of influence. Ideologies were foreign to him, and so were the causes of violence. Concerned with methods rather than objec-

subject
be so
n were
dealt in
f classic
ve about
t Russia
s of the
y to the
ation. He
maintain
iet Union,
d stressed
to attack
ediness of

he fault of
wn bargain-
s a price for
inst Britain's
eme that they
to attempt to
ation in order
me meaty ma-
visionists who
hat Hitler was
ians and their

Russia he wrote
rtment "that we
appear that we
to have entered
e Russian cause
t." He remained
wartime alliance
e "in opposition
from left to right
look in the years
once more in the
nd highly mili-

man for causes." Yet this is only
he is a man whose entire career
dgments, whose code of morality
any of the Scotch Presbyterians
ded. It is simply that his morality
s outraged by the Nazi tyranny
ce state, less by the barbarities
han by those of the Russians,
d cultural poverty of average
Americans.

l no doubt honestly considers
tist. Yet he is typically, and
s idealism and in the high
ades his writing and his
splaced European, nor the
ry *philosophe* that he may
quarely in the American
Henry Adams and Jay
had vanished and the

Russia (eventually as
covered in this book)
l attitudes, and filled
to the system he ob-
had a considerable
erhaps a far greater
nsistently were the
e in upon me dur-
ow—so prolonged
mpressions, each
the other—that
ough he had a
eople (whereas
ect), he so de-
bted whether
d States. On
with Moscov
at any lat
ally or

If this sounds like John Foster Dulles on the
of Communist China, the resemblance may no
coincidental as it seems. Both these statesme
basically religious fundamentalists, even if one
ideology while the other spoke in the language o
diplomacy. Although he was far more percepti
the nastiness and untrustworthiness of Stalinis
than were the woolly-headed American libera
1930s and early 1940s, his emotional antipat
Soviet regime led him to questionable exagger
deplored FDR's belief that it was possible to
mutually advantageous relations with the Sov
had little sympathy for it during the war, a
the extent to which "Hitler's final decision
Russia was influenced by the stubborn gr
Soviet diplomacy."

The war, one might suspect, was all t
Stalin, who "would so seriously overrate his
ing power as to make upon the Germans—a
Russia's collaboration in the wider war aga
world position—demands so greedy and extr
would convince Hitler he had no choice but
eliminate Russia as a factor in the world sit
to get on with his principal job." Here is so
terial for a new generation of German re
will no doubt one day try to demonstrate
pushed into the war by the greedy Russ
Western dupes.

Two days after the German attack on
an influential associate in the State Depa
should do nothing at home to make it
are following the course Churchill seem
upon in extending moral support to th
in the present Russian-German confli
faithful to this position throughout the
with the Russians and would contin
ntil the movement of the pendulum
uld bring it close to my own ou
6 to 1948, only to carry it away
direction, with the oversimplifi

tarized view of the Russian problem that came to prevail after 1949." He had no use for those who sentimentalized the Russians because they were our allies. At best they were fools or dupes, at worst agents of the Soviet Union. He even castigated the American military establishment as early as 1945 for being "still deeply affected by what I had felt to be the disgraceful anti-British and pro-Soviet prejudices that certain of our military leaders had entertained during the war."

Even before the war was over he was ready to reverse the alliance and urged the U.S. to cut off all aid to the Soviet Union as punishment for her refusal to aid the non-communist Polish underground during the Warsaw uprising. The threat to cut off aid would also, he believed, force the Russians to be more cooperative in the problems of organizing the United Nations and plotting the political future of Eastern Europe. Russia's behavior during the Warsaw uprising was, in his mind, "the moment when, if ever, there should have been a full-fledged and realistic political showdown with the Soviet leaders" over Eastern Europe. So much for the lingering impression, totally refuted by the record, that Kennan ever had anything but contempt for the communists, their methods, and their goals. He was a hard-liner from the beginning. The great difference between him and those who later took his warnings to heart was that he did not allow his moral indignation to militarize his thinking.

The Russians, in his eyes, were not only untrustworthy allies, devious schemers, and moral hypocrites, but Oriental brutes carrying on the traditions of Genghis Khan. He was moved to agony over "the wild brutalities and atrocities being perpetrated by a portion of Soviet troops . . . as they made their way into Germany," although he does not show such indignation at the uncountable brutalities and atrocities committed by the Germans. So extreme are his anti-Soviet, pro-German prejudices, that he condemns the Nuremberg trials of the Nazi war criminals on the grounds that we lost the right to judge the Germans once we became allies with the Russians. "The day we accepted the Russians as our allies in the struggle against Germany," he wrote in 1947, "we tacitly accepted as facts, even if we did not ourselves adopt, the customs of warfare which have prevailed generally in Eastern Europe and Asia for centuries in the past and which will presumably continue to prevail long into the future." Better, in his view, to have shot the Nazi war criminals on the spot than to have held a public trial which "could not expiate or undo the crimes they had committed," and admitting a Soviet judge whose presence "was to make a mockery of the only purpose the trials could conceivably serve."

It was not only the presence of a Soviet judge that bothered him about the Nuremberg trials, but the belief that "history, in judging the individual cruelties of this struggle, will not distinguish between those of victor and vanquished." By a not unsimilar logic he opposed the postwar efforts at de-Nazification of German society, arguing that it would be difficult to accomplish, that it would endow the victims with the cloak of martyrdom, and that it was unnecessary. "It must be demonstrated to Germany that aggression does not pay," he advised the State Department in 1943. "But I do not see that this involves the artificial removal of any given class in Germany from its position in public life." This is indeed the long view of history, but one wonders whether, if the situation were reversed and it was the Russians whose territory was being occupied by the American army, Kennan would still have argued against the "artificial removal of any given class" in the Soviet state.

Although sympathetic toward Germany, a country whose language he spoke fluently and in which he had lived for some six years as a student and as a diplomat, and intensely hostile to Stalinist Russia, Kennan prided himself on being a political realist rather than an ideologue. He recognized that peace did not depend on the "intimate collaboration with Russia that Americans had been taught to envisage and to hope for," but rather "all that was really required to assure stability among the great powers was the preservation of a realistic balance of strength between them and a realistic understanding of the mutual zones of vital interest." The Russians understood this, and the problem was to get the Americans to understand it as well—to see the cold war not as a moral struggle for the soul of mankind, but as a conflict of interests that could be dealt with by an unemotional show of strength. He chided the "chimera of Soviet collaboration," but he stressed that the primary problem faced by the West was political rather than military. "Moscow would have no reason to contemplate a further military advance in Europe," he wrote in May 1945; "the danger for the West was not Russian invasion—it was the Communist parties in the Western countries themselves, plus the unreal hopes and fears the Western peoples had been taught to entertain." He wrote this not during the anxieties of 1947, but in the full flush of Russo-American cooperation two years earlier. In this assessment of Russia's intentions he was right, while those who criticized him at the time later embraced views far more sweeping and militarily oriented than any envisaged by Kennan.

These recommendations later appeared in the famous "X" article that he originally wrote in January 1947, as a memo for Secretary of the Navy James Forrestal, a man who became Kennan's protector in the government, and who was instrumental in having him assigned to the prestigious National War College and later chosen by General Marshall to head the Policy Planning Staff in the State Department. The article made Kennan famous, largely for its espousal of the "containment" doctrine. It was received so enthusiastically because it came at a time when the wartime alliance with the Soviet Union had turned into a cold war rivalry. A new foreign policy was needed, and Keenan provided its intellectual substance by urging a program of resistance to further Soviet penetration in Europe. Kennan was a hero overnight. The containment doctrine became the foundation of American foreign policy, and we have been living with its heritage ever since.

For Kennan the whole thing became a source of acute embarrassment. Although it made him famous, he believed that his recommendations were misinterpreted and distorted so that they no longer represented his assumptions. Instead of a doctrine for the *political* containment of the Soviet Union in Central Europe, it became the justification for an enormous rearmament program aimed at *military* containment. It was the "X" article that provided the foundation for the NATO pact, a construction Kennan viewed with alarm and dismay.

Looking back, Kennan singles out the deficiencies in the article that led so many people to interpret it differently from the way he says he intended it. Walter Lippmann, for example, took him to task for conceiving containment as a military posture, and for failing to offer any program that might lead to the mutual withdrawal of Soviet and American troops from Europe. Kennan deplores this misinterpretation and assumes much of the blame for not making himself clearer. "The Russians don't want to invade anyone," he wrote in an unsent letter to Lippmann. "They don't want war of any kind." Containment, he insisted, was designed to encourage Western Europeans to resist domestic, not international, violence. Eventually the containment policy was supposed to provide the stability that would allow us to negotiate with the Russians to end the partition of Europe. This was the link, he argued in a much later reassessment of his own doctrine, between containment and disengagement.

Yet if all this was clear in Kennan's mind, it was not so in anyone else's; neither in the minds of those who were preparing for a military showdown with the Soviet Union, nor of those who hoped that the division of Europe could be eased before it became rigidified and militarized. However much Kennan may regret this, much of it was his own fault—not only because he failed to make himself clear, but also because his vehement antipathy to the Soviet Union made it impossible for him even to envisage a cooperative approach. Perhaps such an approach would have failed. That is certainly Kennan's belief, and he reproaches those who continued to believe otherwise. But by virtually precluding any hopes of such cooperation and by favoring initiatives, such as the creation of an independent West German state, that "aroused keen alarm among the Soviet leaders" and so forced the Russians to respond in kind with equally drastic measures of their own, Kennan accepted as inevitable the very partition of Europe that he deplored. He accepted that the Russians were going to remain dominant within their sphere of influence, and urged we should take every step necessary to solidify our own. Although he did not believe that conflict between the two blocs was necessary or even likely, he could see no prospect of reaching a meaningful accord with Stalinist Russia.

As early as 1945 he argued that "the idea of a Germany run jointly with the Russians is a chimera," and stated that "we have no choice but to lead our section of Germany . . . to a form of independence." From this flowed logically all the things he deplored: the partition of Europe, the creation of NATO, the rearming of Germany. He may have been surprised, but he shouldn't have been. Urging us to protect our own sphere of influence, he saw no reason why the Russians should not do the same in theirs. He was not surprised by the communist coup in Czechoslovakia, nor by the attempt to force the Western allies out of Berlin—both of which he viewed as "defensive reactions on the Soviet side" to the Marshall Plan and our decision to set up a West German government. He could not understand why people in Washington were so alarmed, why they rushed to set up NATO and rearm Germany. He tried to explain the reasons for his equanimity to the people in the State Department and expresses surprise that officials accepted the "tough" part of his analysis but were unmoved by his more subtle qualifications. "The only answer," he comments with curious naïveté, "could be that Washington's reactions were deeply subjective, influenced more by domestic-political moods and institutional interests than by any theoretical considerations of our international position."

He admits that the policy of containment later failed.

This was not because it was impossible to halt the Russians, or because Soviet policies did not mellow. "The failure," he writes in retrospect,

> consisted in the fact that our own government, finding it difficult to understand a political threat as such and to deal with it in other than military terms, and grievously misled, in particular, by its own faulty interpretations of the significance of the Korean War, failed to take advantage of the opportunities for useful political discussion when, in later years, such opportunities began to open up, and exerted itself, in its military preoccupations, to seal and to perpetuate the very division of Europe which it should have been concerned to remove. It was not "containment" that failed; it was the intended follow-up that never occurred.

The follow-up never occurred because it was not the way official Washington saw the problem—particularly after the outbreak of the Korean war.

According to Kennan, the Soviet signal to unleash the attack in Korea probably stemmed directly from Washington's decision to set up permanent bases in Japan, and to sign a peace treaty without Russian participation. But by then Washington was thinking almost exclusively in military terms, and the Korean war seemed like the prelude to a Soviet probe in Central Europe, rather than a defensive measure designed to frustrate the American effort to turn Japan into a military bastion. Along these lines Kennan reveals that in July 1950, only a few weeks after the outbreak of war, the Chinese reportedly accepted an Indian proposal to end the conflict by a restoration of the *status quo ante*, and by the admission of Communist China to the UN—and that the U.S. government turned this down flat, although Kennan thought it a sensible compromise. Later, as we know, MacArthur marched toward the Yalu, the Chinese intervened as they had warned they would, and the war dragged on for three more years.

Perhaps none of this would have happened had Washington followed Kennan's advice. Perhaps we would have been spared the worst excesses of the cold war, the agonies of Korea and Vietnam, the waste of NATO and the Warsaw Pact, and the rearmament of Germany which solidified the partition of Europe. With an uncommon lucidity, an intellectual acuity, and a deep sense of humanity, Kennan would have been a far better guide than any we had during the squandered later years of the cold war. Yet he bears a share of responsibility for the hardening of our own attitudes—and perhaps that of the Russians as well—in the early post-war years.

Perhaps the most depressing part of these memoirs is Kennan's puzzlement over the fact that his advice was taken only selectively—that official Washington finally in 1947 came around to his point of view when he urged a crackdown on the Russians, but that nobody listened when he insisted that the real danger was political rather than military. Yet this should not have been surprising. His influence was not so great—he could not, after all, persuade any of his superiors to do anything they were not ready to do in the first place. Rather, he provided the intellectual framework which permitted them to rationalize what they were ready to do anyway—confront the Russians—for reasons that had little to do with Kennan's memos.

Although at the center of the storm, he remained very much on the fringes of power: one of the many intellectuals who are drawn into the government, whirled around the vortex until they produce something that is useful to their superiors, and then disgorged like dried sponges. This has been the fate of countless others, and it would have been Kennan's as well had he not had the courage and the good sense to get out of the State Department and try to influence policy from the outside.

The Kennan who is so respected today throughout the world is not the architect of the containment doctrine distorted by the military minds of four administrations, nor the free-talking ambassador who was declared *persona non grata* by the Soviet Union, but the historian who has since used his remarkable intellectual gifts and his eloquent pen to question some of the most persistent myths of the cold war.

Organization Man

Like George Washington, whom he resembled in other ways as well, Dwight Eisenhower was first in war, peace, and the hearts of his countrymen. He led the great wartime coalition (the "crusade," he called it) that defeated Hitler's armies; returned home amid wild acclaim to preside in the White House during eight years of what we would now call "benign neglect," and so embodied all the virtues of Middle America that his reputation both as General and as President has become nearly as sacrosanct as the flag.

But, like the flag, it has a new meaning to a generation of young Americans who barely remember the Eisenhower Presidency, and who were not even born when the Allied armies finally crushed Hitler's Germany and lifted the scourge of Nazism from Europe. To them V-E Day, whose twenty-fifth anniversary was marked by the publication of the first five volumes of the Eisenhower papers, must seem as remote as Gallipoli or Austerlitz. All the more reason, therefore, to welcome these papers, which cover the war years from December 1941 to May 1945. Not only do they provide valuable historical documentation of the military and political decisions made during the war; they also reveal how Eisenhower carried out his responsibilities as Supreme Commander of Allied forces in Europe.

Through these volumes we gain new insight into the disputes among the Allies over policy and strategy, into the problems of organizing a mass army over a front covering two continents, and, above all, into the personality of a man whose genius lay not in strategy (several of his subordinates, particularly Field Marshal Montgomery, were far superior to him in this respect), but in an ability to organize, delegate authority, and mediate. Eisenhower dealt with the Allied armies the way he dealt (less happily) with the Presidency—as head of an enormous bureaucracy.

Ike was, in many respects, the ideal bureaucrat: patient, firm, charming, nonintellectual. He was a committeeman who forged a consensus from the advice given him, and turned it into a plan of action. As Alfred Chandler, the editor of these volumes, notes, one of the unique qualities of these papers is that there exists "no comparable record of the thought and activities of the head of a huge modern bureaucratic enterprise." It was as a bureaucrat that Eisenhower contributed his greatest service in reconciling divergent opinions among such forceful generals as Patton, Montgomery, Clark, and Alexander, and in coping with such stubborn political personalities as Churchill, de Gaulle, Giraud, and Darlan.

Eisenhower did not interfere in politics and never overstepped the role assigned to him. But, as these volumes make clear, he took actions that were essentially political—e.g., the famous deal with Darlan to end the resistance of the Vichy forces in North Africa. He disagreed forcefully with Churchill over the strategy for defeating Hitler and circumvented Roosevelt's hostility to de Gaulle by conferring directly with the Free French leader on problems concerning France. In disputes between political leaders regarding strategy he would be the bureaucrat-diplomat, defining his position in military terms and expressing his readiness to be overruled on political, but not military, grounds. Because there was considerable disagreement at the top, Eisenhower's position often carried the day.

Eisenhower was elevated from obscurity because of his ability to organize, speak frankly, and act decisively. A year before the outbreak of the war he was only a lieutenant colonel. His first involvement in high-level planning did not begin until a week after Pearl Harbor, when he came to Washington to serve in the War Plans Division. There he won the admiration of George Marshall, who catapulted Ike along the road that within a few months led to his becoming Commander-in-Chief of Allied forces in Western Europe, and eventually President of the United States. It is one of the great success stories of our time, and it is no less a tribute to Eisenhower to note that his achievement was based to a large degree on his bureaucratic talent. "Others could— and did—provide expert and experienced leadership in the field," Chester Wilmot wrote in *The Struggle for Europe,* "but nobody else revealed Eisenhower's remarkable capacity for integrating the efforts of different Allies and rival services and for creating harmony between individuals with varied backgrounds and temperaments."

Eisenhower gave his subordinates considerable freedom in carrying out their assignments and, for the most part, ignored their excesses (Patton's, for example) when these did not interfere with basic strategy. But, for all his charm and willingness to accommodate minor differences, he could be adamant when he felt a vital issue was at stake. One of Eisenhower's tasks on arriving in Washington in December 1941 was to forge a unified command from the British and American units. Having managed their campaigns by a committee of commanders, the British were against the idea of a supreme commander. Instead they proposed that a committee, the Combined Chiefs of Staffs, conduct the war. Marshall agreed to this but in the end Eisenhower, through the force of his personality and the administrative arrangements he worked out, succeeded in creating the unified command structure that the CCS had formally denied him.

The integrity of the unified command structure was his guiding principle, and he defended it with grim determination. The most serious challenge to his conception of the Supreme Commander's role came from Field Marshal Montgomery, who in the autumn of 1944, after the unexpected swift Allied victory in France, sought to place all available troops and matériel under British command for a single thrust to Berlin. The plan was a daring maneuver to end the war quickly by capturing the Ruhr and destroying the German war machine.

Eisenhower, however, favored a broad-front strategy based on the capture of all territory west of the Rhine and an advance into southern as well as northern Germany. When Montgomery—a daring loner who was the antithesis of Ike's genial committeeman—asked Chief of Staff Walter Bedell Smith to place him in command of the 12th Army Group in order to achieve his goal, Eisenhower's patience snapped. The indecisiveness with which he had been charged by Montgomery and Alan Brooke was replaced by an assertion of his authority as Supreme Commander.

The problem, he wrote Montgomery, was not the integrity of battlefield commanders, but the fact that in a "battlefront extending from Switzerland to the North Sea, I do not agree that one man can stay so close to the day-by-day movement of divisions and corps that he can keep a 'battle grip' upon the *over-all* situation and direct it intelligently." Eisenhower stressed the need for agreement on command arrangements; he also emphasized his decision that first priority must be the capture of the port of Antwerp, and stated that if Montgomery continued to "feel that my conceptions and directives are such as to endanger the success of operations, it is our duty to refer the matter to higher authority for any action they may choose to take, however drastic."

Montgomery loyally acceded to Eisenhower as his

superior, and the crisis was resolved. But the dispute
over the wisdom of Ike's strategy has continued. Part
of the difficulty lay in the difference of personalities: to
Montgomery the easygoing geniality of Eisenhower often
seemed like vacillation, and he agreed with Alan Brooke,
Chief of the Imperial General Staff, who found Eisenhower continually shifting, "inclining first one way, then
the other." Such charges grew out of Eisenhower's lack
of battlefield experience, his willingness to give his field
commanders wide latitude, and his desire to work out a
compromise whenever possible. He would issue a *diktat*
only if he felt that it was unavoidable. Montgomery's
strategy posed both a military and a political problem.

Montgomery's plan to seize the Ruhr in a lightning
thrust was indeed bold, but it involved halting Patton
and confining the Third Army to a defensive role. It was
obvious that this would trigger a political uproar on the
home front, which might have been tolerable had Eisenhower been convinced of the merits of Montgomery's
strategy—which he was not. Instead, he preferred to
stick to his policy of advance on a broad front for, like
Marshall's, his faith lay in the smashing power of overwhelming force. Ike's formula for an offensive, it has
been said, was that everybody should attack all the time.
He stuck firmly to this theory, dividing his supplies
between Montgomery in the north and Patton in the
south.

The result was that neither commander had the resources to attain his objectives. Refusing to choose
between the two rival plans, Eisenhower gave limited
approval to both and hoped for the best. But the very
situation he feared came to pass: his armies were
stretched over a long front and immobilized by a shortage
of supplies. By trying to seize both the Ruhr and the
Saar-Frankfurt area he delayed the opening of Antwerp;
to quote Chester Wilmot, "[Eisenhower] failed to capture
the one objective in the West that the Germans could
not afford to lose, and he had failed to secure the one
port the Allies had to have if they were to maintain

the broad front on which he had deployed his armies."

Although Eisenhower's strategy misfired—the Allied armies became bogged down and the Germans had time to regroup their forces and counterattack at the Battle of the Bulge—there is no assurance that Montgomery's plan would have worked. It depended on massive supplies, which Eisenhower contended could not be delivered through the Channel ports. Montgomery's own staff had grave doubts about the wisdom of his single-thrust scheme and believed he would run into fanatical German resistance once the Rhine had been crossed. Montgomery, however, argued that Eisenhower's policy would not guard against such resistance and would simply result in a long war of attrition that would sap Britain's strength and delay her recovery. For him time was of the essence, and he believed he could reach Berlin by winter and end the war. The risks were great, but Montgomery felt they were worth it, and he was convinced that Eisenhower had failed to take advantage of the opportunities to destroy the German army before winter.

At the core of the dispute over the single thrust versus the broad front lay an inescapable political reality that Eisenhower could not avoid. Not only would American public opinion have been inflamed were Patton halted and Montgomery given priority, but Eisenhower needed a broad front on which to deploy the American divisions that were piling up. To end the war without using those divisions would have been politically embarrassing to Marshall and Roosevelt. And, above all, as Stephen Ambrose points out in his excellent essay on the broad-front dispute, the fact was that "no matter how brilliant or logical Montgomery's plan for an advance to the Ruhr, and no matter what the nature of Montgomery's personality, under no circumstances would Eisenhower willingly give all the glory to the British. The American people would not have stood for it, nor would Patton, Bradley, Marshall, or Roosevelt."

We shall never know if Montgomery's or Patton's strategy would have worked for neither was ever tried. All we know is that Eisenhower's policy of compromise did not.* The war dragged on through the winter with enormous casualties, and the Allied armies never did reach Berlin. The American strategy rested on killing as many Germans as possible, which meant encounters resulting in an appalling rate of American casualties. This, with certain modifications, was also Westmoreland's strategy in Vietnam, and it produced equally terrible losses before he was replaced.

More than one kind of politics was involved in the different strategies proposed by the British and the Americans. We know that Churchill, who put high priority on the capture of Berlin, tried to dissuade Eisenhower from his plan to move toward Leipzig and Dresden and to meet the Russians at the Elbe. "If the enemy's resistance should weaken," he wrote on March 31, 1945, ". . . why should we not cross the Elbe and advance as far eastward as possible?" In a subsequent letter to Roosevelt he stressed the urgency, in the postwar negotiations, of not letting the Russians believe they had defeated Germany. Churchill maintained that in this sense Berlin had great symbolic importance even though the postwar occupation zones had already been established. Eisenhower admitted these political considerations but quite properly, as befitted his role, stressed that military factors came first. Once the Allied forces had linked up with the Russians at the Elbe, the British, he promised, would be given what they needed to reach the Baltic and Berlin. In this Eisenhower had the approval of Marshall and Roosevelt.

After the disintegration of the war-time alliance and the subsequent cold war dispute over Berlin, Churchill's strategy for outflanking the Russians gained many converts. But it is well to remember that the scheme was contrary to the spirit of Allied cooperation, and that it

---

* In a recently-published posthumous work, the British strategist B. H. Lidell Hart has charged that the war could have been won in September 1944 if Eisenhower had given Patton the gasoline he needed for his thrust into Germany, instead of diverting supplies to Montgomery.

no doubt fueled the Russians' suspicion of Western motives—a suspicion that later led them to consolidate their
hold over Eastern Europe by the most brutal means.
Churchill's policy was based on minimizing Russia's post-
war political influence and maximizing Britain's; Eisenhower's on destroying German power and emphasizing
military considerations designed to end the war as soon
as possible. It was inevitable that they would disagree on
questions of strategy because these also involved politics.

Eisenhower shared the belief of American military and
political leaders that a second front should be quickly
opened in Europe. Here they ran into the staunch opposition of Churchill, who by grim determination and wily
diplomacy was able for two years to stave off the cross-
Channel invasion and divert Western forces to North
Africa and Italy. When Eisenhower arrived in Europe
in June 1942 to take command of the European theater
of operations, the British had—largely from a fear that
the Americans would divert their resources to the Pacific
—accepted Washington's plan for a cross-Channel invasion in 1942 or '43. But Churchill reneged, announcing
instead that the British favored a landing in North Africa.
The Americans reluctantly allowed themselves to be persuaded, and for the next two years were bogged down on
the periphery of the Nazi empire.

Stalin was furious at what he regarded as a betrayal of
the Allied promise to open a second front in Western
Europe no later than mid-1943, and he suspected that
Churchill wanted to see the Soviets bled white by the full
force of the German army. It was only under the strongest pressure from Stalin that Churchill finally agreed to a
cross-Channel landing in June 1944. Whether or not
Stalin's suspicions were correct, Churchill also favored a
peripheral strategy of gradually tightening the noose
around Germany because he wanted to keep down casualties and avoid trench warfare. Churchill put a high
priority, too, on air power as the means of destroying Germany's war machine. Also it is clear, as later critics have
suggested, that he wanted to exert maximum British influence in the Mediterranean.

Because the British had their way, Eisenhower was not involved in the formulation of grand strategy after mid-1942. However, once the decision for a cross-Channel attack was definitely made, he played an important role. After January 1944 he crossed swords with Churchill on three major issues: the landings in southern France to back up the Normandy invasion, the use of air power to knock out rail transportation, and the single-thrust plan to capture Berlin. On each issue Eisenhower carried the day by his persistence, by the force of his military arguments, and ultimately by his support from Roosevelt and Marshall.

He was sometimes wrong, although it is far from certain that those who disagreed, such as Churchill and Montgomery, were right. Ike was not a brilliant strategist and had never been a battlefield commander. Reluctant to impose his own ideas in tactical matters, he sought the opinion of those concerned and tried to work out a compromise. The qualities of an Organization Man, which made him such a superb Supreme Commander, hampered Eisenhower in the field, where bold decisions were essential.

Being a compromiser, he rarely rose above the consensus. This made him invaluable as commander of a vast wartime operation composed of military and political prima donnas. It served him less well in the Presidency, where vision, even more than management, was the prime requirement for political leadership. But as commander of Allied forces Eisenhower performed his role well. He listened carefully to the arguments of others, gave each position consideration, showed the greatest patience toward the idiosyncrasies and demands of those who served under him, never overstepped his role by trying to usurp that of the political authorities he represented, and made sure that he had weighed every aspect before he made a decision. Throughout a long war during which the very survival of nations was at stake, when the lives of many thousands hung on the decisions he made, and powerful personalities vied for authority and dominance, Eisenhower retained his dispassionate sense of authority and won the respect even of those who disagreed with him.

Partly because it was seemingly so lackluster, his was a remarkable accomplishment.

Empire Builders

Since the beginning of the cold war there has been happy agreement about the methods and goals of American foreign policy. We were, most Americans believed, the torch-bearers of liberty, the "watchmen on the walls of world freedom," in John F. Kennedy's overwrought phrase. We launched NATO and the Marshall Plan to stop the aggression-bent Soviets from engulfing Western Europe. We fought in Korea and Vietnam to preserve the rule of law and hold the line against what Hubert Humphrey once referred to as "militant, aggressive Asian Communism, with its headquarters in Peking, China." Although we frequently had to revert to arms in the defense of freedom, our ambitions were noble and disinterested. "What America has done, and what America is doing now around the world," President Johnson declared shortly after he began bombing North Vietnam, "draws from deep and flowing springs of moral duty, and let none underestimate the depth of flow of those wellsprings of American purpose."

Few bothered to investigate those "deep and flowing springs of moral duty" because the assumptions of American foreign policy were taken for granted. The cold war against communism became its own justification, and all the acts carried out in its name explained in the noble rhetoric of American idealism. We were not doing anything so base as protecting our investments when we financed an invasion against the government of Guatemala and overthrew Mossadegh in Iran. We were not playing power politics when we saved the royalist government in Greece and helped put down the Stanleyville secessionists in the Congo. Nor were we concerned with such nasty concepts as spheres of influence when we launched the Bay of Pigs operation, sent the Marines into Santo Domingo, and plunged head first into the Vietnamese civil war.

Some might consider such acts as the subversion of foreign governments, the dispatch of military forces to preserve friendly regimes, the direct intervention in the internal affairs of other nations, the use of trade and aid as instruments of political warfare, and a dedication to the prevention and extermination of radical-minded revolutions as typical acts of an imperial power. Some, like Richard Barnet in his devastatingly detailed study, *Intervention and Revolution*, would argue that "from the Truman Doctrine on, the suppression of insurgent movements has remained a principal goal of U.S. foreign policy."

Nothing, however, could be further from the mind of the average American, or from the vocabulary of the government official. Everyone knows, or ought to know, that American policy is motivated by self-sacrifice. Empire is a nasty European word. Our diplomacy is not venal or self-seeking. It is, to use the jargon dear to the hearts of what Barnet calls the National Security Managers, "responsible." Let us listen, for example, to George Ball, renowned for his dove-like murmurings on Vietnam. The United States, he declared when he was Under Secretary of State and U.S. planes were pounding North Vietnam, is engaged in "something new and unique in world history—a role of world responsibility divorced from territorial or narrow national interests."

How satisfying to serve a government engaged in such a noble task, as Mr. Ball did during his six years as chief deputy to Dean Rusk. How inspiring to know that there is no conflict at all between American national interests, as defined in Washington, and those of other countries, since what we want for them is what they want—or ought to want—for themselves. We have occasionally dissipated our resources by failing to think ahead properly. But, as George Ball writes, with the self-assurance that is the hallmark of an important National Security Manager, "there is no historical precedent for the generosity of our policy."

This certainty that American power is being used beneficently, if not always efficiently and wisely, pervades Ball's revealing study, *The Discipline of Power.* The title is drawn from Senator Fulbright, and the main part of Ball's argument is that our power is not being used arrogantly, but rather that it simply lacks discipline. His concern is the "political organization of power" and how various "structures" and "disciplines" can be devised to guide our policies. Indeed, he concludes his study with an appeal for "better structures and concepts and disciplines" which will guide us in "finding our way to a safer and more decent world." It is a curiously bureaucratic and inconclusive appeal, but one not inconsistent with Ball's view of the world and America's place in it.

He is no critic of American foreign policy, although he spares his friends responsibility for the "heresies" he apparently believes his book contains. Rather, he is an ardent believer and defender, who faithfully served both Kennedy and Johnson. His mild criticisms of U.S. policy concern the way it has been applied, not its underlying principles. This "book of argument" based upon his "personal experience covering more than three decades near the center and on the periphery of foreign policy on both sides of the Atlantic," is perfectly conventional in its wisdom, though instructive in what it tells us about the making of American foreign policy.

While opposed to the bombing of North Vietnam (although never to the extent of resigning in protest from the administration conducting it), he saw in late 1967 "no serious option but to continue the course we are presently pursuing . . . until we further wear down the enemy in South Vietnam." This, let it be remembered, is the counsel of the administration's most publicized dove. Having become so deeply involved, we will, he states, have to keep 100,000 men in Southeast Asia for another ten or twenty years. "This does not arise from any desire on our part to play an imperial role . . . but when the United States undertakes to help build a nation and to provide the political assistance and security to maintain that nation against what is almost certain to be a constant effort of subversion, we have signed up for the duration." One has to search far to find much heresy in phrases like "nation building" and "signing up for the duration."

"What our experience in Vietnam has taught," Ball declares in a key statement, "is that there is clearly a point of no return beyond which national options tend to fade and disappear. Once America passed beyond that point in Vietnam, her only course was to go forward; otherwise, she would have disclosed her weakness rather than demonstrated her strength—and this could have had serious political consequences all over the world." In other words, once a mistake has been made, magnify it until it becomes a catastrophe.

As Barnet has observed in a critique of just such thinking: "Once military forces are committed . . . it is usually impossible to limit the objectives to those which originally impelled the intervention." Questions of prestige and power are raised, and the reputation of the nation becomes identified with that of the policy-makers. Withdrawal becomes ignoble, even if the original intervention was ill-advised, and there is no choice but to "go forward." Ball, of course, argues that we should never have become so involved in Vietnam in the first place. But with the commitment already made, he sees no way out. It is not surprising that President Johnson's dove-in-residence made so little headway against the hawks, since he had already accepted their logic, even while rejecting the premises on which it was based.

The portrait that emerges from the pages of this book

is of a rather arrogant and impatient man. Those who do not share his ideas about European unification disclose their own "ignorance of history and innocence of the world today"; their attitude reflects an "ignorance of the facts"; and their views are "arrant nonsense." Those who carry placards and burn their draft cards in opposition to the Vietnam war evoke the condescending assurance that "I revere anyone's constitutional right to make an ass of himself"; while private individuals who tried to open communications between Washington and Hanoi are suspected of a "zeal to win Nobel or Pulitzer prizes." The author expresses indifference to "world peace through world law," rejects the capacity of the UN to solve problems, and makes wisecracks about capital cities with names "like a typographical error"—unfortunate observations for one who served as U.S. representative to the United Nations.

Following a tradition in American diplomacy, he is, like Dean Acheson, John Foster Dulles, and Clark Clifford, a lawyer by training, with both the virtues and the weaknesses that a lawyer's thought processes often involve. In Ball's case there is a tendency to rely on formulas—European unification being his favorite one—and to treat opposing views as without any conceivable merit, or, as he would say, "arrant nonsense."

While Ball is a man of many convictions, his burning passion is the cause of West European political unification, one born in "the yeasty years" when he worked in Paris with Jean Monnet, "one of the towering figures of the age." Like a good lawyer arguing for a client he admires, he apparently has not the slightest doubt that a politically unified West European community will join the U.S. in exercising the agonizing responsibilities of power. He prods the Europeans to form "a second Western great power, capable of sharing with the United States the burdens and decisions of the West in a way the individual European nations can never do." "By and large," he argues. "we would see things in the same general terms and react with the same humane impulses." Britain, he believes, has no real alternative but to enter the European federation, and should be discouraged from thinking it has any such thing as a "special relationship" with the United States.

Ball argues for a politically unified Western Europe with the kind of ardor that fur-draped American matrons plead for birth control in underdeveloped countries. With the touching self-assurance of one who would consider it lèse-majesté to question his convictions, he envisages a Europe which would be "our mature good friend, giving us from time to time sound advice, bringing to world councils its own insights, agreeing or disagreeing as the case may be, but acting always from the same larger purposes that it shares with us."

The question, however, is whether a European community would share Washington's idea of the "larger purposes," or whether, on the contrary, it could define its identity only by being something separate and different from the United States. Europe as a "third super-power" could perhaps serve as a buffer between the U.S. and the Soviet Union, as Ball urges. But once it gained such power a United Europe might find that it has more in common with Russia, which holds the key to the division of the Continent, than it does with an America trying to carry out an imperial "white man's burden" in Asia.

Ball's formula for European federation may be the wave of the future, and many Europeans seem to agree. But even the most ardent federalists resent having their arms twisted by the United States. It is widely believed that Ball's pressure tactics on the Common Market, during the delicate negotiations over Britain's entry, contributed to de Gaulle's famous veto of January 1963. For Ball such attitudes are incomprehensibly reactionary, and de Gaulle is an evil genius who "has been one of the destructive elements in the larger chemistry of the West." But as Stanley Hoffmann observes in *Gulliver's Troubles:*

> There is a gang of rebellious European urchins who see no point at all in European unity unless it results not in a European echo of American policy but in a European policy. . . . America's advice and promotion of

supra-nationality have also had divisive and delaying effects on Europe's search for a new mission. Inevitably, people resentful of dependence were bound to be suspicious of any scheme so ardently embraced by the leader.

In his enthusiasm for a European super-power allied to the U.S., Ball was an ardent champion of the ill-fated multilateral nuclear force (MLF) of missile-carrying cargo ships under NATO command. It was a "good idea," he declares, "an educational instrument and a healing ointment" that collapsed "largely because our own government failed to take a sufficiently decisive position during 1961 and 1962." But at best the MLF was a political monstrosity that was militarily superfluous, designed to assuage non-existent German fears and isolate a nuclear-armed France.

Vigorous and opinionated, George Ball's "book of argument" is a lucid exposition of the conventional politics of the cold war era we are now moving out of. For all its minor iconoclasms—opposition to the bombing of North Vietnam and indifference to communist regimes in small African states—it is profoundly rooted in an imperial view of American world responsibility and the immutable struggle against Soviet communism. Ball is neither an ideologue (although his "pragmatism" sometimes rises to the level of fervor) nor a militarist, and he probably does not think of himself as a nationalist, although he seems to assume that American power confers a special moral responsibility. He is, like the other National Security Managers so well described by Barnet, one who sees "no better alternative model for world order than the imperial model, to be constructed, hopefully, with as light a touch as possible." Unable to make a connection between the wealth of the industrialized Northern nations and the poverty of the exploited Southern ones, he is one of those for whom, in Barnet's words, ". . . underdevelopment is a fact of the natural order. There are lucky nations and unlucky ones, energetic creative peoples, and peoples whom history has passed by. Stifling the Calvinist impulse to call wealth virtue, the American bureaucrat is convinced that the misery of the underdeveloped world is no one's fault except possibly its own."

Barnet's book offers a devastating examination of the bureaucratic mentality that has led the United States on the path of intervention and counter-revolution. "The United States government," he declares, "has seized upon the moral ambiguity of revolution to justify a global campaign to contain it, to channel it into acceptable paths, or to crush it." In case histories of key post-war U.S. interventions, he furnishes a powerful dramatization of his thesis that "The United States will oppose where it can or where it dare the establishment of new communist or communist-leaning governments, whether they come into being through foreign invasion, domestic revolution, or election."

In seeking the roots of intervention, Barnet makes a detailed analysis of what American officials did when confronted by insurgent movements, how they explained their actions, and what the effects of their policies have been. The result is an absorbing document of great utility to a new generation of Americans who are questioning the traditional explanations of the cold war and are rejecting the concept of an American guardianship over the world. It helps put the current crisis into perspective by examining its roots, and demonstrating how the doctrine of containment led to a policy of counter-revolution.

II. NUCLEAR DIPLOMACY

Tho unleaohing of the atom has given us not only nuclear weapons, but nuclear strategists, nuclear strategy,
and even nuclear diplomacy. The universities have been
called into the service of the empire, with billions of
dollars of federal funds flowing into government-ap-
proved research projects designed to increase the power
and efficiency of the military machine. Entire faculties
have been set up to carry on government-supported
activities—whether it be the perfection of new weapons
or the techniques of "nation-building" in the more remote reaches of the "free world." The cold war has
spawned the federally-financed, military-blessed "think
tank," and with it a whole generation of ex-mathemati-
cians, economists, and political scientists whose careers
(as well as whose prestige and salary) are based upon
ways of making nuclear warfare thinkable, and explaining, to the satisfaction of their Pentagon employers, why
an unending succession of new atomic weapons systems
is essential to national survival and self-respect.

The Bomb, by its promise of instant obliteration, may
have made total war between the great powers less
likely than during a period when the stakes were lower.
But in raising the threshold of total war, it has also
made possible a variety of lesser conflicts, such as wars
of "national liberation." In trying to devise an imperial
diplomacy for the nuclear age, American policy-makers
have relied heavily on the strategists who, to our good
fortune and theirs, have not had their theories put into

practice. The following essays deal with the interconsion to use the first atomic bomb against Japan, to the confrontation that nearly took us beyond the brink during the Cuban missile crisis.

Why the Bomb
Was Dropped

More than two decades after the scientific triumph that became a political nightmare, we are still trying to come to terms with the decision to use the bomb. Burdened as we are with the terrible legacy of Hiroshima —the shame, the responsibility, and the fear—that decision strikes us as one of the most momentous this nation has ever taken. Yet at the time, when the feverish work at Los Alamos was coming to a conclusion, there was no problem of a decision at all. To General Leslie Groves, who directed the Manhattan Project, "There was never any question in my mind that we would use the bomb when we got it ready and also that we would get it ready just as fast as we could." It was an opinion reflected at the highest levels of government and later expressed by President Truman himself when he wrote: "I regarded the bomb as a military weapon and never had any doubt that it should be used." Not only was there no doubt that it should be used, there was never
any di_____ the matter. It was simply *assumed*. As
_____ itten in words which today seem re-
_____ eir matter-of-factness, "The decision
_____ use the atomic bomb was never an

If it was not an issue in 1945, it has become one today. Why? Perhaps because our consciences are nagged by the suspicion that the sacrifice of Hiroshima and Nagasaki may not have been necessary. Perhaps because we have become more skeptical about the rhetoric which nations use to justify the impersonal violence of war. Perhaps because we are no longer so callous about the slaughter of the innocent, whether at Hiroshima or in the villages of Vietnam. And perhaps because today, unlike 1945, we feel the hot breath of the atom upon our own necks and know that our fate hinges upon a decision similar to the one made, or assumed, by American policymakers in the last months of the war against Japan.

At the time it was tested, the bomb seemed like an extension of the weapons already in use—different in degree, but not in kind. Being a weapon of war, it was used as a weapon of war. Today we find it shocking that it was dropped without warning on unprotected civilians as a device of terror quite divorced from any military significance. And it is. But the indiscriminate slaughter of civilians did not begin at Hiroshima. It was launched at Guernica and in Ethiopia, and developed on a larger scale at Rottendam, Leningrad, and Dresden. It was refined by the U.S. Air Force in the fire raids against Japanese cities where civilians were the primary target. In a single raid on Tokyo, 83,000 people were burned alive—a toll greater than that taken by either of the atomic bombs. Few, however, bothered to question such brutality, although among the few was Secretary of War Henry Stimson, who later told Robert Oppenheimer that "he found it appalling that there had been no protest over the air strikes we were conducting against Japan which led to such extraordinarily heavy losses of life . . . He did think there was was something wrong with a country where no one questioned that."

Belatedly, but in growing numbers, such questions are being asked by a new generation of Americans, who see the dropping of the bomb on Japan as a decision which weighs heavily on all of us who are its descendants coming to terms with the legacy of Hiroshima, there is no better point of departure than *The Decision to Drop the Bomb* by Len Giovannitti and Fred Freed. This is an intricately detailed, scrupulously fair, and totally engrossing study which grew from two NBC White Papers the authors prepared for television. With objectivity and an impressive knowledge of their material, they analyze the personalities, the decisions, and the forces in operation during those four momentous months between the death of Roosevelt and the surrender of Japan.

In this recreation of history the authors have helped put the tensions and the conflicts of that period into perspective, and to wrench the struggle of human wills out of the gray hulk of documents. Here is Harry Truman suddenly become President on April 12, without ever having known that the bomb project existed; here is Averell Harriman telling him only a week later that we were faced with a "barbarian invasion of Europe" by the Russians; here is Stimson advising Truman to hold off negotiations with Moscow until the bomb was tested; here is Secretary of State James F. Byrnes suggesting to Leo Szilard that "the demonstration of the bomb might impress Russia with America's military might"; here is Undersecretary of State Joseph Grew desperately searching for a way to end the war before the Russians got in; here is Assistant Secretary of State Archibald MacLeish trying to sabotage Grew's plan to speed surrender by retaining the Emperor; here are the scientists, often intimidated by the generals and politicians, and divided among themselves on the wisdom of using the bomb; and here in the middle of it all is Truman, endowed with a titanic military power he was incapable of using politically. It is a dramatic story, and Giovannitti and Freed make the most of it.

From their mass of documents and interviews they determine, along with most other observers, that it was not *necessary* to drop the bomb on Japan to win the war. By the time the bomb was ready, the war was virtually over and the Japanese were frantically extending peace feelers. The war could have been ended without a costly invasion—either by a continuation of the air strikes, or by the shock of Russian entry, or by a relaxation of surrender terms—or perhaps even by simply waiting a few weeks. But by the summer of 1945, the makers of U.S. policy were no longer eager to have the Russians enter the war and saw them as rivals, possibly as enemies, in the post-war world. The bomb offered the means to end the war quickly without Russian help. At this point the authors stop. While they point out the diplomatic weight it carried in the Truman administration, they deny that the "sole, or even primary, reason for using the bomb was as a political weapon against the Russians." Rather, in their words, it was "an *additional* reason." It was, it would seem, a question of degree.

If the bomb was not necessary, was it at least justified? Again, the answer is categorical. "In the end," they conclude, "the decision was made because a decision not to use it could *not* be justified." Congress and the public would demand to know why $2 billion had been spent on a weapon that was never used. American soldiers would die, and their families would believe they had been needlessly sacrificed. Maybe the Japanese would surrender if the Russians entered the war . . . if they could keep the emperor . . . if the devastating bombardment continued. But maybe they would not. The alternatives were all so vague—and after July 16, the atomic bomb was a certainty. To nearly everyone concerned it seemed inevitable that the bomb would be used. To refrain from using it would have meant to reverse the wheels that had been put in motion six years before and to make a deliberate decision *not* to use it. It was a decision which virtually no one in authority at the time—neither the major officials of the administration nor the key scientists at Los Alamos —saw the need to make.

This is a moderate and rueful view of the events that culminated in the tragedy of Hiroshima and Nagasaki. It points no fingers, casts no blame, and identifies no villains—unless villains be all men of heavy responsibilities and inadequate vision. But it is not the only view, and, indeed, as far back as 1948, the British physicist and Nobel

Prize winner, P. M. S. Blackett, charged that the dropping of the atomic bomb was not the final blow of the Second World War, but the opening gambit of the cold war between Russia and the West. Blackett's charges, long dormant, have now been revived, expanded, revitalized, and documented with some 1,400 citations by a young historian who has written a devastating attack on those responsible for American foreign policy during the crucial months before and after the Potsdam conference.

In *Atomic Diplomacy: Hiroshima and Potsdam,* Gar Alperovitz, who was only nine years old when the events he describes took place, undertakes a daring and elaborate work of historical reconstruction which questions not only the motives behind the decision to drop the bomb, but the very origins of the cold war. Wading through the published material on the period, plus the unpublished diaries of Stimson, Grew, and Admiral Leahy, Alperovitz arrives at the conclusion that the bomb was not used primarily to spare an invasion of Japan and thus save American lives, as is generally believed, but rather to intimidate the Russians and make them more manageable in Europe.

In brief, his argument runs like this: Almost as soon as he became President, "Truman launched a powerful foreign policy initiative aimed at reducing or eliminating Soviet influence from Europe." Initially he favored Churchill's plan to have an early showdown with the Russians while the British and American armies in Europe were still at full force, but he was talked out of this by Secretary of War Stimson, who told him that because of the atom bomb project at Los Alamos "we shall probably have more cards in our hands later than now." Accepting the new strategy of "tactical retreat," Truman changed his poker face for smiles and became the model of amiability toward the Russians—even to the point of sending Harry Hopkins on a conciliatory mission to Moscow. It was all a ruse, however, designed to stall a confrontation with the Soviets until the bomb was tested. The bomb, as Byrnes told him, "could put us in a position to dictate our terms at the end of the war."

Resisting Churchill's insistent pleas for a Big Three meeting in the spring, Truman decided that Potsdam would have to wait for Los Alamos. The only trouble was that Potsdam could not wait forever. After twice postponing the scheduled conference, Truman reluctantly had to set sail for Europe in July, without knowing whether the "master card" was an ace or a deuce. But his policy was already clear: "If it works, as I think it will," he confided on the eve of the conference, "I'll certainly have a hammer on those boys!"

Back at "Trinity"—as the New Mexico testing ground had been baptized by Oppenheimer—the scientists were working furiously to get the bomb ready in time. By July 16, the date the Potsdam conference opened, Truman had his answer: the bomb would work. The President was elated, and told Stimson that the bomb "gave him an entirely new feeling of confidence." Not only could it be used to make the Russians behave in Eastern Europe, but it now made their entrance into the war against Japan quite unnecessary. The bomb would allow the U.S. to win the war without an invasion and without the Russians. It was the answer to Washington's prayers. Yet oddly enough, the news did not make Truman noticeably stiffer in his attitude toward Stalin, nor in his demands that the Soviets comply with the Yalta accords as the West understood them. If Truman tried to intimidate the Russians in Eastern Europe with the bomb, he failed totally. As Herbert Feis later wrote, the explosion at Trinity "filtered into the conference rooms at Potsdam only as a distant gleam."

Why so dim and distant? Because Truman had decided, presumably on Stimson's advice, that he should not "have it out with Russia" until the bomb had been demonstrated by actually "laying it on Japan." Thus—and here is Alperovitz's attack—the bomb had to be used against Japan in order for it to be effective as a diplomatic instrument against the Russians. Although he does not try to prove this accusation, he strongly implies that there was no military justification for dropping the bomb, and

American policy-makers knew it. "Despite their subsequent assertion," he charges:

> They were no longer primarily worried about having
> to undertake a costly invasion of Japan. They believed
> a Russian declaration of war in itself would probably
> end the war quickly if necessary. They were also pre-
> pared to moderate the surrender terms to end the war
> before an invasion. Consequently, the fundamental ob-
> jective was no longer military, but political—could the
> war be ended before August 8?

And August 8, as the President and his advisers knew,
was the date by which the Russians, as they had secretly
agreed at Yalta, were to declare war on Japan. The bomb
struck Hiroshima on the 6th.

These are serious implications, and it is not surprising,
considering the issues and the reputations at stake, that
they have aroused such controversy. Whatever one's skepticism about some of Alperovitz's assumptions, it is clear
that the central point of his thesis is well-documented and
as conclusive as such things can be until the archives are
opened: the bomb had a determinant effect on American
foreign policy during that critical period between the
death of Roosevelt and the surrender of Japan. It almost
certainly accounted for Truman's two postponements of
the Potsdam conference, for his perplexing shifts in policy, and for the behavior which inspired de Gaulle's acid
comment that "the Americans and British hoped to recover in application what they had conceded in principle"
at Yalta.

This is the backbone of Alperovitz's book, and it gives
some substance to his suggestions that: first, the cold war
began about two years earlier than is generally admitted
in the West, and that it may have even been stimulated as
much by American bomb-rattling in the summer of 1945
as by Soviet greediness in Eastern Europe; and second,
that, *at least to some degree*, the bomb was directed
against the Russians as well as against the Japanese.
Otherwise, why did Truman refuse to demonstrate the

bomb in an uninhabited area (as many scientists urged), or wait until after August 8 to see if Russian entry would shock Japan into surrender? Even Herbert Feis—whose definitive work, *Japan Subdued,* Alperovitz continually refutes—believes that these probably would "have impelled the Japanese government to yield almost as soon as it did." During the past twenty years a variety of reasons have been given for Truman's refusal, but none has been fully convincing.

But it is one thing to maintain that the desire to keep Russia out of the Japanese war and to make her more manageable in Eastern Europe was a reason for dropping the bomb. It is something quite again to state that "Hiroshima and Nagasaki were to be sacrificed primarily for political, not military reasons." Alperovitz doesn't prove this, nor does he try, and on this ground his historical sleuthing is little more than guesswork. Even in analyzing the strategy of Potsdam, he leaves too many loopholes unplugged. For example, Truman is supposed to have twice delayed the Potsdam meeting so that he could use the atomic bomb as a "hammer" on the Russians. He had his hammer the day the conference opened. Why didn't he use it? Why did he wait eight full days before mentioning it to Stalin—and then only so casually that the Soviet dictator could hardly be expected to know what he was talking about? Alperovitz says it is because Stimson reversed himself and wanted to delay the showdown until after "laying it on Japan." But no evidence is offered for this assertion, nor any reason given why Truman would accept such contradictory advice. Isn't it equally possible that Truman *intended* to use the bomb as a diplomatic weapon, turned out to be inept at doing so, and refrained from telling Stalin about its full power for fear he would demand to know how it was made? Further, why did Truman bother beating a "tactical retreat" during the three months before Potsdam—if, as Alperovitz claims, he wasn't really worried that the Russians would renege on their promise to declare war on Japan? What if the bomb didn't work? Then he would have lost his chance to drive a hard settlement with the Russians in Eastern Europe.

Would he have been foolish enough to put all his eggs in one untested basket? Perhaps . . . and perhaps not.

Truman was, like any statesman, almost certainly duplicitous, and no doubt tried to squeeze whatever political advantage he could out of the bomb. That he was so spectacularly ineffectual was not a tribute to his virtue but a mark of his incapacity. To imply, however, that he was a nuclear Machiavelli is to press beyond the weight the documents will bear. More likely, Truman himself, ignorant as everyone else about the effects and the aftermath of the bomb, was swept up in a tide he could not control.

Alperovitz's dissection of American diplomacy during the four-and-a-half months following Roosevelt's death is a provocative work of historical induction that is likely to be discussed, analyzed, and argued about for a long time to come. It would be even better if he speculated less and stuck to the evidence—which is explosive enough. While he throws new light on the role of the bomb in the formation of American policy during the genesis of the cold war, he does not convincingly show that the bomb was dropped on Japan primarily to intimidate Russia, nor that Truman and his advisers had any more than a dim awareness of the political power put in their hands. On this count the judgment of Herbert Feis still holds that "the Americans at Potsdam either did not know how to use their command of the new weapon effectively as a threat, or chose not to use it in that way."

War Games

As a result of the terrible power unleashed by the atom, we are returning to a rather more flexible and subtle theory of warfare than the kind conducted with such disastrous effects during the last two European wars. The baleful influence of the Clausewitz school—which defined victory as the destruction of the enemy's armed forces, and thereby provided the rationale for the mindless slaughter of trench warfare during the First World War—has now been replaced by a broader concept. Instead of wars of attrition where ignorant armies clash by night with no other purpose than to destroy one another, nations now seek to achieve their political ambitions by a limited and discriminating use of force. The concept of victory itself has changed. It is no longer the physical obliteration of the enemy's army (which France and Britain achieved in 1914–18 only by the near-obliteration of their own), but to persuade the enemy that further resistance is undesirable. Now it is generally accepted, in the words of the British strategist, B. H. Liddell Hart, that "the aim of a nation in war is to subdue the enemy's will to resist, with the least possible human and economic loss to itself." War of attrition, as refined with such horrible results in the First World War, has given way to war of intimidation.

In current theories of strategy the psychological element of warfare is at least as important as the military element. Armies locked in combat are just one element of war. They are not the whole thing, and not necessarily even the most important thing. Today we take this for granted, and indeed the whole theory of deterrence is based upon the belief that military strategy can be conducted without engaging in direct battle. We have come so far from the theories in vogue during the nineteenth century and applied so cataclysmically during the First World War, that we have turned Clausewitz on his head. Instead of war being "the carrying out of diplomacy by other means," it is now diplomacy (or nuclear diplomacy, if you will) which is the carrying out of war by other means.

Clausewitz sought to break the morale of the enemy by military victory on the battlefield; today, according to General André Beaufre, one of the most lucid and intelligent of the contemporary strategists, victory is achieved by "exploiting a situation resulting in sufficient moral disintegration of the enemy to cause him to accept the conditions it is desired to impose on him." From the confrontation of opposing armies we have swung over to a totally different concept: the dialectic of opposing wills. Where nations once sought to bludgeon their enemies, they now prefer to demoralize them. Brute force has taken a back seat to psychology, and nations now use the *threat* of military force to achieve the political objectives they would once have been able to obtain only by the *use* of such force. The war of nerves has succeeded the *Blitzkreig*. Strategy is no longer a push-button to unleash a holocaust, but a keyboard on which various levels of intimidation are combined with selective use of force in order to achieve the desired psychological result. The Cuban missile crisis is the true successor to the trench warfare of the First World War—and a dramatic symbol of how far we have come from the theories Foch inherited from Napoleon.

This new strategy of warfare seems natural to us. But if we take it for granted, it is in large part because of the groundwork laid down with such clarity and persistence over the past forty years by B. H. Liddell Hart. The most important and original military thinker to have come out of the First World War, Liddell Hart has had a profound influence not only upon the theory, but upon the practice of warfare. His ideas of mobile warfare, centering around the tank and the airplane, which were so long ignored in his own country, were taken up enthusiastically by the German generals and used with devastating effect during the Second World War.

Liddell Hart was above all a revisionist. He wanted to correct what he believed to be the errors of the First World War. Like many other young officers, he was horrified by the waste and the futility of trench warfare. He sought to break through the deadlock of land armies locked in massive battle, and found a breakthrough in the tactics of mobile warfare. Using the tank as the instrument of what he called the expanding torrent method, he developed a complete theory of tactics which had a powerful influence on military thinking ever since. In addition, he developed a new concept of strategy resting upon the deception of the enemy and the use of nonmilitary means to achieve political ends. It is in this realm, even more than in the field of tactics, that his influence has been so important. He was the forerunner of the theories which have been explored with such chilly organizational precision by the RAND Corporation and similar institutes for strategic studies.

Liddell Hart, it can be said, did not so much innovate a theory of strategy as return to earlier theories, such as those practiced by Alexander and Scipio, in seeking to overcome the enemy's will to resist without first destroying the mass of his army. "The destruction of the enemy's armed forces," he wrote in 1925,

> is but a means—and not necessarily an inevitable or infallible one—to the attainment of the real objective. It is clearly not, as is so often claimed, the sole, true objective in war . . . our goal in war can only be attained by the subjugation of the opposing will. All acts, such as defeat in the field, propaganda, blockade, di-

plomacy, or attack on the centers of government and population, are seen to be but means to that end . . .

In turning the military mind away from the rigid formulas of Clausewitz's followers, he brought a new element of flexibility, and a new element of instability, into the art of warfare. Military strategy has never been the same since, and the impact of Liddell Hart is perhaps more powerful today than it was in the 1920s and 1930s when his theories were first being developed.

While he achieved fame at a very early age, and had a predominant influence upon the generation of strategists who succeeded him, Liddell Hart's career was not an entirely successful one. He was bitterly resisted by the British General Staff, and never more so than just before the Second World War when he became adviser to Hore-Belisha, the Secretary of State for War. By the time he reached a position of influence he had revised his own thinking to emphasize the defensive over the offensive. His advice was taken, and proved to be disastrous against the Germans, who were employing earlier Liddell Hart tactics of mobile warfare.

But the tactical errors of the late 1930s fade to unimportance as compared to the genius of Liddell Hart as a strategist of indirect warfare. *The Liddell Hart Memoirs 1895-1938*, covering the years from his birth to the end of the phony peace, offer a rich, informative and frequently witty insight into the career of a man whose name is known to few, but whose influence is felt by all of us who live in an age when teeth-bared confrontation has given way to the subtle blackmail of nuclear deterrence.

Of all the disciples of Liddell Hart, none has been more outspoken in his appreciation than General André Beaufre, whose new book, *Deterrence and Strategy*, is dedicated to the master—who in turn wrote the preface to the General's earlier book, *An Introduction to Strategy*. The mutual appreciations of master and disciple should not, however, discourage the reader, for General Beaufre is no whispering acolyte dressing up borrowed British

theories in new French *couture*. On the contrary, he is
an original strategist in his own right, and his book on
nuclear deterrence is an important contribution to an
evolving, highly perilous, and gravely misunderstood art.
A clear thinker with an admirably sharp and uncluttered
literary style (ably translated by Major-General R. H.
Barry), General Beaufre offers an impressive analysis of
the new strategy of deterrence which has evolved from
nuclear weapons. This is a slim volume, but an extremely
meaty one, which offers even the uninitiated reader a
high-level, but jargon-free, analysis of the precarious
balance on which the policy of deterrence currently rests.

General Beaufre, who is now director of the Institut
Français d'Etudes Stratégeques, a kind of French RAND,
maintains that nuclear weapons are a powerful stabilizer
in international affairs, and that "it is the risk of nuclear
conflict which keeps the peace so stable." This will come
as a surprise and perhaps a shock to most readers, but
General Beaufre makes a powerful case for his thesis.
According to him, nuclear weapons have introduced an
entirely new factor into military strategy; instead of a
strategy of potential threat, we moved to a strategy of
deterrence. The purpose of deterrence is, unlike former
strategies, not to defeat the enemy, but to prevent him
from taking the decision to use armed force.

Nuclear weapons, to his mind—and here he parts company with a good many American strategists—are not for
defense, but for deterrence only. But deterrence, in order
to be effective, depends upon the *threat* that nuclear
weapons will be used, for "if no one fears that someone
else will fire first, there is no nuclear deterrence." Thus,
"the disappearance of nuclear deterrence would be a
frightful catastrophe . . . for we should then lose the
benefit of the stability created by the atom in our rapidly
evolving world." Impelled by this line of reasoning,
General Beaufre thus sees the current nuclear stability
between America and Russia as being inherently dangerous—because it opens the temptation to violence
below the nuclear threshold—and believes it necessary
to re-establish a certain nuclear instability. His remedy:

the creation of independent nuclear forces in such places as western Europe and China.

Having defined a certain amount of nuclear proliferation as basically healthy, General Beaufre declares it to be "nothing less than a law" that "a conventional armaments race produces instability, whereas a nuclear armaments race produces stability." This may be hard going for most American strategists, but General Beaufre sees the danger of nuclear war between the great powers as virtually nil, and therefore is interested in using nuclear weapons to deter major conventional conflicts as well. "In the nuclear world," he declares in a key passage, "peace and war have lost their traditional meaning because nuclear war has become unthinkable and peace is nothing but the permanent interplay of deterrence. It is for this reason that fears about independent nuclear forces possibly triggering off nuclear war are totally unrealistic. Such forces reinforce deterrence instead of reducing its effectiveness." The remedy for the current woes within the Atlantic Alliance, which he sees as based upon America's monopoly over nuclear control and strategy, is thus an independent European nuclear deterrent.

General Beaufre's conclusions are arguable, just as some of his premises—such as a rather exaggerated fear of the emerging 'Third World'—seems dubious. But his reasoning is rigorous, and his logic has a compelling quality which cannot be easily tossed off. This is original strategy on the highest level, and if it is to be refuted, it will take a mind of the same caliber to do it.

The Experts

If war is too serious to be left to the generals, is strategy safe in the hands of the strategists? Nobody, to be sure, knows more about such mysteries as "deterrence," "options," and "escalation" than the coterie of intellectual technicians we call defense strategists. At a hundred universities and research institutes—from dingy laboratories in Manhattan to leafy retreats in Cambridge and Santa Monica—they plot the vectors of nuclear mishap and balance the threat of disaster against the opportunities of atomic diplomacy. They are the mentors to generals, the advisers to statesmen, the new elite of our global military establishment. Our reliance on them is exaggerated and seemingly inescapable, for when confronted with the awful complexity of the atom there seems nowhere else to turn but to the "experts" for advice.

Some find comfort in the rising power of defense strategists over military policy, and even over diplomacy. These strategists, trained in such traditional disciplines as economics, mathematics, and even statistics, but now turning their energies to defense theories at such places as RAND, the Hudson Institute, MIT, and the Institute for Defense Analysis, have provided the formulas for "deterrence," "counter-force," and "limited warfare" that roll lightly off the tongues of both generals and statesmen.

Among our current Clausewitz strategists, few are more eminent or influential than Bernard Brodie, former luminary of RAND—the California defense research institute —and now professor at UCLA. In his forceful essay, *Escalation and the Nuclear Option,* he argues that we must be far more willing to use our tactical (battlefield) nuclear weapons in order to be really sure of deterring the Russians. Such refusal to be intimidated by the dangers of escalation, he believes, will also discourage our European allies, who might otherwise be tempted to suspect we would cop out of a European land war rather than face a nuclear exchange with the Russians. No admirer of the McNamara strategy of "flexible response"—which is based on the attempt to meet a Russian probe in Western Europe with non-nuclear weapons as long as possible— Brodie believes that the build-up of conventional forces and the downgrading of nuclear weapons during the Kennedy administration led the Russians to believe they could push us around. The 1961 crisis over Berlin and the Cuban missile affair the following year, he suggests, were our own fault because we gave Khrushchev the wrong clues. Had we been less worried about "escalation" we could have intimidated the Russians more easily since, "unless we are dealing with utter madmen, there is no conceivable reason why in any necessary showdown with the Soviet Union, appropriate manipulations of force and threats of force, certainly coordinated with more positive diplomatic maneuvers, cannot bring about deterrence."

Unfortunately, it is hard to see how the Russians could be much more acquiescent in Europe than they already are, and thus harder to see why we should adopt Brodie's prescription for a light finger on the nuclear trigger. This is particularly true since he himself asserts that "it is difficult to discover what meaningful incentives the Russians might have for attempting to conquer western Europe." Brodie's strategy of atomic readiness, it would seem, becomes more pressing with each diminution of the Russian threat. And will our allies find much encouragement in a strategy which, if ever actually put to use, would devastate most of Europe? Rather than revitalizing NATO, Brodie's prescription could be its *coup de grâce*, and rather than dissuading the already deterred Russians, his project for using tactical nuclear weapons "more abruptly than the Russians seem to have bargained for in launching their aggression" could well lead to the full-scale nuclear holocaust he desires to avoid.

Like many of the people in Washington whom he advises, Brodie has apparently over-learned the lesson of the Cuban missile crisis and tends to see American military power as a panacea for a complexity of political ailments. Thus, in a casual footnote to his plea for first use of tactical nuclear weapons in Europe against the Russians, he asserts, with regard to the war in Vietnam, that "imaginative use of special types of nuclear weapons much earlier in the campaign might have gone far toward defeating the Viet Cong." Surely, one assumes, this is meant as a joke—the kind of humor that probably takes place around the water cooler at RAND. Can Brodie seriously believe that a guerrilla war fought by primitively armed peasants in an economically backward country can be defeated by the "imaginative use" of American nuclear weapons? Apparently he does—which leads one to the disconcerting conclusion that Clemenceau's warning about generals holds true for strategists as well.

Skepticism is confirmed by repeated exposure. The strategists, it becomes clear on closer inspection, do not really know much more about war and its prevention than do the generals—armchair and real—who actively concern themselves with such problems. Their "scenarios" are fascinating and their analyses enlightening. But they have no political answers, and a good many of their recommendations are based on slide rule speculation. This is not to deprecate them, for their impact upon defense thinking has been enormous and in many ways beneficial. But it is necessary to try to put them into some kind of realistic perspective.

Among the most perceptive and influential of the civilian strategists is Thomas Schelling, a Harvard-based economist who has pioneered the application of mathematics and games theory to military strategy. Always literate and often witty, Schelling is not unaware of the human element that does, or ought to, determine the choice of strategy. He has learned his Clausewitz well, and recognizes that the rational justification for military force is the attainment of diplomatic ends. In *Arms and Influence* he examines how the power to hurt can be used as a bargaining lever, how it is reflected in such notions as deterrence and retaliation, and how the "diplomacy of violence" results from the measured application of military force to political ends.

Schelling makes a useful distinction between "deterrence" (designed to prevent an adversary from doing something we fear) and "compellence," which is meant to force him to do something we desire. Applying his theory of compellence to Vietnam, Schelling defines it as "the direct exercise of the power to hurt, applied as coercive pressure, intended to create for the enemy the prospect of cumulative losses that were more than the local war was worth, more unattractive than concession, compromise or limited capitulation." All this sounds very reasonable. The only problem, however, is that it doesn't seem to be working in the one place that it has seriously been applied. Hanoi is not, so far at any rate, being coerced into concession, compromise, or limited capitulation, and indeed has referred to our policy of bombardment today, foreign aid tomorrow, as one of "the broken stick and the rotten carrot." "Compellence" by air power is not working any better in Vietnam today than did strategic bombing in the Second World War. Perhaps it is the theory rather than the application that is at fault. Further, even if mounting escalation were able to coerce Hanoi into capitulation, what reason do we have to assume that this would end the war in the South—which is why we became involved in Vietnam in the first place? Schelling seems to share the administration's assumption that this is a simple war of foreign aggression, for otherwise "compellence" is marginal to the real problem of Vietnam. Yet to believe that is to tailor the facts to fit the theory—a process that yields symmetry, but often at the expense of reality.

Schelling's argument is powerful and lucidly presented. But his general theory offers no formula for a world that is more puzzling and more intractable than even such an enlightened strategist would lead us to believe. *Arms and Influence* is a stimulating study and it is perhaps unfair to call Schelling to task for the failure of "compellence" in Vietnam when he is really presenting a general theory. But surely such theories are presented for the purpose of being applied, and, judging from the evidence, "compellence" has not been very successful, or perhaps even particularly relevant, in Vietnam. That war may be an anomaly, but it is a war, we are deeply involved in it, and the ways of dealing with war is what strategy is supposed to be all about.

It is to a large degree, one might suspect, because of the influence of the defense intellectuals, and to their theories of "coercion," "compellence," and "graduated escalation," that we have become so deeply involved in Vietnam. Perhaps without the aid of their analysis, without their carefully delineated rungs of escalation, our policymakers might not have considered it possible to become embroiled in such a conflict without seriously risking a full-scale war with Russia or China. The strategists may be right in their estimation of reasonable "risk-taking," but would reasonable men, weighing the national interest against situations such as those in Vietnam, normally have been willing to take such risks?

The strategists speak with objectivity of "raising the price of aggression"and "forcing the enemy to behave," as though this were a formula that would automatically bring about the desired results. Yet when put into practice, their prescriptions appear to be little more than guesswork, and their results almost contrary to what was anticipated. There is a tone of enlightened reasonableness about the "diplomacy of violence" the defense strategists have evolved, and one cannot help being impressed by their seriousness and intellectual acuity. But unfortunately diplomacy cannot be measured in teaspoonfuls of violence, and successful coercion depends upon a good deal more than the threat, or even the application, of force.

Indeed, judging from our experience in Vietnam, it would seem that the very concept of coercion is inadequate and even self-defeating, regardless of Brodie's assurance that a conflict which is in large part a civil war can be resolved by the "imaginative use" of atomic weapons, and regardless, too, of Schelling's prescription for the "compellence" of Hanoi as though this would end the guerrilla activity in the South. Surely a reasonable strategy should be made of more subtle, and politically perceptive, stuff. If the "diplomacy of violence" cannot take the intractability of politics into serious consideration, then the prescriptions of the strategists must be considered as general hypotheses, rather than as specific recommendations of policy. In this sense, the strategists can tell us what we might do—if we wanted to do it, and if the political situation was such that it was politically relevant or possible to do it. This is, perhaps, a more modest role than they might choose for themselves, but it is one which a wise diplomacy ought to insist upon.

In delineating a "diplomacy of violence" for the nuclear age, the strategists have not made war unthinkable. On the contrary, they have made certain kinds of war quite thinkable, and even possible, by prescribing conditions under which controlled violence can take place. They have taught us not only to think about the unthinkable, but also to engage in a "competition in risk-taking," to borrow one of Schelling's phrases, along the fringes of the unthinkable. The strategists have shown that Eisenhower was wrong when he said there is "no alternative to peace." Apparently there are numerous alternatives, and we are today engaged in exploring some of them. The legacy of Clausewitz hangs heavy over Vietnam.

Having learned to accept, and even to glorify in, Clausewitz's fusion of diplomacy and military power, we are now being faced with the obligation to evolve a theory of politics for a world Clausewitz never knew, and for which his theories are only vaguely relevant, if relevant at all.

Only by unlearning the lesson of Clausewitz, by finding a way of channeling and restraining violence, rather than using it for narrow political ends, may we be able to find a way of living at peace in a world that the atom has made too dangerous for a "diplomacy of violence."

Nuclear Chicken

"Does Herman Kahn really exist?" one critic asked in outrage when Kahn's now-notorious tome, *On Thermonuclear War,* appeared back in 1960. A cold-minded, and to most readers a cold-blooded account of how to wage nuclear war and still "prevail," it brought Kahn the kind of international fame enjoyed by such personalities as Moise Tshombe and Walter Ulbricht. With his slide rule and his atom smasher, he became the monster of our nuclear nightmares, the mad scientist who would reduce us all to radioactive fallout.

Feeling unjustly accused of monsterdom, Kahn swears that he is not really advocating all those terrible things he writes about. Like many a seeming Caliban, perhaps he is misunderstood. Which is not to say that he didn't bring some of his misfortunes upon himself. His first book, *On Thermonuclear War,* was the perfect model of political naivety. Kahn is a mathematician and a physicist —not a political philosopher. Reaching out of his depth by fusing dubious political judgments with computerized strategic options, he made it easy for critics to dismiss the implications of his sharp analysis. His political gaps were reinforced by a looseness of vocabulary that made him seem callous—if not actually sadistic—when he was probably only trying to be unemotional.

Herman Kahn had to learn that there is a delicate line between shaking people out of their apathy and shocking them out of their pants. He applied the lesson in his second book, *Thinking About the Unthinkable,* and seems to have taken an overdose in *On Escalation,* his latest study of atomic unthinkability. Here is not only a more mellow Herman Kahn, but a cautious, and even a benign one. To be sure, many of the old elements are still there: people are optimistically trooping off to their civil defense drills, Russia and America are blasting each other with atomic bombs, and nations are bounding back to their former levels of prosperity in double-time. Even that Strangelove monstrosity, the "doomsday machine," makes a return bout, and at virtually bargain-basement prices (between $10 billion and $100 billion) although it is now dismissed as impractical and "not likely to affect international relations directly." But the old gusto is gone, and with it some of the gems that made the first book such a landmark of (unintentional) sick humor— like the unforgettable comment of one blast victim to a vomiting fellow-victim suspected of malingering: "Pull yourself together and get back to work! You've only received a ten-roentgen dose!"

Instead of such hearty stoicism, Kahn now admits that nuclear war will be no bed of roses. Which doesn't however, make it impossible. Or even unlikely. Like Clausewitz, on whom he seems to model himself, he wants us to consider how force, even nuclear force, can be used for political ends. Deploring our reluctance to use force sparingly for limited objectives, and then to use too much force once our emotions are aroused, he preaches a "cool, restrained and moderate willingness to threaten or use force." And in the atomic age, force means atomic weapons.

A primer on nuclear arm-twisting, *On Escalation* is not designed to shock, but to instruct—to show how we can use our atomic weapons and still, perhaps, come out alive. Or at least kicking. Based on the premise, unexceptionable in the abstract, though deceptive in the specific, that "a very undesirable peace might have consequences . . . worse than those of many wars—even [some] thermonuclear wars," it tells us how to avoid such an undesirable peace by being willing to wage certain kinds of atomic war. Rather than merely thinking about the unthinkable, Herman Kahn now speculates on how we can do the unthinkable—and maybe even get away with it.

Escalation, in Kahn's definition, is a "competition in risk-taking," not unlike the adolescent game of "chicken," in which the players try to gain prestige and humiliate their opponents by taking dangerous risks. Like chicken, it is no game for the faint-hearted, for as Kahn observes, "when one competes in risk-taking, one is taking risks. If one takes risks, one may be unlucky and lose the gamble." And when one gambles with nuclear weapons, he might have added, there may be no return bout. Why, then, play the game at all, the unromantic might ask? Why not reach agreements without threatening to use force? Why not "reason together," as a President impervious to other people's reason keeps suggesting? Because, as Kahn tells us, "if either side desperately desires to make a settlement without harm or risk of harm, it is likely to get a very bad bargain."

Having thus defined *Realpolitik* as a global chicken-playing, Kahn constructs an escalation ladder by which nations can work their way up a series of forty-four graduated rungs from ordinary cold war unpleasantness to all-out nuclear oblivion. With the aid of analogies from history (metaphors) and hypothetical confrontations at various points along the ladder (scenarios), Kahn demonstrates some of the options that are open in the game of chickenmanship.

We begin our climb up Kahn's Ladder with run-of-the-mill incidents like the Tonkin Gulf raids of 1964 (Subcrisis Maneuvering) and progress gradually to the Cuban missile crisis of October 1962 which, although it had us all under our beds, seems to have been only at level 9 (Dramatic Military Confrontation). From there we push on steadily, breaking off diplomatic relations, fighting land wars, and issuing nuclear ultimatums up to rung 17, where we start evacuating our cities for limited nuclear war. On reaching rung 21 we find ourselves in "bizarre crises" where we use atomic weapons in a frugal manner, stepping up the pace bit by bit (unless one side turns chicken and swerves off) until we finally arrive at rung 44 (Spasm or Insensate War). At this point the game is over. "All the buttons are pressed," Kahn writes, with what I presume is mordant humor, "and the decision-makers and their staffs go home—if they still have homes; they have done their job." In this case, escalation was presumably a success, although the patient unfortunately died.

With his doomsday ladder, Kahn has built a ladder, not an elevator, and to set foot on rung 1, we are told, doesn't automatically whisk a nation up to rung 44—at least if it keeps its wits. In the abstract, nations always have the option of climbing off the ladder if the going gets rough. Whether in fact they would be able to do so once the bombs start falling in a "barely nuclear war" is another story.

In this quest for demystification of nuclear war, escalation becomes the means by which it is possible to open the atomic cupboard and take some of the small bombs off the shelf. In a world of atomic stalemate, limited nuclear battles are offered as the alternative to "all-out spasm war or peace at any price." By taking the mystery out of nuclear war, Kahn transforms the traumatic into the ordinary. Which is why there was such an outburst of horror when his earlier books were published. We do not want nuclear war to be demystified, because we fear that the more ordinary it seems, the more likely it will be to occur. For most people, its unthinkability is the only guarantee of its improbability. Even Kahn seems to sympathize with those who fear "that the more both sides believe in the possibility of nuclear bargaining . . . the more likely it is that such bargaining will be tried and that it will escalate." But his answer is that nations are going to engage in escalation anyway, so they might as well do so with some knowledge of the risks involved, rather than in total ignorance.

Though escalation may not be an automatic process, it requires cool nerves on both sides. Even more importantly, it demands a mature political judgment which can distinguish between essential risks and foolish ones, between vital interests and crude displays of power politics, between a Cuba and a Vietnam. For all its temptations, as Kahn points out:

> The probability of war eventually occurring as a result of "chicken" being played once too often may be very high . . . After a while, the hypothetical danger of war may look less real than the tangible gains and the prestige that are being won and lost. It may turn out that governments learn only after peace has failed that it is not feasible to stand firm on incompatible positions . . . To rely even on slow, rung-by-rung escalation in international crises is a dangerous strategy.

As an escape hatch from his nuclear nightmare, Kahn counsels arms control which would limit options and thereby reduce the dangers of escalation open to sovereign states. Although so long as states are sovereign, it seems unlikely that they would forego the temptations that escalation provides. Failing such self-restraint, the only other hope is some form of world government—which Kahn vaguely espouses, but for which he sees little prospect except as the result of a nuclear Armageddon.

As this book makes clear, the psychological wraps are slowly being stripped off atomic weapons, and what was once untouchable is now entering the military arsenal as just another weapon. Like the crossbow, gunpowder, and high-explosive bombs in an earlier age, nuclear weapons have become part of our mental furniture. The unthinkable has become a commonplace, and if the President should decide to use "little" atomic bombs in Vietnam tomorrow in the defense of "freedom and democracy," who will be shocked? The major threshold may already have been crossed: the one in the public mind. With that barrier gone, escalation simply becomes a matter of logistics and of risk-taking in which the only limitation is the self-restraint of the players involved.

Herman Kahn has shown us how it can be done. Clausewitz with a computer, he demonstrates, in the words of his mentor, that even nuclear war may be "a real political instrument . . . a carrying out of [policy] by other means." By reducing nuclear strategy to its logical conclusions, he has made nuclear war banal. And that which is banal, as Hannah Arendt has taught us, is rarely resisted. He is not telling us we *should* wage nuclear war; he is telling us how we might still survive if that is what we insist on doing.

The global game of chicken, after all, is not conducted by academic strategists, but by political leaders. It is they who will be tempted to use atomic weapons to impose unfavorable settlements on weaker rivals, and they who will hazard the risks of escalation to reap tantalizing rewards. In the new Augustan age now dawning in Washington, it is not American military power that limits the degree of escalation, but the hesitations of a democratic society which has not yet accepted the imperial role that has intoxicated its leaders. Unorganized and politically inarticulate though it may be, it is still the public which seems to be blocking the nation's steady ascent up the escalation ladder.

The authority for this is no less than Herman Kahn himself who, in a recent lecture recounted by the astute Washington correspondent of the London *Times,* described how the United States was in a position to do almost anything it wanted to do in Vietnam, even bombing China. "I asked," the reporter wrote, in words that speak for us all, "why it did not exercise that enormous power, and quite simply he said 'public opinion.' " *Vox populi:* a restraint which Clausewitz never felt, but which may now have become our court of last resort.

Peace Is
Our Profession

"The 12th of October dawned like any other day for the Strategic Air Command, poised as always to spring into action at a moment's notice." So reads the opening sentence of General Thomas S. Power's *Design for Survival*, describing how SAC gave Khrushchev the heave-ho and chased the Russians from Cuba. It is a story with overtones of Zorro and even a heartwarming account of "the little old lady who adopted a B-47 detachment and regularly brought the alert crews home-baked cookies and hot coffee."

But somehow one can't help wondering if there isn't a little more to it than that. Which is pretty much the impression left by this glowing account of how SAC does everything, from cleaning up dirty guerrilla wars to defending the American Way of Life—and would do it even better if only stingy politicians would vote it more money. The man who had his finger on The Button for the past seven years describes how a little more SAC in the arsenal can give us "peace on *our* terms" (without saying what the terms are) in the cold war, and "military victory" (whatever that is) if the button ever gets pushed.

As commander in chief of SAC from 1957 until his retirement in 1964, General Power deserves our attention.

He also deserves our gratitude, both for *not* pushing the button during the seven years he had his finger on it, and also for letting us know what he has been thinking all this time. In fact, he would have liked to let us know sooner, but the Eisenhower administration turned thumbs down on an earlier version of this book in 1959—presumably in the belief that generals with their fingers on the button are better seen in Omaha than in print. Now it can be told, and in his book—part Air Force brochure, part lecture on why you can never trust a communist, part critique of current defense policy—he eagerly lays it on the line.

Responsible, as he says in his ghostwriter's style, for "over 90 per cent of the nuclear firepower of the entire Free World," General Power has been a very powerful man indeed. And whatever the demands of his office, silence on matters of public policy has always been a relative one. The hearing rooms of Congress and the columns of the press are always open to the man responsible for all that nuclear firepower—whether it be General Power or his garrulous predecessor, Curtis LeMay. No gag, after all, prevented General Power, in his capacity as SAC commander, from testifying in the Senate against the nuclear test-ban treaty—despite the fact that the treaty was endorsed by his bosses: the President, the Secretary of Defense, and the Secretary of the Air Force. Nor did it prevent the officers of SAC, with the help of a breathless Joseph Alsop, from publicizing a terrifying "missile gap" during the late fifties—a gap which after the 1960 election suddenly turned out to be as nonexistent as Eisenhower claimed it was all along. While the publication of this book makes General Power's voice heard across the land, it is hardly the first time.

Surrendering to an impulse most retired officers find irresistible, General Power treats us to his own interpretation of world affairs—one which seems to rest upon the belief that "agreements with the Soviets can be expected to be meaningless" since they are dedicated to the "ultimate Communist objective, which is the annihilation of the capitalist system." While such a concern with free enterprise might seem a bit overdone from one who has spent most of his adult life on the public payroll, enjoying such socialistic benefits as free medical care and officers' clubs, it is perfectly common in the upper echelons of the military where the oil depletion allowance is equated with the right to vote—and perhaps one notch above freedom of speech. We are even warned that the tendency "to impose certain controls on private enterprise" may continue piling up "until we reach the 'point of no return' and have, in fact, a controlled economy." But then the book itself, as we are informed in the Preface," is intended mainly as a report to the nation's stockholders—almost 200 million of them," which I suppose is meant to endow it with the virtues of the reports issued by such Air Force suppliers as Dow Chemical or North American Rockwell.

Since communism is defined as "the most insidious and gigantic plot in history," and since "many of the Russian intellectuals are not educated in our sense," it is obvious that there is scarcely "any possibility at all of reaching an agreement with the Soviet Union." Aside from being uneducated, the Soviet rulers are "merely tools of the system" and thus "are not easily deterred from anything or by anything—except that which threatens them personally"—which might lead one to assume that the most effective deterrent would be a bomb hidden in a samovar in the Kremlin basement. But that would eliminate the need for the Strategic Air Command, which could hardly be what General Power has in mind.

In fact, it is sometimes hard to know what he does have in mind. At one point we are told that we need a "war-winning capability" which will insure "military victory," and thus deter the Russians from aggression. But even that is not enough, since "deterrence is not a goal in itself; it can contain Communist aggression but it cannot defeat Communist ideology which must be our ultimate goal if we are to survive as a sovereign nation." Whether this is to be done by some act of mass conversion—an *auto-da-fe* in Red Square under the guidance of the Reverend Billy Hargis—or through the mailed fist of the organization whose motto is "Peace is Our Profession," the

General does not tell us. But we can get a glimpse of his thinking when he muses wistfully on that period in the late forties when we had the Bomb and the Russians didn't: "It is academic to reflect whether, in the long run, we have done a greater service to the cause of freedom and democracy by listening to the voices of restraint and caution, or whether we should have used every opportunity to crush Communist aggression—as long as we had such an opportunity."

Leaving behind General Power, foreign policy analyst, we are left with the counsel of General Power, strategist. Aside from deterring (personally threatening?) the Soviet rulers, he describes how an all-purpose SAC can be used to stamp out rebellions in troublesome countries "without excessive drain on our military resources." Writing in 1964, on the war in Vietnam, he suggests that we warn the communists that "unless they ceased supporting the guerrillas in South Vietnam, we would destroy a major military supply depot in North Vietnam." We would continue this strategy—is it all beginning to sound familiar?—until Peking and Hanoi run up the white flag. Thus General Power assures us, in the same firm tones which no doubt convinced Lyndon Johnson, "within a few days and with minimum force, the conflict in South Vietnam would have been ended in our favor." Fanfare, trumpets, and jet trails into the wild blue yonder.

Except that it hasn't worked out that way. Which is not to knock General Power for making a mistake. After all, he has distinguished company. But it does raise a few questions about the rest of his strategic advice, and makes us wonder whether the case against disarmers, one-worlders, minimum deterrers, limited warriors, test ban treaties, and arms control is nearly so clear-cut as he would have it. Or for that matter if the manned bomber really is the key to world peace. In an eloquent plea for more strategic bombers, at a time when virtually everyone who doesn't wear an Air Force uniform or manufacture airplanes considers them obsolete, General Power confesses endearingly: "I may be accused of being prejudiced in favor of bombers because of my long association with SAC which, until not so long ago, was strictly a bomber force." Which is like a man who has spent his life as an elevator operator remarking that he really does prefer manually operated elevators to automatic ones.

But then the gradual obsolescence of the bomber has been an unkind blow to SAC's share of the defense pie, which fell from 13 per cent of the total in fiscal 1962 to 8 per cent in fiscal 1965. Small wonder that there are screams from the men in blue. And small wonder that those screams find an echo on Capitol Hill among Congressmen determined to cut their districts in on the lucrative contracts handed out by the Pentagon. More than one Secretary of Defense, from James Forrestal on, has fallen victim to the Air Force Lobby, an informal pressure group combining the talents of Air Force generals who just love planes and missiles, powerfully placed congressmen for whom a big defense budget means vote-getting jobs and factories in their districts, and manufacturers who whisk them both away on handsome (tax deductible) expense accounts to weekends in the Virgin Islands where they are gently persuaded of their patriotic duty to plonk down public cash for their new products.

Rarely has mutual back-scratching developed into such a fine three-way art. Over the years the Air Force lobby— part of that "military-industrial complex" that Eisenhower denounced, better late than never, during his last month in office—has secured billions of dollars for flying hardware for which there was no need, and which occasionally (as in the case of the Atlas missile) was obsolete even before delivery.

General Power, not surprisingly, doesn't deal with that particular aspect of SAC's activities. Nor does he tell us about the bitter inter-service rivalries that have led to duplicate weapons systems and ferocious empire-building among Pentagon generals. This is unfortunate, because the General could have given us a rare insight into the inside operations of that mammoth machine controlling "over 90 per cent of the nuclear firepower of the entire Free World" with its 52 bases, its 260,000 men, its 2,200 tactical aircraft, its 800 ICBMs, and its $6 million a day budget. Instead, he has chosen to treat us to his quaint views on foreign policy and explain how SAC can do everything—except wrong. In so doing he has convinced us of his patriotism and sincerity, but also made us once again agree with Clemenceau that war is, after all, too serious a matter to be left to generals.

Endgame

It was a time, in Khrushchev's memorable phrase, "when the smell of burning hung in the air." Robert Kennedy's account of those Thirteen Days in 1962 from October 16, when he and his brother were presented with proof that the Russians were secretly building long-range missile bases in Cuba, until October 28, when the Kremlin agreed to dismantle them—shows the view from the inside by one of the key participants.

This short, terse memoir—bloated by the publisher with superfluous introductions, photographs, and documents—does not, of course, tell the whole story of the missile crisis. There is a good deal about the events leading up to the crisis that is gone over too lightly or deliberately clouded over. The clash of personalities and ambivalent motives is muted and the tone rather detached. But behind the measured prose we see the spectacle of rational minds swayed by passions and the euphoria of power, governmental machinery breaking down into the struggle of individual wills, and decisions affecting the future of humanity made by a handful of men—the best of whom were not always sure they were right.

We have come to take the balance of terror so much

for granted that it is hard to imagine any situation in which the two super-powers would actually use their terrible weapons. Yet more than once during those thirteen days it seemed as though the unthinkable might actually occur. SAC bombers were dispersed to airfields throughout the country and roamed the skies with their nuclear cargoes. At one point President Kennedy, fearful that some trigger-happy colonel might set off the spark, ordered all atomic missiles defused so that the order to fire would have to come directly from the White House.

The first showdown came on the morning of October 24, as Soviet ships approached the 500-mile quarantine line drawn around Cuba. "I felt," Robert Kennedy wrote of those terrible moments, "we were on the edge of a precipice with no way off. . . . President Kennedy had initiated the course of events, but he no longer had control over them." Faced with this blockade, the Russian ships turned back, and the first crisis was surmounted. No more missiles could get into Cuba. But what of the ones already there that Russian technicians were installing with feverish haste? President Kennedy was determined that they had to be removed immediately and on Saturday, October 27, sent his brother to tell Soviet Ambassador Dobrynin "that if they did not remove those bases, we would remove them." The Pentagon prepared for an air strike against the bases and an invasion of Cuba. "The expectation," Robert Kennedy wrote of that fateful Saturday, "was a military confrontation by Tuesday."

We know, of course, how it turned out. On Sunday morning the message came through that Khrushchev would withdraw the missiles in return for a U.S. pledge not to invade Cuba. Kennedy had pulled off the greatest coup of his career—the first, and one hopes the last, military victory of the nuclear era. Not a shot was fired, although we came a good deal closer to war than most people realized at the time, or have cared to think about since.

It was a victory not only over the Soviets, but over

many of Kennedy's own advisers who favored a more militant course from the start. The drama was played out among a hastily assembled group, which later took on the formal title of the Executive Committee of the National Security Council, that met several times a day in the White House. The sessions were frequently stormy, although the lines were loosely drawn at first. Several of the participants, according to Robert Kennedy, shifted their opinion "from one extreme to the other—supporting an air attack at the beginning of the meeting and, by the time we left the White House, supporting no action at all." A few, such as Dean Acheson and Douglas Dillon, were hawks from the start, and argued for what they euphemistically called a "surgical strike" against the air bases. They were eventually joined by John McCone, General Maxwell Taylor, Paul Nitze, and McGeorge Bundy. Favoring a more moderate course, which settled around a naval blockade to be "escalated" to an attack on the bases only if absolutely necessary, were the doves, led by Robert Kennedy and Robert McNamara, and including George Ball, Roswell Gilpatric, Llewellyn Thompson, and Robert Lovett.

Dean Rusk, for the most part, avoided taking a stand, or even attending the sessions. The Secretary of State, in Robert Kennedy's caustic words, "had other duties during this period and frequently could not attend our meetings." It would be interesting to know what these duties were. Robert Kennedy does not elaborate, although he does offer the further intriguing aside that "Secretary Rusk missed President Kennedy's extremely important meeting with Prime Minister Macmillan in Nassau because of a diplomatic dinner he felt he should attend." That was the meeting, one will remember, where President Kennedy agreed to help out Harold Macmillan on the eve of the British elections by turning over Polaris missiles to Britain after the Skybolt fiasco that had embarrassed the Tories. De Gaulle, predictably, was furious, declared that Britain still valued her trans-Atlantic ties above her European ones, and vetoed her entry into the Common Mar-

ket. The Nassau accord was a colossal error of judgment
that an astute Secretary of State should have been able
to prevent.

Some of the hawks were, of course, predictable. It is
not surprising that the Joint Chiefs of Staff were eager to
use their expensive hardware. "They seemed always
ready to assume," Robert Kennedy wrote, "that a war was
in our national interest. One of the Joint Chiefs of Staff
once said to me he believed in a preventive attack against
the Soviet Union." Nor is it surprising that Dean Acheson,
among the most recalcitrant of the cold warriors, should
have come down on the side of the military. "I felt we
were too eager to liquidate this thing," Elie Abel reports
him as saying in *The Missile Crisis*. "So long as we had
the thumbscrew on Khrushchev, we should have given it
another turn every day. We were too eager to make an
agreement with the Russians. They had no business there
in the first place." Ever since his crucifixion by Congress
during the Alger Hiss affair, Acheson has become increasingly reactionary and eager to prove his toughness
toward the communists. His bomb-first-and-talk-later argument found receptive ears in such pillars of the Eastern
Republican Establishment as Douglas Dillon, John J.
McCloy, and McGeorge Bundy.

Many who were not aware of the drama being played
out in the White House during those thirteen days, however, will be surprised to find Robert Kennedy as the
leader of the doves and the moral conscience of his
brother's administration. Although he does not dramatize
his own role, we learn from his account and those of
others that he argued against a first strike as contrary
to American traditions. "My brother," Abel quotes him as
saying, "is not going to be the Tojo of the 1960s." This
impassioned plea against a Pearl Harbor in reverse moved
even Maxwell Taylor. The general, Abel quotes one of
the participants as commenting, "showed what a moral
man he is by recommending that we give the Cubans
twenty-four hours' advance notice—and then strike the
missile bases."

The other outstanding dove of the deliberations was

the man in charge of the military establishment, Robert McNamara. The Secretary of Defense, in Kennedy's words, "became the blockade's strongest advocate" and argued that "a surgical air strike . . . was militarily impractical." McNamara was not only a consistent dove, fighting off the belligerent advice of his service chiefs, but disputed the prevailing view that the Russians were trying to upset the strategic balance between East and West. "A missile is a missile," Abel and others have quoted him as saying. "It makes no difference whether you are killed by a missile fired from the Soviet Union or from Cuba." Observing that the Russians had ICBMs and that the only effect of the Cuban-based intermediate-range missiles would be to reduce by a few minutes our warning time in case of attack, McNamara's advice, in effect, was to sit tight.

However valid such advice might have been from a military point of view, it was quite unacceptable politically. John F. Kennedy was especially vulnerable on Cuba, having used it as an issue against Nixon during the 1960 campaign, and then having suffered the ignominy of the Bay of Pigs. The Republicans were pressing him hard on his "do-nothing" policy toward Castro, and former Senator Keating of New York was leading a wolf pack in charging that the Russians were turning Cuba into a base for offensive weapons. Kennedy, as Democratic Party leader, could not tolerate Soviet missiles in Cuba, even if the civilian head of the Pentagon could.

"If the missiles," Roger Hilsman, head of intelligence in the State Department and then Assistant Secretary of State for the Far East, comments in his book, To Move a Nation, "were not important enough to justify a confrontation with the Soviet Union, as McNamara initially thought, yet were 'offensive,' then the United States might not be in mortal danger, but the administration most certainly was." And, according to John Kenneth Galbraith, then ambassador to India, "once they [the missiles] were there, the political needs of the Kennedy administration urged it to take almost any risk to get them out."

Did we, then, nearly go up in radioactive dust to shore up the Kennedy administration's fading image before the November, 1962, elections? Not necessarily, for if the missiles did not upset the strategic balance, even a President less image-conscious than John F. Kennedy could not easily accept such an abrupt change in the status quo —least of all the Caribbean. "To be sure," Theodore Sorenson observed in his *Kennedy*, "these Cuban missiles alone, in view of all the other megatonnage the Soviets were capable of unleashing upon us, did not substantially alter the strategic balance *in fact*. . . . But that balance would have been substantially altered *in appearance* [italics in original]; and in matters of national will and world leadership, as the President said later, such appearances contribute to reality." In fact, Kennedy himself leaned heavily on the prestige argument when he announced the blockade to the nation on October 22.

> This sudden, clandestine decision to station strategic weapons for the first time outside of Soviet soil is a deliberately provocative and unjustified change in the status quo which cannot be accepted by this country, if our courage and our commitments are ever to be trusted again by either friend or foe.

Elevating his rhetoric, as usual, above the needs of the occasion, Kennedy set the stage for a direct military confrontation.

He was acutely conscious of any questioning of his courage, and with the ashes of the Vienna encounter with Khrushchev still in his mouth and another Berlin crisis brewing, he had to get the missiles out of Cuba. But did he have to get them out before the end of October? What would have happened had he negotiated with Khrushchev instead of issuing the ultimatum—delivered to Ambassador Dobrynin on Saturday evening, October 27, by Robert Kennedy—that "we had to have a commitment by tomorrow that those bases would be removed." What would have happened had the negotiations dragged on for a few weeks and some kind of quid pro quo arranged?

The Russians, of course, would have had the already delivered missiles in place by then. But their withdrawal could still be negotiated and, in any case, the continuation of the blockade would have brought Castro to his knees within a few months. Assuming that the missiles had to be removed, was it necessary, in Robert Kennedy's words, "to have a commitment by tomorrow?"

At the time, a good many people believed Kennedy had politics in mind during the missile crisis. General Eisenhower, when informed by McCone about the discovery of the missiles, "took a skeptical view," according to Abel, "suspecting perhaps that Kennedy might be playing politics with Cuba on the eve of Congressional elections." The thought also crossed the mind of Kennedy's old chum, David Ormsby-Gore, then British ambassador to Washington, who felt that "British opinion must somehow be persuaded that the missile crisis was the real thing, not something trumped up by the President for vote-getting purposes." Nor did the elections go unnoticed by the participants in the Executive Committee. I. F. Stone has pointed out Sorenson's comment that during one of the meetings a Republican member passed him a note saying:

> Ted—have you considered the very real possibility that if we allow Cuba to complete installation and operational readiness of missile bases, the next House of Representatives is likely to have a Republican majority? This would completely paralyze our ability to react sensibly and coherently to further Soviet advances.

It is not to denigrate John F. Kennedy's patriotism to assume that he was aware of such possibilities. Nor is it to question the motives of those who took part in those exhausting, often stormy, meetings during the thirteen days. It would have been political folly for Kennedy to have broached the subject of the elections before the Executive Committee, where it would have fallen on a good many unsympathetic ears, and it is exceedingly unlikely that the question was ever formally raised. Nor did the participants believe they were behaving by the rules of partisan politics when they decided that the mis-

siles had to be removed immediately. But of the fourteen-
odd people who participated in most of the meetings,
only a few—Sorenson, Robert Kennedy, and, of course,
the President—could be considered politicians. As politicians who had to fight elections, as leaders of the party
which was about to be tested at the polls, they could not
have been oblivious to what was going to happen in early
November—even if they never mentioned it in the meetings, or to one another.

To do nothing about the missiles, as McNamara's position would imply, or to take the issue to the United Nations, or to compromise by trading the Soviet missiles in
Cuba for the obsolete American missiles in Turkey, would
have been bad politics at that particular time. Obsessed
by his image, Kennedy feared that Khrushchev would
not take him seriously if he again backed down in Cuba.
This questioning of "our courage," he believed, could
tempt the Russians to a policy of adventurism, perhaps
in Central Europe. Indeed, the first reading of the missile
crisis was that Khrushchev was prepared to force a Berlin
settlement on his own terms. Thus did considerations of
high strategy and party politics reinforce one another and
convince Kennedy that the Russian withdrawal had to be
complete, unilateral, and secured by the end of October.

The question of a quid pro quo revolved around the
American missiles in Turkey and Italy. These had been
placed there five years earlier during the Eisenhower
administration's panic over the Sputnik. Designed to redress the strategic balance during a time when the U.S.
had no reliable ICBMs, these relatively primitive liquid-
fuel missiles had become, in Hilsman's words, "obsolete,
unreliable, inaccurate, and very vulnerable." Shortly after
his inauguration, Kennedy asked that they be removed
and was discouraged by the State Department. He raised
the question again in early 1962, and despite objections
that the Turks disapproved, instructed Dean Rusk to
negotiate the removal of the missiles. "The President,"
Robert Kennedy has written, barely concealing his contempt for Dean Rusk, "believed he was President and

that, his wishes having been made clear, they would be followed and the missiles removed."

But his instructions were not carried out, and Kennedy discovered that the obsolete Turkish missiles had become a bargaining foil for Khrushchev. "We will remove our missiles from Cuba, you will remove yours from Turkey," read the note received from the Kremlin on the morning of Saturday, October 27. ". . . . The Soviet Union will pledge not to invade or interfere with the internal affairs of Turkey; the U.S. to make the same pledge regarding Cuba." This note, with its quid pro quo, added a new condition to the emotional message received the night before, in which the Soviet premier indicated he would pull out the missiles in return for a U.S. promise not to invade Cuba.

Adding Turkey to the bargain filled the White House advisers with consternation—not least of all because it appeared perfectly fair. "The proposal the Russians made," in Robert Kennedy's words, "was not unreasonable and did not amount to a loss to the U.S. or to our NATO allies." Categorically to reject such a trade would make the U.S. seem vindictive and threaten the support of its allies—none of whom had any wish to be dragged into nuclear war over the issue of Cuba. But to accept the trade would be to invite accusations of weakness and dishonor by the Republicans. Kennedy, needless to say, was furious at the State Department for putting him in such a vulnerable position.

The Kremlin was not the first to raise the issue of trading the Cuban bases for the Turkish ones. In his column of Thursday, October 25, Walter Lippmann suggested a diplomatic solution to get the missiles out of Cuba:

> There are three ways to get rid of the missiles already in Cuba. One is to invade and occupy Cuba. The second way is to institute a total blockade, particularly of oil shipments, which would in a few months ruin the Cuban economy. The third way is to try, I repeat, to negotiate a face-saving settlement. . . . I am not talking about and do not believe in a "Cuba-Berlin" horse

> trade. . . . The only place that is truly comparable with Cuba is Turkey. This is the only place where there are strategic weapons right on the frontier of the Soviet Union. . . . The Soviet military base in Cuba is defenseless, and the base in Turkey is all but obsolete. The two bases could be dismantled without altering the world balance of power.

This position had already been argued by Adlai Stevenson who, according to Robert Kennedy, on October 20 "strongly advocated what he had only tentatively suggested to me a few days before—namely, that we make it clear to the Soviet Union that if it withdrew its missiles from Cuba, we would be willing to withdraw our missiles from Turkey and Italy and give up our naval base at Guantanamo Bay." With this suggestion Stevenson went a good deal further than Lippmann, who never included Guantanamo in the trade. This won Stevenson the wrath of several of the participants, including Robert Kennedy, who prevailed upon his brother to send John J. McCloy to the UN to handle the Russians during the missile crisis. But time healed some of Robert Kennedy's wrath, and in *Thirteen Days* he wrote:

> Stevenson has since been criticized publicly for the position he took at this meeting. I think it should be emphasized that he was presenting a point of view from a different perspective than the others, one which was therefore important for the President to consider. Although I disagreed strongly with his recommendations, I thought he was courageous to make them, and I might add they made as much sense as some others considered during that period.

Stevenson's proposal was not so heretical as it was treated at the time, or as it was in the inside stories that appeared shortly after the crisis. Kennedy was prepared to give up the Turkish bases, but for political reasons could not make it a quid pro quo—although there is some reason to think that he might have done so *in extremis*. On Saturday—when the Russians sent their second note calling for the Turkey-Cuba base trade—Kennedy, according to Abel, told Roswell Gilpatric to prepare a scenario for removing the missiles from Turkey and Italy, and have it ready for the meeting that night. That evening he sent his brother to Ambassador Dobrynin with the demand that the Russians had to promise to withdraw the missiles from Cuba by the following day. The Joint Chiefs of Staff were preparing to bomb the missile sites on Tuesday. Dobrynin, according to Abel, "gave it as his personal opinion that the Soviet leaders were so deeply committed they would have to reject the President's terms."

But while he ruled out an explicit deal, Robert Kennedy told the Soviet ambassador that there need be no problem about the Turkish missiles. "President Kennedy," he said to Dobrynin, "had been anxious to remove those missiles from Turkey and Italy for a long period of time . . . and it was our judgment that, within a short time after this crisis was over, those missiles would be gone." Dobrynin sent on the message to Moscow; President Kennedy, at his brother's suggestion, accepted the more moderate first message from Khrushchev and ignored the second Kremlin note; and an apprehensive Washington awaited the Kremlin's response as plans proceeded for an air strike against the Cuban bases. On Sunday morning the word came through that the missiles would be withdrawn in return for a simple U.S. pledge not to invade Cuba. The worst crisis of the cold war was over. But even at this moment of triumph, some were not satisfied. "On that fateful Sunday morning when the Russians answered they were withdrawing their missiles," Robert Kennedy revealed, "it was suggested by one high military adviser that we attack Monday in any case."

The resolution of the Cuban missile crisis ironically set the stage for a more cooperative policy from Moscow, culminating in the test-ban treaty of 1963. It also contributed to the euphoria of power that led Kennedy's successor, urged on by Kennedy's advisers, to have his little war in Southeast Asia. Had the U.S. been forced to back down in Cuba, or to work out a Cuba-Turkey trade with the

Russians, perhaps Washington might have awakened from the dream of American omnipotence before Lyndon Johnson launched his crusade in Vietnam.

Cuba, in Hilsman's words, was "a foreign policy victory of historical proportions," but in the long run the Russians did not come out of it too badly. They lost a certain amount of face, particularly among the Communist parties of Latin America, and they revealed once again that the interests of the Soviet state take precedence over the world revolution. Peking, for its part, lost no time in gloating that it was "sheer adventurism to put missiles into Cuba in the first place, but capitulationism to take them out under American pressure." Perhaps the Cuban setback contributed to Khrushchev's demise, although it is dubious whether that was a net gain for the West. But the blow to Soviet prestige was washed away with passing time, and the Russians, perhaps because they had their fingers burned in Cuba, refrained from exercises in global management of the kind that obsessed President Johnson and ultimately drove him from office.

What was the lesson of the Cuban missile crisis? There were several: first, that diplomacy gave way to military ultimatums; second, that there was a failure of intelligence interpretation; third, that the Kremlin's motives were never adequately understood; and fourth, that there is something basically wrong with the whole process of decision-making.

1. *The suspension of diplomacy.* Kennedy's mistake was not, as former Secretary of State Dean Acheson would have it, in failing to brandish the big stick more quickly. Rather it was in deliberately rejecting diplomatic contact when it might have made unnecessary precisely the kind of confrontation that occurred. Instead of using traditional diplomatic channels to warn the Russians that he knew what they were up to, and thus give them a chance quietly to pull back, Kennedy chose to inform the Kremlin of his discovery by a nation-wide radio-TV hookup. He put them, in other words, in the position where a sub-rosa withdrawal was impossible, and public dismantlement of the bases meant humiliation. In doing so, Kennedy vio-

lated the first rule of diplomacy in the nuclear age, a rule he himself expounded in his famous speech at American University in June 1963:

> Above all, while defending our own vital interests, nuclear powers must avert those confrontations which bring an adversary to the choice of either a humiliating retreat or a nuclear war.

To be sure, he did not gloat over the Russian withdrawal, and insisted on treating it as a statesmanlike move. But the Kremlin's withdrawal under a public American ultimatum was a humiliation nonetheless.

President Kennedy certainly had ample opportunity to play it otherwise. There were available not only the Soviet ambassador and the famous "hot-line" direct to the Kremlin, recently installed with such fanfare, but also the Soviet Foreign Minister, Andrei Gromyko, who came to visit the President on Thursday afternoon, October 18— three days after Kennedy learned of the secret missile sites, but four days before he announced the blockade. Gromyko's visit had been scheduled some time before the discovery of the missiles, and the wily Soviet diplomat did not, of course, mention them. Instead he insisted that the Russians were furnishing purely "defensive" arms to the Cubans and wanted to relieve tensions with the U.S. over Cuba.

Robert Kennedy reports that his brother "listened, astonished, but also with some admiration for the boldness of Gromyko's position." Why should he have been astonished? Did he expect the Soviet Foreign Minister to confess that his government was secretly setting up long-range missile bases in Cuba? Mastering his astonishment, the President read aloud his statement of September 4, which warned the Russians against putting missiles or offensive weapons in Cuba. Gromyko assured him this would never be done and departed, returning to the Soviet Union a few days later.

The unavoidable question is why didn't President Kennedy tell Gromyko that he knew the truth, and give the Russians a chance to pull back? Robert Kennedy says it was because he hadn't yet decided what course of action to follow and was afraid of giving the Russians a tactical advantage—a judgment, Abel reports, supported by Rusk and Thompson. But Robert Kennedy reports that the President decided on the blockade on Saturday, October 20, two days before his speech to the nation. Why didn't he tell Gromyko on Saturday? The question was raised at the time by Walter Lippmann who, in his column of October 25, warned Kennedy against repeating the mistake of suspending diplomacy that plagued both world wars:

> I see danger of this mistake in the fact that when the President saw Mr. Gromyko on Thursday, and had the evidence of the missile build-up in Cuba, he refrained from confronting Mr. Gromyko with this evidence. This was to suspend diplomacy. If it had not been suspended, the President would have shown Mr. Gromyko the pictures, and told him privately about the policy which in a few days he intended to announce publicly. This would have made it more likely that Moscow would order the ships not to push on to Cuba. But if such diplomatic action did not change the orders, if Mr. Khrushchev persisted in spite of it, the President's public speech would have been stronger. It would not have been subject to the criticism that a great power had issued an ultimatum to another great power without first attempting to negotiate the issue. By confronting Mr. Gromyko privately, the President would have given Mr. Khrushchev what all wise statesmen give their adversaries—the chance to save face.

Roger Hilsman argues that Gromyko somehow erroneously assumed that the President really knew about the missiles all the time. He gleans this from various warnings given to the Russians about putting offensive weapons into Cuba—warnings by Chester Bowles, U.S. Ambassador to Moscow Foy Kohler, and the President himself. With all these lectures the Russians might, perhaps, have assumed that Kennedy knew what they were up to, but was keeping it under his hat until after the elections. "The best explanation for Gromyko's behavior," he writes, "seemed to be that the Soviets were hedging, trying to avoid a direct confrontation with the United States in the hope of leaving their hand free for negotiations or, if faced with extreme danger of war, for withdrawing the missiles with the least loss of face." Yet if the Russians assumed that Kennedy knew, presumably they were not plotting a surprise attack. In any case, Hilsman's argument, while it might excuse Gromyko of duplicity, does not justify Kennedy's behavior, and is not offered as a hypothesis by Robert Kennedy.

2. *The failure of intelligence.* Why were the missile sites not discovered sooner? Discovery of the missiles was a total surprise to the President, Robert Kennedy affirms. "No official within the government had ever suggested to President Kennedy that the Russian buildup within Cuba would include missiles." The United States Intelligence Board, in its most recent estimate, dated September 19, advised the President "without reservation . . . that the Soviet Union would not make Cuba a strategic base." It based this on the fact that the Russians had never taken such a step in any of their satellites, and that the risk of U.S. retaliation was too great. Although a number of unconfirmed reports had been filtering through the intelligence network, Robert Kennedy maintains "they were not considered substantial enough to pass on to the President or to other high officials within the government."

But the fact is that Washington had been buzzing for weeks with unconfirmed reports that the Russians were secretly introducing long-range missiles into Cuba. According to Abel, as early as August 22, CIA chief John McCone told President Kennedy that the Russians were putting SAMs (surface-to-air missiles) into Cuba to protect offensive missile sites, and urged reconsideration of the September 19 intelligence estimate. Meanwhile reports kept flowing in from agents inside Cuba that missiles much longer than SAMs were being delivered, and Castro's pilot had reportedly boasted "we have everything, including atomic weapons." According to Arthur Krock's *Memoirs*, the French intelligence agent, Thiraud de Vosjoly (the celebrated Topaz) came back with eyewitness evidence for McCone.

Robert Kennedy says "there was no action the U.S. could have taken before the time we actually did act," since no films were available to offer proof to the rest of the world. But why were photographs not made earlier? When McCone returned from his honeymoon in early October, he discovered that the eastern part of Cuba had not been photographed for more than a month. He immediately ordered the entire island photographed, and the U-2s returned from the flight of October 14 with the proof we now know.

What happened was nothing less than a failure of intelligence. Suspicious signs were ignored, Republican charges were dismissed as election year propaganda, and there was a disinclination to probe the evidence. What induced this state of mind? First, the conviction of the analysts that the Russians would never dare do anything so risky. Second, skepticism about charges made by Republican politicians. Third, reluctance to face a new Cuban crisis on the eve of the Congressional elections, Fourth, a personal message from Khrushchev, delivered by Ambassador Dobrynin to Robert Kennedy on September 4, assuring the President that the Soviets would create no trouble for him during the election campaign and would place no offensive weapons in Cuba.

Kennedy had every reason to want to believe Khrushchev, and none of his trusted advisers presented him with any proof to the contrary. There was, of course, McCone. But Kennedy had been burned once over Cuba by the CIA and no doubt was doubly skeptical of its surmises. This skepticism, reinforced by his own desire to accept Khrushchev's assurances, at least until after the elections, and the failure of the intelligence community (and his own advisers) to argue differently, led to the failure to draw the proper inferences from the evidence.

3. *The misreading of the Kremlin's motives.* Why did Khrushchev do it? There is little speculation about this in Robert Kennedy's memoir, for he is concerned with what happened in Washington rather than with Russian motivations. To this day we do not know why the Soviets took such a colossal gamble. The rewards, one must

assume, could only have been commensurate with the risks. The first reaction—that the Russians would try to force the Western allies out of Berlin in return for their withdrawal from Cuba—was unconvincing at the time, and is even more so in retrospect. It showed the New Frontier's vulnerability on the Berlin issue, particularly after the disastrous Vienna meeting. But it offers no reason why Khrushchev could rationally have believed that the Western allies would give up their rights in the former German capital. Perhaps the main reason why the Kennedy administration was caught so flat-footed was that it could never figure out why the Russians might find it advantageous to put missiles in Cuba.

An intriguing explanation has been put forth by Adam Ulam in his study of Soviet foreign policy, *Expansion and Coexistence*. The Russian leaders, he suggests, installed the missiles in Cuba in order to negotiate a package deal to be announced at the UN in November. The deal would include a German peace treaty, with an absolute prohibition on nuclear weapons for Bonn; plus a similar arrangement in the Far East, with a nuclear-free zone in the Pacific and a promise from China not to manufacture atomic weapons. The Chinese, of course, could be expected to balk at such a proposal, but their support might be won by demanding the removal of American protection from Formosa as the final price of withdrawing the Soviet missiles from Cuba. This, Ulam argues, "would add an almost irresistible incentive for the Chinese at least to postpone their atomic ambitions."

This is highly imaginative, and almost certainly an explanation that never occurred to Kennedy and his advisers. It may never have occurred to Khrushchev either, although anything is possible. But without being quite so fanciful, one might speculate that the Russians installed their missiles in Cuba for the purpose of having them there, not in order to withdraw them as part of some future bargain. The placing of the missiles, in short, can be explained as a desperate attempt to compensate for a "missile gap" that put the Soviet Union dangerously far behind the United States.

The so-called "missile gap," it will be recalled, was one of the issues used by John F. Kennedy to club the Eisenhower-Nixon administration in the 1960 campaign. Uncritically accepting the propaganda of the Air Force and the aerospace industry, he charged that the Republicans had allowed the nation to fall hostage to Soviet missiles. Shortly after assuming the Presidency, however, Kennedy discovered that the "missile gap" did not exist. U-2 flights over the Soviet Union and the revelations of Colonel Oleg Penkovsky confirmed that the gap was quite the other way around, with the U.S. possessing a crushing superiority over the Soviet Union.

After returning from Vienna, where Khrushchev reportedly badgered him about the Bay of Pigs and led him to fear a new Berlin crisis was brewing, Kennedy decided to let the Russians know that the missile gap was actually in our favor. About the same time he engineered the bomb-shelter scare to show that he was willing to face nuclear war if necessary. Deputy Secretary of Defense Roswell Gilpatric was chosen to unveil the news to the Russians. In a speech on October 21, 1961, he deliberately revealed that we had penetrated Soviet security and knew where their missile sites were located. "Their Iron Curtain," he declared, "is not so impenetrable as to force us to accept at face value the Kremlin's boasts." For the Russians, the implications were, in Hilsman's words, "horrendous." What frightened them was not that we had military superiority, for they knew that all along—but that *we* knew it.

The U-2s had pin-pointed the Soviet missile sites and Colonel Penkovsky had revealed that they lagged far behind in missile production. Since the Russians at that time had mostly a vulnerable "soft" ICBM system that could be used for retaliation only if the sites were kept secret, the American discovery meant that their entire missile defense system was suddenly obsolete. Had the United States launched a pre-emptive attack, they would have been largely incapable of retaliating. The balance of terror had broken down and the Russians found themselves, for all practical purposes, disarmed.

Naturally this was intolerable to the Soviet leaders (we can imagine the reaction in Washington if the situation were reversed), and perhaps a cheap answer to the problem was installing some of the older missiles in Cuba. This would help redress the strategic imbalance by confronting the U.S. with additional targets to be knocked out. It would also allow the Russians to stretch out the production of the new "hard" ICBMs without putting a further drain on their resources, help satisfy Castro's demands for protection, and strengthen the Soviet position in the Caribbean and Latin America.

Khrushchev made a serious mistake, the folly of "adventurism," as Peking would say. But could he reasonably have assumed that the Kennedy who had been so ineffectual at the Bay of Pigs and unimpressive at Vienna would suddenly become so intransigent? Nothing fails like failure. But in the context of the times, the effort to redress the missile gap seemed like a gamble worth taking. The worst that could have happened, the Russians probably assumed, was that their deception would be discovered and that they would quietly be told to take the missiles out. By immediately escalating the issue to a public confrontation, Kennedy had created a situation that was getting out of hand. In this respect, Khrushchev's message of October 26, when he offered to withdraw the missiles in return for a U.S. pledge not to invade Cuba, is instructive. "If you have not lost your self-control," he wrote,

and sensibly conceive what this might lead to, then, Mr. President, we and you ought not to pull on the ends of the rope in which you have tied the knot of war, because the more the two of us pull, the tighter the knot will be tied. And a moment may come when that knot will be tied so tight that even he who tied it will not have the strength to untie it, and then it will be necessary to cut that knot, and what that would mean is not for me to explain to you, because you yourself understand perfectly of what terrible forces our countries dispose. Consequently, if there is no intention to tighten that knot, and thereby doom the world to the catastrophe of thermonuclear war, then let

> us not only relax the forces pulling on the ends of the
> rope, let us take measures to untie that knot. We are
> ready for this.

Whatever his motives, Khrushchev certainly did not
intend a nuclear confrontation, nor in retrospect did the
situation demand it. It seems clear that Russian policy
was basically defensive and, as John Kenneth Galbraith
has commented, "in the full light of time, it [national
safety] doubtless called for a more cautious policy than
the one that Kennedy pursued." One of the hallmarks of
the New Frontier was a nagging sense of insecurity that
manifested itself in inflated rhetoric (the classic being
Kennedy's inaugural address) and self-assumed tests of
will, such as Cuba and Vietnam. While Kennedy won his
victory, he also had Khrushchev to thank, and as Hilsman
has observed, "although putting the missiles into Cuba
was threatening and irresponsible, the Soviets handled
the ensuing crisis with wisdom and restraint." Kennedy
showed his skill in throwing down the gauntlet, but it
required greater courage for Khrushchev to refuse to pick
it up.

4. *The vagaries of decision-making.* The basic decisions
of the missile crisis, as we have seen, were reached in the
informal group known as the Executive Committee. Most
of the members of the Cabinet were excluded from this
group, and, indeed, did not even learn about the crisis
until a few hours before Kennedy announced it to the
nation. Nor were America's NATO allies, who would
have been blown up along with us, consulted at any
point along the way about plans or strategy. When Dean
Acheson arrived in Paris to tell de Gaulle of the blockade,
the General asked, "Are you consulting or informing me?"
Informing, Acheson confessed. "I am in favor of independent decisions," de Gaulle replied, and remained
consistent to that policy.

Some of Kennedy's independent decisions were made
in the most curious way. For example, on October 20 it
was decided that the U.S. Navy would intercept all ships

within an 800-mile radius of the Cuban coast. Three days later David Ormsby-Gore happened to be dining at the White House and observed that 800 miles seemed to be a bit far out. Perhaps, he suggested, the quarantine line could be drawn at 500 miles, thus giving the Russians a bit more time to think. A good idea, replied the President, and on the spot redrew the line—no doubt wisely—over the protests of the Navy. One wonders if any other ambassadors, had they been on as close terms with the President as Ormsby-Gore, might also have had some good suggestions.

We have already learned that the Secretary of State was too busy with other matters to act as chairman of the Executive Committee, or even to attend many of his meetings. It is also instructive to learn how Kennedy, while excluding most of his Cabinet from knowledge of the affair, reached outside the government to tap such venerables as Robert Lovett, John J. McCloy, and the redoubtable Dean Acheson. Recently Acheson, having been bested by Robert Kennedy over the issue of the blockade, has reached into the grave to take a swipe at his old adversary by declaring that the successful outcome of the missile crisis was "plain dumb luck."

In a sense he is right, but for the wrong reasons. He means that President Kennedy was lucky that the Russians didn't make the bases operational before they were discovered. Acheson wouldn't have fiddled around with a blockade or negotiations, but would have joined LeMay in bombing them from the start. As it turns out, there was more time than the participants thought, or accepted, at the time, or that Acheson is willing to admit even today. According to Hilsman, who, as former intelligence chief for the State Department, ought to know, "the two-thousand mile IRBM sites, which were not scheduled for completion until mid-November, never did reach a stage where they were ready to receive the missiles themselves." Kennedy, in other words, had at least two more weeks and could have postponed his ultimatum. Also, it appears that Khrushchev was planning to be true

to his word and not make trouble for Kennedy until after
the election, when he would unveil the missiles for whatever political purposes he had in mind.

Kennedy was lucky, however, in the sense that Khrushchev chose to withdraw rather than make Cuba a test of
national or personal virility. Had Acheson and the other
hawks had their way, probably none of us would be here
to conduct these post-mortems. Robert Kennedy had
something quite interesting to say about this. In an interview given just two days before his death, he commented
on the advice given in the Executive Committee during
the crisis:

> The fourteen people involved were very significant—
> bright, able, dedicated people, all of whom had the
> greatest affection for the U.S.—probably the brightest
> kind of group that you could get together under those
> circumstances. If six of them had been President of
> the U.S., I think that the world might have been blown
> up.

None of these six is particularly malicious or fanatical,
and none is in the government today. Yet if a similar
crisis were to occur, would the response of the President's
advisers be very different from that given by these six
in 1962? The lesson of the *Thirteen Days* is to show us
just how slender is the thread of our survival, how the
fate of mankind rests in the hands of a few individuals
driven by perfectly ordinary fears, anxieties, and rivalries.
The Cuban missile crisis was a very close call, and it
could have gone the other way.

Were the stakes worth it? Even Robert Kennedy was
no longer sure. He intended to complete this memoir by
adding a discussion of the ethical question involved:
what, if any, circumstances or justification give this
government or any government the moral right to bring
its people and possibly all people under the shadow of
nuclear destruction? It is our common loss that this
complex man, who in the last years of his life learned
to doubt much of what he had taken for granted, was
murdered before he could deal with this question.

III. ALLIANCE POLITICS

The cold war spawned the alliance with Western Europe, thereby endowing an essentially colonial relationship with the verbal trappings of equality. So long as Russia seemed menacing and the Allies remained weak, NATO was in a healthy state—which is to say that there was no challenge to Washington's hegemony. But the passing of these two conditions—dramatized, though hardly caused, by the impertinence of General de Gaulle—undercut the purpose of the alliance. NATO went into a chronic state of crisis, and indeed has now become so irrelevant to both America and Europe that its demise is scarcely considered important enough to merit serious comment.

The alliance, in any case, was never much more than a security pact, with the United States supplying the security and the Europeans the bases. When we stopped needing the bases and they were less concerned with security, the more lofty pretensions of the alliance were revealed as pure rhetoric. The United States never had any intention of giving the Europeans the slightest control over its foreign policy any more than over its nuclear weapons. The Cuban missile crisis made this obvious, and the Vietnam war brought it home.

Atomic Wedlock

"The atom bomb," Raymond Aron wrote in the early 1960s, in his book *On War*, "developed at a moment when two states were overwhelmingly more powerful than all others, has reinforced the bipolar structure of the diplomatic field. On the other hand, once the bomb is at the disposal of every state, it will contribute to the dissolution of the structure." As the coda of the cold war alliances this is eminently concise and irrefutable.

With this prognosis fulfilled by the decay of NATO and the fission of the Sino-Soviet bloc, Aron, in *The Great Debate*, focuses on the problem of nuclear strategy.

Starting from the generally accepted premise that atomic weapons have thrown most of the old theories of warfare—defeat on the battlefield, disarming the enemy, occupation of his homeland—out the window, Aron shows how both offense and defense have given way to something quite different: the art of deterrence. Nations don't build hydrogen bombs to use them, but to prevent enemies from using theirs. Now that the victor can expect to suffer the same fate as the vanquished, the recourse to atomic warfare becomes in itself the acceptance of defeat. Thus all nations possessing the Bomb dare not use it as an instrument of warfare, yet they must *threaten* to use it in certain circumstances if the deterrent is to work. "It is," Aron comments of this paradox, "as if the non-use of these weapons for military purposes were inseparable from their continuous use for diplomatic ends."

Deterrence being a juggling act by definition, the balance is constantly changing as new nations and weapons are thrown into the arena. Kennedy came to power with the inheritance of a doctrine of "massive retaliation"—itself based on U.S. invulnerability—that had been obsolete for years. In a serious crisis it offered only the choice between loud-mouthed paralysis (viz. Dulles on Hungary) or nuclear hari-kari. Deterrence had become the enemy of diplomacy, making the State Department the all-too-willing prisoner of the Pentagon's outmoded strategy. At this point McNamara moved in with the whiz kids and computers and hammered out a new defense policy designed to reduce the real danger facing both America *and* Russia: that they would be sucked into an atomic war against their will either through misunderstanding, "escalation," or the mischief of their own allies.

The result was the theory of "graduated response." It called for a U.S. nuclear monopoly within the West to prevent the allies from pressing the button and sending everybody up in fall-out; beefed-up land forces in Europe to keep any skirmish limited to conventional weapons; and the "hot line" to provide constant communication between the Kremlin and the White House. To reassure those Europeans who thought they glimpsed a blueprint for a gradual American deatomization of the continent, the Pentagon brought out the old and creaking "counterforce" strategy and promised that it could ensure Europe's defense by wiping out Soviet missiles before they were fired. While no one was expected to believe this strategic improbability, it became a handy bludgeon for attacking the *force de frappe* and other pretensions to nuclear self-reliance.

Predictably enough, the Allies were more disturbed than pleased by the new strategy. Each of them saw in it the confirmation of his own anxieties. The French, having just given birth to their little Bomb believed the McNamara doctrine was deliberately designed to discredit the atomic force they were building at such expense. The Germans, in their congenital state of alarm, envisaged a *Götterdämmerung* nuclear "pause" taking place on their territory so that Russia and America might be spared the horrors of escalation. The British Tories, desperately trying to preserve the last fragments of their not very "independent deterrent," feared that the U.S. strategy meant the end of their defense policy—and their term in office as well. All of the allies were perplexed by the Pentagon's soothing assurance that the Russians could be held at bay if they would only boost NATO's land army by five more divisions, up to a total of thirty. Whatever happened, they asked, to those Russian "hordes" that Washington used to brandish at every NATO meeting, those 175 divisions panting to march to the Bay of Biscay? Gone without a trace. Or perhaps they never existed. Somehow it all seemed very suspicious. But the case of the disappearing Cossacks was the key to the whole doctrine of "graduated response," for only if the Europeans boosted their armies would it be possible to halt the Russians without using atomic weapons—and thereby stop the process of escalation before it began. And only if some kind of conventional balance seemed possible, would the Europeans make the effort.

For all its dubious statistics and discomforting "options," the McNamara doctrine was the first serious attempt to combine deterrence with defense, and hopefully to prevent war, by prescribing the conditions under which nuclear weapons would be used if the deterrent broke down. From a narowly American point of view it seemed an eminently sensible and long overdue response to the missile age by which the U.S. itself had become vulnerable to atomic devastation. But it could hardly be expected that the allies would be enthusiastic once the "options" began to sink in. However admirable from the point of view of the United States, "to keep hostilities from escalating," as Aron points out, "means turning Europe into both the theater and victim of operations."

Having only recently cleared away the rubble of the last conventional war, Europeans had no desire to put more men in uniform to fight another. And they suspected that if they did, U.S. soldiers would then be free to leave the continent, taking their atomic artillery with them. Rather than a policy of no-escalation, which seemed more to America's advantage than to theirs, they clung to the doctrine of "massive retaliation," which had the double advantage of costing them little and of promising to pull America into any atomic war from the start. Even a staunch Atlanticist like Aron finds continental reservations "easily justifiable by the geographical situation of the European half of the Atlantic bloc and by the dependence on the United States to which the non-dissemination of nuclear arms has reduced the European continent."

Is the new strategy wrong? Not from an American point of view, at least, for it reduces the danger of escalation, which is the major problem facing the United States. Unfortunately, that is not Europe's problem, or at least not the problem as Europeans see it. They are more worried about a conventional assault by the Russian armies than a full-scale nuclear war, which they consider both unlikely and unthinkable. What the new strategy has done is to emphasize that America and its allies face different kinds of risks—risks rooted in the stubborn realities of geography.

What, then, are the Europeans to do? For the time being, they can only accept it, since, as Aron observes, their "security will depend on the American deterrent for at least another fifteen years." Eventually they could build a deterrent of their own, but even if they do, he argues, they would probably have to adopt some version of "graduated response," though not necessarily the one Washington has decreed for them. To restore peace to NATO, Aron would have the U.S. and its allies split the difference over the strategic dispute: the Europeans would "accept the American conceptual scheme and relinquish the illusory doctrine of massive retaliation," while the Americans should "not concentrate their attention on the strategy of use and on ways to avert escalation."

But is this not to prescribe a Band-Aid for an ulcer? The real problem, as Aron notes, though he does not pursue it, is that "even if the United States were to behave with the greatest of wisdom and . . . inspire total confidence, they [the Europeans] would still resent the place accorded to them in the Atlantic alliance." Here is the nub of the dispute, one which is likely to drive America and Europe further from the false consensus within NATO because it rests upon such elemental questions as national identity and the will to independence. The Europeans resent their subsidiary place within the Atlantic alliance, yet they cannot expect a better one so long as they are totally dependent on America for their defense. And they cannot hope to be militarily independent unless they create a European consciousness that will make the sacrifices of sovereignty worth the pain.

There is a price to be paid for European unity, and Aron is under no illusions as to what it will probably be: "The creation of a superior political unity," he wrote in *A New Europe?* "embracing old nations weighed down in history like Great Britain, Germany or France, demands a real political will—unless it is to be a sort of abdication. But a political will is inseparable from a will to be independent, even if it is not equivalent to a will to power. Many of the Brussels Eurocrats are conscious of this fact and see the constitution of a European state, capable of taking a stand and defending itself, as the inevitable final outcome of their efforts."

Here the two strands of defense and diplomacy come together, and an independent deterrent becomes, if not the precondition of European political unity, at least its logical result. Aron, despite his blistering assault upon the *force de frappe* as a purely national force in the service of French diplomacy, admits that on the question of nuclear self-reliance, "General de Gaulle seems to me absolutely right; to exist as a political unit, Europe would have to acquire the capacity to defend itself." Thus while de Gaulle may have put a roadblock in the kind of federalism favored in Brussels, his *force de frappe,* combined with his policy of resistance to the U.S., may succeed in stimulating the creation of a European political will, which Aron sees as inseparable from the will to independence. Ironically, de Gaulle's embryo Bomb, which has already forced the U.S. to enter into a dialogue with Europe over nuclear strategy, even to the point of pursuing the chimeras of the MLF, already "constitutes an incipient protection against the unpredictability of future diplomacy" and "may someday form the nucleus of a European deterrent."

Torn, like many thoughful Europeans, between Atlantic and continental loyalties, Aron wants to see the creation of an independent and united Europe, yet deplores the atomic responsibility that is likely to be its price. But the great debate he outlines so well cannot be dodged, since the U.S. cannot give its allies a finger on the nuclear trigger without running intolerable dangers, and the allies must remain satellites so long as the final decision between life and death remains in American hands.

In the atomic age NATO is an anachronism which must lead either to an atomic wedlock of Europe and America in a politically unified Atlantic "community," or else to the nuclear independence of two friendly, but distinct powers. "What thermonuclear weapons have rendered obsolete," as Aron points out, "are not alliances as such, but alliances of the traditional type." Nations will still band together in common defense, but only if they are so politically and geographically united that an attack upon one really is an attack upon all. "Alliances will either evolve toward communities or else dissolve altogether." Which is to say that nations which can only pray together, are unlikely to stay together.

The Lesson of Suez

To those whose memories of antiquity stretch back to 1956, the remarkable events of June 1967 seem like the time machine moving backward. Here is President Nasser threatening to destroy Israel, and then watching the ignominious defeat of his own armed forces; here is General Dayan sweeping his armies across Sinai to the gates of the Suez Canal and the banks of the Red Sea; here is the Middle East once again aflame and threatening to ignite an even greater conflict. To many this must seem like Act Two of the Suez drama that shook the world in late 1956, and left the Middle East a cauldron of resentments and hatreds.

But this time it is different. The issues are simpler and the actors are fewer. This time it is basically a question of Israel's right of survival, not the proprietary rights of Western powers in the Middle East. Gone from the equation are two of the central actors, Britain and France, both of them far removed from the power struggles of the Middle East: one now counseling moderation and faith in the United Nations, the other proclaiming her neutrality and seeking the friendship of the Arab states. Where Paris and London once breathed fire and called for blood, they now sit back and hope that Washington and Moscow will somehow hammer out a settlement.

Gone, too, are those who staked their reputation on the Anglo-French intervention at Suez. Gone is that sad, perhaps even tragic, figure of Anthony Eden, who believed that the Western powers had to stop Nasser in 1956 as they had failed to stop Hitler in 1938. Now in the guise of Lord Avon, Eden is a retired, indeed an almost forgotten, statesman whose brief career as Prime Minister is remembered only for the fiasco of the Suez adventure. A scapegoat for national illusions now laid to rest, Eden has curiously emerged with his honor, if not his judgment, intact. Gone, too, are the British Tories who thought it their role to punish petty dictators who became too uppity. The Tories will one day return to power, but their taste for Empire has long since been transmuted into the quest for affluence.

Gone is the French socialist leader Guy Mollet, who as Premier in 1956 forged the secret alliance with Israel that served as a pretext for the Anglo-French invasion of Suez. Ultra-nationalist and a convinced imperialist, Mollet wanted to bring down Nasser for helping the Algerian rebels, as well as for having the temerity to nationalize the Suez Canal.

Britain and France are no longer the instigators of the drama in the Middle East: they have been reduced to the role of bystanders. Yet they are bystanders precisely because of what happened at Suez a decade ago—because their intervention against Nasser failed and the assumptions that made such an intervention possible reduced much of their foreign policy to ruins. The Suez affair of 1956 was not only the prelude to the events which have just taken place; they were the death-knell of the imperial dreams of powers. The impact of Suez is still being felt, but its lesson has not yet really been learned.

The purpose of the landings at Suez was to punish Nasser for nationalizing the Suez Canal and for inciting anti-Western sentiments throughout the Arab world. The seizure of the canal was an intolerable affront to the British, and Eden was hardly alone in believing that Nasser should be punished. "We can't have this malicious swine sitting across our communications," Churchill told the man he picked as his successor. The British, although they hoped to get rid of Nasser through political and economic pressure, were prepared to use force, and said as much to the U.S. government, whose backing they sought in any military move. Dulles, however, preferred to seek a *modus vivendi* with the Egyptian dictator, and devised a series of delaying tactics which infuriated Eden and Mollet, and finally induced them to undertake the invasion without the knowledge of the United States. The French were particularly eager to go ahead, and found in Israel's planned assault upon Sinai a convenient pretext for an Anglo-French invasion of the canal. Their intervention would be justified by a desire to separate the combatants.

To the planners in London and Paris, the intervention seemed necessary and desirable. Necessary because Dulles' temporizing was allowing Nasser to get away with his seizure of the canal; desirable because the regime in Cairo was threatening pro-Western governments throughout the Middle East. Each of the participants had his own illusions. Eden apparently believed that with the first show of Western force the Egyptians would overthrow the evil Nasser and install a government more suitable to Whitehall's taste—perhaps one like the puppet regime of Nuri Es-Sa'id in Iraq. The French, for their part, apparently believed that the Algerian rebellion would immediately collapse if deprived of Egyptian support (Egypt presumably being to the French what North Vietnam today is to the Americans).

These ambitions, which seemed reasonable enough to those planning the intervention at Suez, were soon mocked by events. Instead of toppling Nasser, it shattered the career of Anthony Eden, who soon retired from office in broken health and disgrace. The Egyptian leader, on the other hand, was made to seem a victim of Western imperialism, and when the intervention collapsed because of American pressure to withdraw, became a hero throughout the Arab world. Suez drove one more nail into the coffin of the Fourth Republic in France, reinforcing Mollet's determination to stamp out the Algerian insurrection, and contributing to the crisis that brought Charles de Gaulle back to power barely 18 months later.

Rather than buttressing the positions of Britain and France, the Suez affair disastrously revealed their real weakness—weakness which was even more of a surprise to the Arabs than it was to London and Paris. Suez did not end the Algerian revolution, nor save Nuri Es-Sa'id in Baghdad, nor bring Nasser to heel, nor did it even achieve the internationalization of the canal—the only ostensibly legal basis for the intervention. In terms of its objectives, the operation was a total failure. Further, it caused a grave rupture in the Atlantic alliance—a rupture that was intensified by Dulles' repudiation of the intervention and his joining with the Soviet Union in demanding an immediate withdrawal. The alliance has never been the same since. Rightly or wrongly, Eden and Mollet felt themselves to be betrayed, and the British bitterly resented Washington's refusal to support the pound sterling until they agreed to withdraw.

From the Suez adventure London and Paris drew opposite conclusions. The British believed that it was impossible to pursue any policy without the support, or at least the acquiescence, of the United States, and proceeded posthaste to repair the "special relationship" with Washington. The French, on the other hand, feeling abandoned by Britain and stabbed in the back by the United States, sought security in a strong currency and an independent nuclear deterrent. The contrary lessons drawn by Paris and London from Suez destroyed the short-lived *entente cordiale* and fortified de Gaulle's suspicion of Britain's European credentials—a suspicion which continues to exclude her from the Common Market.

Suez was thus a turning point of history, one of those extraordinary adventures which, like the placing of Russian missiles in Cuba, do not seem of monumental importance while being planned, but which have repercussions far beyond the action itself.

It is one of the strangest military adventures of modern times, and from the pages of Hugh Thomas' *Suez*, we gain a revealing insight into the curious combination of factors that made it possible. *Suez* is a book about Anthony Eden—(the French and Israelis play very subordinate roles in Thomas' account) and how his emotions and illusions—his belief that Nasser was another Hitler, that he could override Dulles' objections by appealing directly to Eisenhower, that Suez was a life-or-death matter for Britain, that he could take the country to the brink of war without so much as confiding in his Cabinet—led to the disaster that occurred. To Eden the Nasserite threat had to be met by force, for as he wrote Eisenhower, ". . . it would be an ignoble end to our long history if we accepted to perish by degrees."

Britain, of course, did not perish by degrees or otherwise. What she did lose was the illusion that she had the power in 1956 to play the world role that was possible 20 years before. It was not only the end of empire; it was the end of the independent power that made empire possible. Suez was an adventure doomed to disaster, but as Thomas says, "It is nevertheless tragic to see great imperial countries (especially our own) ending their pretensions in comic style." In retrospect the whole adventure seems so misconceived and unnecessary that one can scarcely imagine why it appeared so essential to its protagonists at the time. Perhaps this is what we shall say about Vietnam a decade from now. Eden and Mollet were not fools, but they were vain and self-deceiving men, swept away by emotional considerations, persuaded by false historical analogies, and obsessed by narrow assessments of prestige. The real mark of their error was not that the Suez affair failed, but that it could not have succeeded under any circumstances. Even had they not been forced to withdraw barely a day after they landed, Britain and France could not have hoped to hold the Canal Zone indefinitely. Even had they toppled Nasser they could not have assured a puppet regime in Cairo, nor could they have squelched the anti-colonial nationalism that has swept the Middle East and the rest of the

Third World. We don't live in that kind of world any more, and Britain and France learned it the hard way.

As it turned out, Nasser was not Hitler, Suez was not the Rhineland, and Britain and France have long since ceased to worry about who owns the Suez Canal. Events have overtaken old passions, and what happened at Suez in 1956 already has the smell of history about it. There is a lesson there for those who are willing to learn it, while those who are not willing are condemned to repeat it elsewhere.

The Day They Buried NATO

The day they buried NATO was warm and sunny, and everybody was too busy to come to the funeral. The French were off flirting with the Russians in Siberia, the British were immobilized by strikes, the Greeks and Turks were threatening war over Cyprus, the West Germans were busy debating with the East Germans on television, the Italians were having a governmental crisis, the Portuguese were fighting in Angola, the Belgians were rioting about what language they speak, and the Americans were launching a new intervention in the Caribbean. It was, in short, a typical day, and all the members of the family sent their regrets. The deceased was quietly laid to rest in a filing cabinet overlooking the Potomac, and nobody seemed to pay any attention, except for a Russian with binoculars. The nearest of kin held a brief wake in NATO's elegant Paris quarters—which was soon to become the new Chinese Embassy—and then went their separate ways exchanging vows to write one another regularly.

If this is a fanciful scenario, it is not a particularly exaggerated one, judging by the various convulsions that continually shake the alliance. If NATO is still alive, nobody would ever know it from the actions of its members, all of whom are behaving as if they were responsible to no one but themselves. For better or worse we seem to be getting back to that "wholesome state" described by British Foreign Secretary George Canning in the last century: "Every nation for itself and God for us all."

Although the Atlantic alliance is falling apart, just like its Soviet counterpart in the East, the sky does not seem to have fallen. The General has marched his troops out of NATO, but the Russians aren't sprinting to the Channel, and nobody in the West feels any more insecure than he did before. The disintegration of NATO, which in earlier times would have been greeted as a catastrosphe, is now generally accepted with the quiet resignation of a woman counting her gray hairs. As the military form of U.S. dominance over Western Europe, NATO is now under assault by a whole generation of Europeans who may find de Gaulle's methods irritating, but who share his assumptions.

Gaullist diplomacy, as David P. Calleo observes in *Europe's Future: The Grand Alternatives*, "invariably appears puzzling, idiotic, or sinister to those who cannot imagine why anyone except a communist would want to be independent of the United States." Thus it is not surprising that the General has become the favorite scapegoat for the Atlantic theologians in Washington who are currently tearing out their hair over the disintegration of NATO. To their eyes the very substance of Western civilization is enshrined in the sub-clauses of the NATO pact, and anyone who would want to change a word of the scripture as it was written eighteen years ago is either demented or, worse yet, "inward-looking."

Since the late 1950s, the nature of the Soviet threat and the relations between Russia and the West have changed so profoundly that the arrangements set up in the late 1940s no longer seem particularly relevant. Even the vocabulary has become archaic, and we are stuck with concepts like "cold war," "iron curtain," "containment," and "Red menace," that no longer mean what they did, or even describe anything much at all. They simply make it harder for us to grope with the changes that have been taking place.

Take the argument over the principle of integration of military forces within NATO, for example. De Gaulle says that integration is no longer tolerable now that Europe is back on its feet, and so he yanks French troops out of NATO. Washington pleads that integration lies at the very heart of the Atlantic alliance and that without integration no defense of Europe is possible. Does this mean de Gaulle is crazy? Or that he wants to invite a Russian invasion? Not at all. It means that both sides have set up straw-men which they proceed to knock down as it suits their pleasure. Integration may be a sacred principle, but it has never been much of a reality.

What was the Nassau Pact, signed by Kennedy and Macmillan without inviting or consulting the other Allies, if not bilateral? What, for that matter, was the little-publicized but wide-ranging 1964 arms accord between the U.S. and West Germany? In diplomacy, as on the home front, integration is not always observed by those who talk the most about it. De Gaulle was calling for the integration of allied diplomacy as far back as 1958. Neither Washington nor London was interested then or since. Except for a joint supply system and an air defense alert network, integration has been mostly a cold war fiction. Every nation's armed forces have been ultimately subject to its own control, and if de Gaulle has found such integration "intolerable" it is hard to see how it has tied his diplomatic hands so far. The U.S. has certainly never let integration prevent it from fighting a war in Vietnam that could at any moment involve its allies in a conflict with Russia, or from withdrawing seasoned troops from Germany without so much as bothering to inform its NATO friends.

Integration was always a polite word that was supposed to make German rearmament respectable. It was never meant to be taken seriously by the other allies, and it never has been. The bloated NATO bureaucracy never had any more authority than the national governments were willing to give it—which was not very much. The big boss of NATO has always been an American general, and although he wears two caps, his orders always come from Washington, D.C. Nor has there ever been any pretense about this. The Pentagon, under the direction of a man who is not only a brilliant strategist but a clever salesman, has penetrated the miasma of State Department propaganda about the Atlantic family and has seen Western Europe for what it is: a vast, lucrative dumping-ground for U.S. military equipment. Thus, under the lofty banner of integration, the Allies are being told that they must either balance the U.S. trade deficit by buying U.S. arms exports, or else the GIs will silently fold up their tents along the Rhine and go away . . . presumably to Danang.

The Allies know that their defense does not rest in the hands of the variegated generals roaming around NATO headquarters saluting one another, nor even in the GIs sitting in tents along the frontier between the two Germanies, but in the American nuclear deterrent. And there has never been anything integrated about the Bomb. It is under the exclusive control of the President of the United States and all the State Department's pious evocations of integration cannot change that one iota. Britain and France excepted, the Allies have so far been willing to go along with it because they prefer the promise of American protection to the expense of providing for their own defense. Call it realism, call it laziness, call it cynicism—but please don't call it integration. It is about as integrated as a Mississippi swimming pool with a Negro janitor.

This is why nobody in western Europe is particularly worried about de Gaulle's departure from NATO. They know that the United States is obliged to cover France with its nuclear umbrella, just as it covers neutral Switzerland and the rest of Western Europe. The reason has nothing to do with treaty commitments, but with realities of national interest. Western Europe is too rich and too important to be allowed to fall into unfriendly hands. This would be just as true whether NATO existed or not. For purposes of deterrence, NATO is irrelevant. Now that the cold war is running out of steam, the fear of Soviet attack has all but vanished, and the super-powers are discovering a whole range of common interests, the old equation in Europe is being re-written. On both sides of the iron curtain there is a desire to emerge from under the thumbs of the nuclear giants, to break down the barrier across the Elbe, and integrate the communist states back into a wider European community.

Whatever settlement is reached in central Europe, it is obvious that the new equation is going to be very different from the one that is still such an article of faith in Washington. There has been much sanctimony, and even more self-deception, in America's attitude toward postwar Europe. Our policy has been dominated by pious generalities, wishful thinking, and hypocritical rhetoric.

Paramount among these is the federalist approach to European unification which has so entranced official Washington. On it rests the whole extraordinary record of American interference in postwar European affairs. Inspired by the dream of a united (Western) Europe linked to the U.S. through the eternal bonds of an Atlantic "community," Washington has behaved like the field marshal of European federalism: declaring who should be permitted to enter the Common Market, playing favorites among the Allies, trying to break up the Franco-German accord reached by de Gaulle and Adenauer, and in general behaving as though the unification of Europe were an affair to be decided in Washington, D.C. It is not surprising that these strong-arm methods culminated in de Gaulle's veto at Brussels—and it is indicative of where the pressure lay that the blow was taken a good deal harder in Washington than in London.

De Gaulle did not take anything away from the British that they showed any signs of seriously wanting, but he did destroy a certain conception of Atlantic "community," and for this the State Department has never forgiven him. While it never had any intention of pooling its own sovereignty with its European Allies, the U.S. has persistently told the Europeans that they should tear down their national frontiers and build a United States of Europe on the American model. But such a Europe is opposed by both France and Britain, and even if it could be created it is doubtful that Washington has ever given any serious thought to what a truly united Europe would be like.

It would hardly be the mute and obliging partner that Washington seems to imagine. It would demand access to the American nuclear arsenal, or else it would build a Bomb of its own. Nor would it be content to play deputy sheriff to America in the unruly states of the southern hemisphere, applauding every landing of the U.S. Marines and dutifully chipping in to help our foreign aid bribes. A unified Europe would want to work out its own arrangements with Russia—in whom it might find a useful ally to balance off the overwhelming weight of American power—and it would almost certainly not share Washington's mania about China. Indeed, it would have every reason to build up China as a counter to Russia in the East.

In no case would a unified Europe tolerate the continuation of the present situation in which it can automatically become involved in a major war as a result of some unilateral American action in a place like Vietnam. There has been a good deal of cant in Washington's daydreams about European unification, and Calleo is quite right in pointing out that:

> . . . before allowing her power to be enlisted to impose an ideal on others, America had better give that ideal a close look to see whether it corresponds to her real interests, whether it cannot be achieved in some other way, and whether it appeals to her better or worst instincts.

This is a lesson worth remembering, and one already becoming apparent as the Europeans try to shake off the Russo-American protectorship over the Continent and find some new form of association that will combine their desire for independence with their quest for security.

The old formula, which decreed that Europe should indefinitely remain divided into rival military blocs, has
been rejected by the Europeans themselves, and even the
Rumanians are declaring that the cold war alliances are
"anachronisms incompatible with national independence
and sovereignty." The nationalism which we have ap-
plauded on the other side of the iron curtain is now
spreading westward and is expressing itself in a growing
European discontent with the premises of an Atlantic
alliance which seems based on the perpetuation of the
status quo.

    With the U.S. apparently dedicated to an anti-commu-
nist crusade in Southeast Asia, the Europeans have become fearful that they may be dragged into a war against
their will. As a result, the appeal of some kind of armed
neutrality has grown proportionately, and Gaullism has
gained converts throughout the Continent. The desire to
detach Europe from the perils of American globalism
may yet be the greatest impetus to European unification,
and its implications are already being glimpsed in new
Gaullist overtures to bring Britain into the Common Market. The old dream of a "little Europe" west of the Elbe
is being absorbed by the vision of a greater Europe
stretching to the Vistula, one which will be liberated from
both Russian and American dominance.

    Papa's NATO is dead, and clearly it is now up to the
Europeans themselves to start lifting the iron curtain by
dismantling the cold war military blocs, and bringing Russia back into the European community. If the Atlantic
theologians in Washington have a more appealing program than that, they had better unwrap it quickly before
they find themselves sitting all alone at NATO's next
family reunion.

Who Needs the UN?

The inestimable virtue of the United Nations, indeed the key to its longevity, is that it knows its place. It has not been allowed to interfere with the vital interests of the super-powers, nor to intervene in areas where world peace is really threatened. Except for the lunatic fringe of Maoists and Birchites, the UN has no real enemies. Liberals sing its praises, conservatives accept it as a minor inconvenience, and virtually everyone agrees with U Thant's assurance of "how much sorrier a state the world would now be in if the United Nations had not existed."

It is, of course, easy to take the name of the UN in vain, but few people would be tempted to dispense with it altogether. It is too useful, too sacrosanct, and, when it comes to the really crucial issues, too irrelevant. Therein lies the secret of its success. It has won the world's heart because it has not stepped on any powerful nation's toes —or at least not hard enough to do any damage. Having settled for weakness as the price of survival, the UN has been absorbed into the world power structure. Why attack it for not being more than it is, when what it is serves most people's interests so well? If the UN did not exist, we would have to invent it, and what we would invent would probably be very much like what we have today. This is the tragedy of the UN, and also the reason for its endurance.

However, the fact that we are stuck with the kind of UN we deserve does not prevent us from yearning for something better, or from berating the failure of the organization to live up to our own romantic expectations— expectations which would probably horrify us if they were ever realized. We are all victims of our own illusions about what the UN is supposed to be, and we make the UN itself the scapegoat for our disappointments.

Every country has its own view of the proper function of the UN. The United States wants to use it to contain communism and to smother left-wing revolutions. The Europeans see it as a useful forum for the airing of grievances and as a convenient center for diplomatic contact among nations. The Russians view it as a necessary evil in which they must participate, lest the "imperialists" monopolize it. And the economically backward, ex-colonial states cling to it as the instrument by which they can make their anxieties felt and can shame the wealthy nations into providing more economic assistance. Every country, then, wants to use the UN for its own purposes, and those who fail to recognize this fall victim to their own mythology.

Professor Alf Ross, a Danish philosopher of international law, has no illusions about the motives that inspire the member-states of the UN, nor does he betray much sentimentality about the organization's utopian ambitions. Nevertheless, he thinks that the UN can be a significant instrument for allowing the major powers of the world to defend their interests by means less primitive than periodic slaughter. In *The United Nations: Peace and Reality*, he argues that unless the great powers have a vested interest in preserving the UN, and unless it can be made relevant to the necessities of their own diplomacy, the UN cannot hope to survive. To breathe new life into the UN, Professor Ross would therefore have it transformed into a benevolent dictatorship by which the great powers keep the peace. With impressive scholarship and clarity of style, he presents his case that world peace, if it ever comes, will more likely be achieved through a dictatorship of the super-powers than through majority voting in the General Assembly. Thus Professor Ross would reform the UN in accordance with the intention of its founders by establishing a great-power directorate in the Security Council.

Given the inability of the great powers to agree on much of anything over the past twenty years, Professor Ross's prescription for great-power unanimity may sound utopian, but it is based on the assumption that the super-powers have a common interest in preventing the UN from being used in a manner detrimental to themselves. This view is confirmed by the increasing tendency of America and Russia to deal with their differences privately, rather than to drag them into the UN, where they are subject to the scrutiny, the diatribes, and the adverse votes of the mini-powers. Over the past few years, there has been a steady movement away from the General Assembly, where the super-powers have to lobby for the votes of states like Chad and Malawi, and back to the Security Council, where they enjoy the prerogatives of the veto. Perhaps it is too late for a great-power dictatorship such as Professor Ross favors, for the super-powers no longer rule the world as they did a decade or two ago, and there are now a good many matters about which they cannot hope to do much more than agree to disagree. But they do share a real disenchantment with the General Assembly, where every nation enjoys an equal vote. Even the United States, which tried to augment the powers of the General Assembly so long as it enjoyed a majority of votes there, has increasingly of late come to look upon the Security Council with new affection.

Up to now the United States has been able to avoid using the veto in the Security Council. Its abstinence, however, stems less from respect for principle than from the ability to protect its interests in other ways so effectively that the UN has rarely dared to approve resolutions considered unfriendly to Washington. Anyone entertaining any illusions about the role of the United States within the UN will find them ably demolished in John G.

Stoessinger's *The United Nations and the Superpowers*, a compact and enlightening study of great-power interactions in the world organization.

The author, a professor of political science at Hunter College, is well aware that America has at times seen fit to support an expansion of the powers of the General Assembly and the Secretary-General, but he points out that there are also periods "when the American interest dictates a more conservative role for the UN." In the past, therefore, "the United States has employed the hidden veto [pressure in the General Assembly], attacked the Secretariat, prolonged the membership stalemate, fought for the exclusion of Red China, withdrawn support from the IRO [International Refugee Organization], bypassed the IAEA [International Atomic Energy Agency], and attacked the unanimity principle of the Special Fund."

But according to Mr. Stoessinger, such moves—as well as those undertaken by Russia to protect her national interests—have strengthened rather than harmed the UN; they have forced it to develop its own political resources for circumventing the great-power impasse. The UN, he argues, "has moved forward *because* of the superpower struggle as well as in spite of it." He sees the UN as a pawn which "has had to learn to live between the giants and, ultimately, to capitalize on that position." By so doing, he believes, it may continue to augment its strength and perhaps one day become a powerful political force.

If, however, the UN were to develop such power, would it be a force for peace or for greater instability? To make the UN relevant as a political body is to give it political power, and this can be done only at the sufferance of the great powers. But is a great-power dictatorship any more likely to secure the peace than great-power antagonisms held in check by a balance of forces? And if the great powers should refuse to play such a role, can the disparate member-states of the UN evolve any system that is more likely to approximate international justice than the current system? Those who would augment the political effectiveness of the UN, who would endow it with an independent army and vastly expanded "peace-keeping" powers, usually fail to come to terms with the likely consequences of such a move. It would mean either the collusion of the great powers and, in effect, the imposition of a great-power dictatorship—which has been tried before and has failed—or it would mean that the great powers would be willing to allow a majority in the General Assembly to impose its will on recalcitrant minorities. Yet to accept this is to endow the member-states of the UN with virtually unlimited powers to punish a nation even for its domestic policies.

The problem inherent in this punishment-power is being dramatized in the case of Rhodesia, whose internal policies are repugnant to a majority of nations in the General Assembly. For this reason, Rhodesia has been declared a "threat to the peace," thereby permitting Chapter VII of the Charter to be called into use. Under this provision the UN has, for the first time in its history, made economic sanctions obligatory upon all UN members, and even upon non-members. A failure to observe such sanctions is thus a violation of international law. These are extraordinary powers, and, if followed to their logical conclusion, would result in the dispatch of a UN "peace-keeping" force to subdue the government of Rhodesia.

Since it is exceedingly unlikely that economic sanctions will succeed in bringing down the Smith regime, there will probably be demands from the General Assembly for more stringent action: for a blockade of South Africa and the Portuguese territories to plug the holes in the embargo. The African nations, incapable of providing such a blockade themselves, must call upon the great powers to do so. Is the United States willing to blockade South Africa, Angola, and Mozambique? Is it willing to support the invasion of Rhodesia by an African army wearing UN helmets? Is it willing to dedicate itself to the overthrow of governments because their internal policies are repugnant to a majority in the General Assembly, or to the views of most Americans? If so, why single out Rhodesia, whose racist policies, however obnoxious, are no more obnoxious than the domestic policies of many of the nations which voted for sanctions?

What is involved here is not a principle, but an act of expediency. Sanctions were imposed upon Rhodesia because the British government has been incapable of either defeating the Smith regime or coming to terms with it. In desperation, it therefore turned to the UN, where nations which are unable to agree on anything else are able to form a majority to denounce white colonialism. The UN has allowed itself to be used as a dumping ground for London's failure, and has responded with a gesture that could conceivably set the stage for a race war in southern Africa.

After having shown its inability to deal with such real threats to the peace as the Berlin crisis, Suez, Budapest, and Vietnam, the UN has bravely pounced upon Rhodesia and has unleashed its vast legal powers to punish her as a "threat to the peace." While bombs are falling and people are dying in Vietnam, while millions are suffering from malnutrition, while uncontrolled population growth breeds misery, frustration, and perhaps future aggression, the UN has decided that the real danger to the peace of the world is a government in Salisbury which will no longer accept instructions from London. By the kind of irony that is becoming the hallmark of the UN, the very nations which so pride themselves on their anti-colonialism are trying to punish Rhodesia for refusing to behave like a colony.

Before we lend our own power to the support of such actions, we would do well to ask whether they might not be a greater threat to the peace than the policies of the government they are designed to punish. Then, too, we ought to ask ourselves whether we would ever be willing to tolerate this kind of intervention in our own internal affairs.

By using Chapter VII to interfere in a nation's domestic policies, the UN might well be laying the ground for a crisis within its own ranks. Gestures against a small and friendless state like Rhodesia are cheap, but to expand the powers of the UN in this way is to make the organization itself an instrument of aggression by temporary majorities. Intervention in a nation's domestic affairs rarely ensures justice; in many cases it is likely to furnish the pretext for the imposition of puppet governments by the great powers, or for the kind of military conflagration that the UN is supposedly designed to prevent. The justification of intervention as a way of helping a lawful government deal with its internal problems—or of forcing it to deal with its problems in a manner congenial to the intervening powers—is, as Alf Ross comments, "one of the most unfortunate principles of international law of our time," for it "opens the way for infiltration and camouflaged invasions."

The UN charter is flexible, to be sure, but it cannot be stretched too far without endangering the existence of the organization itself. If the UN should founder, the small nations would be the ones to suffer, not the great ones, for it is the mini-powers that benefit most from the UN. It gives them a forum to express their grievances and, what is more important, it provides the technical assistance on which they are so dependent. The UN is a luxury for the great powers, which use or ignore it at their pleasure. It is, however, a necessity for the small powers, for without it they would have an even harder time than they do now in making their presence felt and their wishes known. Basically, the UN is their organization, but unless they are willing to show a sense of restraint about the use of its political powers, they may well provoke the very crisis that could lead to its demise.

The UN ought to survive because its virtues are numerous, its idealism desirable, and its drawbacks—so far—minimal. The world deserves something better than the deification of the nation-state, and if the UN can provide the possibility of an alternative, it merits our continuing sympathy and support. But the price of survival in this world is relevance. Unless the UN is able to bring its actions into line with its principles, and unless it can be made into something more than the plaything of the super-powers and the instrument of irresponsible mini-powers, it may suffer the fate of its predecessor. This would be regrettable and perhaps even tragic. But it would be even more tragic to allow the UN to be twisted into an arbitrary international gendarmery which places small and defenseless nations at the mercy of great-power opportunists and mini-power Machiavellis.

Today it is Rhodesia's turn to have the vast legal powers inherent in the UN Charter applied against her by states whose domestic policy is, in many ways, no better than her own. Tomorrow it could be the turn of other isolated and weak states such as Portugal—or Israel. The precedent is a dangerous one that liberals, idealists, and even one-worlders should be wary of. It may be important to make the UN powerful. It is even more important to ensure that it does not use its potential power to enforce a tyranny of the majority.

Grand Illusionist

A great leader must possess "something which others cannot altogether fathom, which puzzles them, stirs them and rivets their attention." So wrote Charles de Gaulle some thirty years ago, and so has he been practicing ever since. To his critics he is a Machiavelli of double-dealing, but for de Gaulle all this is part of the game of statesmanship. He may be deceitful, but he has never deliberately lied in public, for that would be to diminish his standing and narrow his options. "What distinguishes his political style and what makes him unique," as Herbert Luethy has pointed out, "is precisely that he knows how to be an opportunist without appearing to be one, and how to compromise without compromising himself." De Gaulle's style depends upon guile, dissimulation, and illusion—and he is a master of them all.

Je vous ai compris, he assured a screaming mob of Algerian colonists in 1958 shortly after returning to power. They thought he was promising never to let Algeria go. But within four years the North African colony was independent, the *pieds noirs* retired to southern France and de Gaulle managed to convince most people that it all happened exactly as he planned.

Perhaps it did, but nobody will ever know, for de Gaulle refused to give his cards away in advance. He is all things to all men ("I am a man who belongs to no one and who belongs to everyone," he declared in 1955), cutting across party lines and ideological platforms, a man of the Right who attracts admirers on the far Left, an ex-officer who is contemptuous of the army, an imperialist who gave away the Empire, an autocrat who saved the Republic. "De Gaulle," as Jean Lacouture remarked in a biography, "is more left-wing than the Popular Front ever dared be."

As a master of *trompe l'oeil*, de Gaulle has long wielded an influence out of all proportion to the actual power he is able to marshal. It is this above all which seems to infuriate his critics and to drive even such perceptive and normally mild-mannered men as Senator Fulbright into paroxysms of anti-Gaullism. In any scale of raw power, France today—even with her hoard of gold nuggets and her atomic *bombette*—is a pygmy compared with the giants across the Atlantic and beyond the Vistula. Yet such are de Gaulle's powers of manipulation, that he frequently manages to make Paris sound like one of the arbiters of the universe.

How does he pull it off? Partly with his extraordinary sense of style and bravado, and even more importantly because he is willing, when every other course has failed, to say *non*. This willingness to put his foot down when he thinks France is being dealt a dirty hand has aroused the irritation, if not the enmity, of virtually every ally France has ever had. It is one of his most unappealing qualities. But when one is weak and surrounded by powerful adversaries, sometimes the ability to say no is all that is left. If used properly, it can be a powerful tool.

It was this stubbornness as head of the French government-in-exile which led Churchill to call him his Cross of Lorraine—a sobriquet which almost certainly must have pleased de Gaulle. When he left London in 1943 to set up Free French headquarters in Algiers, Anthony Eden told him that he was the most troublesome of all the exile leaders. "I do not doubt it," de Gaulle replied, as though receiving a compliment. "France is a great power."

De Gaulle = France. This automatic connection in the General's mind between himself and his country lies at the core of Gaullist policy. It reflects a belief that nations rise to greatness only under leaders who incarnate and stimulate the virtues of their people. Frenchmen are fallible and must constantly be prodded by leaders who are inspired by "a certain idea of France." This conception of leadership harks back to Maurras and even to Machiavelli, but it also has strong elements of Rousseau, for it sees the great leader as translating the general will into action. De Gaulle, like that other anti-ideologue, Lyndon Johnson, would reach across party barriers to establish a great consensus in which all men, having reasoned together, would agree on the ineluctable wisdom of his will.

This attitude does not make de Gaulle a dictator ("What dictator ever had to face a run-off ballot?" he commented after the December 1965 elections). For all his monarchical qualities, he has also absorbed the revolutionary, republican traditions of France—and thus in the recognition of China or the ending of the Algerian war, has been more effectively radical than the French Left. Rather, he has a mystic view of leadership, one in which the leader has a symbolic significance separate from the mere individual who exercises the role. So we have third person Gaullism. "Try to get this into your head, monsieur," the General explained to a bodyguard who, after one of the innumerable assassination attempts by OAS die-hards, warned him against plunging into crowds to shake hands. "De Gaulle does not interest me except as a historical figure."

It is as a historical figure that he interests everyone, for he has become a legend in his own lifetime, the only survivor of the great wartime alliance, the soldier who revolted against his own government in 1940 to lead a resistance movement and defend the values of the *pays réel* when the *pays légal* had collapsed into the arms of

Hitler, the wartime hero who retired into exile rather than play post-war politics, the almost-forgotten leader who returned to power again in 1958 to save the Republic a second time, the recalcitrant ally who under Johnson and Kennedy, just as under Roosevelt, defies Washington's blueprints for an orderly world. It is an extraordinary life, one which embodies a double resurrection and spans three historical epochs.

De Gaulle's arrogance has served to compensate for the weakness of France, both during the war and since, when confronted with allies who were ready to take her for granted. "I understood and admired, even while I resented, his arrogant demeanor," Churchill wrote of the war years. "Here he was—a refugee, an exile from his country, under the sentence of death, entirely dependent upon the good will of the British government and then of the United States. The Germans had conquered his country. He had no real foothold anywhere. Never mind, he defied them all!" Churchill's respect was not echoed by Roosevelt, who under-estimated, despised, and frequently ridiculed de Gaulle—urging Churchill to break with him and suggesting contemptuously he be made Governor of Madagascar. De Gaulle, as Milton Viorst showed in detail in *Hostile Allies*, brought out the pettiness that marred Roosevelt's noble character. But he rarely succumbed to it himself. His weapon was not ridicule, but irony, and he has used it with devastating effect on all those visions—Roosevelt's "American Century," Kennedy's "grand design," or Jean Monnet's federated Europe—which to him seem to compromise the integrity of France.

A nationalist at a time when only super-powers and under-developed nations have the right to practice nationalism, de Gaulle pursues his dreams of Gallic glory: blasting the "twin hegemonies" (us and them), making eyes at the hopeful Cinderellas of the Third World, praising the virtues of national independence, and ploughing the French taxpayers' money into atomic adventures, space extravaganzas, and foreign aid bribes for the new nations. In short, he is behaving just as though France were a great power. It is all very expensive, some of it is ineffective and unnecessary, and a good deal of it is meringue. But it is all part of the quest for *grandeur*—one of those words that sound faintly ridiculous until they are translated into English where—as greatness, glory, and self-respect—they strike all too close to home. Should the French, unlike everybody else, be denied their grandeur—even if much of it is sham? Without the Gaullist cushion of status-symbols—the *force de frappe* which keeps a rebellious army happy, the gold hoarding, the pep talks, the jibes at America and Russia, the prestige junkets to the capitals of the Third World—without all this could France, which since 1940 has known capitulation, collaboration, occupation, parliamentary anarchy, and sixteen years of colonial warfare, be the stable, democratic, territorially-satisfied society she is today?

De Gaulle trumpets grandeur, but France is not at war with anyone, does not have army garrisons overseas, and is quite content to let others live under whatever regimes they please. Under him France has been a troublesome ally, but before him, as we seem to have forgotten, France was the joke of Europe with her musical-chairs premiers, her stagnant economy, and her futile colonial wars. Without de Gaulle she would today quite likely be a fascist dictatorship with General Salan in the Elysée, General Massau in the Matignon, and half a million soldiers still fighting in Algeria. De Gaulle has been a nuisance to Washington, but when the chips were down at Berlin and in Cuba he was the first to pledge his support. He has little use for the present form of NATO, and even less for a world gendarmery run from the LBJ ranch. But then why should he? His job is not to be deputy sheriff to Washington, but to restore to France her self-respect—and this he has done triumphantly.

His methods have not always been consistent, nor above-board. "If one walks through mud," he said of the circumstances surrounding his return to power, "one cannot help being stained." He has deceived many and disappointed even more. He almost certainly never intended to liberate Algeria and dismember the French Empire. But he was willing to come to terms with the inevitable, and in doing so managed to transform into a personal triumph and a curious kind of national victory an act of surgery whose mere suggestion brought down the Fourth Republic. For all his nationalism, de Gaulle understood what Lyndon Johnson has yet to learn: that a great nation's prestige does not depend upon the tenacity with which it clings to obsolete involvements, but upon its ability to distinguish national interest from national pride. It takes a great realist to make this distinction, and a great illusionist to render it palatable.

Ugly Americans

"Anti-Americanism," an Italian literary magazine commented in a symposium on the subject, "is a state of mind which has spread all over the world." Nobody seems to doubt the truth of the observation. The writers and scholars asked for their opinion tried to explain *why* the United States was disliked, not *whether* this was indeed the case.

Yet the reasons for it are hard to pin down. Why this rash of feeling against the United States? Why this resentment of American power, American culture, and even an American presence? Nothing quite like this has ever happened to this country before, and many Americans are sincerely puzzled by the growing hostility around them.

Anti-Americanism has become a kind of indoor sport around the world. Nowhere is this more true than in Europe, where even our most faithful allies have declared open season on Uncle Sam. In London, students picket the American embassy. In Berlin, earnest young men in duffle coats and girls in mini-skirts distribute leaflets accusing the United States of Hitlerlike tactics in Asia. In Paris, intellectuals echo General de Gaulle's scathing critiques of American policy and applaud the departure of U.S. troops from France. And in Madrid, Rome, and Athens, fashionable people denounce the "Americanization of Europe" as though it were an insidious plot hatched by Washington to undermine the fiber of the Old World.

It is hard to be in Europe for very long and not feel this anti-Americanism—even though as a visitor you may be spared a personal attack. You read it in the press, which berates the U.S. for its foreign policy. You see it in the movies. You hear it in the conversations at parties, in cafés, and even on trains. And you cannot help but feel it in the reaction you get when you meet a stranger and, in answer to his question, reply, "I'm an American."

The answer itself seems to unleash a whole set of emotions in the European—emotions of curiosity, antagonism, superiority, or even incredulity. You may well be asked to justify the racial problem, or the Vietnam war, or the spread of "materialism," as though you were personally responsible for them. And you may find yourself, or your country, or both, attacked for virtually every sin from the corruption of Europeans with Coca-Cola, to the murder of innocent women and children in Southeast Asia.

Most Europeans have the courtesy, and the good sense, to spare you personally from their assault on American influence and American ways. If they like you, they will assure you that you are "different" from other Americans. They may even pay you the compliment of asking if you are *really* an American. And although they mean this to be flattering, it is hard not to take it as a kind of insult. Which indeed it is.

This antipathy toward America is relatively new in Europe. Before World War II, only a handful of snobs thought it fashionable to berate Americans for their "vulgarity." During the war and immediately following it, Europeans were deeply grateful to the United States for having liberated them from the Nazi invaders, and then for having saved them from communism and rebuilding their cities. Those were the years when Europeans were very pro-American, and Uncle Sam was looked on as a protector rather than as an international menace.

Since then, however, things seem to have changed drastically. Whereas many Europeans once thought the Old World was finished—a victim of its own self-destructive civil wars—and America offered the bright hope for the future, now they seem to feel just the opposite. If America once appeared to be an El Dorado of equality, plenty, and tranquillity, it now strikes many Europeans as a mire of inequality, misery for the underprivileged, and violence. "After the war we envied you and wanted to be like you," a Danish doctor said. "Now we wouldn't be in your shoes for anything."

Suddenly America seems to many Europeans like a nation where everything has gone wrong, where the dream of equality has turned into a war between the races, where the quest for prosperity has brought only insecurity, and where the desire to preserve freedom has turned into an obsessive preoccupation with communism. Today it is Europe that is at peace and America that is at war; Europeans who are planning for the future and Americans who are dying in foxholes; Europeans who are building modern cities and Americans who are burning theirs down.

It is as though all the old roles were reversed. It is now America that is accused of fighting colonial wars and trying to hold together an unwilling empire. It is now America that is torn by civil disorder and social unrest. It is now America that is under assault nearly everywhere in the world—not only from her enemies, but also from her friends. "America today," the Italian journalist Oriana Fallaci has written, "is perhaps the most hated country in the world." And she speaks in sorrow rather than in anger.

America is distrusted, and the new anti-Americanism is something that should give us all some concern. Its sources are complex and not easy to sort out. It is compounded of fear and envy, of irritation and fascination, of impatience and incomprehension. America has become a kind of puzzle for Europeans. They see a society that in many respects is not so very different from their own. People dress more or less the same, eat similar foods, drive to work in similar cars, and see the same movies. On the surface, America and Europe are very much alike. Yet when you probe a little deeper, you find enormous areas of misunderstanding. Also, there are differences of attitudes that no amount of information seems to bridge.

When viewed from the other side of the Atlantic, the United States looks rather different than it does from these shores. Whereas we see our country as a disorganized, often ineffective series of groups struggling for influence, Europeans see a monolith over which they have no control, and which threatens to flatten them simply by shifting its weight around. By any standard of measuring power—economic, military, political—the United States is stronger than all of Europe combined. And Europe is a long way from being combined. There is an old saying, dating back to the Depression of the 1930s, that "when America sneezes, Europe catches pneumonia." Never has this been more true than it is today, and most Europeans find it alarming.

They fear American industry, which is so powerful that it is gobbling up European firms right and left. Over the past few years, billions of American dollars have flowed into Europe to set up American-style factories producing American-type goods for the European market. "Soon Europe will be little more than a multilingual U.S. branch office," a British economist warned. He and others have urged Europeans to join together to combat what French editor Jean-Jacques Servan-Schreiber calls "the American challenge" to the independence of Europe.

Europeans also fear American military power. They feel themselves totally dependent on this vast power for their protection, yet they have little control over its exercise. They fear that the United States may drag them into a war with Russian over an issue, such as Vietnam, in which they have little stake. Or they fear that the U.S. and Russia might make some private arrangement over

Europe's head, at the expense of her interests. These fears may not be consistent with one another, but they are widely expressed, and they represent Europe's jitters over American leadership.

All of these anxieties have come to a head over the war in Vietnam. While they may not feel directly affected by it, Europeans are very much aware of the war. They see it every night on their television screens, and read about it on the front pages of their newspapers. Some find the war puzzling and do not understand what the United States is doing in Vietnam. "If you're there to defend democracy, you're kidding yourselves," a French novelist has commented, "and if you're there to play power politics with the Chinese, you can count us out." A growing number of Europeans are expressing the desire to be counted out of U.S. involvements in places such as Vietnam.

The war has been deeply troubling to those who have until recently considered themselves ardent friends of the United States. Take, for example, the German historian, Golo Mann. He lived for many years in this country when his father, the famous novelist Thomas Mann, came here as a refugee from Nazi Germany. But Mann now sees a similarity between the situation in the U.S. today, and the one in Germany that he and his family fled from in the 1930s. "The Levy court-martial, U.S. atrocities, the bombing of civilian areas, and the burning of draft cards, all remind Germans of the stern moralizing by Americans during the Nuremberg war-crimes trials," he writes. "Germans were told they should have resisted Hitler, but Americans who refuse to fight in the dirty war are sent to prison."

Not all Europeans, of course, share these views. There are those who fervently support American leadership and American policies. British columnist Bernard Levin, has commented, "I have admiration and gratitude for the United States and for the *pax Americana* which is keeping the world imperfectly free." The novelist Kingsley Amis believes that "the U.S. is still different from other great powers because of her idealism," and sees the Vietnam war as an example of that idealism. For the Italian journalist Luigi Barzini the problem is rather different. "The image is not of the U.S. being wrong to be in Vietnam," writes this long-time admirer of America, "but of spending millions and getting nowhere. The image is one of ineffectiveness."

Our critics do not even agree among themselves. Some say we are too idealistic, others too ideological; some say we are domineering, others that we are ineffectual. It would be hard to be all these things at the same time, but not impossible. Europeans expect too much of Americans. They expect us to be better than they are, or at least as good as we ourselves think we are. In a symposium on anti-Americanism, the Italian writer Giorgio Bocca touched on this when he commented: "Perhaps we have imagined America more beautiful and virtuous than she really is, and it is painful to think that she may be ridden by the appetites and violence of the old empires."

In a similar vein, the French journalist Yves Chabas believes that our faults may stem from an excess of our virtues—that by wanting too much to be liked, we end up by being detested:

> American friends, you wanted so much to be liked. But though some nations fear you or admire you or make use of you, very few like you. I ask myself whether the disesteem in which you are held does not result precisely from your yearning to be liked. Because it is very difficult to like one who is rich and powerful, who —rightly or wrongly—sets himself up as the defender of Christian civilization and of the "free world." Messianism is always suspect. . . . Why do you want to play at being the world's policeman, the universal moralist?

Such a criticism, however, may not be very helpful. Of course Americans want to be liked, and it is probably true that we worry too much about this. But wanting to be liked is our problem, not that of the Europeans. If they dislike us, it is not because of what we feel or what we secretly yearn for, but because of what we do, and the way they react to our influence.

In actuality, this anti-Americanism is neither consistent nor uniform. It depends on the country you mean, and the kind of person you are talking to. It is more pronounced in France, for example, than it is in Holland or Austria. The French are ultra-nationalists and have never been particularly enthusiastic about any other country—especially one bigger and richer than theirs.

More important than anti-Americanism in France is the fact that it is spreading to other countries which have traditionally been very warmly disposed toward the United States: to Italy, West Germany, and Scandinavia. In Stockholm, students have attacked the American Embassy in protest against the Vietnam war; in Hamburg they sign petitions denouncing U.S. "war crimes"; and in Milan it is now fashionable to criticize the United States for subverting European civilization.

The degree of anti-Americanism also differs according to the level of society. Workers and farmers, for example, are not particularly aware of the Americans. Insofar as they think about Americans at all, it is in terms of relatives who live in Brooklyn or Detroit. For Europeans near the bottom of the economic scale, America is still the golden land of opportunity. The middle class, which tends to be conservative by instinct, is less kindly disposed toward the United States. Traditionalists see American influence upsetting their customary way of life. They hate discothèques, hamburgers, and bowling alleys. They don't like their children to read movie magazines or to wear blue jeans. They feel that their familiar world is disappearing, and they blame this on the United States.

But these people are not vehemently anti-American, and their feelings do not really influence foreign policy. The most serious source of anti-Americanism is among the amorphous class of people known as intellectuals: scholars, journalists, writers, artists, and government officials. These are the most influential people, and their opinions filter down to the public at large.

Although they resent America for not fully living up

to her own ideals, and they publicly scorn what they call the American Way of Life, these intellectuals are not consistent in their denunciation of America. On the one hand, they accuse America of being obsessed with the ideology of anti-communism, and of abusing the great power that she possesses. Unsurprisingly, they detest the Vietnam war, and openly sympathize with the Viet Cong. "The guerrillas on the banks of the Mekong—these are my people," a professor at London University proclaimed to 800 cheering students at the first British teach-in. They also are genuinely puzzled by the racial problem in the United States and are convinced that the fault lies entirely with the whites, who are trying to suppress the Negroes.

On the other hand, they admire the products, the techniques, and the restless dynamism of American culture. They damn America for her "materialism" in one breath, and in the next breath tell of their dreams to acquire all the shiny gadgets they associate with American living. They tell you how America has corrupted their cultivated European ways, but they rush down to *il supermercato* (or *le supermarché, or el supermercado*) to buy frozen peas or barbecued chickens. Without intending to, and sometimes even without knowing it, they emulate the very American Way of Life they are constantly berating.

Some Europeans are very much aware of this inconsistency. For them it is a terrible dilemma. Increasingly, as the relentless process of technological change continues, Europeans are getting to live like Americans. Five years ago, a housewife would not think of buying frozen food—if she could afford it. Today, she stocks her home freezer just like her American counterpart. Europeans now drive American-styled cars made in American-owned factories, live in American-style apartments or ranch houses, spend their evenings watching TV, drink sugary soft drinks instead of wine, and make plans for spending *le week-end* out of town.

They dress in American clothes, dance to American music, and dream of a holiday in San Francisco. They fly around the Continent and across the Atlantic on American-built jets where stewardesses in American-designed uniforms welcome them with noncommittal American-type smiles. Their pop singers adopt names like Johnny Hallyday or Sheila, their discothèques are called the Top Ten (in Hamburg) or the Piper Club (in Rome), and they sip Coca-Cola and smoke Marlboros as a mark of sophistication. Part of the antagonism Europeans feel toward Americans comes from their own rootlessness: they no longer know who they are. As Italian critic Franco Fortini has said sadly: "We have become half-Americans, and New York is our Jerusalem."

Anti-Americanism in Western Europe thus is rooted not so much in an antipathy toward the United States, but in a fear of being smothered by American culture— a culture so pervasive that it threatens to submerge their own identity. They want to be modern without being American, and they find that it is not always easy to distinguish one from the other. So much of what they admire in pop culture and modern living flows from across the Atlantic. They want the soul music and the vinyl pillows without accepting racism and the Vietnam war. But they don't know how to separate one from the other. So they are verbally anti-American while adopting many of the implements and attitudes of American culture.

The case, however, is rather different in the communist states of Eastern Europe. Whereas the West Europeans see us every day, feel our influence everywhere, and have (to say the least) grown rather tired of having us always around, East Europeans still look on American tourists as a novelty. They think of America as a land of milk and honey, where every shop is brimming over with blue jeans, mini-skirts, and knee-high boots, and every bar is equipped with strobe lights. If there is anyplace in Europe where it is a positive advantage to be an American, it is in the countries on the other side of the iron curtain.

In Prague, Warsaw, and Budapest, Americans are objects of curiosity, and often treated like fabled visitors from another world—visitors who have the latest word on Op art and Mod fashions, and who know how to dance the bugaloo. America and Americans attract them like forbidden fruit. East Europeans want to know what Americans are wearing, how they live, and what music they listen to. To be American, in their eyes, is to be modern. Curiously, they seem less interested in politics than their counterparts in the West, and not nearly so critical of American policy in Vietnam and elsewhere. These indoctrinated young Communists of the postwar era are often sick of politics, and they visibly yearn for a relief from the everyday drabness of their lives. For them, America represents glamor. Theirs is a strange America: a place where everybody drives a Mustang and has a remote-control TV in living color. It is more a state of mind than a real geographical spot, but nonetheless real in their minds.

What is happening is that Europe, on both sides of the iron curtain, is being shaken from its traditional ways and being plunged into a fluid, confusing modern world. The old order, with its rigid class structure, its semi-feudal privileges, and its authoritarian manners, is breaking down. This is not Americanization so much as it is modernization. But since America is the country where this process happened first, and where it has proceeded the farthest, it is called Americanization.

Traditionalists find this process disturbing, and blame America for all the ills that go with the breakdown of the old order: the increasing freedom of young people, the permissiveness in relations between the sexes, the loosening of parental discipline, the tendency to live in the present rather than building for the future. Even modernists who welcome these changes find them hard to deal with, because they feel that by becoming too modern, too "Americanized," they may lose whatever it is that makes them distinct. They want to be contemporary, to be with it, to be switched on—but not to be Americans.

There is much about the American way of life they do not admire: the violence, the hostility between the races, our interference in the affairs of smaller nations, the attitude of superiority displayed by many Americans abroad, and the sheer pervasiveness of our influence. They want (whether or not they openly admit it) to adopt many of our ways, but they also want us to leave them alone.

Maybe this is asking too much. But until the Europeans get it, or until they are able to band together into a new great power more independent of the United States, they are likely to continue demanding it. We can sympathize with this, and to some degree we can even do something about it. We can be more understanding of European sensitivities; we can try to observe our own actions through the eyes of Europeans; we can try to behave in a way—both at home and in places like Vietnam—that will not offend those peoples with whom we are so intimately linked by ties of blood and culture as well as by treaties.

We can, and we should, do all this, for America is neither so wise nor so powerful that she can afford to stand alone in a hostile world. But we shall also have to learn to live in a world where we are not necessarily liked. Then we may find, as Yves Chabas has suggested to us Americans, that "if you no longer seek to be liked, you will find that many of us here in Europe hold you in esteem. Those who are saying they don't like you are disappointed lovers."

IV. COUNTER-REVOLUTION

One of the ironies of the cold war is that its two major adversaries have discovered that they share a community of interest in subduing recalcitrant allies and keeping their respective empires intact. The Soviets brutally suppressed the democratization of Czechoslovakia by invoking the Brezhnev doctrine, granting themselves the right to intervene whenever they feel that "socialism" (that is, Russian control) was being threatened. But was this very different from the Johnson doctrine, by which the Marines were sent to Santo Domingo to prevent "another Cuba?" Washington and Moscow piously denounced one another's interventions, but each dutifully respected its opponent's right to do as it pleased within its self-appointed sphere of influence.

Whatever lip-service they may pay to their own distant revolutions, both America and Russia are deeply and determinedly counter-revolutionary. The reports in this section were mostly written from the outposts of their respective empires: from unhappy Prague, which learned that in the Russian empire independence takes a back seat to "socialist unity"; from Havana, which escaped American control only by becoming dependent on the Soviets; from Athens, where the Truman Doctrine "to support free peoples" ended in a military dictatorship of colonels pledging allegiance to NATO; from Haiti, where Washington winks at repression in the name of stability, and where the demise of Duvalier may lead to another invasion by the Marines; and finally, from Oakland, home of the Black Panthers, the Mao-quoting militants who call themselves the vanguard of the revolution that will vanquish the American empire.

Athens:
The Wrong Coup

"We went to bed like men," the bartender said, glancing to see whether any of his customers might be listening, "and we woke up like sheep. That's what happened to us Greeks." The scene was a sun-baked island in the Aegean, a mecca for pale tourists in search of a fast tan, picturesque peasants, and a wine-dark sea. But it could have been anywhere in this wounded land which overnight was transformed from a parliamentary democracy into a military dictatorship.

By now many months have passed since the lightning coup of April 21, 1967 when a band of obscure colonels seized control of the Greek state—confounding not only the napping politicians, but the King and their own army superiors as well. During those long months the ruling junta—a brigadier, two colonels, and a council of nine—has tightened its grip on the nation and ruthlessly moved to crush potential sources of resistance. To make its dictatorial rule more palatable, it has enacted some economic and administrative reforms, but it has yet to show any serious interest in relinquishing power to the politicians it overthrew so easily and views with such contempt.

In Greece today there is resentment and shame mingled

with visible acquiescence. Above all, there is a sense of impotence, a belief that nothing much can be done for the present, and that it is best to wait and see what the colonels will accomplish. Greek self-respect—*filotimo,* that untranslatable word—has been deeply wounded by the kind of military coup common to banana republics and former colonies. But there is no organized resistance to the ever-tightening rule of the colonels and little sign of any appearing in the near future—unless it be a counter-coup by other disgruntled officers. Greece today, to use one of the junta's favorite analogies, is very much like a patient etherized upon a table, waiting mutely for the surgeons to perform their operation and hoping that it will not be fatal.

Gradually the pattern of the new regime is becoming clear: it is a humorless, puritanical and basically unstable junta, with overtones vaguely reminiscent of Nasser and Peron, but without the charismatic leadership or the ideology to inspire popular loyalty. This is a government of middle-echelon army officers, most of them country provincials who sincerely believe in the platitudes of clean living (no miniskirts or long hair), patriotism and obedience, and the virtues of military government ("Anarchistic democracy is dead," said Brigadier General Stylianos Patakos). These are officers seething with resentment at the politicians who have lately made such a charade of parliamentary government, at the press and the intellectuals who express disturbing ideas, at center-left programs which they equate with communism, and even at the very rich who milk the country at the expense of the peasants and the urban poor.

The junta, composed largely of politically unsophisticated provincials, has behaved in ways that are crude, nasty, and occasionally comic. It is obsessively worried about its image, yet given to the promulgation of decrees —such as the banning of beards and mini-skirts, and obligatory church attendance for civil servants—that make it appear ludicrous. It declares that it has saved

Greece from the clutches of international communism, yet by its own repressive measures is making the once discredited Greek Communist Party (KKP) seem a fount of patriotic resistance. It declares its allegiance to NATO, with seemingly little interest in the democratic principles that organization is supposed to defend. And it blithely jails its own citizens for listening to the music of communist composers or making unfavorable comments about members of the royal family.

Yet whatever its nastiness, or its inconsistencies, or the foreign opposition it faces, the military junta is unflinching in its determination to remake Greek society along authoritarian lines, and to form, in the words of Brigadier Stylianos Patakos, Minister of Interior in the ruling triumvirate, "a new Christian society in which man will approach near-perfection." To help its citizens achieve this near-perfection, the junta has imposed the most severe restrictions on political liberties this side of the iron curtain. It has now become clear that the assumption of many Western liberals that the regime would soon collapse of its own incompetence, or that it would retire in shame because of the barbs of its foreign critics, is mere wishful thinking. The colonels are solidly entrenched, and every passing day solidifies their control over a restless and dissatisfied, but basically acquiescent, nation.

Ever since April 1967 the Greeks have been under martial law: their parliament closed down, their Constitution suspended, and their political parties proscribed. The press has been gagged, most youth organizations disbanded, trade unions brought under government control, the civil service purged, mayors and local officials dismissed, and strict censorship imposed over radio, films, and the theater. People are picked up off the streets and disappear for weeks, eventually to be discovered in an army prison. Telephones are tapped, private mail perused, idle conversations reported to the police by numerous informers, and any overt displays of criticism severely punished.

Not only are potential leaders of an organized opposition being locked up, but virtually anyone who spreads what the regime calls "malicious lies." This is a category that includes anything from questioning the stability of the junta to speculations about the politics of Queen Mother Frederica. The military has taken over the courts, and there is no appeal from its judgment. Recently it has sentenced students to jail for twenty years for distributing anti-government handbills, imprisoned a housewife for criticizing the colonels over the telephone, and arrested a woman for listening to the music of the banned communist composer, Mikis Theodorakis, on her home phonograph.

It is estimated that the regime has imprisoned more than 40,000 people since it seized power, many of them on such vague charges as "leftist sympathies." Most of these people have been released after promising to support the regime and to refrain from future political activity. While such promises may seem of dubious value in the West, they are highly valued in Greece where political leaders discredit themselves among their followers by signing such recantations. Of the 6,000 "hardcore" prisoners sent to the concentration camp island of Yaros, more than half have signed the pledge, while the remaining 2,500 have been transferred to another camp on the island of Leros, where they defiantly await the collapse or overthrow of the junta.

From all signs it looks as though they are likely to have a very long wait. The colonels have solidified their authority by conducting a sweeping purge that has not spared any potential source of opposition. They have cleaned out the police and the army, retiring hundreds of officers suspected of insufficient loyalty to the new regime, and promoting others who now have a vested interest in the regime's survival. The hope that the King could launch a counter-coup by calling on loyal officers has been made even more hypothetical by the junta's purge. High-ranking civil servants have also been dismissed for political reasons. Even the Orthodox Church has been brought under control of the junta by the installation of Ieronomos Kotsonis as Archbishop. Control over education has been tightened by making teachers responsible for the conduct of their students outside the schools, and by threatening dismissal if "the actions and behavior of professors and assistant professors indicate that they are not inspired by a spirit which befits the existing social regime and national ideals."

The press remains under the heavy hand of the censor, even though controls have been slightly eased, and the seven remaining newspapers (of the fourteen that existed before the coup) are little more than illustrated government handouts—often with exactly the same make-up and photos, and always with similar editorial comment. A new press law was recently decreed which theoretically ends preventive censorship, but nonetheless makes it a crime to criticize the April "revolution," the armed forces, Cabinet members and the decisions they make, or members of the royal family. It is no longer necessary to reprint government decrees verbatim, and the implementation of the junta's policies may now be criticized— although not, of course, the policies themselves. The Athens press, which in the past was the intemperate servant of various political factions, has now become the drab mouthpiece of the regime.

The slightly relaxed censorship law was announced with great fanfare as though it were an extraordinary demonstration of the regime's magnanimity. Its primary purpose, however, was not to encourage criticism, but to persuade the stubborn right-wing publisher, Mrs. Helen Vlachos, to resume printing her two popular dailies. A conservative with little sympathy for the Left, Mrs. Vlachos is nonetheless a determined republican, and suspended publication of her papers after the coup in protest against the abrogation of press freedoms guaranteed by the Constitution. When the modified press law failed to win her over, the regime put on economic pressure by cutting off the unemployment benefits of her employees. This induced Mrs. Vlachos to break her long silence and scathingly denounce the colonels as "mediocrities"—an act which furnished the regime with the pretext for putting her under house arrest pending trial for defaming the government.*

The attempted wooing of Mrs. Vlachos may seem strange behavior for a regime which has shown no scruples about throwing suspected leftists into concentration camps, and which ruthlessly punishes any overt sign of opposition to its authority. But Mrs. Vlachos is a thorn in the junta's side precisely because she is well known as a conservative. Her opposition cannot be dismissed as left-wing subversion and undercuts the excuse by which the colonels have tried to justify their seizure of power— that they were short-circuiting a communist-organized revolution. Conservatives such as Mrs. Vlachos should normally be the backbone of a self-declared anti-communist regime, and their refusal to accept the legitimacy of the junta has now goaded the colonels into taking more direct action against its right-wing opponents. The sentencing of Evangelos Averoff, Foreign Minister in the rightist Caramanlis government, to five years in prison for holding an unauthorized cocktail party, and the arrest of George Rallis, Minister of the Interior under Caramanlis, on a similar charge, were deliberately designed to silence opposition from the Right. This action, however, backfired when an international outcry ensued, and the regime was forced to pardon Averoff and suspend the Rallis trial.

An even greater source of embarrassment to the regime has been Panayiotis Cannelopoulos, head of the right-wing National Radical Union (ERE) Party, and Prime Minister at the time of the coup. Although the major opponent of George Papandreou's Center Union party, Cannelopoulos was not one of those who favored an "extra-parliamentary solution" to the Greek political crisis—that is, a camouflaged military dictatorship under control of the royal palace. A dedicated republican who opposed the Metaxas dictatorship and participated in the resistance against the Germans, Cannelopoulos collabor-

---

* Mrs. Vlachos escaped house arrest, fled the country, and is now living in exile.

ated with the Left before joining the royalists during the communist uprising at the end of World War II. Having refused to sign a decree transferring his powers to the colonels at the time of the coup, the former Prime Minister was placed under house arrest. In late September he broke a five-month silence by denying that "freedom of speech is an exclusive privilege of those who possess automatic weapons and tanks," called for the colonels "to rid Greece of themselves," and ridiculed the excuse that their seizure of power saved the country from chaos. The junta responded by placing Cannelopoulos back under house arrest and by launching a new crackdown on the right-wing opposition.

A recent new decree has been issued granting sweeping powers to Colonel George Papadopoulos, the real strong man of the regime. The Colonel is consolidating his power and placing control of the key ministries increasingly in the hands of the military. Although publicity-shy, Papadopoulos is the chief organizer of the coup, and because of his strong-arm methods and ideological sympathies he is pleased to be known as the "Greek Nasser." Content to leave the puritan moralizing to General Patakos, the crafty Papadopoulos is laying the foundation for indefinite military rule under his direction.

To assuage international opinion, the regime has made promises to present a new Constitution by the end of 1967, and then, after appropriate review to ensure that it does not contain, in the words of General Patakos, "those clauses which allow politicians to make mistakes," to submit it to a plebiscite for approval. While the recommendations of the Constitutional Commission have not yet been made public, it is assumed that the new document will reduce the number of deputies from 300 to 150, eliminate proportional representation, and augment the power of the executive branch. Such reforms had been discussed long before the April putsch, but it is rumored that the colonels are also demanding the disqualification of all "extremist parties" such as the EDA and the left wing of the Center Union, and is contemplating the formation of its own political party.

Even if the Constitution is approved by the junta and eventually by the voters, it is doubtful that parliamentary elections would be held within the foreseeable future. According to the Athens daily, *Elefteros Kosmos,* which is considered to have close ties to the regime, "The government did not come to power for a fixed period. It has undertaken to guide the nation into a safe harbor. How long will the voyage last? Circumstances and the skill of the crew will decide that. Only when the government has completely fulfilled its mission will it be permissible to think of an evolution of affairs." Junta members estimate that the fulfillment of their mission may take a decade or more.

Drastic as its methods have been, the junta has garnered a good deal of sympathy among ordinary Greeks. Bureaucratic inefficiency, widespread nepotism, and a paralyzing corruption in virtually every area of public life had sapped public confidence in the old regime. Halfway between western Europe and the Middle East in more ways than geography, Greece is a country where the palms of civil servants had to be crossed with silver for the simplest service, and where parliamentarians and cabinet officials expected, and took, a sizable cut of government contracts. Under the old regime it took half a day to retrieve a package from the post office, and three months to receive a reply from a government agency. Parliament was viewed as a charade for the enrichment of a few officeholders, and even sophisticated Greeks had little but contempt for most deputies.

While Greek politicians are no better or worse than most, the system under which they operated was hardly a model of democratic government. The King, as the bulwark of the Greek upper class, was able to manipulate parliament through his control over the armed forces.

The present situation in Greece has occurred in large part because the monarchy has insisted upon using the army for political purposes, a tradition which long preceded Constantine's accession to the throne in 1964. It was in 1936 that General Metaxas became prime minister and installed a dictatorship with the consent of King

George to forestall a left-wing threat to the throne. The Greek monarchy, which was imposed upon the nation only a century ago by the European powers, has never been able to sink its roots deep into the national life. It is the repository of the Establishment—the rallying point for the church, the army and big-business interests— but it is not content to stand above politics as in Britain and Scandinavia. The infusion of the palace into politics has made the monarchy an object of contention rather than a symbol of national unity. Feeling itself threatened by republican forces in the society, the palace has formed a close alliance with the army, purging it of disloyal officers and removing it from control by parliament.

It was this control of the army by the palace which was threatened by George Papandreou, leader of the Center Union Party. A middle-of-the-road democrat with a weakness for demagoguery, Papandreou was not anti-monarchist—indeed, he was brought back by the British in 1944 to restore the monarchy and crush the communist insurrection. But after the elections of 1964, when his party won an unprecedented 53 per cent of the popular vote, Papandreou tried to purge the army of its more extreme right-wing elements and to advance officers whose primary loyalty was to the Center Union government rather than to the palace. Simultaneously, he put his own men in key positions of the Greek intelligence agency, KYP.

While the palace had little to fear from the moderate reforms of George Papandreou, it became alarmed by the rising influence of his American-educated son, Andreas, and particularly by his declared intention to reduce the political role of the monarchy. This alarm was shared by conservative Greeks, who feared Andreas' vaguely leftish pronouncements, and also by the American Embassy, which strongly disapproved of his intransigence on the Cyprus question, his denunciation of Washington's "intolerable interference" in Greek affairs and his hints that Greece might retire from NATO and seek a more neutral role.

In a country with bitter memories of the civil war, in

which communism is more than an abstraction, Andreas' pronouncements became highly controversial. The Right, with the support of the palace, moved to discredit him by revealing the existence of a secret left-wing organization within the army. This group, known as Aspida, was presumably intending to overthrow the monarchy, and was ostensibly led by Andreas Papandreou. Whether or not such a group existed, whether it had any serious political aims, and whether Andreas was involved, has never been proved. Probably Aspida was little more than a mutual protection society. Despite a lengthy secret trial of its alleged military participants for treason, no convincing evidence of a plot has been demonstrated.

Aspida now seems to have been a red herring dragged across the trail by the Right to prevent Papandreou from purging the armed forces. By discrediting Andreas, the Right hoped to bring down the government of his father. They probably would not have succeeded had not George Papandreou overestimated his power by dismissing his own defense minister, the beer baron Petros Garoufalias, and demanding the portfolio for himself. At this point the Palace balked. Papandreou dramatically threatened to resign, and Constantine called his bluff by accepting his resignation.

Papandreou's demand of the defense portfolio, however necessary it may have been to carry through his army purge, was a strategic mistake at the time, for the defense ministry was also responsible for investigating the charges against Andreas. By demanding, in effect, to be his own son's judge, George Papandreou furnished his enemies with the ammunition they needed to evict him from office.

Never known for his modesty, Papandreou thought he could force the King to capitulate, and spurred on his followers to months of riots and strikes. The palace, however, stood firm, and the shaky coalition government of Stephan Stephanopoulos managed to stay in power all through 1966. Finally, tired of cooling his heels, Papandreou decided to work around, rather than against the palace. He patched over his feud with Constantine—

which was not difficult since he had always been a royalist, and was even entrusted by Churchill in 1944 to pave the way for the restoration of the monarchy. Eager to secure new elections which he hoped would return him to power, Papandreou, it is widely believed, reached a secret accord with Cannelopoulos and the royal palace, under the good offices of the publisher Christos Lambrakis, to form a coalition government if neither party won a clear majority. Such a coalition would exclude the extremists: the pro-Caramanlis rightists with the ERE, and Andreas' followers within the Center Union. Andreas was becoming a threat not only to the Right, which feared that he would abolish the monarchy, take Greece out of NATO, and bring the communists into the government, but also to his own father. The King agreed to parliamentary elections only on the assurance that Andreas would be kept leashed.

Constantine, however, was taking no chances, and to make sure that he would not be faced with a left-wing regime under Andreas, he approved the "Prometheus" plan by which his senior military officers were to launch a preventive *coup d'état*. While Constantine had patched up some of his old quarrels with George Papandreou, he feared that Andreas would soon take over control of the party from his octogenarian father. And Andreas had frightened the palace and the Right by questioning the validity of the monarchy as well as attacking the "interference" of the United States, particularly through the CIA, in Greek politics. As the opening of the election campaign approached, Left and Right were moving toward a showdown, and there was open talk of a military coup.

When the coup came, it nonetheless astonished everyone because it was launched by the wrong people. Instead of the King seizing power through his general staff, it was a group of relatively unknown colonels who moved against their own superiors. By setting forward the date for Prometheus—which was set to take place only if the Papandreous won a clear victory—the colonels beat the King at his own game and won for themselves the fruit of his plotting. Immediately upon seizing power the colonels declared that they had saved the country from a communist coup that was to take place a few days later. While few with any political sophistication believed this fabricated cover story, a surprising number of Greeks seemed relieved that the long dreaded confrontation between the palace and the Left was not going to take place. Optimists hoped that the colonels would end the anarchy of the past two years, chasten the politicians, put an end to corruption, and then gracefully retire from the scene.

Once in power the colonels quickly moved to establish their Populist credentials ("We belong to the class of toil, and we will stand by the side of our poor Greek brothers"), and made a bid for public support by pushing through some desirable reforms. They increased the education budget, cut price-support subsidies, lowered transit fares, raised pensions, slashed the over-staffed bureaucracy, told civil servants to answer letters in three days or be fired, attacked the palm-greasing and corruption within the government, and even passed a law forbidding anyone to earn more than the Prime Minister. To stimulate the Greek economy, which has been growing at a healthy rate during recent years even though heavily overloaded toward tourism, they opened the door wide to foreign investors, and signed a long-stalled contract with Litton Industries to develop Crete and the southern Peloponnesus. Economic neophytes, the colonels may be putting too much emphasis on private investors without sufficient public control. But their primary concern is development that will provide jobs and thus win them public support.

In foreign affairs the junta has followed a considerably less chauvinistic line over the Cyprus issue than either the Rightists or the Papandreous on the Left. Without the need to prove its patriotism by intransigent postures, it has made several initiatives, although so far unsuccessful, to strike an accord with Turkey that would return the island to Greece. If it can overcome the fears of the Turks by granting enclaves on the island, and achieve the *enosis* (union) of Cyprus with Greece (despite the reluctance of many Cypriots themselves, including Archbishop Makarios), the junta will win itself not only enormous public esteem, but also the approval of Washington for ending a long-festering wound along NATO's southern flank.

But this is easier said than done. While General Grivas, the extreme right-wing leader of the Cypriot resistance against the British, commands the 14,000 man Greek army on Cyprus, the moderately leftist Makarios is furnishing his own police force with arms from Eastern Europe. Markarios is determined to ensure that Grivas, in cooperation with his army friends who now rule Greece, does not depose him through a *coup d'état* or impose a *diktat* settlement upon him.

For the time being this Gordian knot remains untied, and the colonels have their hands full trying to keep Greece's shaky economy afloat. Colonel Nicholas Makarezos, Minister of Coordination and least conspicuous member of the ruling junta, has signed up a number of foreign firms to build new plants in Greece or expand their present ones. But the regime is suffering a hemorrhage of talent as a result of its own political inquisition, and is discovering that tank commanders do not necessarily make good economists.

While the regime has its economic problems, they are not new ones for Greece, and certainly not enough, under present circumstances, to bring it tumbling down. It is premature to speak of a serious recession, and even if one were to occur, there is no guarantee that this would mean curtains for the junta. There are countries far poorer than Greece with authoritarian regimes, and one would be hard-pressed to think of a dictatorship that was replaced by a democracy because it got into economic trouble. The tourist boycott of Greece observed by many liberals, and even the cut-off of economic aid from the EEC, may be desirable demonstrations of opposition to dictatorship. But they are unlikely by themselves to bring down the junta, and their major effect may be to make the lot of the average Greek a bit worse than it is already.

The fate of the junta, it is becoming increasingly apparent, will be determined by the attitudes and the actions of the Greeks themselves. Foreign pressure may help, but it could also backfire. It should be applied with a cold appraisal of the real factors involved, and not simply to express the indignation or salve the consciences of well-wishing liberals who are outraged at dictatorship in Greece, but indifferent to it in Eastern Europe.

Despite its blunders, its brutality, and its dictatorial methods, the regime is still accepted by the majority of Greeks. It retains the support of the conservative peasants who have contempt for the professional politicians of Athens and are pleased that simple, honest men like themselves now run the state. Even a good proportion of the bourgeoisie, however much it may grumble about the bad manners and simple minds of the junta members, seems in no particular hurry for the return of the old parliamentary game. "These clowns may yet do the country some good," a small textile manufacturer declared as we sipped *ouzo* amid the clanging horns and exhaust fumes of fashionable Kolonaki Square. Instead of making martyrs of the politicians by jailing them, the junta has heaped even further discredit on a system which has never worked very well in modern Greece. There is still a widespread willingness to give the colonels a chance, and a hope that they can somehow set the country back in order before it is returned to the hands of the politicians.

Labeling the colonels as simple fascists is neither very helpful nor accurate. While they are vehemently anti-communist, they also condemn the large landowners and have little use for the King and his entourage. They are weak on ideology, and while determined to sweep out the old regime, do not yet have much of an idea what they will replace it with. "Communism is fascism," General Patakos declared not long ago. This is the kind of slogan that now passes for politics in Greece. The junta firmly believes in patriotism, and sometimes behaves as though it alone would solve Greece's many ills. Teachers have been instructed that "the first and chief objective of the school is to stimulate the national conscience," and are warned of their obligation to "guide youth toward the eternal values of our Hellenic-Christian civilization." The regime's idea of the good society, it would seem, is not so much the mass rally, as favored by Hitler and Mussolini, but the conversion of the entire nation into an orderly barracks where everyone keeps his area clean and follows the instructions of his superiors.

If Greece is to be transformed into a para-military state—a "guided democracy," if you will, as the term is used throughout the Third World—there can be no room for politicians or for any organized group that poses a serious alternative. This is why the King has been reduced to a figurehead, why the haute bourgeoisie has had its influence sharply cut, and why the political power of the Left is being dismantled. Now that Constantine is little more than a gilded mouthpiece for the regime —even allowing himself to be used recently as a messenger-boy to Washington, where he unsuccessfully requested the resumption of full-scale U.S. military aid— there remain only the politicians to be disposed of. The severe sentence against Averoff and the house arrest of Cannelopoulos were meant as warnings to the moderate Right; the coming trial of Andreas Papandreou for "high treason" is designed to break the resistance of the democratic Left.

The regime is clearly embarrassed by the foreign attention the younger Papandreou has attracted, and particularly by the pressure which his academic colleagues have been able to put upon the American government. This may have saved Andreas's life during the early days of the coup, and may yet succeed in having him deported from Greece rather than imprisoned for his alleged involvement in the Aspida group.* The coming trial has already been compromised not only by the flimsiness of the charges against Andreas and by the alleged bribing of two major prosecution witnesses, but by the obvious intention of the regime to use the Aspida affair as the justi-

Andreas Papandreou was exiled by the Greek government and lives in the West.

fication for its own illegal seizure of power. Whether he is ultimately exiled or kept in prison, Andreas has had his reputation enormously enhanced by having been made to appear as the junta's number one enemy. If the regime is overthrown and democratic government restored, he will almost certainly become the leader of the non-communist Left.

For the time being, however, the only real threat to the junta is not on the decimated, disorganized, demoralized Left, but on the moderate Right, where such politicians as Cannelopoulos, Averoff, and Rallis are now openly challenging the authority of the regime. In this bold move they have the covert support of the American Embassy, which fears that the communists may ultimately benefit from prolonged military rule and is unhappy about the current dissension within NATO caused by a military regime in Greece. They are also supported by King Constantine, who fears his throne slipping out from under him. No matter what happens, Constantine is in serious trouble. If the colonels remain in power they will tolerate his presence only so long as he is useful to them. They are not dedicated royalists, and if the King ever crossed them he would be given a one-way ticket to Estoril.* This, in fact, might even win the regime a good deal of approval, since the monarchy has never been popular, and Constantine's prestige has slumped lower than ever as a result of his abject submission to the junta. At the very least this would embarrass the Left, which has long talked about the anachronism of the monarchy, but has never had the power to do anything about it. Already the colonels, in the name of defending the crown, have reduced Constantine's power far more than old Papandreou would ever have dared. It would be an even greater irony if they carried out the Left's dream and deposed him altogether.

Whatever secret intrigues it may be carrying on, Washington has so far been willing to work with the colonels rather than against them, urging them to restore parlia-

---

* After one inept attempt to overthrow the colonels, Constantine fled to Rome with his family and remains in exile.

mentary government and hoping, with unjustified optimism, that the promised new Constitution will somehow put a legal face on it all. Whether or not the CIA or the Pentagon had a hand in the colonels' coup, the United States helped set the stage for it by its support of the most stridently anti-communist, and thus extreme right-wing, elements in the Greek armed forces. There is little quarrel with the regime's foreign policy, which is vociferously pro-NATO and anti-communist, and a widespread fear that the collapse of the regime might bring to power a left-wing government under Andreas Papandreou. Also, U.S. diplomats are reluctant to push the colonels too hard for fear they may look to Moscow for support. So Washington remains content with a largely symbolic suspension of military spare parts for the Greek armed forces and hopes that no one will notice the gap between its rhetoric and its policies. Perhaps no one will notice, for everyone knows that the U.S. intervenes only to overthrow dictatorships of the Left, not those which pledge their allegiance to the "free world."

Burdened with a King more interested in saving his throne than in restoring democracy, with politicians whose past behavior has engendered little respect for parliamentary government, with an army which has never accepted the supremacy of civilian control, with a regressive social system which has prevented the poor from effectively challenging the authority of the rich, and with a powerful ally whose cold war obsessions have augmented the control of anti-democratic forces in the army and the palace, the Greeks may be plagued with military rule for a long time to come. It will not be permanent, for the Greeks are a courageous, factious people insubmissive to tyranny. But the replacement of the junta may take a good deal longer than anyone imagined a few months ago, and it is not going to happen of its own accord. Only the Greeks can decide how long they are going to live with the colonels, and what price they are willing to pay.

While they remain in power the colonels have a chance to accomplish certain reforms: to eliminate corruption, speed economic development, improve the condition of peasants and workers, stop the hemorrhage of Greek skills and manpower to other nations, reduce the power of the rich, end the feud with Turkey over Cyprus, and implement a workable Constitution. "Getting things done" is the traditional justification for authoritarian regimes, and perhaps this band of conspiratorial colonels will have something positive to show for its reign. Whether or not they will do it, and even more important, whether the price is worth it, is quite another matter. The majority of the Greek people are ready, perhaps too ready, to give them the benefit of the doubt, and their acquiescence to military rule is in itself an indictment of the inadequacies of the parliamentary system it replaced.

But instead of a social revolution on the Nasser model —a tyranny that at least offers some hope of economic advancement to the poor—the junta seems to be modeling itself on the banana dictatorships of Latin America. Instead of bringing stability to a nation tormented by political strife, it has merely imposed a surface conformity that may yet erupt into violence. Unless the colonels can find a way of restoring some semblance of popular rule, they are likely to instigate the very civil conflict that they claim to have thwarted by seizing control of Greece.

Prague: Heretic on the Doorstep

First came the dream: a society that could be both communist and free—where men could speak and write without fear of punishment, where rewards would be based on merit rather than loyalty, where socialism meant experimentation instead of numbing conformity. That was all they wanted—the Czechs and the Slovaks who in January 1968 overturned the Novotny dictatorship. They had no intention of reinstating capitalism, of leaving the Warsaw Pact, of conspiring with "revanchists," or even threatening the communist party's political monopoly. Their goal was to humanize a system that had become economically inefficient and bureaucratized—to see whether a Marxist society could be run by consent rather than by intimidation. That was the dream.

Then came the reality: Soviet tanks rumbling across the frontiers, joined by token contingents from East Germany, Poland, Hungary, and Bulgaria. They said they were saving socialism and combatting counter-revolution, which is what they said in Budapest a dozen years ago. What they meant was that they were stopping a gangrenous infection before it spread to the restless states of the Soviet empire and even to Russia itself—the infection of reform and democratization.

Twilight fell once again over Prague, as it did in 1938 when Britain and France told Hitler he could have the Sudetenland, as it did in 1948 when the communists seized total control of a coalition government and transformed a democratic society into a bureaucratic police state. The world stands by today, as it stood by then, as democracy in Czechoslovakia, for the third time in a single generation, has become a victim of great power politics.

The sin of the Czech and Slovak reformers—of the writers, journalists, and intellectuals who eagerly joined them, of the millions of quite ordinary people who became actively involved in the remarkable struggle taking place—was that they thought they might be able to build their own form of socialism according to their "national specific features and conditions," as the Bratislava declaration solemnly affirmed only three weeks before Soviet tanks rolled into Prague. They thought that a Marxist society need not be a prison, that people should be allowed to express unorthodox opinions without losing their jobs or disappearing, that communists do not have a total monopoly on the truth, and that the Soviet road to socialism is not the only one—nor even the one best suited to a nation which knew prosperity and democracy long before it experienced Marxism-Leninism.

They were wrong, and today they are paying the price. Or at least they were wrong in thinking they could get away with it in the shadow of Soviet power, sandwiched between "comradely neighbors" hostile to their experiment in democratization, in their strategically vulnerable position as a corridor linking West Germany to the Soviet Union. The Kremlin was no more willing to tolerate what it believes to be threatening political and social experimentation in Eastern Europe than is the United States in the Caribbean. Where the great powers have staked out their sphere of influence, freedom of maneuver is possible only on the sufferance of the authorities in the seat of empire.

In a sense the handwriting was on the wall all along, but nobody wanted to read it. It was hard to believe that there could be another Budapest. Too much had happened in the world during the past twelve years—the two rival power blocs were gradually loosening at the seams, Moscow and Washington had learned to live together in uneasy symbiosis, and the cold war had degenerated into an institutionalized balance of power. The Czechs and the Slovaks had posed no direct threat to the security of the Soviet state. Not even if they pulled out of the Warsaw Pact—which they had not the slightest intention of doing. The alliance with Russia, confirmed by the Anglo-French betrayal at Munich and cemented by the liberation from the Nazis by the Russians in 1945, is a fact of life. It is, as Alexander Dubcek said before the invasion of his country, "the alpha and omega of our foreign policy."

An independent communist government in Czechoslovakia today, or even a neutralist non-communist government, is no more a physical threat to the Soviet Union than was a socialist Guatemala to the United States in 1954, a communist Cuba in 1961, or a neutralist Dominican Republic in 1965. But weak states in the shadow of powerful ones enjoy a marginal independence. In principle the Russian invasion of Czechoslovakia was not a great deal different from the landing at the Bay of Pigs, although the force employed was considerably greater and the methods more brutal. Politically they were equally disastrous for the invaders, both of whom apparently convinced themselves that what they were doing would somehow win the support of those they were invading.

The great powers have shown little tolerance for diversity within what they arrogate to themselves as their sphere of influence, and each respects the right of the other to stamp out whatever heresy it finds inacceptable. The Russians would not have tried to save Castro even had the Bay of Pigs turned into a full-scale American invasion, and the United States has made it clear that it has no intention of intervening in Eastern Europe. The current Russo-American détente, as Dean Rusk and others have stated on numerous occasions, rests upon a mutual respect for the lines of demarcation drawn after the Second World War. The Russians do not encroach on what is generally regarded to be U.S. territory—the Caribbean, Latin America, Japan, Western Europe—and the U.S. does not poach on their sphere of influence in Eastern Europe. Within these recognized spheres, there has been general stability. Trouble has occurred basically in the peripheral areas where both sides are jockeying for advantage: the Middle East and Southeast Asia.

It is argued that the U.S. has behaved with far more tolerance to challenges from within its system of alliances: for example, we have not invaded France although she has virtually withdrawn from NATO. But the parallel is not a convincing one since it ignores geography. Czechoslovakia lies on the invasion route into Russia; France is separated from the United States by an ocean. The parallel with France is Albania, which has persistently defied Moscow, but is geographically so remote and militarily irrelevant (as well as inaccessible to the direct application of Soviet power) that its heresy can be tolerated. The parallel with Czechoslovakia is the Dominican Republic, where the United States launched an invasion to prevent a change of government, and justified it by saying it was on the invitation of certain Dominican leaders, and that unspecified agents of a foreign power threatened to take over the country. Morally the difference was minimal, even though the conditions and the methods cannot be equated.

The system of great power reciprocity has never worked better than during the crisis over Czechoslovakia. It has been reported, on generally good authority, that the Russians launched their invasion only after confirming that the gentleman's agreement with the United States on spheres of influence was still valid. Reluctantly Washington replied that it was. In a sense the United States was powerless to do anything about the decision to intervene, once the Russians decided that a compliant regime in Prague was crucial to their interests. But it is also true that very little effort was made to dissuade the Russians, to warn them of the dangers such an invasion would pose to the détente, or to reinforce the arguments of Kremlin doves. Once the intervention came, President Johnson waited a full twelve hours before condemning it. The fact is that Washington, preoccupied with Vietnam and committed to the policy of super-power diplomacy, had no serious interest in rocking the boat over the regrettable but peripheral fate of Czechoslovakia. As Dean Rusk said at his first staff meeting after the invasion, Czechoslovakia did not deserve that much sympathy because she was a major supplier of arms to North Vietnam. The Russians were holding up their part of the unofficial bargain in Latin America; the United States could do no less in Eastern Europe.

The question, of course, remains: why did the Russians do it? The official reason was the much-proclaimed threat of counter-revolution, that the reformers were, according to *Pravda*, "preparing the ground for reorienting the Czechoslovak economy on the West," that "reactionary, anti-socialist forces which relied on world imperialism for support were rearing their heads in the country," and that, most dangerously of all, events were "turning the Czechoslovak communist party into an amorphous, ineffectual organization." Behind these charges lay the more serious unofficial reasons: that the Czechs and the Slovaks had failed to carry out fully the accords reached with Moscow at Cierna, and ratified in the presence of its allies at Bratislava.

While the Cierna accords have never been made public, the Russians allege that Dubcek, as head of the Czechoslovakian communist party, agreed to reimpose press censorship, prevent the formation of political parties outside the communist-controlled National Front, strengthen the army and the militia, halt any purge of conservative communists, and cease all press polemics with the Soviet Union and its allies. In addition the Russians demanded the removal of two leading liberals: Cestmir Cisar, secretary of the central committee, and Frantisek Kriegel, a member of the party presidium. When Dubcek failed, in Moscow's view, to carry out this agreement, the balance was tipped in favor of those who demanded military intervention to save the situation.

What these hard-liners particularly feared was that the Dubcek-led reformers would purge the central committee of Moscow-oriented conservatives at the special party congress scheduled for September 9. Once the central committee was cleared of those opposed to the new reforms, there could be no hope of turning back the clock in Prague without a full-scale military occupation. By beating Dubcek to the draw, the Russians thought they could, with a minimum show of force, restore the situation to what it had been during the Novotny regime. Like Kennedy at the Bay of Pigs, they seem even to have convinced themselves that the majority of Czechs and Slovaks actually wanted to overthrow their government in favor of one more amenable to Moscow's wishes.

The Russians were clearly contemplating military intervention for several months, and the long refusal to pull their troops out of Czechoslovakia following Warsaw Pact maneuvers was designed to intimidate the reformers. At Cierna they thought they could separate the liberals from the conservatives and impose a harsh settlement. When this split failed to materialize, however, they agreed to a compromise that accepted the basic principles of the reform movement. A few days later their allies were brought in at Bratislava to ratify the accords, and there were strong objections from Gomulka, Ulbricht, and Zhivkov of Bulgaria. But the agreement was signed, and when the Czechoslovak leaders returned to Prague, they believed that the danger of invasion had been surmounted. To placate the Soviets, Dubcek discouraged popular demonstrations during the brief state visits of Tito and Ceausescu, and told the press to tone down its criticisms of the hard-line regimes in Warsaw, East Berlin, and Moscow. The tide turned on August 12 at Karlovy Vary, where Ulbricht demanded that Dubcek live up to the Bratislava agreements, while the Czechoslovak leaders argued for the principle of non-interference in the internal affairs of communist states. From that moment on the conservatives in the Czechoslovak party presidium and central committee dug in their heels, and the hawks in the Kremlin became convinced that they could not tame Prague without a military intervention.

The final decision to intervene was made not because

there was a misunderstanding over the terms reached at Cierna, but because the Soviets and their allies feared that the Czechoslovak defection from Communist orthodoxy would imperil the solidity of the alliance and spread heresy to their own lands. They saw the experiment of the Czechs and Slovaks not as a variation within the socialist system, but as an infection that could undermine their conception of what a communist state should be. They believed it would weaken the communist party's control over the state apparatus and unleash an uncontrollable range of opinion.

In a sense they were right. Even in the most rigidly authoritarian states, such as Poland and East Germany, not to mention the Soviet Union itself, there are forces pushing for a loosening of arbitrary economic controls and for greater freedom of expression. The intellectuals, scientists, and technicians, the "new class," of these societies are increasingly resistant to the dogmatism of the party bureaucracy and the arbitrary controls exercised by the apparatchiks. While committed to the values of socialism, they, like the Soviet physicist Sakharov, in his remarkable manifesto, are beginning openly to demand greater freedom of expression and artistic creation and to repudiate the neo-Stalinist restrictions. When Prague eliminated press censorship, encouraged freedom of discussion and the confrontation of ideas, allowed the creation of non-communist political groups, and tried to make the bureaucracy responsive to the vocalized demands of the hitherto silent population, East European liberals were heartened.

But the orthodox communist leaders in the Soviet Union, Poland, and East Germany decided that the situation was getting out of hand. It was not so much that they distrusted Dubcek's motives as his ability to keep in check the political and social forces unleashed in Czechoslovakia. They were alarmed by the free-wheeling iconoclasm of journals like the literary-political weekly *Literarni Listy*, which played a crucial role in the liberalization drive. The magazine became a spearhead of the Czechoslovak revolution, and its circulation shot up to over 300,000 in a nation of only fourteen million. Three of its editors had been expelled from the party last fall for their attack on the Novotny regime, and one of them, Ludvik Vaculik, later wrote the famous manifesto, "Two Thousand Words," signed by leading intellectuals in support of the reformers. Prodding the Dubcek leadership from below and openly satirizing such unsympathetic foreign comrades as Ulbricht, the magazine symbolized everything orthodox communists feared from the reform movement.

This was simply the most outspoken element of an attitude that had deep roots in the communist party itself. It is precisely what was unique about the Czechoslovak experiment—that it came from within the ranks of the party hierarchy. The reformers were dedicated Marxists, dissatisfied with the rigidity of the party structure and eager to breathe new life into ossified, bureaucratic institutions. They wanted to make the economy work more efficiently, reward initiative, and decentralize the economic machinery. They resented the unequal trading relationships with the Soviet Union, where they processed Russian raw material at little benefit to themselves, and they wanted to expand economic links with the West so that they could modernize their outdated industrial plant. While it had been the most industrialized state of Eastern Europe before the war, Czechoslovakia had fallen behind such neighbors as Austria. In many cases its industry had become inefficient, outdated, and uncompetitive—locked in the communist trading bloc, but unable to operate on the world market. The economic crisis had become so severe that Novotny was forced to accept some of the reforms proposed by Professor Ota Sik, including production geared to demand, and the decentralization of authority.

But the reforms were being held up by economic conservatives with a vested interest in the status quo. Last year the regime resumed its repression of intellectuals, and the Slovaks became increasingly resentful of their domination by the Czech majority in Prague. With only four million of the country's fourteen million people, the

Slovaks have felt discriminated against by the more numerous, industrially advanced Czechs. Considering themselves to be a separate nation, with a somewhat different language and different historical and social traditions, the Slovaks have never assimilated easily into the hybrid state formed in 1918 at the break-up of the Austro-Hungarian empire. Where Prague had been administered by Vienna, the Slovak capital of Bratislava was absorbed in the Hungarian part of the empire, and the differences have been crucial.

During the Stalinist terror of the early 1950s the Slovaks, with the few remaining Jews, were singled out as "bourgeois nationalists," and repressive efforts made to ignore or stamp out their separate identity. Even after the terror, Slovakia was treated more like a colony than a theoretically equal member of a federated state. Novotny was particularly contemptuous of Slovak feelings and became an object of contempt for both nationalists and reformers. Resistance to his regime became centered in Bratislava, where the Writers' Union demanded a purge of Stalinists, the release of political prisoners, and an abolition of censorship. When the Czechs realized this involved more than simply an expression of Slovak nationalism, they joined forces with their colleagues and sparked a whole progressive movement.

Faced with the resentment of the Slovaks, the demands of the intellectuals, and its own economic failures, the Novotny regime began to crack around the edges. It needed only a push to crumble, and that push came in October 1967 when the relatively obscure first secretary of the Slovak communist party stood up in the meeting of the Central Committee and attacked the Novotny leadership. Progressives and conservatives rallied around Alexander Dubcek, including a majority of workers. After a bitter struggle Novotny was ejected first as head of the party, and then as President. Once the rotting foundation had been removed, the barriers fell faster than anyone could have anticipated. Within a few months freedom of the press was restored, political prisoners liberated and rehabilitated, the economy decentralized and opened to the play of market forces, and the communist party itself democratized to provide for secret ballots and minority criticisms of majority decisions. Although he began as a moderate reformer, Dubcek himself was caught up in the tide and became a leading advocate of democratization.

From the 5th of January, when Novotny was ejected from office, to the 21st of August, when Russian tanks rolled across the frontiers, Czechoslovakia experienced an exhilarating freedom. People who had been circumspect, or even silent, for a generation, suddenly were able to voice their feelings. Workers held debates on the streets, housewives stood in line to sign petitions, the press cast off two decades of censorship and began subjecting the government to a blinding scrutiny. Various non-party groups were allowed to form, such as Club 231, of former political prisoners, and KAN, an organization of non-party political activists. While they posed no counter-revolutionary threat, some of their members spoke of the day when the communist party might be willing to compete for power with a non-communist party. The communists, after all, had won 38 per cent of the vote in 1947 during Czechoslovakia's last free election.

"The creation of an opposition party in Czechoslovakia is a necessity," stated the young playwright Vaclav Havel, "and this party should enjoy the same rights and the same chances as the communist party." This was also the position of Ivan Klima, one of the three writers temporarily evicted last fall from the communist party by Novotny. "The press can remain free," he wrote in *Literarni Listy*, "only within a functioning democratic system, and this is scarcely imaginable without the existence of several independent political parties." Other reformers, however, argued that this was unrealistic, given the political situation in Czechoslovakia, and its relation with the Soviet Union. Even such an outspoken liberal as Professor Eduard Goldstücker, president of the Writers' Union, has argued that "a parliamentary opposition as a system for the control of power exists only in a class society. Since Czechoslovakia has gone beyond the struggle between classes, we have to find and create another system for controlling power."

The government leaders did not want to break the communist party's monopoly on power, but simply, in Dubcek's words, to eliminate "the discredited bureaucratic-police methods"—to infuse communism with the humanism that had been lost in decades of conspiracy and repression. They realized that what they were proposing was radical—dangerously so in the eyes of the Soviet Union and its allies—and they were not sure they would be able to get away with it. We knew there were risks involved in the "effort toward social renewal," Josef Smrkovsky, president of the National Assembly told the Czechoslovak people after returning from his abduction to Moscow, "but we never thought we would have to pay the price we paid the night of August 20-21." That price was a return to communist orthodoxy, reimposition of censorship, permanent stationing of Soviet troops on the West German frontier, dissolution of non-communist political groups. Nobody wanted to admit it, yet all along the reformers realized in the back of their minds that they might not be able to get away with their experiment.

"What we are trying to do here," one of the most outspoken advocates of the reform movement told me in Prague just two weeks before the invasion, "is to find a form of communism that is relevant to advanced, technological societies where people have to be given the latitude to think for themselves. This is the only kind of communism that is ever going to have any appeal to Western Europe. The reform-minded parties in Italy, and even in France, are with us. But I'm afraid the Russians aren't ready to understand what we are doing. They see it as a threat to their own system, and so they accuse us of being 'counter-revolutionaries'—which means that we don't slavishly imitate their ways. They know we're not going to embrace the West Germans or apply for membership in NATO. But they are afraid that our 'heresy' of free speech and non-communist political groups might infect their own citizens. Beneath the crust of neo-Stalinism, the Soviet Union is seething with the demand for reform.

If the Czechs and Slovaks can get away with this 'heresy,' why not the citizens of the Soviet Union, Poland, and East Germany? That's the question the Russians are asking themselves, and I'm afraid what the answer might be."

In the balmy air of an early August night in Prague, the warning seemed a bit exaggerated. With Czech hippies playing their guitars on the baroque Charles Bridge, with rock-and-roll music wafting through the streets from student discotheques, and with the moon rising above the spire of Hradcany Castle, the prospect of a Soviet military intervention seemed highly improbable. But Prague is a city where dreams can turn into nightmares, and Hradcany is also the Castle that tormented Kafka's Josef K. Central Europe is not a place for easy optimism. The history of the Czechs and the Slovaks is riddled with failure and betrayal: the burning of Jan Hus at the stake in 1415, the defeat of the Reformation army at the Battle of the White Mountain in 1620, the stab in the back at Munich.

It is not so remarkable that the Czechs and the Slovaks failed to retain everything they won during the exhilarating months since the Novotny dictatorship collapsed last January. The Soviet Union simply behaved with the arrogance and the blindness of a super-power that knows it has a free hand within the area it claims as its sphere of influence. What is remarkable is that the people of Czechoslovakia, by bravely defying the occupiers without militarily provoking them, by painting swastikas on their tanks and telling the Russian farm boys to go home, and by supporting their ousted and imprisoned leaders, have for the time being been able to retain a considerably greater degree of autonomy than anyone would have imagined when the Russian military machine first struck. The hands of the reformers are now tied, the secret police is silencing opposition, and the people have once again retreated into stony silence. But Russian military government has been averted, for the time being at least, and in the long run the Czechs and the Slovaks are likely to win back some of their reforms, just as the Hungarians did after the brutal invasion of 1956.

This is not the end of the story of revolution within the communist empire, but only the beginning. The forces of reform and democratization which have been released in Czechoslovakia, and momentarily restrained by Soviet military power, are not unique to that country. They exist in Poland, where stagnation and political repression have created great instability beneath surface conformity; in East Germany, where even the Ulbricht regime has not been able to silence support for the Czechoslovak liberals; and in the Soviet Union itself, where the new technocracy and the intelligentsia have grown increasingly restive under the reactionary, autocratic rule of the party bureaucrats who replaced Khrushchev. The system of political repression practiced by the Soviet Union and its orthodox allies could not withstand the kind of public criticism that was the hallmark of the Czechoslovak reform program. The Soviet system demands authoritarianism at home and obedience of national communist parties abroad.

But this system, which was workable during the time when the Soviet Union could with some justice claim to be the leader of the world communist movement, is now in ruins. It is not world communism which has suffered from the invasion of Czechoslovakia—for there is no longer any single seat of communist authority—but the Soviet Union. The prestige it has enjoyed within the communist movement has been shattered, and it has revealed itself to be simply another dynastic state with dynastic ambitions. Moscow, not Prague, is the greatest casualty of the intervention against the Czech and Slovak reformers, and its actions have been repudiated by the major European communist parties, including the French, the Italians, the Yugoslavs, and the Rumanians. Unity within the communist world was long ago destroyed; it is now being broken down within the repressive communist bureaucracies of Eastern Europe.

The initial reaction in the West to the Russian intervention was a call for greater vigilance against the "communist conspiracy" and for increased arms budgets to meet the Soviet threat. Even the normally liberal *Times* of London hoisted the cold war flag and called for the Western powers to "look seriously at the state of their defenses." Many fear that the cold warriors here and abroad will get a new shot in the arm, and the détente will be seriously imperiled. This may be exaggerated. The Russians pose no more a threat to the West than they did two days, or two months, or two years ago. They are neither more aggressive nor more pacific. They simply want to hold on to the empire they believe is rightly theirs and which they consider vital to their security. No political leader in Washington has challenged this principle, even though they all lament its implementation. The truth is that Washington is willing to let Moscow play its game, so long as the Russians do not infringe on our territory. The détente is unlikely to be endangered because both political parties are committed to it and respect super-power diplomacy. Washington will forget Czechoslovakia even faster than it forgot Budapest. But it has a vested interest in the détente, regardless of which party is in power.

Revolutions of the kind that occurred in Czechoslovakia are troublesome to the super-powers. They cannot accept them without undermining their control over their client states and eroding their traditionally conceived spheres of influence. They cannot intervene forcibly against them, however, without diminishing their international prestige and, perhaps more importantly, unleashing disruptive forces within their own societies. This is what the United States learned at Santo Domingo and in Vietnam, and it is what the Soviet Union is now discovering in Czechoslovakia.

The Czechs and the Slovaks had their moment of glory, and they will have it again. For the time being they must play the good soldier Schweik and sit out the storm that is now enveloping them. But their vision of a humane communist society was an inspiring one that will have a profound impact on nations that are trying to achieve social justice without undergoing a brutalizing dictatorship. In the Soviet empire itself, the rumbling echoes of the Czechoslovak heresy have only just begun to be heard.

Santo Domingo: The One We Got Away With

Remember Colonel Elías Wessin y Wessin? Or Donald Reid Cabral? Or José Molina Ureña and Antonio Imbert? How about W. Tapley Bennett and Hector García Godoy? Or surely John Bartlow Martin, Juan Bosch, Joaquín Balaguer and Ellsworth Bunker? Don't they ring a bell somewhere in the dim recesses of the mind where we store the personalities of our various interventions? These gentlemen, of course, were part of the cast of that little affair in the Dominican Republic, a couple of interventions ago, back in 1965. You know, the one we got away with.

For those who have pushed aside these names to make room in their heads for the dramatis personae of our current road show in Cambodia, let us recall that Col. Wessin in 1963 overthrew the legally elected government of the Dominican Republic and sent President Juan Bosch into exile, that the military junta replaced him with Cabral, a smooth businessman from a distinguished (that is, rich) Dominican family, before his incompetence led him to be overthrown in April 1965 by a countercoup from the Left designed to restore Bosch to power. Although they had widespread public support and had set up a provisional government under Molina, the "con-

stitutionalists," as they were called, were opposed by
more conservative elements of the military, who hated
Bosch. Led by Wessin, some military units decided to
resist the revolution. They were vastly outnumbered, however, and were weakened by the defection of many of
their own soldiers. Just as they were on the point of defeat, the American ambassador, the courtly Mr. Bennett
from Georgia, sent a telegram to Lyndon B. Johnson
calling for help.

At this point the story becomes more familiar. American troops rushed to Santo Domingo, ostensibly to protect imperiled American citizens, but actually, as soon
became apparent, to defeat the revolution and prevent unnamed "communists" from seizing power. The consti-
tutionalists were defeated by Col. Wessin, with a little
help from his friends, and John Bartlow Martin, former
ambassador to the Dominican Republic under Kennedy,
was dispatched to straighten things out. Martin promptly
made a mess of everything and soon was replaced by a
succession of emissaries, including McGeorge Bundy and
Cyrus Vance—but not before he had set up a government
under Imbert, who was so detested that no responsible
Dominican would agree to serve in his dictatorial regime.
Exit Martin, enter Ellsworth Bunker, former businessman
(director of the National Sugar Refining Corporation)
turned ambassador, and currently proconsul to Saigon,
who installed a provisional government under Hector Gar-
cía-Godoy which set the stage for the withdrawal of U.S.
troops and for free elections. In 1966 the conservative
Balaguer defeated Bosch, and was reelected in May 1970,
to Washington's audible relief.

Happy ending? Not exactly. The Dominican economy
is stagnating, with per capita income lower than in 1960,
between one-quarter and one-half the labor force is un-
employed, the Left is subject to a continuing terrorism
that sees daily political murders and "suicides" of political prisoners. Unwilling or unable to control this political violence and economic unrest, Balaguer has lost support to Wessin, who poses the danger of a rightist
dictatorship, and to the splintered Bosch forces on the

Left which are rejecting electoral politics in favor of revolution and "popular dictatorship." Even should the Dominican Republic not explode again, the intervention took a high political toll on the participants: The Organization of American States has been discredited as a supine instrument of the State Department, Latin American oligarchies have been confirmed in their belief that Washington will bail them out when the going gets rough, Latin generals have been encouraged to intervene in political affairs, and in the eyes of many at home and abroad, the U.S. came off as a clumsy imperialist ready to crush any client state that threatens to get out of hand.

It could, of course, have turned out even worse. Had it not been for a combination of fortuitous circumstances, we might now be fighting against a Dominican guerrilla army of "national liberation." The fact that we are not has less to do with the wisdom of American policy in the Caribbean than the fact that there was no political base for a national resistance movement against the foreign invaders (us), and that the communists were few and ineffectual (which meant there was no reason to intervene at all).

From the beginning it was a sordid affair, based on a heritage of intervention stretching back to the occupation by the U.S. Marines from 1916-24, thirty years of accommodation to the tyrannical Trujillo regime, a neo-colonial relationship that makes the Dominican Republic dependent on the U.S. for some 75 per cent of its trade, an interpretation of the Monroe Doctrine that considers the Caribbean a U.S. lake, a knee-jerk anti-communism that sees a threat to the national security wherever a handful of Marxists gather, and a failure to examine the tired assumptions that American policy makers have been chained to for the past quarter century. Lyndon Johnson sent American troops to the Dominican Republic, Jerome Slater sums up in *Intervention and Negotiation*, because "in 1965 the United States was a prisoner, both at home and abroad, of its own oversimplifications, myths, and outmoded policies."

Slater, an associate professor at the State University of

New York at Buffalo, has written the most complete, the most objective, and the most authoritative account of the Dominican intervention, one that will remain a source book for anyone interested in what happened, why it happened, and, alas, why it may well be repeated elsewhere unless some attitudes are radically revised. While his sympathies lie with the reformers, and while he looks upon the intervention as a disastrous mistake, he does not heap the entire blame on Lyndon Johnson, and indeed makes clear that the overall policy that led to the invasion was "much more a creation of the Kennedy administration than of the Johnson administration." He also takes to task those such as Theodore Draper and Senator Fulbright who maintain that the U.S. intervened to prevent the return of Bosch or to restore the status quo.

Johnson, Slater argues, was committed to free elections from the outset of the intervention, and while opposed to Bosch, would not formally have prevented his return to power if freely elected. But he does severely criticize the administration for intervening at all, showing that there was no serious risk of a communist takeover, and stating that, even if there were, "another Cuba" would not represent a security threat to the U.S. The Johnson administration, however, could not admit this. It was a prisoner of its own oft-proclaimed cold war rhetoric, and it was fearful of public opinion. In Slater's caustic words,

> reasonable men could and in fact did fear that a successful communist revolution in the Dominican Republic might well jeopardize the future of the Democratic party in the United States.

Like the Cuban missile crisis three years earlier, the Dominican intervention was dictated in part by domestic political considerations. Having failed to revise its policies in the light of new realities, the Johnson administration, like its predecessors and its successor, made itself the prisoner of its own bankrupt premises. There is more to the story than this, for U.S. policy makers, irrespective of real or imagined attitudes held by the public, are deeply hostile to revolution in the authoritarian, impoverished countries of the Third World. Even if it were a victim of its own (perhaps mistaken) view of what the voters would tolerate, nonetheless the Johnson administration, as Slater points out, "refused to use the opportunity to effect really sweeping military reform" to bring about social change after it had intervened to "save" the Dominican Republic from "communism."

U.S. policy was, and remains,

> conditioned on the very explicit premise that whatever its faults, the Dominican military is an essential force for "order" and "stability" and that, therefore, nothing must be done that would seriously weaken it.

So long as that attitude remains unchanged, we have probably not yet seen our last intervention in the Caribbean. No more Dominican Republics? Don't bet on it.

Haiti:
Papa Doc and
the Free World

It doesn't take long to discover that nothing is ever quite what it seems in Haiti. Not what you see, not what you hear, and not even what you suspect. It is all wrapped in ambiguity and contradiction, like the people themselves. Ask a direct question, and you get a bemused reply that simply raises more questions. The Haitians— all charmers, even when at their most sinister—speak in a strange double-talk designed to conceal what they really mean and transform the obvious into mystery.

Least of all can you trust your own senses. On the surface life seems placid and uneventful. The people go about their business in the dusty streets of Port-au-Prince, the shanty-town capital that houses a third of a million souls in various degrees of misery. Scarcely anyone ever gets shot up in public anymore by the Tonton Macoutes, President Duvalier's own private militia of sportshirted, pistol-packing thugs. And at night you can walk down the darkest alleys in absolute safety. Law and order is a dream come true in Duvalier's Haiti, and at first glance it seems literally like an island of tranquillity.

As indeed it is, for the sun-seeking North American tourists who paddle around the kidney-shaped swimming pools of the luxury hotels in suburban Pétionville, high above the steaming capital. From the hill the view is scenic, the vegetation lush, the souvenir vendors amusing, and everyday life blissfully uneventful. But in the humid streets of Port-au-Prince and in the teeming slums that rim the waterfront and spread into the countryside, life is neither calm nor picturesque.

In Haiti today everyone is waiting for something to happen. No one is quite sure what is going to happen; when or how or if it will happen. But tension is in the air, and the stability of Papa Doc's regime seems shakier than at any time during the past half dozen years. Ever since last May the Haitian dictator has been a recluse in his palace, emerging only on ceremonial occasions, such as Governor Nelson Rockefeller's breathless Latin-American tour that brought him to Port-au-Prince for a few hours in July 1969. The event induced Papa Doc to leave his palace for the first time in two months. He was cheered by thousands of Haitians who had been brought in trucks from their villages and forced to stand for hours in the ninety-degree sun to greet their leader and his American visitor.

The precise cause of Davalier's seclusion has not been divulged, and rotating rumors fill the knowledge gap. Instead of putting to rest the rumors of his illness and possible departure from office, the brief appearance of the sixty-two-year-old President triggered a new round of speculation about palace intrigue and what might succeed his regime.

The regime has been badly shaken by attacks from without and within. In April 1969 the government announced that it had tracked down and summarily executed some thirty rebels in the hills outside Port-au-Prince. They were labeled "Communists" (the customary term for anyone who opposes Duvalier) and accused of collaborating with foreign powers. A government decree banned all communist activities, defined as "crimes against the security of the nation," and applied the death penalty to those committing or abetting such vague crimes. Scores of people, denounced as "agents of international Communism" or simply as "Communist sym-

pathizers," were arrested and disappeared into the notorious Duvalier prisons.

But the attacks against the regime continued, and in
May government troops were fighting against a group
of "exiles and mercenaries" on the northern coast. The
airborne exile landing was combined with an attempt
to bomb the presidential palace—ascribed to the machinations of former President Paul Magloire, now in exile in
New York. In an appeal to the UN and the Organization
of American States, the government's spokesman described the attacks as "international brigandage" which
would not have been possible without the tolerance of
such neighboring countries as Jamaica, Cuba, the Dominican Republic, and the United States. While there
are a good many Haitian workers in Cuba, some of
whom no doubt have been trained as guerrillas, it appears
that the old B-25 which made such an amateurish job
of bombing the President's palace came from a base in
Florida. The regime reacted with a new roundup of
suspects, charged that the Cubans were behind it all,
and called for the United States to resume its military
aid to Haiti.

Duvalier has been trying to convince the Nixon administration that his government is threatened by a Communist conspiracy. The accusation holds little water, for
the Cubans have been very circumspect toward Haiti,
and the Haitian Communists are divided and weak. But
it is an argument that has wrung money out of Washington before, and Papa Doc can hardly be blamed for
trying to get the old dog salivating again.

The regime has been threatened not only by the
capricious activities of the exile groups, with their periodic, and invariably ill-fated, landings and bombings,
but also by an increasingly high mortality rate among
the Tonton Macoutes. A growing number of Duvalier's
private militia of killers have been murdered recently.
Some believe that this is the work of resistance groups
preparing the way for the dictator's downfall. Others,
rather more cynical and perhaps used to Duvalier's ways,
believe that he secretly ordered their murder himself

since the Macoutes were becoming so strong that they represented a threat to his one-man rule. Papa Doc's formula for survival has always been divide-and-rule.

Despite the spate of strange activities, compounded by the disappearance of various suspected opponents of the regime, Haitians gingerly avoid political discussions. Wise people have learned not to talk about politics, and those with an acute sense of survival try not even to think about it. "Let's talk about Susan Sontag," a young Haitian intellectual said to me in his office crammed with highbrow American film quarterlies and literary reviews, "and about your student revolution." When I tried to steer the conversation back to the Haitian scene, he deftly began to lecture on the African origins of voodoo. Later I learned from another source that his uncle had been killed by the Macoutes and that he himself had been held in the infamous political prison known as Fort Dimanche.

Self-censorship also extends to foreigners, such as the lovely American woman who has been working in Haiti for the past decade. Once as I gently tried to shift our conversation from the richness of Haitian musical lore to the problems of everyday life under Papa Doc, her usual smile froze, and she replied testily, "Nothing's the matter here. Anyway, politics isn't my business." Her reply was typical of the small American colony in Haiti— resident businessmen and plant managers, a hotel proprietor or two, a few Negroes in exile from racism and the black revolution, and a variety of amateur ethnologists, escapists, sybarites, and artists. These people stay on good terms with the government by keeping their nose out of politics. Papa Doc has nothing against the resident Yankees, who live in great splendor on little money (a full-time servant costs $30 a month, and a palatial house under $100), and the Haitians treat them with their usual kindness and hospitality.

Officially the American presence has been subdued since Washington cut off direct economic aid to Haiti in 1962, when President Kennedy declared Papa Doc's regime to be dictatorial and incompetent. The diplomatic personnel who remain are discreet and usually appreciative of Haitians and their culture. They work hard, lament over the bad relations between Port-au-Prince and Washington, and feel cut off from one of the few Latin-American governments that is relatively independent of the U.S. Embassy. They sit ensconced in a shiny white cube on the edge of the sea, besieged by an unending file of Haitians seeking immigrant visas to the United States, and enjoy the pleasures of being rich in a poor country. At lunchtime the station wagons line up in the Embassy driveway, where their wives and pink-skinned children wait to take them back to hillside homes that are trimmed in bougainvillaea and stocked with supplies from the PX at Guantánamo. Yes, Guantánamo in Cuba, where they periodically go shopping for U.S. goods at tax-free, duty-free prices.

These American officials readily admit that there is oppression in Haiti, that the press is stifled, the trade unions muzzled, the intellectuals driven into exile or forced into silence, and that justice is dispensed at the whim of Papa Doc. But this is old hat, and they tend to treat it as a matter of course. Politics in Haiti may, literally, be a life-and-death matter, but it is not *sérieux*. What seems to engage their interest are the problems of what used to be called "nation building." They want to bring in more foreign (particularly U.S.) private investment, raise health standards, improve education and transportation, and steer Haiti along the path of sustained economic development. They tend to view Haiti as an engineering problem which can be set right with diligence, cooperation, and the proper tools.

They are unhappy about the absence of a formal U.S. aid program to Haiti, although they are quick to point out that the aid program was allegedly misused by the Duvalier regime. "Much of the aid money was wasted," one explained, "and a lot of it found its way into Duvalier's pocket." This, of course, Papa Doc vehemently denies, and in turn charges that the aid cutoff in 1962 was part of a plot by Kennedy to overthrow his government.

This, however, was a long time ago, and Papa Doc is now ready, indeed eager, to kiss and make up with Washington. Aside from citing his anti-communist credentials, he argues that his government is economically responsible and is trying to follow an orderly development program within its drastically limited means. Even today there is a small U.S. aid program trickling into Haiti, most of it consisting of food and medicines funneled through the UN and the OAS. This program has been extremely helpful in the countryside, where the people are even more destitute than in the capital.

Americans in Haiti, even while disapproving of the Duvalier regime, believe that the direct aid program should be resumed. "The ones who suffer," they argue, "are the people, not the government." They believe that if the regime would accept the strict controls Washington favors, Haiti could benefit greatly from inclusion in the aid program. Most Haitians tend to agree, even those who are bitterly anti-Duvalier. But they have mixed feelings. They berate the United States for neglecting Haiti and imply that Washington's motives are really racist. At the same time they resent American interference in Haitian affairs and say that Duvalier could only exist with U.S. tolerance. While the intellectuals hate Papa Doc, they admire him for defying Washington and for refusing to accept American control as the price of economic assistance.

The wily Duvalier plays the strings of Haitian nationalism like a virtuoso, evoking the indignation and wounded pride that arose from the American occupation that began in 1915 and did not end until 1934. At the beginning of that occupation, ordered by Woodrow Wilson for the ostensible purpose of subduing disorder and preventing foreign intervention, the U.S. Marines landed in Port-au-Prince, went to the Haitian National Bank, and carried off $500,000 in gold, as part of an arrangement between Secretary of State William Jennings Bryan and the directors of the Haitian Bank, which was in turn owned by the National City Bank of New York. The

Haitians argued that they had injured no Americans, defaulted no debt, and violated no obligation of the United States. This plea went unanswered. A puppet government was set up, the legislature dissolved, and a new constitution favoring U.S. investments forced upon the Haitians. An officer of the Marine detachment Colonel Smedley D. Butler, later wrote that in Haiti he was "doing the dirty work for the National City Bank." Haitian resistance against the invaders turned into guerrilla warfare. In the "pacification" effort 3,250 Haitians were killed. The bitterness engendered by the occupation, which continued in the form of an economic trusteeship until 1946, has lingered on to this day.

Aside from paying off U.S. and foreign creditors, the American occupying forces did what they were best at: they built roads, schools, hospitals, and a workable telephone system. They also trained a strong gendarmerie which ended rural resistance and centralized political authority in the capital. When the Americans left, the things they built gradually fell to pieces: the roads have washed away, the schools and hospitals have become inadequate, and the telephone is little more than a decorative object which emits static. But the idea of centralized control caught on. Through the Tonton Macoutes and the militia-like National Security Volunteers, the idea has played a part in the long, unhappy reign of François Duvalier, self-declared President-for-life.

Thus the American impact on Haiti has not been negligible—indeed the U.S. dollar is the semi-official currency of the island—but it is not quite what many Americans imagine. The impact is economic: Haiti has provided a safe haven for American investors in search of raw materials, rich land, and cheap labor. It is political in that the country, whether ruled by dictators or democrats, remains firmly in the American orbit. But it is not cultural, unless one counts a few American schools and the pervasiveness of English among young people.

The good country doctor Duvalier gives the Americans very little credit. His relations with the embassy are cold, but correct. He seems to feel that the U.S. government is responsible for his "bad press" abroad, and particularly for the disastrous drop in tourism following the withdrawal of aid in 1963. There is an element of truth in this, for Washington did discourage Americans from visiting Haiti. But the reason given was internal instability, and it can be said that Papa Doc helped substantiate this charge by unleashing a reign of terror against his political opponents.

Fearing an invasion of Haitian exiles abetted by Washington, and perhaps convinced of this by the sudden appearance of American warships in the Bay of Port-au-Prince, he decided to wipe out the last vestiges of political opposition. His private militia, the Tonton Macoutes, were called into action. Suspected opponents of the regime were dragged from their homes at night, others were shot down in the street. Thousands fled the country, others cowered in terror and silence. Those were the days Graham Greene wrote about in *The Comedians*, and they are still spoken of in whispers.

The situation is a good deal calmer now, and one could walk the streets of Port-au-Prince without necessarily being aware that Haiti is anything more than another happy-go-lucky, *merengue*-dancing Caribbean island. The people are remarkably beautiful, even though many seem malnourished and suffering from debilitating diseases such as malaria, pellagra, and tuberculosis. The cotton clothing is brilliantly colored, although it is often little more than bits of rags patched together. By day the marketplaces and streets teem with activity, even though few, except the occasional tourist, have money to buy anything. At night the air is heavy with the perfume of tropical flowers, and the dark streets are quiet and perfectly safe. "A lot safer than Washington, D.C.," as the embassy people kept telling me.

In a sense Haiti is a perfect holiday spot—so long as one has no squeamishness about poverty and no qualms about authoritarian regimes. The hotels are well run and remarkably cheap by Caribbean standards, the pools are ice-cold and palm-fringed, the sun is hot and the vegetation lush, and the paintings produced by Haitian artists are imaginative and powerfully evocative. Unfortunately, the roads have so fallen to pieces that going to the beach is a two-hour chore, and a trip to Cap-Haïtien and the ruins of Henri Christophe's magnificent, crumbling Citadel by road takes three days (plus a travel permit from the Ministry of the Interior). But there is a great deal to do in the capital. And for those who prefer not to look at the slums on the edge of town, there are the marvelous, decaying Victorian gingerbread houses of the Haitian elite, the cooler hillside suburbs of Pétionville and Kenscoff, the art galleries and curio shops, and the sad little nightclubs, where tourists, government bureaucrats, the miniscule foreign colony, and the remnants of the local elite gather to do the *merengue*.

For the amateur sociologist the Haitian elite is a study in itself. Until quite recently the word *elite* was virtually synonymous with *mulatto*. Light-skinned Haitians, descended from the union of African slaves with French colonists, are only a tiny minority of the population. But even before the formal declaration of independence in 1804, they dominated the country through their key positions in commerce, agriculture, and government. Speaking French as a sign of education and "culture," rather than the rich Creole language of the Haitian peasant, practicing Roman Catholicism rather than the folk religion of voodoo, and educated abroad whenever possible, the elite has been not only a separate class but a caste within Haiti.

Periodically, black faces have been allowed into the elite, for the mulattoes have often found it convenient to deflect the indignation of the peasantry by ruling through black presidents and black generals. But their economic and political control was undiminished. This began to change during the late 1940s under Estimé, when an increasing number of blacks were brought into the government bureaucracy. Under Duvalier, who considers himself a Populist and the ideological descendant of Estimé, this movement became a deliberate policy to eradicate the old elite and form a new one. Thousands of blacks moved into positions of economic and political power, creating a new class, which is a product of the present regime, and perhaps dependent upon it for survival.

The Duvalier regime has been called a mulatto-hating dictatorship. But it is also something more: an expression of powerful forces which have long been submerged by a selfish, exploitative, culturally alienated elite. Elevating voodoo to official approval and bringing its *hoggans,* or priests, under his control, breaking the power of the Catholic Church and driving many foreign priests from the country, and preaching a kind of Black Is Beautiful philosophy, which emphasizes Haiti's African heritage rather than its veneer of French "culture," Duvalier has won considerable support from the peasantry and the urban proletariat.

In this sense, the so-called "Duvalier revolution," to which he constantly refers, is real. But it is a revolution that literally is only skin-deep. The elite now has a darker hue, but it is no less oligarchic. Haiti is still a country where 95 per cent of the people—illiterate, undernourished, and politically voiceless—are manipulated and exploited. Duvalier has not changed the economic structure of the society, even though his "revolution" is phrased in the vocabulary of Third World nationalism. It is what our own Black Panthers would scornfully call "cultural nationalism"—substituting black capitalists for white capitalists.

So far the "revolution" is mostly verbal, confining itself to a new airport, a paved road that ends a few miles outside the capital, and a semi-abandoned, deteriorating model village appropriately named Duvalier-ville. Government officials hurry to explain that great plans are in the works. An Italian firm is now building generators for the long-stalled hydroelectric project at the Peligre Dam, and a Canadian company is working on pipelines to provide a fresh-water supply for Port-au-Prince. If these projects are completed, they could help attract new industry, which is already beginning to dribble into Haiti to take advantage of the low-cost labor.

Coffee is still the major export crop, with sugar, bauxite, and copper accounting for most of the remainder. Industry has been virtually non-existent in Haiti, partly because there is no domestic market with the available cash to buy manufactured products. Most Haitians live on the subsistence level and cannot afford even canned foods (most of which are imported from the United States) let alone common consumer goods. Also the foreign-owned (largely American) firms controlling the mines and plantations do not want their products to be refined locally. Thus there are no plants in Haiti for making soluble coffee or turning bauxite into aluminum.

Recently, however, there has been a small-scale influx of U.S.-based firms setting up plants in Haiti for the processing of materials imported from the United States. These plants produce embroidered cloth, electronic components, and nearly all the baseballs and softballs imported into the United States. They have been set up to use Haitian low-cost labor, which is less than $2 per man day. The American firms find it cheaper to send the raw materials to Haiti and import the finished products into the United States than to manufacture them at home with union labor. This is a rather shaky base for economic development, but at least it is providing jobs for a good many Haitians who would otherwise be unemployed.

Unemployment is a chronic problem in Haiti, particularly among the urban proletariat which has drifted away from the countryside but has been unable to find jobs in the cities. Port-au-Prince, with a population of 300,000, is in fact the only large city in the country, and here the problem can be seen most dramatically. The dark hovels of the slums, with neither running water nor electricity, make rural Sicily seem affluent by comparison. In the pathetic open-air markets, prematurely-old young women sell rotting fruit and rusty bits of metal. Children roam the streets, too poor to go to school.

The statistics are not very helpful, but do give an indication of conditions in the country. The average annual income (whatever that means in a country like Haiti) is about $50. This is the lowest for any nation in the Western Hemisphere, and puts Haiti on a par with such poverty-stricken areas as the Brazilian Northeast and the Bolivian altiplano. Population density, which is one of the highest in the world, is kept in check only by a high mortality rate. There are about five million Haitians, although nobody knows for sure, most of them living off the land. Their average life expectancy is 40 years, compared to 65 in the United States, and there are only about 250 doctors in the entire country. Of the 675,000 children of school age, only a quarter are actually enrolled in classes. At the university in Port-au-Prince, there are some 1,500 students, and from dawn until long after sundown, one can see them strolling along the tree-shaded walks of the park outside the presidential palace, notebooks in hand, memorizing their lessons and reciting them aloud, like a troupe of black Hamlets.

While these students are the cadre of the new elite, the prospects for most of them are not very promising. "Of course it's nice to be one of the privileged few who get an education," one student at the law faculty complained, "but what am I supposed to do with it—sharpen pencils at the Ministry of Underdevelopment?" In a stagnant economy there are not nearly enough professional jobs for the qualified people being trained at the universities. Young people are either forced into jobs beneath their capacities or obliged to emigrate. Tens of thousands of trained Haitians have left the country, many of them for political reasons, others because there is little economic opportunity. An estimated 50,000 Haitians live in New York City alone, not to mention some 300,000 who work in the Dominican Republic.

The political-minded *émigrés* are badly splintered; often their only common ground is their opposition to Duvalier. New York is the headquarters for the major bourgeois-liberal opposition group, the Haitian Coalition. Its membership ranges from the moderate left of its young director, Raymond Joseph, to the center-right of ex-President Paul Magloire. The Coalition has Washington's unofficial blessing and represents the kind of vaguely progressive, property-respecting, pro-American government that the State Department would like to see installed in Port-au-Prince.

The left-wing opposition groups hold the coalition in contempt, charging that it is little more than a tool of the State Department and financed by the CIA. The two Marxist-oriented parties, PEP and PUDA, recently fused to form the Unified Party of Haitian Communists (PUCH), with headquarters in Havana. Like the Coalition, PUCH has an extensive information network within Haiti. In its two-hour daily radio program in Creole, it declares Duvalier to be a tool of American imperalism and calls for an armed peasant revolution. PUCH cadres have been organizing in Haiti for several years, and in 1967 held up the Royal Bank of Canada in Port-au-Prince, walking off with $60,000 for the purchase of arms. PUCH has set up contacts in the university and has tried to organize peasant groups in the mountains so that it may be in an influential position when the Duvalier regime ultimately crumbles.

The government has seized upon and greatly exaggerated the communist danger. Shortly before the Rockefeller visit, Gerard de Catalogne, whose *Nouveau Monde* is the unofficial mouthpiece of the regime, wrote in his newspaper: "Under the government of President François Duvalier, Haiti will never become a Communist spearhead directed against the heart of the United States."

This is a continuing litany of the regime, for Duvalier knows how to play on Washington's fear of communism. Despite occasional criticisms of the U.S.—meant for Haitian domestic consumption—Papa Doc is safely within the American camp. He poses no threat to U.S. hegemony in the Caribbean, has no intention of nationalizing American private investments, or allying himself with the Russians. Tyrannical though he may be, he is a tyrant in Washington's pocket. So long as he is in power there will be no immediate danger of communism—and no reform.

What Haiti needs is a social revolution that will break the grip of the ruling oligarchy; organize the peasants into rural cooperatives; provide housing, education, and medical attention for all; and undertake a system of economic development based upon national needs rather than foreign profits. Perhaps the well-meaning liberals in the New York-based Haitian Coalition can provide this leadership. But it is far from certain that they will have a chance to try, even if Duvalier suddenly disappears. More likely, is a continuation of the same repressive system, with new faces and more unfulfilled promises. Should serious reformers come to power after Duvalier, they will almost certainly be accused by their opponents of being "communists." Will Washington reply as it did in Santo Domingo in 1965?

Papa Doc lingers on in his gleaming white palace as the unhappy people of the hemisphere's second oldest independent nation wait for something better: for the revolution that may never come; for the return of the exiles who are comfortably settled abroad; for the new regime which could be no better than the one they have; for the return of the U.S. Marines should their leaders be accused of communism; for another Toussaint or Dessalines to again raise the red and blue flag and astonish the world.

Mysterious Cuba

While nobody was looking, Cuba disappeared. It vanished from the headlines and presumably has been quietly removed from the secret list of areas worth blowing ourselves up about. A few years ago it was an "intolerable menace only 90 miles from our shores." Today it is nowhere, at least for Americans. It has been reduced to a briefly glimpsed patch of green 30,000 feet below the Jamaica-bound jets, a moment's idle conversation between the frozen dessert and the transparent coffee.

Washington, of course, continues to blacklist the perfidious Castro regime, forbidding U.S. businessmen to trade with Cuba, and even preventing Americans from visiting the island. The State Department's passport restrictions were recently struck down by the Supreme Court, but no mass influx of *yanqui* tourists seem likely —particularly since it is virtually impossible to get to Cuba. Air service from the U.S. has been suspended, and the island's only link to the entire Western hemisphere (highjacking aside) is via a twice-weekly flight from Mexico City. There all Havana-bound passengers are obligingly photographed by a CIA agent, perhaps to make them feel that Somebody Up There cares.

Locked in America's inland sea, unable to trade with her Latin neighbors, denied a share of the U.S. sugar quota on which her economy has long depended, refused diplomatic recognition by every nation in the hemisphere except Mexico and Jamaica,* forced to depend on the communist world for her survival, fifteen minutes flying time from the most powerful nation in the world, and 5,000 miles from her nearest protector, Cuba is hopelessly vulnerable, isolated and dependent. By all reasonable standards of economics and power politics, the Castro regime should have crumbled long ago. Some U.S.-approved judge or general should be running the show in Havana, and United Fruit should be reclaiming its land.

Yet the Cuban revolution hobbles on. Like North Vietnam's triumph over American military technology, it couldn't have happened—but it did. Cuba is beset by consumer shortages and administrative inefficiency, bureaucratic incompetence and political suppression, social conformity and censorship. The government is loaded with Fidelista zealots and communist hacks, style often serves as a replacement for substance, and the regime—particularly in its relations with its neighbors—sometimes gives the impression of being its own worst enemy.

Why does it hang on? If the people are miserable and starving, as our mass media would have us believe, why do they not rise up and overthrow the regime? The conventional answer is that they live in terror and would be ruthlessly repressed if they tried to overthrow Castro by themselves. This is the logic of the CIA, which persuaded President Kennedy to launch the Bay of Pigs landing on the assumption that the Cuban people would rush to embrace the Florida-based exiles. We all know what happened there. The invaders were routed not because Kennedy refused to supply air cover, as the distinguished exiles charged, but because there was no

* The Marxist government of Chile recognized Cuba in November 1970.

uprising in Cuba itself. The regime proved to have a good deal more popular support than anyone in Washington had been willing to concede.

The hard truth seems to be that the majority of Cubans has no desire to overthrow the government. It is a government, like a good many others, that has made serious mistakes, antagonized people, and interfered unjustifiably in the private lives of its citizens. It is far from representative, and in many ways it is totalitarian and repressive. It has destroyed the old class structure, taken away many privileges of the middle classes, and caused some 300,000 people to emigrate. It is not surprising that many Cubans hate the Castro regime—because it took away their riches, or betrayed its own early promises.

Virtually no Cuban ever wanted or expected to have a communist government. Certainly none ever dreamed of being cut off from the United States and Latin America, and living under the constant fear of invasion. And yet even though all this has happened, most Cubans are incontestably better off under Castro than they were under Batista. The regime has provided homes, schools, hospitals and jobs for millions of people who lived in ignorance and apathy. It has eliminated illiteracy, stamped out racial discrimination, raised the living standard of peasants and unskilled laborers and restored national pride to a people mired in the mentality of colonialism. And it has won the allegiance of the young generation of Cubans, who feel that this is their revolution and that their future depends on its survival.

Although Castro has been in power for nearly ten years, historians are still gnashing their teeth over the question of whether he started out as a communist and secretly plotted to lead Cuba into the Soviet camp ever since his days in the Sierra Maestre, or whether he turned to Marxism-Leninism only after seizing power. The difference is crucial. If Castro started out as a dedicated communist, nothing the United States did in the early months of the revolution would have made much difference. But if he became a communist later—either to carry out his revolutionary reforms, or to seek Soviet support in case of a U.S. invasion—then Washington shares a good deal of responsibility for the course of the Cuban revolution.

Would Fidel have turned to Moscow if the Eisenhower administration had not drastically cut, and then abolished, the Cuban sugar quota? Would he have sought Soviet missiles if Kennedy had not ordered the landing at the Bay of Pigs? We can probably never be certain. But according to Castro himself, as reported by Lee Lockwood in an interview with the Cuban leader, he became a communist only gradually, in response to the internal needs of Cuban society, and to Cuba's place in the world. While Castro does not say that a different U.S. policy would have changed his course, he apparently believed that the only safe way to escape American domination was to seek the security of the Soviet camp. What is remakable is that Cuba, while dependent on the Soviet Union for protection and for economic survival, has been able to follow a policy of such outspoken independence from Moscow.

Andrés Suárez, an exile who briefly served in the first Castro government, seeks to demolish the argument that communism came to Cuba as a result of mass pressure from below. Cuba is a communist state, he maintains, not because the people wanted it, or because the old-guard communists plotted it, or because Fidel became enamored of Marxism-Leninism, but because he sought Soviet nuclear protection to spread his subversive doctrines throughout Latin America. *Cuba: Castroism and Communism, 1959–1966* is a detailed study for specialists. While his thesis is well documented, Professor Suárez' historical objectivity is marred by his hatred of Castro, whom he refers to as a "tyrant," "cruel and implacable," and a "consummate opportunist." All of this may be true, but it does not do much to clarify the debate.

A better written and wider-ranging study is Ramon Eduardo Ruiz' *Cuba: The Making of a Revolution*. Professor Ruiz, who teaches at Smith College, argues that the Castro revolution, rather than representing a sharp break with the past, was the culmination of a struggle that began in the 19th century. Its origins lay in the frustrated nationalism of a people who were formally independent but under an American protectorship, in periodic economic crises and unemployment, and in a middle class incapable of governing. Castro, he believes turned to communism for three reasons: his fear and distrust of the U.S.; his need to organize support for the revolution; and his belief that communism could solve Cuba's socio-economic problems. "The Cuban Communist movement offered Castro both the ideology and the political apparatus he required to manipulate labor and to commit the populace to his revolution." His book is not so much about Castro's Cuba as about the forces of Cuban history that led up to the revolution. It is about the roots of Cuban nationalism, the economic system that "transformed Cuba into a vast plantation exploited for the benefit of Americans," the frustrated dreams of such patriots as José Martí, and of American policy toward an island that was a colony in everything but name.

For all the new titles that have spilled off the presses recently, few have given us any accurate idea of what life is like in Cuba today. There are eulogies like Edward Boorstein's *The Economic Transformation of Cuba,* which would have us believe that all of "Cuba's problems . . . resulted from the simple presence of the U.S. monopolies and the monopoly-dominated U.S. government engaged in their normal business." There are novels like Tana de Gámez' absorbing account of the guerrilla struggle against Batista, *The Yoke and the Star.* There is the semi-autobiographical memoir, *Inconsolable Memories* by Edmundo Desnoes, a Cuban who returned to the island after the revolution, and is now a leading cultural figure in Havana, even though his book has been considered mildly critical of the government. ("Not even the workers are satisfied with the Revolution," says one of his characters.) And there is the remarkable *Autobiography of a Runaway Slave,* by 108-year-old Esteban Montejo of his life as a runaway slave in the forests of Cuba, his participation in the war for Cuban independence and his disillusionment with the society that was created under the American protectorship. Montejo's autobiography, as told to Miguel Barnet, is a work of art—crude but authentic.

Descriptive portraits of today's Cuba, however, are all too rare. This gap has been partially filled by José Yglesias' account of life in a Cuban country town. An American of Cuban ancestry, Yglesias spent three months in a village in eastern Cuba, interviewing the inhabitants and trying to understand the impact of the revolution upon their lives. While *In the Fist of the Revolution* makes no claims of objectivity ("I sympathize with your Revolution and I have come to see how it is," he tells the hotel clerk on his arrival), Yglesias does not try to hide some of the seamier sides of life in Castro's Cuba—the punishments it metes out to those critical of the regime, and the way the Committees for the Defense of the Revolution pry into private lives to ferret out nonconformists and dissenters. These he deems to be a "revolutionary necessity." But if Yglesias is a committed observer, his pen is sharp, and he has given us the most graphic portrait of the Cuban revolution in action that has yet appeared.

The revolutionary government remains firmly in power, Fidel is slowly assuming the role of an elder statesman, and a whole generation of Cubans which can scarcely remember anything before the revolution is coming of age. The fight against Batista is becoming part of folklore. Nothing makes this more apparent than the publication of Carlos Franqui's *The Twelve*, first-person narratives by the twelve survivors of the original eighty-two guerrillas who landed in Oriente province in 1956, or by Che Guevara's *Reminiscences of the Cuban Revolutionary War*. Che's book, particularly, not only seems dated, but dry, turgid and totally lacking in feeling for the thrust and passion of the guerrilla struggle against Batista.

Far more moving are the recently published diaries of the guerrilla campaign in Bolivia. It was here that

Che met his death and the revolutionary movement in Latin America received a devastating blow. Stolen from under the nose of the Bolivian government, *The Diary of Che Guevara* has now been released by the Cubans with an explanatory introduction by Fidel Castro. There seems to be no doubt as to the authenticity of the documents, which form a chronicle of the heroism, idealism and ultimate despair of a man who has become a universal symbol of revolutionary fervor. It is an anatomy of a revolution that failed, and the last entries are marked by a courageous lucidity and indomitable humanism. This is an exciting—and depressing—document of the utmost importance.

"Only 90 miles from our shores," Cuba might as well be on the other side of the moon. Most of us know less about it than the average ten-year-old child knows about Vietnam. Passionate denunciation has given way to bored indifference. But someday we may learn to live with Communist Cuba, just as we have learned to live with Communist Poland or Communist Yugoslavia. When that day comes we will regret the wall of ignorance and distrust that cuts us off from an island and a people with which we have so intimately associated. In the meantime, these few books are all we have to bridge ninety miles that is an ocean.

Havana:
The Unalienated
Society

The hardest thing about going to Cuba is not getting permission from suspicious officials in the State Department, or persuading the Cubans to give you a visa, or taking the round-about route to Havana via Mexico City, Madrid, or Prague—although all of these are bad enough, and would discourage any but the most determined traveler. These hurdles, however, are merely preparations. The hardest thing is to avoid being seduced by the Cubans.

Anyone can be trained to resist the blandishments of sunshine and palm trees, of art galleries that stay open until midnight, and even of teen-age traffic policewomen who wear their skirts short and hang their handbags on the traffic lights. You can resist being flattered when everyone calls you *compañero* as though you were just another comrade-in-arms, being uncritically impressed by the new housing projects and schools, and wondering why all countries don't have free medical care, funerals and local telephone calls.

You can approach the Cuban experiment critically, and cast a cold eye on the excesses of a revolution that has turned the country upside down and remade it in a new image. You should have grave reservations about the

methods of a regime that still incarcerates thousands of
political prisoners, that has made some grievous economic mistakes, that has neither a parliament, a free
press, nor a constitution guaranteeing civil liberties, and
that has become nearly as dependent on the Soviet Union
as it once was on the United States. You can deplore the
consumer shortages that force people to wait hours for a
quart of milk, the propaganda machine that urges them
to "volunteer" for hours of extra labor or weeks in the
sugar fields, and the absence of any legal alternative to
a government that rules by decree.

You can do all of this, and maybe even feel a bit self-
righteous as you contemplate the shortcomings of the
Castro regime. But if you stay on awhile, as I did in
January 1968, when I went to observe the international
cultural congress on under-development and colonialism,
you cannot help being impressed by the spirit that an-
imates the Cuban revolution and by the people who are
carrying it out. Even the most jaundiced Western journalists seem to fall under the spell, if only momentarily,
and speak with grudging admiration of the ability of the
Cubans to survive the U.S. economic blockade and build a
new society that has clearly brought enormous benefits to
the majority of the population.

The longer you stay in Cuba the more you become
aware that it is not simply a state like any other, nor
even a communist bureaucracy similar to the ones of
eastern Europe. Rather it is a continual "happening," a
vast and somewhat chaotic laboratory where nothing is
taken for granted and experimentation is the order of the
day. Everything is subject to analysis and modification:
the concept of government, the structure of society, the
sanctity of the family, the purpose of work, the justification of art, and even the nature of the human personality.
At a time when communism has come to seem like
merely another form of bureaucracy, somewhat more
rigid and no less heartless than the more advanced varieties of capitalism, Cuba offers something unique. It
offers the phenomenon of a revolution in progress.

This is why it seems natural to speak of the Cuban

"experiment," for it is a society in a perpetual state of fermentation. Today's orthodoxy may well turn out to be tomorrow's heresy, and none are more ready to admit it than the Fidelistas who run the country on what can only be described as a trial-and-error method. Shortly after ousting Batista they decided, for example, to cut their dependency on sugar by launching a huge industrialization program. This, however, proved to be an expensive failure, and the revolutionaries-turned-economists discovered the hard way that Cuba can produce sugar better than anything else. Today the emphasis is once again on cane as the money-maker which will pay for the modernization of the Cuban economy. The 1968 crop will be under 6 million tons—far below the target figure —but the government is reaching for 10 million tons by 1970. If anything like this figure is reached, it should take the edge off the current economic hardship and consumer shortages.

As it is, these shortages are not the result of an economic breakdown, but rather of a deliberate policy to restrict consumption in favor of investment. Food is rationed because beef cattle and citrus fruit are exported to pay for industrial equipment. The government has been investing heavily in agriculture, livestock, dams, fertilizer, roads, and power plants. When these begin to pay off, as they are expected to do within a few years, the Cuban economy could take a dramatic leap forward. Then it could serve as a model to Latin Americans who despair of ever achieving serious reforms by grace of the oligarchies, or through the ballot box. It is the ambition of the Cubans to show that it is not only possible to have an anti-capitalist, anti-*yanqui* revolution, but that it can succeed on economic grounds.

The Cubans have made a good many mistakes in the past, particularly in the early years of the revolution, when it was assumed that enthusiasm and a dedication to the common cause were sufficient to assure expert performance. That assumption was soon eroded when the economy ran into serious trouble in the early 1960s, and today the emphasis is on technicians rather than upon veterans who won their battle scars in the Sierra Maestra. In referring to the old days, which are still not so very far back, the Cubans tell a story about Che Guevara, who once held the post of minister of economics. When his inexperience became obvious, Fidel reproached his friend by saying: "Why did you raise your hand when I asked which of the comrades was an economist?" "Oh, I misunderstood," Che replied. "I thought you asked who was a communist."

Recently the joke has worn a bit thin, particularly since Che has now been deified as one of the martyrs of the Cuban revolution. His name is uttered with profound respect, and even with awe, for the myth of Che has already transfigured his earthly achievements. He has become an international culture hero, a symbol for a generation of young people who reject the bourgeois society of their elders, and despair of ever changing it by the conventional political process. Che is a made-to-order hero for intellectuals: a man of action who was also a superb political theorist, a brave *guerrillero* who penned an eloquent justification of the Cuban revolution, a romantic figure as agile with a rifle as he was with a pen. A man who made the CIA tremble. His tragic, futile death in the mountains of Bolivia has sanctified the legend, turning the revolutionary hero into the existential martyr.

Che has become more than simply one of the great heroes of the Cuban revolution. He is the symbol of the Fidelista program to bring about revolution in Latin America through guerrilla warfare. The fact that this program has not worked out very well in practice, that the *guerrilleros* are on the run in Colombia, Venezuela, and Peru, that the peasant insurrection in the Brazilian Northeast has fallen flat, and that Che's Bolivian adventure was a fiasco—none of this seems to have diminished Fidel's enthusiasm for world revolution. This has put him at odds with his Russian protectors, who favor working through the traditional communist parties of Latin America; it has also made it virtually impossible for Cuba to reach a *modus vivendi* with her neighbors.

The Cubans, however, argue that they can survive in a hostile world—just a few minutes flying time from the colossus that is their deadly enemy, and 5,000 miles from their protector—only by identifying their cause with that of revolutionaries everywhere. "Socialism in one country," they say, is a prescription for encirclement and eventual eradication. Thus the clumsy efforts to stimulate guerrilla insurrection in Latin America, the perpetual "anti-imperialist" pronunciamentos issued from Havana, the formation of the Organization for Latin American Solidarity as a revolutionary rival to the U.S.-sponsored Organization of American States, and the international conferences that are basically exercises in propaganda—such as the Tri-Continental in 1966, the OLAS meeting in 1967, and the Cultural Congress in January 1968. Thus, too, the inescapable presence of Che in the posters that line the streets of Havana, that decorate shop windows and billboards, that are blown up across the façade of giant buildings. One proclaiming the continuous revolution and exhorting the Cubans to struggle and sacrifice: "*patria o muerte*," "*hasta la victoria siempre*," "*creer uno, dos, tres Vietnam*."

The vocabulary of Cuba is revolution and its idiom is international. Everywhere there is an earnest, almost a desperate, attempt to reach beyond the narrow confines of this isolated island and find friends in the world outside. The countries that geography would normally decree to be Cuba's friends —the United States, the islands of the Caribbean, the nations of South America— mostly fear her example and are hostile to her survival. They refuse to buy her products or to sell her their own, and nearly all, under pressure from Washington, have broken diplomatic relations with Havana. Only Mexico, as a gesture to her own revolutionary past, has resisted U.S. pressure and maintains a tenuous air link with the island. Twice a week a propeller driven Cubana plane makes the round-trip from Havana to Mexico City, carrying journalists, diplomats, tourists and refugees along the only cord connecting Cuba to the rest of the western hemisphere.

As a result of this economic blockade imposed by the United States, Cuba has had to find new friends and trading partners. These are, of course, mostly in the communist countries of eastern Europe and, above all, the Soviet Union. They furnish the technical assistance needed to develop the Cuban economy, the oil to make it run, and the sugar subsidy that provides desperately needed foreign exchange. Without the Russians to help fill the gap left by the Americans, Cuba's economy would long ago have collapsed, and the Fidelista experiment thereby strangled at birth. Although they have grave differences with their protectors, particularly over the strategy of revolution in Latin America, the Cubans are too dependent on the Russians to risk an open break. They bitterly resent Moscow's efforts to normalize relations, with the Latin American oligarchies, while the Russians criticize the Fidelista formula for instant revolution as sheer adventurism.

The dispute broke out into the open in early 1968 when Castro jailed Anibal Escalante, one of the old-line leaders of the Cuban communist party, and some forty of his lieutenants for spreading "malicious lies" about the revolution and committing "treason." They were, in other words, threatening the Castro leadership and they were summarily sentenced to prison after a secret trial. The Russians, who were accused of complicity with Escalante, remained calm throughout the affair, and the Soviet oil tankers continued to unload their precious black cargo from Baku. Cuba is too valuable to the Kremlin as a communist showcase to let the revolution collapse. Fidel knows this, just as he knows he can push the Russians only so far before they might feel obliged to put on the screws. He loudly proclaims Cuba's independence, but he must pay at least formal allegiance to his alliance of convenience with Moscow.

The Cubans are far more dependent on the Soviets than they would like to be, and are now trying to break out of the confines of the communist economic bloc by increasing their trade with western Europe and Japan. This has been exceedingly difficult, because of U.S. pres-

sure on allied countries. We are, one might assume, trying to make Cuba totally dependent on the communist
nations so that we can justify our economic blockade.
But the blockade, although it has caused considerable
hardship and inconvenience, has not threatened the stability of the regime, and has proved to be an economic
failure. Today the Cubans carry on nearly one-quarter
of their foreign trade with non-communist countries—
the leading partners being Spain, Canada, Britain and
Japan.

Despite these efforts to break out of the U.S.-imposed
quarantine, Cuba remains very much a communist country in America's anti-communist inland sea. It has the
face of a misplanted, strangely exuberant, tropical
"people's democracy." With its consumer shortages, its
long lines at grocery stores and bakeries, its near-empty
department stores, its paucity of private transportation,
and its lack of neon glitter, it bears a superficial resemblance to some of the less oppressive communist states
of eastern Europe. There is a restaurant called "The
Volga" (but also a shop named "5th Avenue"), a "Vietnam Bookshop," and a large office of the Czech air lines,
which links Havana to Prague and the communist East.

Yet this is about as deep as the resemblance to eastern
Europe goes, for what is most dramatically evident about
the Cuban revolution is that it is deeply, ineradicably,
defiantly Cuban. Beneath the surface conformity of a
Marxist society caught in the struggle of economic development, there remain the peculiar passion, intensity, and
torpor of the Caribbean. Cuba is a land deeply marked
by Catholic pessimism and rural superstition, by an infat-
uation with the spoken word and a respect for the violent
gesture. It is a society rooted in Spanish colonialism and
transmuted by a profound African influence. Where else
could a leader like Fidel talk for eight solid hours to adoring, attentive multitudes? Where else could one imagine
a night club like the Tropicana—now proletarianized but
just as flashy as in Batista days—so crowded that reservations are necessary weeks in advance? Cuba professes a
unique kind of communism, a fusion of Spain and Africa

that honors the theories of Marx and pays homage to the cult of *machismo*.

In the Vedado section of Havana, where the tourists used to come to gamble, and young Cubans now congregate at movies and discotheques, there is a futuristic-looking structure known as Coppelia. It is the pride of the Castro regime, and has small-scale offspring all over the island. Open all day and most of the night, it is continually crowded by people of every age and description who patiently wait in line for a chance to sit at one of the tables perched on a glassy cantilever or in an attractive garden. From a distance it looks like an exhibition hall, or perhaps an Italian railway station. But on closer inspection it turns out to be an ice-cream parlor, serving fifty-four exotic varieties.

Coppelia is hardly the most important accomplishment of the Castro government, but it is integral to an understanding of what the Cuban revolution is all about. More than the new hospitals, schools, and communal nurseries, more than the rural cooperatives and experimental farms, it symbolizes the spirit animating the revolution, and explains the continuing support it receives from the majority of Cubans. Coppelia is for the people. It reflects the democratization that is the greatest achievement of the Cuban revolution. Whatever happens after Castro, Cuba can probably never go back to being the class-ridden, exploited, seigneurial society that it was only a decade ago.

The fears of some Americans about the dangers emanating from this communist state "only 90 miles from our shores," seem rather ludicrous from Havana, where the American colossus—which sends its reconnaissance planes over Cuban skies, its warships outside Havana harbor, and has its own troops on Cuban soil at Guantanamo—sits only 90 miles off *their* shores. So long as Washington remains hostile, the Cubans have to look to Moscow for protection, for this is their only guarantee of survival. Even if they wanted to cut their ties with the Soviets and follow a path of social democracy, they could not be sure that the U.S. would allow such a government to survive. The fate of Guatemala still stands as an object lesson for any Latin American radical.

Not much has changed since then to undermine the belief that a real social revolution must either take the Cuban path (and be driven to seek Russian protection), or else face extinction by the United States. Thus the Cubans continue to prescribe revolution as the only solution for the ailments of Latin America, and they are encouraged in their assessment by the political failure of the Alliance for Progress, and by the toppling of civilian governments by military juntas in Latin societies where the oligarchies were threatened with serious reforms.

Is there any hope for a rapprochement with the United States? Many Cubans speak of it wistfully, as though the present enmity were some horrible family misunderstanding—which in a sense it is. A few years ago Fidel seemed receptive to improved relations with Washington and felt that, despite the Bay of Pigs, he could get through to Kennedy and work out some kind of *modus vivendi*. But then came the Johnson administration, the U.S.-approved *coup d'état* in Brazil, the intervention at Santo Domingo, and the extension of the war to North Vietnam. The fact is that even without the war, it is dubious that Fidel, for the time being at least, would want to establish normal relations with the United States. This would make Cuba less useful to the Soviet Union, less certain of Russian protection and support, and deprived of a foreign enemy to justify the smothering of dissent at home.

There is a good deal of common griping in Cuba over consumer shortages, and a certain amount of "counter-revolutionary activity" that is not necessarily armed insurrection. There are secret police and jails containing some 10,000 political prisoners, maybe more. The government is ruthless with those it considers to be dangerous enemies, as the Escalante trial demonstrated. The party, under the control of Fidel and his lieutenants, dominates the state, and the state dispenses "revolutionary justice," which often means secret trials and indefinite prison terms. Cuba is a one-party, dictatorial state that tolerates a certain freedom of discussion, but which in no sense is a constitutional democracy. Nevertheless, it is possible to complain about the regime without being hauled off to jail. Some of the people I talked to in Havana told me of their grievances quite openly. It is also possible, for those who do not have needed skills, to leave the island, as some 4,000 do every month, for the nearby glitter of Miami. This emigration has taken the edge off much of the internal opposition, leaving those who either acquiesce in the new order, or who are active enthusiasts.

Much of this enthusiasm is merited particularly in the fields of education, housing, and the arts. A crash program in education has eliminated illiteracy and doubled the number of students in school. Today there are 1.3 million children in grade school, 140,000 in secondary school, 40,000 students in the university. Many of these are children of peasants and workers who formerly had little access to a decent education. The quality of education is not often as high as it should be, and the emphasis is heavily on technical skills, so that there will be enough engineers, scientists, agronomists, and doctors to pursue rapid economic development. There is a good deal of political indoctrination in the schools, and it is extended even down to the *becado* system under which children spend five-and-a-half days a week at state boarding schools, seeing their parents on weekends. When fully operative within a few years, these schools will transform the primary responsibility for raising children from the family to the state.

The accomplishments of the revolution are visible and extensive. Visitors are taken to visit schools and hospitals, housing projects and model farms, libraries and experimental theaters. Many of these are impressive, such as the Mazzora mental home outside Havana, where patients are allowed to roam freely and to work on various jobs, or the futuristic Cubanacan art school on the site of a former country club. Even more impressive to the skeptical North American, because he is not prepared for it, is the vigor and inventiveness in the arts: the electronic music wafting through the galleries exhibiting the latest in op and pop paintings, the theaters where new Cuban dramas are performed together with polished versions of foreign plays (*Quien tiene miedo de Virginia Woolf?* is the big hit of the season), and public exhibits that subtly purvey propaganda as entertainment. Like the Russians shortly after their own revolution, the Cubans have turned posters into a form of art as well as a vehicle of exhortation. There are cleverly designed, colorful posters on every wall and along every roadside, carrying virtually every kind of message: from a plea to cut more sugar cane to one urging the artificial insemination of cows.

The aim of Fidel and his lieutenants is to mobilize the entire society into the task of economic development. The means, however, are not physical coercion so much as moral persuasion. Students, soldiers, workers, intellectuals, and housewives are exhorted to do hours of extra work in their spare time, and to volunteer for weeks in the sugar fields during the harvest. For many these hours of extra labor are not a punishment but a way of building the revolution, and they approach it with enthusiasm and even exhilaration. Those who refuse are not punished, but suffer a kind of social ostracism—as Americans might treat those who refused to help pile sandbags when a town is threatened by flood. The compulsion is moral, but it is incessant, and there are few who are able to resist it—even though they might like to. Everyone, for example, is virtually compelled to participate in the *zafra*, or sugar harvest—from cabinet officials to actors and dancers. "This," a Cuban director said to me about his own imminent departure for the sugar fields, "is our theater of cruelty."

The party plays a leading role in this "moral persuasion" of the Cuban population, just as it does in virtually every aspect of political life. Since Fidel took control of the party back from Escalante and the Stalinists in 1962, there has been some liberalization, but the regime can still be oppressive and puritanical. Until recently, for example, homosexuals were confined to forced labor camps. Currently there is a great dispute going on among writers over the party's decision to do away with authors' royalties. The theory is that this will eliminate the exploitation of culture, but in effect it could make writers dependent for their survival on the party bureaucrats who usually control the writers' union—and the writers' union in a communist society is the dispenser of most literary jobs. A debate is also raging over the future of the Cubanacan art school. Many, including the current minister of education, argue that this futuristic new structure should be closed down because it encourages the formation of a cultural elite—and this is clearly contrary to the objective of a classless society.

To Cubans these are not parochial questions, but involve the very meaning of the revolution. You cannot be in Cuba more than a few days without realizing that the revolution is a continuing phenomenon, even a way of life, and not simply a description of a historical event that overthrew the Batista regime. It is more than a panoply of heroes or a form of political rhetoric; it is a mystique that encompasses virtually every aspect of Cuban life. The revolution is a theory of man, a way of reforming society, and even of re-structuring human beings. The social program of the Castro government is a deliberate and carefully conceived attempt to achieve a new kind of society based upon its interpretations of Marxist humanism. The implementation may be harsh and the goal unattainable, but the theory, at least, is that, in Che's words, "the ultimate and most important revolutionary aspiration (is) to see man freed from alienation." Liberals would argue that in doing so the Cubans are enforcing a new kind of servitude, but the Fidelistas do not see it that way.

The system, as it is being evolved in Cuba today, rests upon the double base of material security and moral incentives, in contrast to capitalist (or even East European communist) societies where the incentives are mostly material. The Cubans are reducing the possibility of material incentives by eliminating the number of things one can buy. Already a number of services are free, such as local telephone calls, medical care, meals on the job, education, day nurseries, wedding banquets, funerals and sports contests. Others are due to be added within a few years, such as rent, basic foods like milk and fruit, and public bicycles.

There are plans to do away eventually even with money, the very symbol of capitalism and the instrument of private property. The Cuban will presumably work extra hours not for material gain, but because it is his obligation to society. "If everyone has the need to consume, then everyone has the inescapable duty to work," read the billboards of Cuba, quoting Fidel. The more the Cuban worker can obtain free, the less he will be driven by material incentives and the desire to amass possessions. "One of the fundamental aims of Marxism," according to Che, "is to do away with personal gain as a psychological motivation," The greater the stake that the workers have in the revolution, the more they will contribute to it. It is a noble theory. Whether it will work in practice remains to be seen.

The Cubans have made remarkable strides during the past nine years, and furnish one of the few examples in Latin America of a society that is actually achieving the social reforms that the others talk about in the meetings of the Alliance for Progress. That they are doing so despite the efforts of the United States to bring down the government is a tribute to the quality of Castro's leadership and the fortitude of the Cuban people. One should never underestimate the agility of Fidel, who used the old-line Cuban communists for the purpose of the revolution, and has refused to be used by them; who has maintained his indepedence of Moscow even while being dependent upon Russian aid and protection for survival. He is one of the great political figures of our time, and his misfortune is to have been born in Cuba, rather than in Brazil or Argentina, where he would have had the scope and the means to carry out his vision on a major scale, and without the continual fear of an American invasion.

Cuba, for the first time in her history as an independent nation, is trying to work out her destiny free from U.S. control. The kind of society the Cubans are building is—like many others in Latin America—hardly a model of political democracy: there is no guaranteed freedom of speech or assembly, parliament doesn't exist, individualism is a suspect word, and there is little chance of swimming against the tide. On the other hand, there is no unemployment in Cuba, or racial antagonism, or violence in the streets, or abject poverty alongside enormous wealth.

It is a society, perhaps one of the few in the world, where people give the impression of actually liking their government—or at least not looking upon it as an enemy. It is a perplexing society: exhilarating and repressive, experimental and puritanical, idealistic and expedient. It is a country, an experiment, a state of mind, quite unlike any other; a seductive place that is perhaps dangerous to take at face value, but impossible not to admire for the courage of its people and the daring of its vision.

Oakland:
The Panthers Bring
the Revolution Home

I went to Oakland, dead end of the westward
course of empire, and home of the Black Panthers, to
take a look at a conference of the revolutionary Left.
Oakland is where the American dream ends at the Pacific,
and the nightmare begins. It is a familiar kind of industrial city: high-rise office buildings and apartments downtown, plasticene shopping centers on the fringe, and
slowly decaying wooden houses in between. West Oakland, facing the Bay and the gleaming hills of San Francisco beyond, is the ghetto where the Black Panthers were
born. It is a California-style ghetto, with one-family
houses and neglected yards, where poverty wears a more
casual face and despair is masked by sunshine.

The Panthers in July 1969 summoned their friends—
a mixed bag of revolutionaries, radicals, pacifists, and
liberals—to assemble in Oakland to form what they called
a "united front against fascism." The phrase itself had
a defensive ring, reminiscent of the ill-fated Popular
Fronts of the 1930s, and it seemed to indicate that the
Panthers were in trouble. White radicals, few of whom
were consulted about the agenda, privately expressed
doubts about the usefulness of such a conference, and
many SDS chapters did not send representatives. As it

turned out, they would not have had much of a role to play anyway, since the Panthers were very much running their own show and not accepting criticism from those who came to hear them.

Like so many other gatherings of the radical Left, the conference produced little unity but a great deal of dissatisfaction. Most of the sessions were disorganized and, with a few exceptions, the speeches were little more than an interminable series of spot announcements denouncing the evils of rampant fascism. No one seemed interested in discussing whether fascism had indeed arrived in America. This, like so much of the other rhetoric of the revolutionary Left, was simply taken for granted.

When the three-day conference finally rambled to an end, the dwindling band of white radicals drifted away in dismay, wondering what kind of bag the Panthers had got themselves into. The more militant radicals from Berkeley feared that the Panthers had turned reformist, while socialists and Trotskyites complained about their dictatorial methods. The "united front," whose creation was the ostensible purpose of the conference, had not been formed and most participants expressed doubts that it ever would be. The general consensus was that the Panthers didn't have a very clear idea of what they were up to. They wanted to enlist allies, and they hoped that some kind of united front would develop. But they had no real plan worked out, and certainly no intention of letting anyone else supply one.

Why did the Panthers call such a conference in the first place? At least in part because they had been under increasing harassment and intimidation by the police and the FBI. During the first few months of 1969 more than forty leaders and a hundred members had been arrested, and some of them were facing life imprisonment or the death penalty. The party's founder and chief theorist, twenty-seven-year-old Huey P. Newton, was serving a fourteen-year sentence for allegedly shooting an Oakland policeman. Its most articulate spokesman, Eldridge Cleaver, had chosen to go into exile rather than return to prison on dubious charges of parole violation. Its treasurer, seventeen-year-old Bobby Hutton, had been killed by police during last year's Oakland shootout. And its acting chairman, Bobby Seale, is under federal indictment for conspiring to incite a riot at last year's Democratic convention, although he was not a member of any of the organizations sponsoring the protests, and spent less than a day in Chicago.

The Panthers see a concerted plot by the federal government, with the assistance of local police, to destroy them.* † Spiro Agnew has described them as a "completely irresponsible, anarchistic group of criminals," and J. Edgar Hoover has called them, among black militants, the "greatest threat to the internal security of the country." In the summer of 1969 the Justice Department set up a special task force to investigate the party in the hope of nailing it on violations of some twenty federal laws, including those making it a crime to cross state lines to foment civil disorder, to interfere with persons participating in programs supported by the federal government, and to damage government buildings. Senator McClellan's Permanent Subcommittee on Investigations has been

---

* Huey Newton was released on bail in August 1970 and granted a new trial. Bobby Seale was severed from the Chicago trial, and conspiracy charges against him were dropped after he was extradited to New Haven to stand trial for having ordered the murder of Alex Rackley, a New York Panther who was a suspected police informer. If convicted, Seale could face the death penalty, even though he was not in New Haven at the time of Rackley's murder.

† Panther offices around the country have been raided by both local police and the FBI. A number of Panthers have been killed in these raids, including Fred Hampton, chairman of the Illinois branch, who was murdered in his bed by Chicago police in a pre-dawn attack on his apartment in December 1969.

Panther leaders have also been imprisoned, often under harsh conditions and with prohibitive bail, on various grounds, including the catch-all charge of conspiracy. In April 1969, for example, twenty-one New York Panthers were indicted for conspiring to blow up several department stores and a police station. Few could raise the $100,000 bail set by the court, and most of the indicted Panthers remained in jail for nearly two years waiting to be tried for plotting to commit a crime that, in fact, never took place.

providing a forum for police officers and their inform-
ants to denounce the Panthers, as well as white radical
groups.

Now that the federal government has joined the local
police in operations against the Panthers—Attorney-
General Mitchell is trying to get the courts to admit wiretap evidence against the Panthers and other groups
ostensibly threatening "national security"—the strength-
ening of their links with white radical groups is more
important than before. This is partly a question of
ideology, for the Panthers—popular impressions to the
contrary—insist they are not racist, and are almost the
only black militant group that actually welcomes white
allies. It is also a question of survival, for without support
from the white community they fear they will be picked
off and destroyed.

The Panthers are convinced that those in power are
out to get them as much for their socialist ideology and
their efforts to organize the black community into an
effective political force as for their defensive actions
against the police. Heavily into the economics and
sociology of Marxism, the Panthers see racism in this
country as an integral part of the capitalist system.
"Capitalism deprives us all of self-determination," Huey
Newton has said. "Only in the context of socialism can
men practice the self-determination necessary to provide
for their freedom."

The Panthers speak earnestly of the need for "socialism"; and this is what distinguishes them from the other
black militant and black power groups. They see themselves as "revolutionary nationalists," as opposed to
"cultural nationalists," who seek black pride in separatist
movements, religious cults, and emulation of ancient
African culture. "The revolutionary nationalist," according to Huey Newton, "sees that there is no hope for
cultural or individual expression, or even hope that his
people can exist as a unique entity in a complex whole
as long as the bureaucratic capitalist is in control." On
the other hand, "cultural nationalism," explained Panther
chief of staff David Hilliard, "is basically related to the

physiological need for a return back to Africa in the culture, and we don't see that that is really relevant to any revolution, because culture never frees anyone. As Fanon says, the only culture is that of the revolution."

The reference to Fanon is instructive, for the Panthers, as can readily be seen from the writings of Huey Newton and Eldridge Cleaver, have been deeply influenced by the black psychiatrist from Martinique who died in the service of the Algerian revolution. *The Wretched of the Earth* is a kind of revolutionary Bible for them, and one with far more emotional impact than the Little Red Books which are so often quoted. Both Newton and Cleaver, freely acknowledging their debt to Fanon, have described black people as forming an oppressed colony within the white mother country, the United States. The colony is kept in line by an occupying army—white policemen who live outside the ghetto—and is exploited by businessmen and politicians.

The exploiters can be black as well as white, for the enemy, they insist, is not so much racism as capitalism, which creates and nourishes it. As would be expected of socialist revolutionaries, the Panthers are opposed to black capitalism, which Huey Newton has described as a "giant stride *away* from liberation . . ." since ". . . the rules of black capitalism, and the limits of black capitalism are set by the white power structure." Explaining his opposition, Newton has stated:

> There can be no real black capitalism because no blacks control the means of production. All blacks can do is have illusions. They can dream of the day when they might share ownership of the means of production. But there is no free enterprise in America. We have monopoly capitalism which is a closed society of white industrialists and their protectors, white politicians in Washington.

According to the Panthers, black power has been absorbed into the establishment, shorn of its horns, and transformed into innocent black capitalism, which even Richard Nixon can praise because it poses no threat to the white power structure.

As an alternative they offer "revolution," to liberate oppressed minorities in the United States and break the stranglehold of capitalism on the economically underdeveloped countries of the Third World. Until there is some form of socialist "revolution" in America, they believe, small countries will remain prey to neo-colonialism and imperialism. The revolutionary in America, therefore, carries the world upon his shoulders. The black man in America will not be free until the white man is free, and until the white man is free, until America is transformed by a socialist revolution, the underdeveloped countries of the world will remain in economic chains.

Such a comprehensive theory clearly has its inadequacies. Although blacks can be described as forming an internal colony within the United States, they do not supply raw materials, labor, or markets to capitalism in the same way as the colonies did. There is, moreover, no evidence at present that the U.S. is entering a revolutionary crisis that will involve the mass of workers. Nor can the Panthers have much success in breaking away into a separate state. What happens, as has been asked, when there's a border dispute? (The Panthers claim neither to favor nor to discourage political separatism; rather they demand that a UN-supervised plebiscite be held on the issue in the black colony. In any case, this is not an immediate problem, and certainly not a major objective for them.)

The Panthers' Marxist-Lennist language, combined with their Fanonist theories of psychological alienation and Third World solidarity, makes them particularly appealing to middle-class white militants, who share their ideology but lack their discipline. White radicals also lack the black man's non-reducible commitment to black liberation: the fact that he is black. A white radical can cop out any time he wants by cutting his hair and behaving like a square. A black man cannot escape. In fighting against the system he becomes, by his very act of resistance, a hero to white radicals. As Huey Newton has explained:

> Black people in America, in the black colony, are op-
> pressed because we're black and we're exploited. The
> whites are rebels, many of them from the middle class,
> and as far as any overt oppression this is not the case.
> So therefore I call their rejection of the system some-
> what of an abstract thing. They're looking for new
> heroes. . . . In pressing for new heroes the young white
> revolution found the heroes in the black colony at home
> and the colonies throughout the world. . . .

While Newton favors alliances with white radicals, he
points out that "there can be no black-white unity until
there first is black unity." Only blacks can decide the
proper strategy for the black community.

White radicals, divided on tactics and ideology, and
split into a plethora of competing, often hostile, groups,
have only recently begun to deal with some of the
problems of "black liberation." There has always been
sympathy for the black struggle, and even participation
when it was permitted during the civil rights movement.
But things have changed greatly since Stokely Carmichael
kicked the whites out of SNCC and the Panthers moved
into the streets with guns. Unable to lead the black
movement, white radicals are no longer even sure how
they can aid it. Uncertain of their tactics, and confused
about their goals, they revert to ready-made formulas,
like "revolution," to deal with a multitude of complexities
that are too difficult to analyze right now. Some assert
that groups like the Panthers are the "vanguard" of the
revolution—as though this justified white radicals' inability to work out a coherent theory or strategy.

The Vietnam war no longer serves as the great rallying
point for the Left that it used to. Radicals have a good
deal to protest about, but they seem to focus their
energies on largely symbolic issues, such as the People's
Park, or on the predictable seizure of university administration buildings. The radical Left is hung up on revolution, but doesn't seem to have the vaguest idea of how
it should be organized, or how the country would be run
if such an event ever took place.

For the time being the Left is divided, confused,
and hopelessly weak. There is, perhaps no more telling

sign of the insecurity of those who hold power in America than that they are seriously worried about its activities. The McClellan committee solemnly listens to the "threats to national security" posed by campus agitators, while Congress debates unconstitutional limitations on dissent and hysterical punishments against demonstrators. Not only do conventional politicians fear the Panthers, who at least carry guns and who can be described as a para-military organization, but even the scholastic debaters of the Students for a Democratic Society.

The SDS, now a decimated and largely ineffectual claque weakened by infighting, purges, and doctrinal rivalries, proclaim their allegiance to the Panthers' view of the class struggle. This makes them useful, if not necessarily helpful, allies for the Panthers, and in Oakland a few hundred SDS people joined others from some forty organizations to form a gathering of about 3,000 people: Trotskyites and women striking for peace, communist party veterans and anarchists, factory workers and ministers. And of course, a contingent of Panthers who, in spite of the inter-racial theme of the meeting, sat in a roped-off section at the back of the Oakland auditorium.

The Panthers ran the conference without help from any of their allies. There were no workshops and no discussion from the floor, until the final night when a few questions were permitted. "When you begin to develop a united front you do not start off with a bunch of jive ideological bullshit," Bobby Seale declared to cries of "Right on" from the Panther cheering section and much waving of Little Red Books. But as the Trotskyite ISC observed in one of the leaflets it surreptitiously distributed at the conference, ". . . A left which lacks respect for its own ideas and programs and cannot stand internal debate cannot possibly hope to win the support of the masses." The Panthers, however, weren't interested in internal debate or jive ideological bullshit (although they produced a good deal of their own in the

course of three days), but support for their own programs—or, as they would say, "solidarity."

The major program they are now emphasizing is
community control of police, with cities divided into
districts, each with its own police force controlled by an
elected neighborhood council, and with policemen living
in the district they control. "If a policeman's brutalizing
somebody in the community and has to come back home
and sleep that night," Bobby Seale explained, "we can
deal with him in our community." Participants at the
conference were urged to get out and work on such
petitions for decentralization—whites in white communities, browns in Latin communities, and blacks in the
ghettos. For blacks and other minority groups such decentralization makes sense. It would not bring about the
millennium, but it could sharply reduce the slaying and
beating of ghetto people by trigger-happy, frightened, or
racist white cops.

The white revolutionaries, however, were put off by
such reformist proposals—particularly the Berkeley contingent, which seemed hung up on violence, with some
members talking about guerrilla warfare in the streets.
Even the pro-Panther SDS leadership felt that decentralization, however good it might be for the ghettos, was a
bad policy for white neighborhoods, where it might lead
to the creation of vigilante teams under the guise of
police forces. The SDS interim committee voted against
endorsement of the petition campaign unless it were
limited to black and brown communities.

This didn't go down well with the Panthers. On his
return from Algiers, where he attended the Pan-African
Arts Festival, chief of staff David Hilliard told newsmen
that "The Black Panther Party will not be dictated to
by people who are obviously bourgeois procrastinators,
seeking made-to-order revolution which is abstract, meta-
physical and doesn't exist in the black or white community." He derided the SDS argument that community
control would make police forces in white areas worse
than they already are, and defined the issue as one of

revolutionary solidarity. "We're not going to let SDS worm their way out of their revolutionary duties," he warned. "If they are revolutionary, then this is what we, as the vanguard of the revolution in Babylon, dictate—that they circulate that petition, not in our communities, but in their own."

Never very comfortable with SDS, the Panthers feel much more at home with the "brothers off the block," the street people, the lumpenproletariat, to use another phrase they are fond of, than with the guilt-ridden children of the white bourgeoisie. With a few exceptions, such as Huey Newton and Bobby Seale, they have had little formal education beyond high school, and some of the most intelligent do not even have that. "We got our education on the street, in the service, or in jail," the Panthers' soft-spoken minister of education, Ray "Masai" Hewitt, told me. The Panther leaders are self-made intellectuals.

"We relate to the Young Patriots" (a white, radical Chicago group), David Hilliard stated, "because they're operating on the same class level as the Black Panther Party." They also share a similar rhetoric. Speaking at the conference on the eve of the moon landing, a leader of the Young Patriots named Preacherman, in black beret and shades, gave a moving speech which was, in effect, a tribute to the Panthers' ability to reach traditionally apolitical, racist white groups:

> Our struggle is beyond comprehension to me sometimes, and I felt that poor whites was (and maybe we felt wrongly, but we felt it) was forgotten, and that certain places we walked there were certain organizations that nobody saw us until we met the Illinois chapter of the Black Panther Party and they met us. And we said, "Let's put that theory into practice about riddin' ourselves of that racism." You see, otherwise, otherwise to us, freeing political prisoners would be hypocrisy. That's what it'd be. We want to stand by our brothers, dig? And, I don't know. I'd even like to say something to church people. I think one of the brothers last night said, "Jesus Christ was a bad motherfucker." Man, we all don't want to go that route, understand. He laid back and he said, "Put

that fuckin' nail right there, man. That's the people's
nail. I'm takin' it." But we've gone beyond it. . . .

The Young Patriots started out as a street gang and
gradually developed a political consciousness that led
them in the direction of the Panthers. A similar attempt
at radicalizing organized labor is being made with the
creation of the League of Revolutionary Black Workers,
a federation of several Detroit-based workers' groups such
as the Dodge Revolutionary Union Movement (DRUM)
and its equivalents at Ford (FRUM), Chrysler (CRUM),
and elsewhere. The all-black League was started, according to John Watson, one of its founders, "because the
working class is already divided between the races, and
because it is necessary for black workers to be able to act
independently of white workers."

White workers have been encouraged to form radical
organizations of their own to work out a common strategy
with black union revolutionaries, but progress has been
slow. Speaking of such a group at the Detroit *News,*
Watson observed, ". . . although a number of the white
guys who were down there had risen above the levels
of racism and understood the exploitative nature of the
company and of the system, they had very little experience in organizing to fight oppression and exploitation." As with the Panthers, these black workers consider
themselves to be in the "vanguard of the revolutionary
movement," and see most whites still on the fringes of
the real struggle.

These "revolutionary" union groups were started to
protect black workers who felt they were being treated
unfairly and even victimized by racist white union
leaders. Also, they believed, together with like-minded
white workers, that union chiefs were in collusion with
the bosses to speed up work schedules and ignore
grievances over intolerable working conditions. The radical union groups are, first of all, self-protective associations for people unprotected or abused by the regular,
bureaucratized unions. Seccondly, they hope to stimulate
a political awareness that will lead to a revolutionary
situation in America.

For the time being, however, it is clear that the ghettos are potentially the most explosive places in the country. This is where the Panthers are organized (although they are trying to establish closer contacts with the revolutionary union movements, as well as with student groups) and where they draw their main support. Much of their appeal for ghetto youths (shared by many whites) is their image of a powerful black man with a rifle. In his book of post-prison writings, Eldridge Cleaver describes his own first encounter with the Panthers at a meeting in the Fillmore district ghetto of San Francisco: "I spun round in my seat and saw the most beautiful sight I had ever seen: four black men wearing black berets, powder blue shirts, black leather jackets, black trousers, shiny black shoes—and each with a gun!"

Since then Cleaver has learned that there is more to being a Panther than carrying a gun. But the image of power and violence is still the basic one created by the Panthers. When ghetto youths learn that party membership is not like joining a street gang but more like taking religious vows, many of them become disillusioned and turn away from the Panthers. They are put off by the strict discipline, the political indoctrination, the discouragement of racism, and such community service projects as the Panther program to provide free breakfasts to ghetto children. The Panthers claim to have purged people who turned out to be basically criminals or racists unable to relate to the party's political and intellectual program.

Lately the Panthers have been emphasizing programs directly related to the needs of the ghetto community, such as free breakfasts and health clinics. They have also set up black "liberation schools," where children between two and sixteen are given party indoctrination, although the Panthers claim that they are correcting the distorted image that black children receive of themselves and their society.

White middle-class revolutionaries tend to patronize such activities as reformist. But the breakfasts, the schools, and the clinics have won the Panthers support within the ghetto that they never could have gained by guns alone or by Marxist-Leninist analyses of the internal contradictions of capitalism. In Oakland, where the party has existed since 1966, it is an important element of the black community. Just as the police have been forced to respect the power of the Panthers, so the white power elite has had to deal with an organized, politically conscious force within the black community. Throughout much of the Bay area, where the Panthers are particularly well organized, they are an articulate, alert defender of black people's interests. The Panthers are there when the community needs them, and they are there when no one else seems to be listening.

An example that occurred while I was in San Francisco concerned a sixteen-year-old boy who was shot in the back by a member of San Francisco's Tactical Squad while he was fleeing the scene of an alleged auto theft. The shooting occurred near his home and was heard by his mother, a practical nurse, who was thrown to the ground by the police when she ran to his side screaming, "Don't shoot my boy again." The wounded boy was thrown into a police truck and nearly an hour elapsed before he actually reached the hospital. It is the sort of thing that happens every day in Hunter's Point and a hundred other black ghettos around America. The only difference is that, miraculously, the bullet was deflected by a rib bone and the boy was not killed, and that the Panthers brought it to the attention of the public by calling a press conference which Bobby Seale, David Hilliard, and Masai, the party's three top leaders, attended.

At the conference were a few representatives of the local press (the television stations were invited but refrained from sending anyone), myself, a few Panthers, their lawyer, Charles Garry, the boy, Jimmie Conner, and his parents. The boy, soft-spoken and composed, spoke of the incident as though it were a normal part of life, and when asked why he ran away, replied, with the tedium of one explaining the obvious, "Why did I run?

Because I'm scared of police." With him sat his parents, an attractive, quiet woman in her mid-thirties and a handsome, somewhat stocky, graying man who works in aircraft maintenance. Both very light-skinned, eminently respectable, and both bitter and confused about what had happened to them.

Had they been white, their son would have been reprimanded, or at most taken to court. But they are black and their son was almost killed, as other boys have been killed in Hunter's Point and elsewhere for even lesser crimes—if indeed Jimmie Conner was guilty of a crime. When asked about the incident, Mrs. Conner replied, "Just another Negro gone, that's the way we believe that they think about the kids up here. Too many of our kids are dying for nothing. They see police three blocks away and they start running because they're scared. I'm gonna fight them. If I have to go to jail OK. If I have to work for the rest of my life, I will. If they shoot me that's fine. I'm gonna fight, this has got to stop."

How did the Panthers get involved in this incident, although none of the Conners is a member of the party? Because a doctor at the hospital where Jimmie was taken was so shocked at his treatment by the police that he called Charles Garry, who in turn called Bobby Seale. What followed was a press conference, followed by a lawsuit under the 1964 Civil Rights Act, followed by press coverage—which of course could never have occurred had the Panthers not been called in.

The cynical would say that the Panthers have something to gain from this publicity, which indeed they have. But by such actions they are establishing themselves, in the eyes of the black community, as the defenders of the black man too humble to interest anyone else. They can sink their roots in the black community and win its allegiance partly because no one else is fulfilling that role. This is one of the things that the Panthers mean by "educating" the people, informing them of their rights and making them activist defenders rather than passive victims. This education is carried on through meetings, discussions, leaflets, and the party newspaper. While their tactics have shifted several times since the formation of the party in October 1966, their objectives remain the ones set out in their ten-point program of black liberation.

Looking at this program and talking to the Panthers, as well as reading their newspaper, *The Black Panther* makes one realize that at least one aspect of the "revolution" they talk about is not necessarily the cataclysmic upheaval that sends the white middle class into spasms. Rather, it is the achievement of constitutional guarantees and economic justice for black people. These gun-carrying, Mao-quoting revolutionaries want what most middle-class Americans take for granted. As Huey Newton has said, if reformist politicians like the Kennedys and Lindsay could solve the problems of housing, employment, and justice for blacks and other Americans at the bottom of the social heap, there would be no need for a revolution. And, it goes without saying, little support for such groups as the Black Panther Party.

The Panthers have a voice in the black community (although not necessarily so large as many whites imagine) because they offer hope for change to ghetto people whom the civil rights movement and the poverty program bureaucrats have been unable to touch. They walk proudly through the streets of Oakland in their black leather jackets, and they hold mass rallies for the liberation of Huey Newton in the shadow of the Alameda County Court House where he was sentenced. They speak to the black man's image of himself. They tell him that he is no longer powerless against the forces that oppress him, and that his struggle for freedom is part of a world-wide liberation movement. In this sense they fulfill a real psychological need.

While they have not yet shed white blood, except in self-defense, does this mean that they never will, that their talk of guerrilla warfare is simply rhetoric? It would be rash to say so, for the Panthers have declared that they are ready to kill anyone who stands in the way of "black liberation." And they are convinced that racism in this society is so pervasive and deeply rooted that there can be no freedom for black people until it is extirpated by some form of revolution. Like some of the white revolutionaries who emulate them, the Panthers seem to have over-learned *The Battle of Algiers*, and have tried to apply its lesson to a society where the situation is totally different. The United States today is not Algeria of 1954, nor Cuba of 1958, nor even France of 1968. It is a deeply troubled, but nonetheless largely stable society which is capable of putting down an insurrection ruthlessly and quickly.

Don't the Panthers realize this? They seem to, at the present moment anyway. This is why they are serving free breakfasts to ghetto children; attempting to form alliances with white radicals, liberals, workers, and pacifists; and urging people to sign petitions for the decentralization of the police. They may be going through a temporary stage, but the direction in which they are heading is clearly marked reformism. Right now they seem interested in maximum publicity, which is why they hold meetings and press conferences, and complain about the way the mass media ignores or distorts their actions. Some of their sympathizers fear that the Panthers are pushing themselves too much in the public eye, and that this only aids the enemies who are trying to destroy them. But since the police and politicians are out to get the Panthers in any case, perhaps such an effort to convince the public that they are not really monsters is their only chance for survival.

The federal government has decided to come down hard on the Panthers at the very time that they are emphasizing ballots and petitions, community self-help, and political alliances, rather than shoot-outs. The severe harassment and repression they are now suffering may, if anything, improve the Panthers' appeal among the black bourgeoisie and white liberals. It would be one of the ironies of our irrational political life if John Mitchell and J. Edgar Hoover, together with the so-called "liberal" mayors of cities like San Francisco and Chicago, succeeded in giving the Panthers a new vitality just at the time when the party seemed in difficulty.

Like radicals in general, the Panthers naturally talk a good deal about revolution, and use such other catch-words as fascism, imperialism, and the dictatorship of the proletariat. They connect racism with the evils of capitalism, and quote freely from the sacred texts of Marx, Lenin, and Mao. Walk into any Panther office and you are likely to find not only Little Red Books lying about, but the officer of the day with his nose buried in the works of Mao, or one of Lenin's many pamphlets. Slogans, often vague and even meaningless in the context in which they are used, become part of the revolutionary vocabulary. This is true not only of the Panthers, who use such slogans to reach an audience with little formal education, but of young radicals generally. The deliberate inflation and distortion of language is a disease of the Left.*

The Panthers, however, realize that racism is deeply embedded in the cultural history of Europe and America and is not, as certain Marxists still argue, simply a by-product of class society. As Huey Newton has said, "Until you get rid of racism . . . no matter what kind of economic system you have, black people will still be oppressed." What revolution seems to mean for the Panthers is the transformation of the ghetto and the "liberation" of black people, and of all oppressed people, from lives of poverty, degradation, and despair. The steps by which this will take place are not specified precisely, but they need not be violent ones unless every other road to radical change is closed.

The Panthers claim they are not racist, but they pointedly refuse to take any instructions from their white sympathizers. Commenting on the anti-white sentiment

---

* More recently—as a sign of their contempt for America (or Amerikkka, as they spell it) and her official foreign policy—they have, in the pages of the party newspaper and in the speeches of some of their leaders, been extolling the virtues of North Korea, glorifying the Palestinian guerrillas, and denouncing what they refer to as "Kosher nationalism" (Zionism).

in SNCC before it became an all-black organization, Huey Newton recently said, "We have never been controlled by whites, and therefore we don't fear the white mother-country radicals." Their willingness to work with allied white radicals is not shared by most black militant groups. When Stokely Carmichael recently left the Panthers, his stormy letter of departure centered on just this issue.

As the Carmichael-Cleaver exchange indicated, the black militants are just as fragmented into feuding factions as are the whites. Their rivalry, however, is a good deal more violent, and the struggle between the Panthers and the "cultural nationalist" U.S. group of Ron Karenga led to the murder of two Panthers in Los Angeles last year. The Panthers are serious about wanting to carry on programs of education, and in spite of the terrible repression they are now facing have an enduring faith in the democratic system of petitions and ballots—far more than do the young white radicals. But like most revolutionaries, they are highly authoritarian and want loyal and unquestioning followers (as Stokely Carmichael rightly pointed out in his letter) rather than critical colleagues.

Unlike the white revolutionaries, however, the Panthers do have some fairly clear ideas of what they want—even though they are uncertain about the best way to get it. Whatever their shortcomings, they did not seem to me self-indulgent or part-time players at revolution. They are in this struggle for keeps. Anyone who is a Panther today, or who contemplates joining the party, knows that there is a good chance that he will be jailed or die a violent death. Panthers have already been murdered by the police, many have been beaten and wounded, and others are almost certain to be killed in the months and years ahead. It takes courage to join the party, to submit to its discipline, and to face the likely prospect of imprisonment or death. But for some there is no other way. As Eldridge Cleaver has written, "A slave who dies of natural causes will not balance two dead flies on the scale of eternity."

The Panthers have come a long way since Huey Newton and Bobby Seale first formed the party in Oakland in 1966. It has spread across the nation and has eclipsed such groups as SNCC and CORE. This expansion has created problems—not only increasing police harassment and repression as the Panthers become more influential within the black community, but also the difficulty of maintaining the standard of membership that its leaders would like. Not all Panthers have the organizing ability of Bobby Seale or the analytical minds of David Hilliard, Eldridge Cleaver, and Huey Newton. The lower echelon of the party has more than its share of racists, simpletons, and thugs, many of whom are drawn to the Panthers by their image of violence—which Cleaver describes so graphically in his book.

The Panthers are prepared for guerrilla warfare, as a last-ditch stand, because they think they may have no other real alternative. There are white revolutionaries, on the West Coast and elsewhere, who, in the impatience of their rage and their inability seriously to change a society whose policies they find oppressive, accept this prescription uncritically, and, in view of the forces marshalled against them on the Right, with a half-conscious quest for martyrdom. As its frustration increases, the New Left becomes more shrill in its rhetoric and dogmatic in its politics. Instead of focusing on the most blatant inequalities and injustices of American life, it is assaulting the periphery. Instead of trying to educate the people to inequities of the social-economic system and the cost of maintaining an empire, it has successfully alienated the working class—without whose support no radical change, let alone "revolution," is possible.

In its resistance to the draft, the war, and racism, the radical Left has aroused parts of the nation. More people now realize there is something seriously wrong with American society but are not certain how to deal with it. Many are frightened and attribute all unrest to a conspiracy of "trouble-makers." Others know that change must come, but would like it to be as unobtrusive as possible. It remains to be seen how many can be reached, whether it be on the plane of morality or self-interest, and convinced that change need not be personally threatening to them. To do this radicals must have plausible ideas on how a transformed society would produce a better existence for the mass of people.

America is not now a "fascist" country, nor is it likely soon to become one, although this is not impossible. Probably it will continue to be an advanced capitalist society in which cruel inequalities and repression, unlivable cities, and inhuman conditions of work continue to exist along with considerable liberty to take political action, while our rulers control an empire of poor nations abroad. It is the duty of the Left to find ways to change this system: to educate people rather than simply abuse them; to understand what is happening in the factories and farms and lower-middle-class neighborhoods and be in touch with the people in them; to use the universities as places where the complex problems of replacing repressive capitalism and imperialism with a better system can be studied seriously; to stop playing Minutemen and begin acting like radicals. If there is ever going to be a revolution in this country, it will have to happen first in people's heads. What takes place in the streets of a society like this one is more likely to lead to repression than revolution.

V. POLITICIANS AND HEROES

Foreign policy is not only about vague notions like balance of power and spheres of influence. It is about people, and groups, and institutions. A nation's diplomacy reflects, to a greater degree than we might like to admit, the kind of society that supports it. If we are following an imperial policy, it may well be that we are still entranced by imperial dreams.

The essays in these sections are about some of the people and institutions that determine our foreign policy —about Congress and the CIA, about legislators, spies, journalists and Presidents. No one of them can be singled out as solely responsible for a foreign policy that has now gone sour, for most of them played a role in creating and sustaining it. We may not deserve the foreign policy we have, but unless we know what we have, we will not deserve anything better. This means looking with cold dispassion, although not without sympathy, at those we have made our heroes, and, in an effort that is even more painful, at ourselves for creating these heroes.

The Vulgar Assembly

On entering the House of Representatives at Washington one is struck with the vulgar demeanor of that great assembly. The eye frequently does not discover a man of celebrity within its walls. Its members are almost all obscure individuals, whose names present no associations to the mind; they are mostly village lawyers, men in trade, or even persons belonging to the lower classes of society. In a country in which education is very general, it is said that the representatives of the people do not always know how to write correctly.

—Alexis de Tocqueville,
Democracy in America.

It is comforting to know that some things never change, or at least not very much. One can still drop into that sprawling chamber where the people's representatives meet in solemn session and wonder how anything of the slightest importance could possibly happen there. A handful of men in baggy suits can be seen in various postures of repose—a few reading newspapers, another picking his nose, one sound asleep—while from somewhere in a sea of mahogany desks a voice rises in droning tribute to the milk-weed pod or the orthodontist. Even high school civics teachers know better than to allow their wards to linger in the House gallery on spring vacation trips to the capital. Lest they all turn into cynics, they are hustled off after a few minutes to see the stuffed Indians at the Smithsonian.

But if de Tocqueville was right, we have to remember that the public spectacle of the lower chamber has always been mostly for show and a few laughs. The real business, then as now, goes on behind the scenes, in the committee rooms where the feudal barons of the legislative process dispose of the public business at their private discretion. As Woodrow Wilson wrote during his professorial days: "The House sits not for serious discussion, but to sanction the conclusions of its committees as rapidly as possible." If the ratification ceremony has little drama and even less debate, nobody seems to mind very much. To expect rapier wit and probing cross-questioning on the floor of the House is to ask of that august body a quality which it does not consider to be a virtue. In the rich heritage of custom the House holds dear, there is little room for question-askers or boat-rockers. Was it not, after all, the late Sam Rayburn, venerated by friend and foe alike as the living incarnation of everything that is most honorable in the House, who summed up the creed governing the institution over which he presided for so many years in the immortal words: "To get along, go along"?

Going along has always been to the House what economic determinism is to Marxists or predestination to Calvinists: an article of faith and a philosophy of life. Those who vote prudently when the chips are down and don't ask too many questions are drawn into the fold and given the sacraments—assignment to a powerful committee, a new federal highway through their district, speedy action on a private bill for an influential constituent. The few others, who for reasons of temperament or conscience have a hard time going along, find the role of a legislator a minefield of bad intentions. As Senator Paul Douglas, a pioneer of the lonesome road himself, reminded a would-be rebel: "The legislation you favor will not go through. The dam your constituents want will not be built. The river improvements your constituents want will not be built."

Yet a few malcontents invariably appear in the House who ignore Sam Rayburn's advice. Among the most poignant are the idealists who think that all issues are decided on moral principle and resolved by the logic of debate. In his collection of round-table discussions, *The Congressman—His Work As He Sees It,* Charles Clapp quotes such a disappointed idealist as saying: "I came here thinking this was for real, that this was the only parliament where democratic processes were at work. That is a myth, I find. You can't stand on the floor and inform people; they don't want to listen. If anybody thinks he is going to come down here and legislate he is crazy. When I first arrived and looked around the Capitol, the White House and the Washington Monument, I had a lump in my throat and I felt pretty humble about being part of this great scene. But now all I see is skullduggery and shenanigans."

There speaks a man who thought he was going to the House of Commons and discovered himself in the House of Representatives, an organization whose leaders have no desire to be informed on the floor by their junior fellows, nor any intention of letting them legislate. While newcomers often complain bitterly about the five-minute limitation on debate, they gradually come to realize that it is not so much a tyranny imposed by the leadership as a handy device for dispensing with the irrelevant— that is, a debate that would not make the slightest difference in the way members cast their votes. With the horse-trading all wound up before the bill ever reaches the floor, the only thing a debate could accomplish would be to tell the voters what was being done to them in the name of their best interests. But since the House does not consider the enlightenment of the electorate to be one of its primary functions, most Congressmen are ardent supporters of the five-minute gag on debate. No temple of rhetoric, the House is a cozy, if slightly seedy, Masonic lodge where the boys swap yarns, the young Turks let off a little harmless steam, and the elders of the community watch over the foolproof system they have developed for keeping things nice and tidy.

One of the most remarkable features of this system is a process whereby speeches are presented but never heard, and where debate often comes only after the vote has been taken. This is accomplished by the device known as the *Congressional Record*, an ingenious publication which offers Congressmen, through their privilege to "revise and extend" remarks, the chance to create the past and go on record *ex post facto*—to be off pinching heifers in Ogalala during a crucial vote and yet break into print with an impassioned speech that gives every appearance of having been delivered in the heat of debate. The fact that this practice provides a deceptive official record which makes it impossible for the courts to determine legislative intent hardly detracts from its self-evident virtues. How useful it is to be in two places at once, to say one thing on the floor and another for the record, to decide one's position after the issue is settled. And how convenient it is for the image-conscious Congressman to have a publication into which he can insert his own public-relations material, or that of a favored pressure group, and then get it distributed at no expense (except the taxpayers') to the voters of his district by means of his Congressional mailing frank. Thus, without recourse to the tedious and time-consuming methods of floor debate, the members of Congress are nevertheless able to fulfill their obligation to instruct the electorate on vital issues of public policy.

To be sure, Congressmen, like everyone else, are subject to persuasion. It is just that the real persuaders are not those who deliver fervent addresses, nor even the President and his various arm-twisting minions, but the handful of venerable figures in the House cat-bird seat: the Speaker, the minority leader, the chairmen of the half-dozen key committees. Theirs are the hands that guide the strange, and sometimes incomprehensible, workings of the House, that hold out rewards and exact punishments, that allow certain bills to be voted upon and consign others to the limbo of the forgotten. These are the men who decide on the assignment of their colleagues to the legislative committees—an act filled with all the darkness and much of the ceremony of the Eleusinian mysteries.

Congressman Bob Wilson, for example, whose political career is mightily helped by a steady flow of defense contracts into his California constituency, told Clapp that he was not exactly sure why he was put on the Armed Services committee, although "one factor of great significance" must have been "that my district has many military installations in it and thus is a logical one to be represented on the committee." Another Congressman, benefiting from Sam Rayburn's dictum that the new Democrats on the Education and Labor Committee must first be cleared by the AFL-CIO, found that his assignment was made "when some labor lobbyists came to me and asked whether I would go on if they could get me on. They went ahead and got me on. I neither asked for it nor lifted a finger for it."

As far as the individual Congressman is concerned, the most awesome seat of power in the House has been the Appropriations Committee. "For a member of the House to fight this committee," writes Neil MacNeil in his long and perhaps overly loving account of House folklore, *Forge of Democracy*, "even in the cause of the President, was to risk dreadful consequences to his own political well-being, for this committee had power over all the federal spending in every Representative's home district. . . . This power over the political lives of the other Representatives gave the committee almost unlimited influence over government spending. Rarely were the committee's bills ever seriously challenged by the House itself. By the 1960s it was not deemed remarkable that the House adopted appropriations of as much as $40 billion without a single amendment being offered on the House floor or a single voiced dissent." It takes either a very brave or a very foolish man to oppose such monolithic authority.

If the Appropriations Committee has the key to the

public purse and the Congressman's heart, another House institution, the Rules Committee, manages to exercise veto power over legislation without having any substantive authority at all. Theoretically empowered only to decide the order in which bills approved by other committees shall be sent to the floor for consideration, it has in reality established itself as the moral overseer of legislation, deciding not merely when the House shall consider bills, but whether it should be allowed to consider them at all. An early chairman of this committee was not speaking through his hat when he said, "In me reposes absolute obstructive powers." Similarly, in 1960, the venerable current chairman, Judge Howard Smith, told two members of his committee who were seeking the release of several key bills: "The only legislation I will agree to consider is the minimum-wage bill. You can tell your liberal friends that they will get that—or nothing. If you try to bring up anything else, I'll adjourn the meeting."

Crafty parliamentarian that he is, Judge Smith has adjourned a good many meetings, with the result that he has usually been able to block the bills he didn't like and speed through the ones he admired—such as the communist control act that bears his name. It is a favorite pastime among liberals to fulminate against the Judge and curse him for having a black heart. Yet the Rules Committee is the House's creation, not his, and it perfectly reflects the political ethos which dominates that institution. Who would vote to remove Judge Smith from the chairmanship of "his" committee—a position which he acquired and maintains by virtue of having been returned to Congress for sixteen consecutive terms —when to do so would be a direct blow to the seniority system from which every Congressman can expect to benefit? Even Sam Rayburn, cunning fox that he was, was unable to pry key administration bills loose from the Rules Committee; nor was he able to purge William Colmer from his second-ranking position on it despite the fact that Colmer, a Mississippi Democrat, actively campaigned against Kennedy in the 1960 election.

To a foreign observer there must have been something

pathetic, if not totally mystifying, in the late President's complaint that much of his program would have been approved had the Rules Committee allowed his bills to come to a vote in the House. After all, the committee had a two-thirds Democratic majority, was headed by a member of the President's own party, and was supposedly acting as an agent of a Democratic-controlled House. But as James MacGregor Burns has told us in his admirable study, *Deadlock of Democracy*, there are two Democratic parties, one controlled by some ninety Congressmen elected by two million voters, and another (when the Democrats are in power) headed by the President and making its appeal to sixty million voters. The Congressional Democrats, with Judge Smith as their rock and Adam Smith as their prophet, view themselves as defenders of the Republic against its wild-eyed enemies "downtown" in the White House and the government agencies. And in this crusade they have found natural allies in Republicans like Charles Halleck, the pugnacious minority leader, who sees the Rules Committee as a "roadblock to unwise, ill-timed, spendthrift, socialistic measures."

Those critics who are trying to save the House from itself and pump some blood back into its congealed arteries naturally seize upon the Rules Committee as the logical place to begin. James Robinson, a young political scientist who has examined the various possibilities for reform in his scholarly study, *The House Rules Committee*, concludes that the most radical solution would also be the most logical: do away with the damned thing altogether and let the majority party leadership determine which committee-approved bills should be considered by the House and in what order. Noting that the Senate sets its agenda by a procedure of unanimous consent agreements, Robinson argues cogently that "if a group of 100 men can agree unanimously on its legislative program, 400 men can surely operate by majority vote." The fact, however, is that both the leadership and the majority of the House seem quite content with the conduct of the Rules Committee and have consistently refrained from any serious attempt to discipline it. It is too handy as a graveyard for legislation that the majority does not want, but dares not oppose openly.

But then has not Congress always looked upon the non-passage of bills as a function at least as important as their passage? As Robert Bendiner says in *Obstacle Course on Capitol Hill,* an informative and witty study of the non-legislative process at work: "A United States Congressman has two principal functions: to make laws and to keep laws from being made. . . . Indeed, if that government is best that governs least, then Congress is designed, by rule and tradition, to be one of the most perfect instruments of government ever devised." Following various bills for federal aid to education on their long and tortuous path to extinction, Bendiner delves into the labyrinth of Congressional obstructionism as it has been refined over the years by the best parliamentary minds in the business. The result is a revealing insight into the non-workings of our legislative system, and a fascinating account of how an intelligent minority has been able to impose its will on a disorganized majority.

Considering all the hurdles and pits that Congress has placed in the path of legislation, it is less remarkable that the system performs so badly than that, like the chess-playing dog, it performs at all. One would be hard-pressed to think of any other functioning democracy where the chief executive could not even persuade the legislature to consider, let alone pass, one fifth of the bills he sent to it. Yet somehow or other the system creaks on, the absolutely vital measures get passed in one form or another, while the controversial ones gather dust until there is sufficient popular demand to force them to a vote—or until the Supreme Court does Congress's work for it. Which is no ground for complacency, but none for hysteria either. Looking back on some of the legislation that has been whooped through the House— such as the perennial wiretap bills, the Smith Act, or the 1950 resolution to cut off Marshall Plan aid to England until the British Parliament ended the partition of Ireland—one might have second thoughts about the desirability of speedy Congressional action.

Perhaps, in any case, it is only the political scientists who take Congress's legislative role seriously. If forced to express an opinion, most Congressmen would probably not place legislating very high on their list of public duties. Faithful servant of the people, the average member of the House takes greater pride in his job of representation. He delights in considering himself a liaison between his constituents and the federal government, serving as a conduit for baffled inquiries about overdue social security checks, veterans' benefits, and draft deferments. The size of the country and the impersonality of the bureaucracy make this function important, although only in the United States is it considered to be the main job of the nation's legislators. While he perpetually grumbles about the time it consumes, the Congressman enjoys playing this role——even to the point of acting as a travel agent for his constituents, reserving hotel rooms for them, and finding them choice seats for the selection of Miss Cherry Blossom. It all gives him a sense of service and it forges ties with the voters that come in handy every second November.

Bendiner, along with a good many other critics of a moribund Congress, believes that this overly tight and narrow relationship between the Representative and his constituents is responsible for the House's failure to educate the public: that is to say, the Congressman doesn't pass the hard truth on to the voters either because he is too busy performing his liaison functions or because he is afraid that they won't re-elect him if he provides unpleasant information. "If," Bendiner writes, "there is any hope of making Congress primarily the nationally deliberative body that it might be and only secondarily the assembly of sectional and provincial representatives that to some extent it must be, the hope lies, I think, in the direction of making its members somewhat freer than they are of local whim and sentiment." To this end he suggests a series of modest, if unlikely, reforms—such as lengthening the term of office and limiting the number of consecutive terms, letting candidates run from whatever district they please regardless of residence, setting up a quasi-judicial agency to relieve Congressmen of the burden of bills for the relief of individual constituents, and reducing the errand-boy role of Congressmen by establishing an office on the Swedish model to serve as an intermediary between citizen and bureaucracy.

Reasonable enough in themselves, these suggested reforms might make Congressmen more independent, but would they also make them wiser—or readier to vote for the legislation so dear to the hearts of the liberals? The answer, I should think, is no. The fearsome old curmudgeons who bottle up medicare, federal aid to education, and home rule for the District of Columbia are not those Congressmen chained to "local whim and sentiment," but precisely the ones who can afford to ignore their constituents because they come from one-party districts and are as firmly entrenched in office as is navy bean soup in the House cafeteria. Of the 435 seats in the House, only 100 at most can be called marginal in any sense of the word, and in recent elections less than one incumbent in ten has been denied another term. John McMillan is not being cowed by the voters of South Carolina when, as chairman of the House District Committee, he decides that his fellow representatives shall not be allowed to vote on home rule for the nation's capital, despite the fact that three successive Presidents have asked for it, and the Senate has five times passed bills which would authorize it. Nor does Judge Howard Smith tremble under the judgment of the central Virginia mountaineers and farmers who have kept him in Congress since 1931; he is all-powerful within his realm because he is an absolutely free agent enjoying autocratic authority under the archaic rules that govern the House in the conduct of its own affairs.

A good many liberals imagine that making every Representative as independent as these Southern gentlemen —or their counterparts in the one-party Republican districts of the Middle West—would bring about a flow of progressive legislation. More likely, however, it would slow such legislation up, since it is precisely the Congressmen from marginal districts who are most receptive to the needs of a changing society. The burden these legislators operate under does not come from the narrow prejudices of their district—a civics-class myth it is time we disposed of—but from a procedural system that prevents a numerical majority from imposing its will upon an entrenched minority. To free Representatives from the pressure of their constituents would in no way threaten the power of the oligarchs who have manipulated the rules of the House to their own purposes, and are responsible to no one but themselves. A more effective remedy, therefore, would lie in freeing Congress from its own procedural prison. Not that this would necessarily bring Congress wisdom, but it could at least help it to function once again.

Nevertheless, it would be foolish to deny that the Representative is a man subject to intense local pressures—pressures which he cannot ignore without sacrificing his political life. He may find these pressures narrow and ignorant, he may even defy them if he thinks he can, but he dare not cut into many bridges of support or he will soon find himself with nowhere to turn and his career in Washington collapsing under him. This is one of the reasons why Congressmen feel it essential to reply to every letter that comes into their office, no matter how undeserving or unnecessary of response. Those from marginal districts where two-party politics is a reality live under the constant terror of offending a single voter. Only an iconoclast like Stephen Young has the courage to reply to crackpots: "Dear Sir, Some damned fool sent me a stupid letter and signed your name to it." But then Stephen Young is not only a free spirit and a man of exquisite sense, he is also a Senator; and Senators can do things that no Congressman would dream of in his wildest flights of fantasy. Blessed with a six-year term and supported by the assumption that voters have short memories, Senators can even court temporary unpopularity by favoring the needs of the nation over the feelings of their constituents. To be sure, even a Senator has to keep the fences mended at home, and never for a minute can he forget that he is an elected official with his state's interests to represent, but at least he has more leeway than his colleagues in the House of Representatives.

The Representative, unless he is permanently entrenched in office by a one-party constituency, takes a national view of public affairs only at his own peril. As D. W. Brogan has pointed out: "An American Congressman who, for the best of reasons, offends local pressure groups, or by not talking for Buncombe, wastes his time on mere national issues of the first order, may be out—and out forever. The history of Congress is full of martyrs to the general welfare, but any given Congress is full of men who have had more sense than to prefer the general welfare to the local interest." Thus, Congressmen from marginal districts feel that they must work both sides of the political fence if they are to be re-elected. This is not always as easy as it sounds, particularly where the Congressman feels strongly about social issues. Speaking for a frustrated minority, one liberal told MacNeil of his disappointment when the state legislature failed to redraw his district: "I could have been a statesman if they had cut off a few of those conservatives. Now I'll have to continue going this way and that way, back and forth. I'm a cracker-ass Congressman—and I could have been a statesman." Perhaps he could have been, but he was in the wrong place, for only those who do not have to worry about being re-elected every two years can afford to be Burkeans.

This, of course, is supposed to be one of the virtues of the House: because Representatives are constantly running for re-election, the House, it is said, more accurately reflects the national will than the Senate. But here we come upon a paradox, for is it not often the case that the Congressman trails behind public opinion, faithfully waving the banner of last year's slogan? The gap between that vast amorphous entity known as The Country and the incestuous little world of Washington has not developed—as most Congressmen like to think—mainly because of the electorate's backwardness. It is a result of the isolation and caution of legislators who are so enmeshed in Congressional gamesmanship that they no longer have any clear idea of what the voters are thinking —and in some cases, they have even ceased to care. Instead of legislating, Congress holds hearings; instead of educating the voters, it bemoans their ignorance; instead of offering leadership, it complains that it is not the President; and instead of drafting its own bills, it merely acts as a receptacle for legislation drawn up by the White House and the federal agencies.

Reflecting on the ways of the House, an institution that fills him with alternating mirth and despair, Murray Kempton writes: "It is argued that the House of Representatives has damaged the country by its persistence in negation. But the real point is that this habit has damaged the House of Representatives more than it has anything else. Negation, long indulged, renders any institution impotent. The House can no longer offer any alternative to Executive discretion on matters truly critical; its attitude has, in fact, turned government into a series of private compacts to do what has to be done without admitting that it is being done. And what should be serious debate ends as only a saber dance. The Congress is content with gestures; it has surrendered to the President what power there is for substantial action."

In the paralysis of its procedures and the negativism of its philosophy, the Senate has been just as irresponsible as the House—and with even less reason, since it cannot fall back on the excuse that a two-year term somehow ties its hands. Together the two chambers form a poignant diptych of Tweedledum and Tweedledee, joined in impotent wedlock by the fetters of their own making. As a result, the role of the Congress in the American system of government has become basically one of obstruction and harassment. It can block administration bills which have overwhelming public support, such as medicare or federal aid to education, but it is unable to offer any constructive alternatives of its own.

It can slash the foreign aid bill to ribbons and hamper the conduct of foreign policy by cutting off aid to countries whose leaders it doesn't like, while shunting off the consequences of its irresponsibility to a frustrated Executive branch. It can annoy the administration, of whatever party, by investigations designed more to embarrass public officials than to enlighten the public, and by indiscriminate hacking at the budgets of administrative agencies that incur the displeasure of one of the Congressional oligarchs. It can drive Cabinet officials to distraction by forcing them to make perpetual appearances before its various committees in hearings which often seem designed more to satisfy Congressional vanity than to provide information. In the face of this collapse of legislative responsibility, even Walter Lippmann, a man not given to dramatic generalizations, has found "reason to wonder whether the Congressional system as it now operates is not a grave danger to the Republic."

What is most alarming about the inability of the Congress to legislate is that it may lead to a breakdown of our peculiarly successful, but not necessarily permanent, democratic system. The checks and balances written into the Constitution are the very fibre of American democracy, and if they are disturbed over too long a period, the system itself must suffer. A self-reliant and responsible legislature is, after all, an anomaly in the world, not a commonplace. For all its sense of drama and lofty standards of debate, the French parliament was so totally incapable of coping with its duties and had fallen to such a level of public contempt that its demise was greeted with indifference or delight. The American Congress, too, could become a purely ceremonial body, providing country lawyers with prestigious titles to cap their careers, and offering a source of harmless entertainment for a cynical public.

This is certainly one way of resolving the Congressional impasse, but it is one over which liberals should contain their enthusiasm. It is only relatively recently that liberals have found such virtue in a strong-arm executive and a politically motivated Supreme Court—

institutions which were both looked upon with considerable suspicion when they were manned by incumbents of different political hue. We have had reactionary Courts and right-wing Presidents before, and we are likely to have them again. We have also had a Congress—although not recently—which took its responsibilities seriously and which was a "great assembly" of the people rather than a museum of stuffed platitudes. Unless that once "great assembly" is put into working order again, we are likely to find ourselves with something even worse —which is no effective assembly at all.

Inside Dope

In our nation's capital, home of the jealously guarded secret and the official lie, uncommon numbers of talented men make their living and reputation as professional insiders. They range from lobbyists and court gossipers to the most widely read journalists. Theirs is an honorable, indeed an ancient, calling, as essential to plutocracies and dictatorships as to democracies. By bringing the human element into the power equation, they play a vital role in every social system.

Only democracies, however, depend upon that special kind of insider whose job it is to pass on the official secret even before the officials are willing to give it up. They are concerned with the public's "right to know," which is invariably wider than any government thinks it has a right to be. Without these insiders we would be even more mystified about what is being done to us in our name and, ostensibly, with our own best interests at heart. We would know even less than we do about who decides which causes we shall die for, what interest groups are the real masters of our public servants, and who lines their pockets with funds meant for the common weal. In a corporate democracy, the most noble service can sometimes be reporting the highest gossip.

For four decades and through six administrations Drew Pearson has been reporting the highest, and sometimes the lowest, gossip to the readers of his syndicated column. In *Behind the Lines,* Herman Klurfeld's adoring biography of this *enfant terrible* of American journalism, we find a portrait of a man who has been braver and more stubborn than most, unafraid of enemies in high places or friends in low ones, tenacious to the point of tedium, and irrepressible in his zest for making an unsavory revelation. For Pearson the well-timed exposé is a kind of carnal delight, to be anticipated, savored, prolonged, and lovingly recollected.

This is the source of his strength and one of his most admirable qualities, for without this attitude he could never have survived all those decades in Washington and done daily battle with the powers of darkness and concealment. An indefatigable and, more importantly, a courageous reporter, Pearson has cast himself in the role of St. George of the typewriter. If he ever has any doubts about the evil of the forces he combats or the virtues of the causes he champions, there is no sign of it in the breathless columns he has turned out with such staggering regularity over the years.

At his best, Pearson displays a stern Quaker passion and courage. At his worst, he can be vindictive, narrow-minded, and less than honorable. His vendetta against the late James Forrestal is legendary, a recent exposé of Reagan descended to the level of attacking the California governor for harboring homosexuals on his staff, and over the years Pearson has not objected to serving as a henchman for various public figures he admires such as Lyndon B. Johnson. On the Vietnam war he has been equivocal (where the conservative Arthur Krock has been bitterly opposed), and has little use for disorderly students, black militants, or radicals. Politically he is a New Deal Democrat of the Humphrey-Johnson variety, and his ideals are sometimes as tarnished as his highly questionable methods.

Pearson's *The Case Against Congress,* written with his colleague Jack Anderson, is a straightforward, documented story of corruption on Capitol Hill. It is a depressing account of Congressmen taking bribes under the table, padding their payrolls with relatives, awarding government contracts to the clients of their law firms, and selling their services to the highest bidder. We learn how many of the most incorruptible Congressmen keep in the good graces of the oil and gas interests, how pressure is put on the regulatory agencies, and the way that lobbyists perform their work. These pages are replete with tales of lawmakers who have abused the public trust and enriched themselves both within and outside the law.

Yet for all their indignation, Pearson and Anderson remain curiously myopic about the nature of the corruption they deplore and the means of combatting it. Their "ten modest proposals" for reform, however desirable and long overdue, are modest indeed and do not even begin to deal with the real corruption of the legislative process. It would be admirable if Congressmen had to divulge all their sources of income, resign from the law firms whose clients they continue to represent on Capitol Hill, refrain from employment with any corporation doing business with the government, and in general behave as though they were repositories of a public trust rather than servants of special interest groups such as the gun lobby, the gas and oil industry, or the insurance companies.

But the real problem is not the malfeasance of a few Congressmen. Rather it is the unresponsiveness, paralysis, and negativism of a legislative system that cannot cope with, or even comprehend, the needs of those it is supposed to represent. The case against Congress is not its venality, for we expect and can live with that. It is its essential triviality and even its irrelevance. Congress has shown itself to be incapable of dealing with the great problems that torment this nation: a war that no one remembers having ever consciously started or knows how to end, a maldistribution of income that aggravates social and political inequality, a breakdown of public confidence in the institutions of society, a corrupting racism that infuses nearly every social institution, and an invisible but unbridgeable chasm between those who wield economic power and those who are manipulated by it.

Congress cannot deal with these problems because it can scarcely admit that they exist without throwing into question the beliefs held by individual Congressmen. There can be no challenge where there is no doubt or disbelief. The balance of power in Congress is held (largely because of the seniority system) by people whose primary interest lies in preserving what is congenial and, in many cases, profitable. Incapable of leading the process of social reform, unwilling to offer a responsible challenge to the arbitrary power of the executive branch, responsive to the demands of economic interest groups at the expense of the public welfare, Congress has fallen into disrepute without even realizing that anything is wrong. This is the real case against Congress, which Pearson and Anderson do not seem to perceive.

To turn from the world of Drew Pearson to that of Arthur Krock is like leaving the stable for the club house. Krock's world is elevated, chummy, and serene, a place where everyone is on a first-name basis and the stench of politics is sweetened by good manners. "In one way or another," the former Washington correspondent of *The New York Times* writes in his *Memoirs,* "I have known eleven Presidents, ten during their incumbency."

It is a phrase that sets the tone of this rambling recollection of bygone personalities, and perhaps explains the reason for its remarkable commercial success. Krock is the ultimate insider, the man who knew eleven Presidents, had lunch with the members of the Cabinet, and played poker with generals and Congressmen. He was privy to military secrets long before they could be revealed, solicited for his opinions on matters of state, and a confidant to the mighty. A Kentuckian of German-Jewish descent, he quickly was assimilated, identifying with the values of Wasp society and maneuvering very well within it. In 1909 he came to Washington as correspondent for the Louisville *Times,* covered the Paris peace conference in 1918–19, became Ralph Pulitzer's assistant on the New York *World* in 1923, and four years later joined *The New York Times,* where he remained until his retirement in 1966.

During a career that spanned six decades, Krock formed strong opinions on the personalities he encountered and the policies they favored. He is fulsome in his praise for Wilson, Hoover, Truman, and Eisenhower, but had a running feud with Franklin Roosevelt and is harshly critical of Lyndon Johnson, the latter for his expansion of the Vietnam war and his pursuit of "a neosocialist welfare state." In this book of reminiscences and opinions we are treated to a revealing portrait of the journalist as Establishment insider.

Krock not only reported on official Washington, he identified with it and saw his role as "The Washington Correspondent" of the *Times* as conferring special responsibilities and advantages. Unlike Pearson, who is a gut fighter, Krock is Olympian, and the difference is not simply one of style. Pearson, for example, fought McCarthyism from the beginning, while Krock was more disturbed by the "infiltration of Communists and crypto-Communists within the official [government] structure," than by the "wild exaggerations" of the late Senator from Wisconsin. Pearson's weakness is his inaccuracy and the not infrequent pettiness of his exposés. Buried just beneath the crusading muckraker lies the malicious gossip columnist. Krock's strength is his detachment and his integrity, but for all his distinction as a reporter, he remains an isolated and dated figure—basically a decent and urbane man who has stood fast as history went rushing by, rather like Herbert Hoover, whom he admired.

The Jewish boy from the South who made good in the East and got to know eleven Presidents, Krock chose to identify with the rich and the powerful. He epitomized what made the *Times* a great, and an often intolerably smug, newspaper, and in the age of mass democracy he remained a pillar of the dying class system. His memoirs are full of shrewd observations and revealing portraits.

But for anyone who does not share the conservative values of Arthur Krock, they are marred by bad temper, narrowness of vision, and a crippling nostalgia for the past. Unlike Walter Lippmann, a contemporary who has remained young by showing the courage to re-examine his assumptions, Krock seems mired in an earlier age.

Not only is he alienated from what he refers to as the "spoiled generations" of younger people and those corrupted by Federal handouts, but he is unsympathetic, perhaps even hostile, to the black American's struggle for equality. He speaks of President Johnson's "radical compulsory racial integration measures that would have infringed the 'civil rights' of the American people as a whole," excoriates the Department of Justice as having "spinelessly established the fact of being a Negro as a grant of immunity for most notorious flagrant violators of both the civil and criminal laws," criticizes "the ethnic groups containing a large percentage of criminals [that] brings constant pressure on Congress to legislate Johnson's Great Society programs," and bemoans the fate of the "Federal judiciary that is constantly defied by the population groups that make a career of violating the law."

What makes Krock's book seem so dated is not that many of the stories he relates happened long ago, but that the personality which infuses these memoirs seems to have stopped its development somewhere in the early 1950s, if not before. From the Age of Eisenhower (which he views as "one of the most notable" in American history), Arthur Krock seems to have found little to rouse his passion other than a condemnation of the young and the dispossessed. One feels in this book that the club house door has been left open too long, that the smell of the stables is seeping into the cozily paneled rooms, and no one knows quite what to do about it except to complain a little louder.

The difference between Arthur Krock and Tom Wicker, the current Washington bureau chief of the *Times*, is dramatized in *JFK and LBJ*, the latter's account of the Kennedy and Johnson administrations. Where Krock is patrician and backward-looking, Wicker, who is also a Southerner, is ironic, serious, and impassioned. His column, since the semi-retirement of Lippmann, is easily the best coming out of Washington, and he is well aware that there is more to reporting than having lunch with Cabinet members and golfing with generals. It is Wicker, and sometimes Wicker alone, who breathes life into the moribund editorial page of the *Times,* and who has that rare ability to put the news into perspective without becoming rarified and abstract.

JFK and LBJ, whose subtitle is "the influence of personality upon politics," seeks to explain why Kennedy could not achieve his legislative goals and why Johnson allowed the Great Society to become a victim of the Vietnam war. It is an entertaining book that is not really up to Wicker's capabilities. The section on Kennedy is rather pedestrian and occasionally descends to bad journalese, but the analysis of Johnson's character is perceptive and fascinating. The book, incidentally, is dedicated to his two predecessors as Washington bureau chief, James Reston and Arthur Krock.

All three of these men—Pearson, Krock, and Wicker— would normally be considered Washington insiders par excellence. That, after all, is their job and they do it well. But behind their success remains the nagging question of whether these famous insiders, through their influence upon their readers, really affect policy at all. We are supposed to live under a government responsive to public will and public needs. But is this in fact the case, and are these insiders, for all their familiarity with the mighty and their ways, any less outsiders than the rest of us? It would be instructive to know the real influence of the press upon politics. There is a topic for Tom Wicker's talents before he retires to write his memoirs.

American Crusader

Among the lonely dissenters of American politics none has been more intrepid or articulate than I. F. Stone. While unfamiliar to most readers on either side of the Atlantic, he has become the self-appointed spokesman of America's bowed, but still unbroken, radical Left. In his four-page weekly newsletter, disillusioned radicals and romantic socialists have found a champion of their cause—and someone to comfort them in their isolation.

The Haunted Fifties offers a revealing insight into the traumas of the American Left, and into the preoccupations of American political life during the Age of Eisenhower. Gone and perhaps better forgotten, the fifties are already surrounded by a mist of vague unreality. If they were not haunted, the fifties were hysterical. The decision to contain Russian imperialism, essential as it was, became a crusade against "atheistic Communism" wherever it raised its head—whether in the trenches of Pusan or in the Fish and Wildlife Service snack bar. American idealism, which if left dormant usually contents itself with Community Chest drives and inquiries into the "national purpose," turned inward on itself in search of "subversives" whose existence alone could explain the frustrations of the cold war. From these frustrations came the witch hunt that paralyzed the Left in a chorus of *mea culpas* over its own naïvety toward Soviet motives. Battered, and decimated, the radical Left retreated into the shell of its own martyrdom, an outcast from a society it could no longer reach and no longer knew how to talk to.

I. F. Stone is as much a product as a historian of those times. Weaned on the absolutes of the thirties— Communism vs. Fascism, progress vs. reaction—he seems never to have come to terms with a world of grays, where black and white are not descriptions, but simply points of reference. Like his small but faithful band of readers, he wears his heart on his sleeve and is ready to fight at the drop of a Cause. Indeed, as he says of himself in a revealing introduction to this book: "For me being a newspaperman has always seemed a cross between Galahad and William Randolph Hearst, a perpetual crusade." With these dubious mentors it is not surprising that courage should sometimes ride herd over contemplation, or that facts should take a back seat to faith.

Stone tends to confuse expedient blunders with evil machinations. Actions he disapproves of become sinister plots against "peace." On the rearmament of Germany, for example, we are told in all seriousness that "the main objective of American policy for several years has been to rearm Germany in order to repeat his [Hitler's] invasion of Russia, this time more terribly than before because supplemented by American atomic bombing."

For all his radicalism, however, Stone is no apologist for Soviet actions. He attacks the Kremlin with the same gusto with which he besieges the White House. Yet beneath his intellectual realization that the dream of Marxist socialism has become the dreariness of the Soviet bureaucratic state, there still lingers an emotional attachment to the tarnished visions of the thirties. On returning from a trip to Moscow in 1956 he confided to his readers: "Whatever the consequences, I have to say what I really feel after seeing the Soviet Union and carefully studying the statements of its leading officials. *This is not a good society and it is not led by honest men.*"

(his italics) While this remark is charmingly ingenuous, one can only marvel at Stone's capacity for surprise, and wonder where he has been all these years.

But with all his emotionalism and the innocent naïvety of his romantic Marxism, Stone is a courageous reporter who has never hesitated to speak his mind, "whatever the consequences." Just as he challenged McCarthy at a time when most liberals were paralyzed by fear, so he charges fearlessly into battle whatever the odds against him and whatever the cause—be it atomic testing, the Cuban blockade, or the war in Vietnam.

His special genius, Murray Kempton observes in an introduction to *In a Time of Torment*, a collection of recent pieces, is that Stone "always remembers the official lie of last month which is contradicted by the official lie of today." Digging behind the headlines, beneath the soporifics of our public officials, and around the miasma of contradictory statistics, he reveals the truths we never quite realized were being concealed. He is the gadfly pricking at the smug rhetorical hide of every administration, be it Republican or Democratic. No wonder that he is both respected and cursed in exalted public places, where the sugar-coated cover-up is considered to be the higher patriotism.

An independent writer-publisher in an era of press monopolies, a political radical who has become a successful capitalist, a scarred veteran of yesterday's ideological battles who has found a belated public recognition in today's guerrilla ambushes, Stone has carved a special niche for himself in the annals of American journalism. There is no one else who combines his pamphleteer's instinct with the historical imagination of a scholar and the unflagging energy of a missionary.

In a Time of Torment is Stone's guide to the sixties, culled mostly from the pages of his own *Weekly* and supplemented by some longer pieces from *The New York Review of Books*—a forum in which Stone has done some of the best writing of his career and where he has found an attentive new audience. A successor to *The Haunted Fifties*, this is an engrossing chronicle of our times and of the decisions imposed upon us by our public officials. The titles of these works may seem a bit dramatic, but only a manic ostrich could call them inaccurate. Today America seems to be living under some kind of curse, yet Stone never takes the easy way out of pessimism or despair. With an abiding faith in human reason, he believes that the truth will set us free —and digs it out whether we want to hear it or not.

Stone's unique service lies in digging out the information and providing the analysis that forces us continually to re-examine our own uncritical assumptions. Lately, for example, the Senate Foreign Relations Committee has been investigating the Pentagon's account of the Tonkin Gulf incident. But back in August 1964, Stone launched his own one-man inquiry with the words: "The American Government and the American press have kept the full truth about the Tonkin Bay incident from the American public" and reached the conclusion that "the second incident seems to have triggered off a long-planned attack of our own." Had a few more Senators been listening at the time, perhaps we would not be where we are in Vietnam today.

A stylist as well as an analyst, he is a master of the felicitous phrase. Of an author given to panegyrics over politicians, he comments: "A writer who can be so universally admiring need never lunch alone"; of General Westmoreland it is suggested that he "may yet go down in history as the first general to be saluted by a yawn." President Johnson is described as a speaker who is losing his audience: "This is the moment," he writes with devastating dryness, "when people begin to feel around for their overshoes and to nudge their way out to the aisles."

For all his moral passion, Stone peoples his world neither with heroes nor with villains. Curtis LeMay, whose simple-mindedness Stone demolishes, is shoved off-stage with a few kind words. While there is no sentimentality about Kennedy, Stone admired him but wrote in an obituary that "Kennedy, when the tinsel was stripped away, was a conventional leader, no more than an enlightened conservative, cautious as an old man for all his youth, with a basic distrust of the people and an astringent view of the evangelical as a tool of leadership."

This kind of irreverent prose and cold eye is all too rare in American journalism, and we remain in I. F. Stone's debt for providing it—even though we may not always agree with his conclusions. He may infuriate or inspire, but he never bores. By being indefatigable in the quest for the buried truth, he has made himself virtually indispensable.

The Reluctant Heretic

"When the proper opposition defaults," Senator J. William Fulbright writes in explanation of his revolt against the foreign policy of the Johnson administration, "it seems to me that it is better to have the function performed by members of the President's party than not to have it performed at all." These are not the words of a natural rebel, but of a distressed idealist who has turned to heresy because it is the only alternative to silence. To reflect upon these words is to understand the poignancy of Fulbright's position as chairman of the Senate Foreign Relations Committee, and thus ostensibly the administration's chief Congressional lieutenant on questions of foreign affairs. It is also to understand the anguish, and the high political courage, that this act of open rebellion must have cost such an essentially loyal and moderate man as Fulbright.

A reflective man who shuns rather than seeks the public spotlight, a party loyalist who prefers to exert influence from within, a believer in the need for strong Presidential leadership, and a political conservative whose natural sympathies are for tradition and order rather than for iconoclasm and rebellion, he has found himself cast as the leader of the Opposition. Darling of the New

Left, despair of the cold war liberals, scourge of the ideologues on both Right and Left, Fulbright is not particularly happy to be the administration's most taunting heretic. But events have forced his hand, and the agony of Vietnam has driven him to take arms against a President he once admired and served so well. "There are times," he writes in *The Arrogance of Power*, "in public life as in private life when one must protest, not solely or even primarily because one's protest will be politic or materially productive, but because one's sense of decency is offended, because one is fed up with political craft and public images, or simply because something goes against the grain."

It is because so much has gone against the grain that Fulbright has rebelled against the leadership of his own party, against the man who once sought his counsel and believed he should be Secretary of State, against the customary role of the chairman of the Foreign Relations Committee, against the beliefs that motivate much of our foreign policy, against certain aspects of the American national character, and even against much of what he himself believed in only a few years ago.

There is a dramatic story in the conversion of Senator Fulbright from administration loyalist, faithful supporter of NATO and the Atlantic Community, defender of foreign aid, and even floor manager of the Tonkin Gulf resolution which gave the President a blank check in Vietnam—to the position of an administration pariah, a grudging admirer of Charles de Gaulle, an enemy of the bilateral foreign aid program, and a vehement critic of the Vietnam war. The story of that conversion could, if put in the proper perspective, tell a good deal not only about the personality of this complex and fascinating man, but also about the traumatic effect of the Vietnam war upon the American conscience. The war, terrible as it is in itself, has become the catalyst for a radical assault upon a good many things that Americans have taken for granted—in our foreign policy and in our domestic life as well. It has called into question the very meaning of the American Dream. That Fulbright should have become a spokesman for those who feel the alienation that has suffused so much of American life, is a remarkable story that ought to be told.

Unfortunately, it is not to be found in the saccharine pages of Tristram Coffin's adoring biography, *Senator Fulbright*. Filled with descriptions of the Senator as a "modern Prometheus," a "public philosopher," and "a prophet," it presents a portrait of a man who has virtually never been wrong, and who is fighting off the forces of evil and darkness all by himself. This is unfair to Fulbright, whose public career is admirable enough to stand up to a fair and critical appraisal, and it is certainly unfair to readers who expect something more than campaign biography in this first full-scale portrait of the Senator from Arkansas. Instead of loving descriptions of Fulbright's charming drawl, intelligent face, and noble instincts, it might be more useful to know something about his relations to his colleagues in the Senate, to explain a voting record that is often discouraging to many of his liberal admirers, to judge his effectiveness as chairman of the Foreign Relations Committee, to examine the role he has played as insider in the formation of foreign policy, to investigate his ambivalent attitude toward the responsibilities and exercise of power, and to reveal, if possible, why this conservative humanist has changed so many of his earlier judgments and adopted many of the attitudes of an alienated radical.

To understand J. William Fulbright, one must turn to his own thoughts as expressed in his book (gleaned and expanded from speeches in the Senate and a series of lectures at Johns Hopkins University) on the use and abuse of power. Etched by a biting skepticism that often seeps over into pessimism, *The Arrogance of Power* marks the passage of Senator Fulbright from a relatively orthodox supporter of the liberal line on foreign policy to a spokesman of the post-cold-war generation. It is a book which could not have been written two years ago, before the Dominican landings and the expansion of the war in Vietnam, for it is a direct response to them. It is a cry of anguish and of anger over the destruction we have caused in the name of righteousness, and pained rejection of the "intolerant Puritanism" that leads us to see ourselves as "God's avenging angels, whose sacred duty it is to combat evil philosophies." This Puritanism, he argues, has caused us to transform every war into a crusade, to dehumanize our opponents to justify the terrible weapons of our technology, to view communism as an unmitigated evil regardless of where or how it is practiced, and "to see principles where there are only interests and conspiracy where there is only misfortune."

In chastising the administration for what it has done, and is doing, in Southeast Asia and Latin America, Fulbright is also calling us to task as a nation for what we are: a people continually obliged to assert authority to prove that we are great because we seem to doubt it ourselves. This is what he calls our "arrogance of power," and compares it to the fatal flaw that led the Athenians to attack Syracuse and Napoleon to invade Russia. Thus his book goes beyond a critique of foreign policy just as, on a different level, Hannah Arendt's study of Eichmann goes beyond the crimes committed by a single man to examine the sources of depersonalization and irresponsibility that affect whole societies and thus make evil actions possible.

Senator Fulbright does not view his fellow Americans as evil, but rather as people caught in the grip of a deep insecurity and intoxicated by the passions of a distorted messianism. Indeed, to his mind, there are two Americas: "One is the America of Lincoln and Adlai Stevenson; the other is the America of Teddy Roosevelt and the modern superpatriots . . . one is judicious and the other arrogant in the use of power." This arrogance comes out in times of crisis and overcomes the fundamentally decent instincts of Americans, causing us to see our extraordinary strength as a sign of superior virtue and leading us to impose our will on other societies. Fulbright sees arrogance in the behavior of Americans abroad, in our interventions in support of various client regimes, in our assumption that other societies have only to follow our example to be wise and prosperous, in our refusal to let others have their own revolutions, in our attempt to create a global Great Society on the American model. This is the kind of arrogance, he warns, that induces "those fatal temptations of power which have ruined other great nations."

In a real sense, this is a work of alienation, one that expresses the corrosive distrust so many Americans feel toward their own government. Reaching across to the angry young radicals, Fulbright defends their dissent by declaring that "criticism is an act of patriotism," recognizes their disenchantment with the values of their society, and questions "whether the sacrifices imposed on the present generation of young Americans are justified by the war" in Vietnam. He raises problems that are more comfortably left unsaid, offers explanations that do not flatter our national ego, and poses alternatives that challenge the cold war mentality.

Some of the ground is familiar: the blistering attack upon the Dominican intervention as an exercise in duplicity, designed "for the primary if not the sole purpose of defeating the revolution," an appeal for sympathy with popular revolutions even where communists are involved, a warning against the "welfare imperialism" of our bilateral foreign aid program, and an appeal to turn away from an excessive preoccupation with foreign wars and foreign crises toward the demands of our own neglected society. The great demands of the Vietnam war are particularly troubling to him because they have taken energies away from the Great Society programs at home and appear to be inducing a "war fever" in certain segments of the population. The latter is an arguable proposition, just as is his assumption that Vietnam has imperiled our accommodation with the Soviet Union. One of the most remarkable facets of the war is the agility with which the administration has been able to keep its lines open to Moscow even while bombing its Asian ally. If the wielders of power are arrogant, they have yet shown no signs of folly in trying to imperil the detente—and indeed President Johnson's policy toward Europe has been exceedingly enlightened.

The Arrogance of Power may be a fitting description of our attitude toward much of the world, but it does not really explain the terrible sacrifices we have undertaken on behalf of our clients, nor the relative restraint with which America has exercised her enormous power. The reality is more complex, more puzzling, and perhaps more elusive than that. Fulbright has done a service by forcing us to re-examine our assumptions.

Foreign policy in a free society is not only, as Senator Fulbright observes, a reflection of domestic policy. It is also a reflection of the countervailing forces within that society, and of the impact of public opinion on the government. There may be arrogance in our attitude toward power, but there is also deep anguish throughout the nation over the use of our power. Senator Fulbright has helped to focus and to channel this anguish into constructive criticism that may yet lead to the changes he desires. Therein lies the courage of his dissent and the importance of this book.

Cloaking the Dagger

Unloved by those it serves as much as by those it subverts, the CIA has entered the popular mythology as a composite demon: half-terrifying, half-ludicrous. Its smoke screen of mystery pierced only when it commits a major blunder, it alternately inspires inappropriate emotions of amusement and indignation. Like our nuclear arsenal, it is one of those regrettable products of the cold war that nobody likes, yet nobody knows how to get rid of. It has lumbered on through four administrations; retained by necessity, it is nonetheless cursed for existing at all.

Any fair-minded account of the CIA and its operations almost inevitably seems to shuttle between distress and resignation, trying to balance the devious diplomacy of the cold war against the traditional methods of democratic government. It is no easy task. In *The Invisible Government,* two enterprising young journalists, David Wise and Thomas B. Ross, have not so much tried to resolve the dilemma as to tell us that it exists. In dramatizing the problem, they have chosen to write an exposé of the CIA, presumably on the assumption that once we know what this thing is, we will then know what to do about it. The cure, unfortunately, doesn't necessarily follow from the diagnosis, but the description of the malady is fascinating—and slightly appalling.

Here, according to the authors, is a "massive, hidden apparatus, secretly employing about 200,000 persons, and spending several billion dollars a year," which gives it, I should imagine, a payroll bigger than the population of Nevada and a budget greater than that of most countries in which it operates. Exact figures are unknown to all but the inner sanctum, since Congress exempts the CIA from such irritating bureaucratic requirements as stating whom it employs, how much it spends, and what it does. Its budget is concealed in those of other agencies, so that every year Congress votes funds "without knowing how much it has appropriated or how much will be spent."

Like Hertz, the CIA has an office nearly everywhere: from Seattle (telephone MA 4-3288) to Ouagadougou (care of the U.S. Embassy). While analysts are sequestered in suburban Washington, *coup*-launchers, spies, and palm-greasers are scattered across the globe, formally touching base at U.S. consulates and embassies where, according to a Senate report, "espionage agents of the CIA are stationed masquerading as diplomatic and consular officials." Such cloaks, however, tend to be even more transparent than the daggers, and any bartender can usually furnish an accurate run-down on the local CIA contingent. In Berlin, for example, where there is about a full division of CIA men, the Russians have found it practical to compile a special spy directory, complete with addresses and telephone numbers. Even though they operate from embassies, CIA agents are remarkably independent, frequently conducting operations without the knowledge and occasionally against the will of the ambassadors who house them. Despite efforts by Presidents Eisenhower and Kennedy to beef-up the ambassadors—the latter went so far as to write them individual letters of support—a Senate subcommittee reported in 1963 that "the primacy of the ambassador is a polite fiction."

Detailing some of the CIA's more lurid activities—such as espionage and government-toppling—Wise and Ross go over fairly familiar ground, but it is not ground the CIA likes to have plowed up and they do it with a high sense of drama that makes engrossing reading. In addition, they throw some much-needed light on the CIA's domestic program. Many will be surprised to learn that right here at home the CIA runs insurance agencies and steamship lines as covers, supports a wide variety of university research programs, such as the Center for International Studies at MIT "which was set up with CIA money in 1950," and subsidizes some excellent magazines and publishing ventures. Branching out into broadcasting, it is behind the scenes at Radio Free Europe, Radio Liberty in Munich, and Radio SWAN in the Caribbean— "organizations that solicit funds from business organizations and the general public, but also receive secret funds . . . and take orders from the CIA." However much it may irritate the invisible CIA officials in Langley, Virginia, these are things we have a right to know about, and we can be grateful to Wise and Ross for performing an important act of public service.

Having been such excellent guides, it is unfortunate that they do not take us one step further, moving from indignation over what the CIA does, to suggestions as to what we are supposed to do about it. While they criticize the vast sums spent on *coups* and espionage, they don't say that such activities are wrong or that the money is badly spent. Although they seem to disapprove of the CIA's ill-concealed finger in every pot of discord, they never question the need for a secret organization of spies. Warning of the "natural human tendency of the leaders of the invisible government to embark upon ventures which might prove their toughness, demonstrate their vision or expand their power," they fail to point out which of the ventures they recount, if any, fall into that category. What they appear to want, as we all do, is a "massive, hidden apparatus" that never gets caught telling a lie or greasing a palm, that never backs the wrong man in a palace *coup*, that both remains shrouded in mystery and is open to public scrutiny.

This is perfectly understandable, but even if our wish were granted, there would still be a problem. The question is not simply how the CIA is to be made efficient and responsible, but how democratic government is to be made responsible to the electorate when an increasing proportion of its activities are deliberately concealed. To single out the CIA as the villain may thus be to bark up the wrong tree. With all its excesses of zeal and inadequacies of vision, it is nonetheless an instrument of the President and submissive to his direction—when it gets direction. If the CIA sometimes becomes a thief of power, it is usually because others are unwilling to make decisions or lay down policy. It is not, after all, entirely the CIA's fault if ambassadors refuse to assert the authority they are given, or if a vacuum of policy results from the State Department's inability to evolve a coherent line of diplomacy. There are means at hand—if anybody wants to use them—for keeping tabs on the CIA and calling it to task. But so far the Congress has refused to set up a watchdog committee to oversee CIA expenditures, while the executive branch has been content to live with the situation as it is.

The problem, then, of reforming the CIA, while an important one, is not crucial; more basic is the use made of the CIA by the Presidency. Rather than a sinister, self-seeking monster, is not this "massive, hidden apparatus" more realistically a tool of the President by which he is able to do with his left hand that which the right hand would never dare try on its own? Is this not the real moral of the Bay of Pigs, planned, financed, and conducted by the CIA at the instigation of President Eisenhower and with the approval of President Kennedy? Is this not the meaning of our role in the slaughter in the Congo where the United States, by means of the CIA, not only supplied Tshombe with planes and bombs to fight the rebels, but paid Cuban exiles to do the bombing?

The CIA in such cases becomes a pair of rubber gloves by which the President keeps his hands clean; Congress in turn disavows all knowledge of what it would rather not know; and the voters remain in ignorance of the activities conducted in their name and with their cash. This may be the price of endurance in the cold war, which has swept a good deal of conventional diplomacy off the board, but we should at least know that we are paying it.

Wise and Ross touch upon this basic question when they observe that the cold war has made our leaders feel that "certain decisions must be made by them alone without popular consent, and in secret, if the nation is to survive." But they neglect to spell out the consequences of such a radical modification of our traditional democratic system. If the critical decisions of government are to be abdicated to a small group of officials who are beyond legislative responsibility or electoral accountability, then the cold war has taken an even greater toll than we have realized. It is little comfort to learn that "there are procedures which call for the approval of any major special operation at a high level in the executive branch of government"; little comfort and not totally convincing, since a good deal of the book is devoted to showing how such procedures broke down in places like Laos, Vietnam, and Costa Rica, where the CIA appeared to be acting on its own. But even assuming that the procedures do work, or can be made to work, is this not to dodge the central issue—that a green light from the White House has not, at least until now, been considered sufficient justification in itself for military interventions which could involve the nation in a state of war? Something has been left out of the question, and that something is the approval of Congress and the knowledge of the electorate.

But that, we are told, is the price of involvement in a cold war we did not choose but cannot avoid. Perhaps it is, yet it is well to get priorities straight and to recognize that the real problem is not the existence of a CIA, but the increasing replacement of visible government by an invisible government which cannot be held responsible for its activities because they are conducted under a cloak of secrecy. The days when we could do without a CIA have unfortunately passed, but the way in which its secret operations can be made consistent with government based upon popular consent has yet to be resolved, or even honestly faced. Wise and Ross do not attempt to solve that problem, but in making us aware of our invisible government, they raise some disturbing questions.

Mr. Clean

In the voluminous pages of *Waging Peace,* the second volume of Presidential memoirs, covering the years from Eisenhower's re-election in 1956 to the inauguration of Kennedy in January 1961, we find Ike taming Khrushchev at Berlin and Budapest, foiling Nasser in Lebanon and the Chinese at Quemoy, blocking Faubus at Little Rock, and defending international morality at Suez. Critics are dismissed as irresponsible or naïve, political opponents are self-seeking or ignorant, fiascos are buried under or forgotten, and failures are so embellished that they become a kind of success. What is left is a succession of triumphs marred only by a few minor disappointments of little lasting importance. Even the abortive 1960 summit conference, which is generally assumed to have been botched by Ike's inept handling of the U-2 affair, is vindicated by the assurance that "the Paris summit, had it been held, would have proved to be a failure and thus would have brought the Free World only further disillusionment." Thus did Ike, by *seeming* to commit a blunder, cleverly save the Free World from disappointment at the hands of an unscrupulous Khrushchev.

Can this infallible man be the Eisenhower we lived with for eight somniferous years? Sometimes it is hard to connect the real world remembered from the late fifties—recession and racial troubles at home, nuclear confrontation and diplomatic stalemate abroad—with the gentle landscape portrayed in *Waging Peace*. So much of the Eisenhower administration, with its quaint nineteenth-century economics and its 1920-style politics of normalcy, has receded into the dim past that it already seems like a historical curiosity, a kind of pre-Lyndon golden age where the toppling of unfriendly governments was left to the bankroll of the CIA rather than to the napalm of the U.S. Air Force, where the entry of a handful of Negro children into an Arkansas school seemed like a triumph for racial equality, where the orbiting of the first Sputnik could be dismissed as a cheap publicity stunt, where Sherman Adams' vicuna coat seemed like the depths of depravity in government, and where an abstract political moralism was tempered by a coldly pragmatic reluctance to involve Americans capriciously in fighting other people's wars. It was an era of insufferable moral posturing abroad and of irresponsible political abdication at home. But it was one which took its moralizing seriously and was not very adept in the arts of cynicism.

Eisenhower's great appeal rested upon the conviction—one which he seemed to share with the voters—that he was above petty limitations of class, interest, or party. Until he ran for President no one even knew what party he belonged to; and the Democrats were quite ready to nominate him in 1952 if the Republicans didn't. He was the apostle of the Great Consensus, a kind of elective monarch whose rare descents into the political arena seemed somehow shocking and out of character. He did not want to dirty his hands, nor did his admirers want him to, for it would have cheapened his political currency and destroyed the image of Ike the Father. This is why, for example, despite his undoubtedly sincere belief in the advancement of civil rights, and the fact that his administration secured the passage of the first civil rights bill since 1875, he refused either to approve or disapprove the Supreme Court's 1954 decision against segregated schools, on the grounds that comment "could tend to lower the dignity of government."

This conception of executive impartiality carried over into foreign affairs, where it led him to see the United States as an arbiter working selflessly to spread the rule of law and the triumph of justice throughout the world. If only other nations would follow America's inspiration there would be no problems, no strife, no oppression. "The difficulties facing the Free World in Cuba, Vietnam, Berlin and elsewhere," he says with an ingenuous simplicity, "*can* be handled with confidence and success if those who love freedom will work together in the knowledge that individual selfish interest must never prevail over the welfare of the total free community." It is all very inspirational, but it seems never to have occurred to him that men may honestly disagree not only about the means of reaching an objective, but about the objective itself; that the American Dream may be somebody else's nightmare; and that U.S. foreign policy may not be quite so disinterested or self-evidently infallible as seems from the vantage point of Foggy Bottom.

His inability to recognize that there may be more than one kind of truth, or perhaps that there may be no truth at all, often led him to see the frustration of his desires as due to veniality, ignorance, or duplicity on the part of his adversaries. Recalcitrant foreign statesmen show "incomprehensible sensitivity" before the brilliance of his proposals; the failure to make any progress on disarmament or the reduction of East-West tensions is entirely the other side's fault, since "no one can justifiably charge the bleak record to any lack of striving on our part"; Kennedy's defeat of Nixon in 1960 "showed again how much elections can be controlled by sentiment and emotion . . . and the importance of successful appeals to large special interest groups," since otherwise "I cannot ascribe any rational cause for the outcome."

This refusal to conceive any opposition as rational, this penchant for always seeking the middle way, is the key to a career which has been truly breathtaking in its triumph of technique over matter. Eisenhower's great role as a wartime leader was never as a strategist, but as a staff officer: a reconciler, an organizer, a delegator of responsibilities. There is a great need for such men in any large organization—be it the army, government, or business—and Eisenhower reached the top in two of them, just as he probably would have been a captain of industry, like his Cabinet officials and golf cronies, if he had had the time. But the qualities that made Eisenhower a great Chief of Staff were the very qualities that failed him as President, for politics is not only logistics and administration, it is passion and commitment and conviction. It is all those things that stand in the way of a good administrator and which are absolutely indispensable to a great political leader.

For all his admirable qualities, and there are many, he was not a great President, nor even a particularly good one. The reasons can be glimpsed even through the curiously opaque and impersonal pages of these memoirs; for they reveal a mind which sought consensus at the expense of conviction, which avoided rather than harnessed responsibility, which delegated so much power that it had little to exert itself, which relied so heavily on the expertise of others that it lacked any apparent direction of its own, which drifted with the tide of events rather than seeking to master it, and which looked upon political leadership as a burden to be borne rather than as an opportunity to be used.

Because his conception of the Presidency was such a circumscribed one, because he often seemed to be quite unaware of the conflict of wills and the struggle for political power that was going on around him, this book is neither "one of the most important memoirs of our time," as the publishers claim, nor even the more modest "personal account" that the author no doubt intended. Although he has furnished a meticulous rendering of the major events of his administration, Eisenhower still remains a hazy and strangely impersonal figure. The portrait that emerges from these pages is blurred, and even the events abstract. What we miss are the qualities in which he presumably excels: a simple honesty, an open di-

rectness, an ungrudging willingness—now that the cares
of office are far behind and there is no reason to dissimu-
late—to go beyond sweet reasonableness and speak can-
didly. This Eisenhower has not done, and without it his
memoirs are little more than a ponderous office diary,
dutifully listing the visits of the Boy Scouts and the musi-
cales of Fred Waring alongside the crises on the Berlin
Autobahn and the downing of Francis Gary Powers's
U-2.

There are few revelations, but they are nonetheless
intriguing, the most celebrated being the "spasm" Eisenhower suffered in November 1957, which prevented him
from expressing himself clearly and which for a time led
him to consider resigning the Presidency. We also learn
that Dulles knew the Israelis were mobilizing six weeks
before the assault on Sinai, and that he was expecting
the British to use force against Nasser as early as July
31—three months before the landings at Suez. His indignation came not from surprise, but from being disobeyed.
With regard to Quemoy and Matsu, Eisenhower reveals
that he was ready to use atomic bombs against Chinese
airfields if the communists invaded the off-shore islands
—this despite the fact that his Secretary of Defense,
Neil McElroy, had told him that Chiang's refusal to reduce his excessive troop forces on the islands was "a
reflection of his hope of promoting a fight between the
United States and the Chinese communists." On the subject of Hungary, Ike wonders whether he might have
intervened if it had been accessible by sea or through
allied territory, but decides that his administration did
"everything possible to condemn the aggression." This
may be the case, but it is hardly the point, since his
Secretary of State had been preaching "liberation" and
"roll-back" for a decade. Without a sigh or even the blowing of taps, those windy campaign promises were hastily
shuffled into a pauper's grave.

In addition to the diplomacy of empty rhetoric, there
was also the special Eisenhower brand of diplomacy by
indirection, an art which reached its apogee in 1959,
when Khrushchev was invited to America *by error* be-

cause the State Department misinterpreted the President's conditions for a summit meeting. Without the loyal Dulles around to protect and interpret for him, Eisenhower was forced to make himself understood by less-than-clairvoyant functionaries and to take over responsibility for foreign policy. The effort was not always crowned with success. "I realized," he writes of the Khrushchev invitation, "that the cause of the difficulty lay more in my own failure to make myself unmistakably clear than in the failure of others to understand me. After all, here were some of the most capable men I knew in their field, and apparently all had failed to comprehend the idea in my mind. It was now up to me to make the best I could of the situation."

All things considered, Eisenhower did not do too badly without Dulles, and the last two years of his administration—the U-2 fiasco apart—were marked by a consistent, although often frustrating, search for an accommodation with the Russians that was never one of Dulles's strong points. Yet Eisenhower sorely missed his Secretary of State, and his deep loyalty and affection for Dulles, his sense of bereavement on his death, is one of the few touching and truly personal elements in the memoirs.

Eisenhower's view of the world was less Manichean than that of Dulles, but it was also a good deal more simple-minded. He quite failed to realize, for example, that as nominal leader of the Free World his visits to Spain and Portugal might have enormous political repercussions among America's European allies and the Latin Americans. "Whatever the reasons for the Spanish revolution," he commented on his trip to Madrid, "it was clear that Franco had proved himself a strong and enduring leader." Which nobody can deny. This simplistic view of the cold war led him to misinterpret the significance of the anti-colonialism that inspires most of the new states, and to confuse nationalism with communism.

In Cuba, for example, with little to go on but his own hunches, he had by April 1959, "become highly suspicious that Castro was a communist"—although Allen Dulles of the CIA had just reported that "Castro's government is *not* communist-dominated"—and refused to see the Cuban leader on his visit to the United States. By July 1960, even though the administration was still unable to demonstrate that Cuba had become a communist base, Eisenhower slashed the Cuban sugar quota, announcing that this "amounts to economic sanctions against Cuba. Now we must look ahead to other moves—economic, diplomatic, strategic." Did Castro jump into Russian arms, or was he pushed by U.S. economic sanctions? The issue is still in doubt, but the portrait that emerges of Eisenhower is one of a man too often given to unexamined assumptions and facile generalizations.

Just as he "knew" Castro was a communist before anyone else did, including Fidel himself, so he decided that Nasser was also a communist, and tried to build up the ineffectual Ibn Saud of Arabia as a counter-weight because "he at least professed anti-communism." It could have been the slogan for the Eisenhower administration's whole foreign policy, for its alphabet soup regional pacts, and particularly for the fatuous Middle East doctrine which provided the cover for the farcical 1958 landing in Lebanon where 14,000 Marines charged up the beaches of Beirut to be greeted by ice-cream vendors and girls in bikinis. Eisenhower never understood then, nor did he apparently even later, that clever nationalists can use both communist and Western aid for their own purposes without having the slightest allegiance or sympathy for either bloc. Like Dulles, Acheson, and all the Good Soldiers who manned the barricades in 1948 and were never able to adjust to the new realities of a changing world, he is today in the mid-sixties still proclaiming the slogans of the late forties. "The truly virulent problems in international affairs," he writes with a staggering disregard for everything that has happened since the Sino-Soviet split and the rise to political consciousness of the have-nots in the southern hemisphere, "spring from the persistent, continuing struggle between freedom and communism." Would that our problems were that simple.

For all his shortcomings, Eisenhower was a man deeply dedicated to the search for peace, and his title, *Waging*

Peace, is a deliberately chosen one. The misfortune, and it is ours even more than his, is that he was never able to translate his yearning for a better world into specific foreign policy objectives designed to bring about his ambitions. He failed not only because the Russians were uncooperative, but also because he never had anything that could be seriously described as a foreign policy. What he, and for that matter his successors, had was a set of Band-Aids for dealing with crises, and a set of vague formulas looking forward to the brotherhood of man. "Our purposes abroad," he writes in describing American foreign policy, "have been the establishment of universal peace with justice, free choice for all peoples, rising levels of human well-being, and the development and maintenance of frank, friendly and mutually helpful contacts with all nations willing to work for parallel objectives." It is an inspirational goal for the long run, but, as Keynes once remarked, in the long run we will all be dead.

One cannot read these memoirs without being once again convinced that Eisenhower was a man of enormous good will, of noble instincts, and sincere compassion. There is a time in the life of nations when such virtues are essential, and such a time was 1952, when the United States lay paralyzed in the grip of McCarthyism and the Korean war. With a steady hand and a mind that eschewed partisanship, he helped restore the nation to sanity. Four years of economic stagnation at home and political foundering abroad were not too high a price to pay for such national therapy. But what was relaxation for four years, turned into paralysis when stretched out into eight. Eisenhower indeed had a *Mandate for Change,* and we have little reason to regret that he fulfilled it, but he was probably right in his suspicion, expressed in this second volume of memoirs, that he should have "withdrawn from politics in 1956 and thus allowed Dick Nixon, or some other nominee, to carry on the campaign of that year as the Republican standard bearer."

By coming when the people needed a reconciler and by healing the wounds of a deeply-divided nation, Eisenhower will always have the gratitude and affection of

Americans; but by staying too long and turning a convalescence into an infirmity, by coddling us in our fears and telling us there were no harsh realities he put the nation into traction and diluted his own considerable achievement.

Brinksmanship

High-level political gossip is the lowest of the fine arts and the highest of the base ones. *Facing the Brink,* by Edward Weintal and Charles Bartlett, manages to combine the highest qualities of gossip with a sense of history and even a gift for analysis. Beneath its lightweight exterior, it helps put our cold war diplomacy into a new—and disconcerting—perspective.

The best parts of this book are the capsule accounts of the crises in Lebanon, Cyprus, Yemen, Cuba, and Vietnam. As for Lebanon, we learn that the National Security Council—ostensibly the President's chief foreign policy advisory body—never even discussed the crisis that led to our 1958 troop landings. Further, it is revealed that only at the last minute did the U.S. Army division decide to leave its atomic weapons behind when it launched an assault on the beaches of Beirut—where it encountered only token resistance from ice-cream vendors and girls in bikinis.

Among our other Arab imbroglios was the anti-royalist rebellion in Yemen, where we simultaneously tried to appease Nasser by recognizing the rebels, and then to placate the Saudis by offering them U.S. Air Force planes to shoot down Egyptian aircraft—an action by which, as the authors observe, "The U.S. could have stumbled into a shooting war with Nasser for the sake of Yemen, a desolate, disease-ridden, primitive tribal enclave." We escaped that one, but the description of the issue at stake would almost fit Vietnam.

Another eastern Mediterranean crisis into which the U.S. stuck its nose was the civil war in Cyprus. Despite the fact that the Greek and Turkish communities had been feuding for more than a decade and that the 1959 independence accords could not possibly hold up, the U.S. had no solution for ending the strife. This, however, did not deter Washington from involving itself and demanding a settlement. Yet when the Greek prime minister asked our emissary George Ball what kind of accord the U.S. wanted, "the Undersecretary fell back again on his contention that the U.S. had no specific plan in mind." Fortunately, the whole problem was fobbed off on the United Nations before there was a call to land the Marines. A fascinating sidelight to this episode is the revelation that President Johnson threatened Turkey with a withdrawal of U.S. support against the Russians if they persisted in their plan to invade Cyprus. So much for NATO's common front against the Red Peril.

The relations of the U.S. with its NATO allies form some of the most interesting parts of the book. There is, for example, an exceedingly useful account of the State Department's efforts to sabotage Gaullist diplomacy in Europe—an effort highlighted by the December, 1962, meeting at Nassau when Kennedy promised Polaris missiles to Harold Macmillan ("We did not even know the meaning of the words we were using at Nassau," Kennedy later confided), and which inspired de Gaulle to veto Britain's bid for membership in the Common Market. After that, anti-Gaullism became the hallmark of U.S. policy toward Europe, and George Ball its high priest. So virulent was this policy—until it was reversed by President Johnson—that the State Department blatantly tried to break up the Franco-German accord and to isolate Paris by making Bonn our favorite European ally. This, too, backfired with the collapse of the Erhard government and the refusal of the Europeans to see the world through Washington's eyes.

In certain circles anti-Gaullism became a kind of obsession. Our ambassador to Paris, for example, decided it was beneath his dignity to try to understand French policy. "Mr. Bohlen," the authors quote an aide as declaring, "not only does not know what de Gaulle thinks but is not even interested." It is to President Johnson's credit that he called a halt to this irresponsible pettiness and refused to engage in anti-Gaullist diatribes. "I keep mum," he told a group of French journalists in 1966. "I told everybody in the government to be polite to General de Gaulle. Just tip your hat and say, 'thank you, General.' " The President obviously does not have any answers for what ails Europe, but he is not trying to push the MLF down NATO's throat, nor the Common Market down Britain's. He knows the limits of European independence— despite the antagonisms of General de Gaulle—and toward Europe he has behaved with statesmanship, restraint, and an enlightened conception of the national interest. One can regret only that he has not done so in Vietnam.

Although the authors claim there are no heroes or villains in their book, their hearts were obviously won by the Kennedy style. Where Johnson is described as "afraid of the unknown," a politician heavily dependent on "his talent for twisting arms," and an impetuous man with "the capacity to unleash forces which could not be recaptured by subsequent remorse," "Kennedy was different." He radiated "seemingly limitless opportunities to exert his capacities in every direction, to achieve noble innovations and reforms and, above all, to take meaningful steps toward world order." During his brief tenure, "Kennedy's buoyant personality brightened the image of the United States," and he was "well on his way to becoming a world leader." "Johnson," on the other hand, "has not taken his first major stride in that direction."

Like Kennedy himself, the authors tend to confuse image with action, and to admire style at the expense of substance. Yet as they themselves reluctantly admit, "there is no evidence that a flow of new concepts and new initiatives was turned loose by liberating the foreign policy machinery from the Eisenhower committee system." The sad truth is that Kennedy's diplomacy was a succession of gimmicks in search of an image. Grandiose plans were announced, such as the multilateral nuclear force, the Alliance for Progress, or the Grand Design for a unified Europe—and then forgotten, or allowed to stagnate long after they proved unworkable.

Kennedy stumbled into the Bay of Pigs—a folly that an astute politician like Lyndon Johnson would never have committed—and then desperately sought to repair his image by exaggerating the Berlin crisis of 1961 (including the deliberately-manipulated civil defense scare) and by increasing the U.S. involvement in Vietnam. "Had he not suffered reverses in the Bay of Pigs and Laos," we are told, "it may well be that President Kennedy would have thought twice before expanding the Viet Nam commitment early in 1962 from 700 to 11,000 advisers. Had he followed a long-range policy plan rather than an understandable concern for his image as a result of the Bay of Pigs fiasco, he might have reduced rather than increased the Vietnam commitment." What kind of comfort is that?

The Bay of Pigs was a fiasco, but Vietnam was a national disaster, and Kennedy cannot be absolved of blame for it. Perhaps he never would have involved us so deeply, as the authors suggest. But it it equally possible that image problems would have involved him ever deeper in the morass of Saigon. It was Kennedy, after all, who decided that the U.S. government could no longer tolerate Ngo Dinh Diem as ruler of South Vietnam, and who in 1963, gave the green light for his overthrow. Yet on the eve of the generals' coup, Diem capitulated. "Tell me what you want me to do and I will do it," he told Henry Cabot Lodge. "If you don't know what you want me to do, cable Washington for instructions and then tell me. I will do whatever you want me to do." But Washington did not know what it wanted Diem to do. The next day he was murdered by his own generals so that the war against the Viet Cong could be waged more effectively. The Viet Cong was then being contained by the South Vietnamese army and 15,000 American advisers. Today only 400,000 American soldiers are preventing the Saigon regime from collapse.

The authors excuse Kennedy a lot and Johnson very little. Pages are devoted to the gaffes of LBJ, and some of these are extremely funny. Yet somehow none are quite so devastating as the explanation of why Kennedy turned down David Bruce for Secretary of State. "A member of the President's family," the authors observe deadpan, "reported that Bruce and his wife, Evangeline, staunch Stevenson fans, had broken into tears when Kennedy was nominated and later elected. Kennedy removed Bruce from his list." Compared to this kind of pettiness, Johnson seems magnanimous. Or at least a paragon of self-restraint, since we are told that Kennedy—unlike Eisenhower and Dulles—never consulted Johnson on matters of foreign policy, "I feel bad about Lyndon because he is miserable in that job," he is quoted as saying. "But when a problem blows up, I never think of calling him because he hasn't read the cables."

Like good sensitive liberals, Weintal and Bartlett are offended by the crudeness of the Johnson style, and look back with nostalgia upon the New Frontier, when Pablo Casals played in the White House and intellectuals found a "tolerant, yeasty climate" in which their ideas could ferment. Yet the qualities of leadership which they admire, as a much-needed antidote to the hazards of accidental diplomacy, were rather less evident in Kennedy than in Johnson. They praise the luminaries of the Administration's foreign policy team (composed almost entirely of Kennedy appointees), and explain its failures by commenting: "If there is one reason why a team of such brilliance and ability has not functioned more effectively, it is lack of leadership. President Johnson, primarily attuned to the domestic scene, has not yet shown his willingness to exercise it." Did Kennedy? The authors are mute on this point.

Aside from their myopia about the shortcomings of

Kennedy as a diplomat, Weintal and Bartlett have written an eye-opening account of crisis diplomacy as seen through the keyhole. This book deserves attention for showing how the United States has become involved—either accidentally, or to overcome unfavorable "images," or from a mistaken concept of the national interest—in crises it could not resolve and which affected its real interests only dimly. Surely a nation embarked upon self-declared global mission should have some better idea of what it is up to.

Who Were the Kennedys?

The king and crown prince are dead, and the heir apparent only slowly emerging from disgrace. But the legend lives on, undiminished by promises unfulfilled, mistakes better forgotten, and doubts stilled by the cold hand of death. It is a tale with all the elements of a feudal chronicle—murders, usurped crowns, vendettas—and no shortage of troubadors to tell it. Theodore Sorensen, alter ego of John F. Kennedy and more recently a spurned aspirant to the public trust, now tells us, in words that will come as no surprise, that he views the Kennedy legacy "as the most important body of ideas in our time . . . a unique and priceless set of concepts . . . that endures and gives us hope."

We need not doubt Sorensen's sincerity—we all take hope where we can find it—to wonder what so great a faith rests upon. Whatever the Kennedy legacy may be, and we are told that it "can no more be summed up in a book than a Mozart concerto in a series of black notes," the Kennedy record was one of great expectations rather than inspiring accomplishments. But Sorensen has a weakness for the overexcited phrase, and his pseudo-Homeric prose ("let the word go forth . . . we shall pay any price, bear any burden . . . now the trumpet summons

us again . . . ask not what your country can do for you
. . .") both shaped and defined the posturing heroics of
the Kennedy era.

We can sympathize with Sorensen's difficulty in defining the exact nature of the legacy he extols, particularly
when we are told that "to love each other like brothers . . .
is the heart of the Kennedy legacy." Lest this hippie message seem sketchy, he also urges us to work hard, have
faith in man's ability to change our society, and not lose
hope. Not by accident is "hope" a recurring word, for if
ever there was a politics cf hope, it was that practiced by
the Kennedys. Our hope that they had a remedy for the
social ills they described so graphically, their hope that
we would be patient while they figured out what to do.
The legacy they left is the enduring faith that somehow
things would have been better were they still here.

Sorensen embellishes the Kennedy legacy in sticky,
though no doubt heartfelt, panegyrics ("there has never
been in American public life a family like the Kennedys"),
ladies' magazine commentary ("good taste and finesse
governed not only their selection of clothes . . ."), political
PR ("the . . . question asked everywhere was when the
Kennedys would return to the White House"), and resentment at the usurper ("Lyndon Johnson . . . wanted to
emulate their graceful wit and intellectual elegance").
The purpose of *The Kennedy Legacy* is to build a platform
for what Sorensen calls a "peaceful revolution for the
seventies."

The program, which appeared in time to publicize, but
not noticeably assist, his effort to fill Robert Kennedy's
old seat as senator from New York, is studded with such
homilies as "we must pre-empt the extraordinary before
the extremists seize it for their own . . . we must devise a
new strategy for living instead of fighting . . . the United
States must become the leading city of the world, not one
of its largest villages." It is not surprising that the voters
were not impressed by such summoning trumpets, for as
John Kenneth Galbraith has pointed out in his pamphlet,
Who Needs the Democrats? "evasion, however disguised

by rhetoric, moral purpose, or soaring phrase, comes over increasingly as crap."

As the brief reign of John F. Kennedy recedes into the historical past, leaving the Vietnam war as its permanent monument, and as Robert Kennedy's unending succession of agonizing reappraisals now seems little more than a footnote to the tribulations of Lyndon Johnson, it is sometimes hard to remember what the Kennedy legend is all about. But it does exist, as one is reminded in Arthur Schlesinger's description, in *A Thousand Days*, of JFK's inauguration when "the future everywhere seemed bright with hope . . . fresh winds were blowing. There was the excitement that comes from an injection of new men and new ideas." We now know that some of those fresh winds were blowing hot air, that a good many of those new ideas were tired clichés, that some of those new men wrought disaster, and that their excitement came from a lust for power. But all that came later. At the time the passing of power from Eisenhower to Kennedy seemed to presage, from the poem that Robert Frost started to read at the inauguration but was unable to finish, "the glory of a next Augustan age."

The old sage knew what he was talking about. The era did turn out to be Augustan, at least in its pretenses (". . . of a power leading from its strength and pride/ Of young ambition eager to be tried . . ."), but the glory was short-lived. It got tarnished somewhere around the Bay of Pigs and never recaptured its former glow. That fiasco was followed by the failure of summit diplomacy at Vienna, the manipulation of public anxiety over Berlin, a dramatic jump in the arms race, the unnecessary trip to the brink during the Cuban missile crisis, timidity on civil rights, legislative stalemate in Congress, and the decision to send the first American troops to Vietnam. Somehow everything went wrong, and increasingly the crusading knight gave way to the conventional politician who had no answers for us. John F. Kennedy's assassination came almost as a reprieve, forever enshrining him in history as the heroic leader he wanted to be, rather than as the politician buffeted by events he could not control.

By the time Robert Kennedy emerged from his grief over the murder of his brother and began maneuvering for the crown he believed was rightfully his, the imperial optimism of the early sixties had given way, under a succession of failures at home and abroad, to disillusionment and rebellion. While the first Kennedy sought to lead us to the lofty peaks in forming "a grand and global alliance . . . that can assure a more fruitful life for all mankind," the second Kennedy faced the less exhilarating but more demanding task of saving us from ourselves. Robert Kennedy stood somewhere between the new politics and the old, increasingly aware of the injustices of American society, yet never quite able to break loose from the traditional beliefs that formed his view of the world. In his radical rhetoric lay his strength with the young and the apostles of change; in his traditionalism was his appeal to the Democratic party machines. It was a powerful combination.

Far more passionate than his brother John, he was essentially a moralist who saw the world as divided between good and evil. He wept for the poor, touched the bloated bellies of starving children, and was outraged by injustice. He was equally emotional and single-minded in his hatred of those he believed to be evil. His obsessive persecution of James Hoffa was the other side of his compassionate plea for the grape pickers. Unlike his brother, he could believe in causes. Indeed, he needed them to satisfy some deep compulsion that could be glimpsed in those icy eyes. Alice Roosevelt Longworth, who has seen generations of politicians come and go, put her finger on the difference between the two Kennedys when she told Jean Stein: "I see Jack in older years as the nice little rosy-faced old Irishman with the clay pipe in his mouth, a rather nice broth of a boy. Not Bobby. Bobby could have been a revolutionary priest."

The complex bundle of emotions that was Robert Kennedy come tumbling out in the interviews taken by Jean Stein and assembled by George Plimpton under the title *American Journey*. These interviews, made mostly with the great, the near-great, and the hangers-on who traveled on the train bearing Robert Kennedy's body from New York to Washington, reveal Kennedy as the symbol to which people responded in different ways—some as a roller coaster to power, others as a politician who would end the war and reform the society, and to millions as a charismatic leader who could somehow understand their anxiety.

The last journey of Robert Kennedy marked more than the death of a leader; it was the end of an era of American politics—one in which it was possible to believe that good government could come from good style, that society could be changed if only the right rhetoric could be found, that a single man could correct everything that was wrong, that things would be all right if we just loved one another. It was not that the Kennedys said it would be easy. They often evoked sacrifice, hard work, and endurance. Rather it was that they nurtured our fantasies. The last fantasy was shattered with the murder of Robert Kennedy. The remarks of those who rode his funeral train —speechwriters, politicians, reporters, advisers, friends, celebrity-hounds—reflected the confusion of people who no longer were sure what they believed in or what the future held. "I'm very narrowly programmed," Adam Walinsky said to someone on the train. "I can do research and write speeches for a candidate named Robert Kennedy. What can I do now?" For Stewart Alsop the long trip through the cities and the scarred landscapes

> . . . had a slightly phantasmagoric, unreal quality to it. A little like that play, *Outward Bound*. All those gay creatures going off into a kind of nothingness. The train went on and on, and you saw those enormous crowds . . . particularly near the big cities and particularly the blacks. You got a curious feeling of disembodiment, as if the experience were unreal. . . . Especially after those people were killed by the train . . . and as the train got later and later. . . .

If the scene inside was a cross between an Irish wake and a Jewish shiva, the scene outside was like the passing of some feudal chief before his assembled subjects. The other America, the people without glamor—housewives in hair curlers, nuns in sunglasses, school-children, blue-shirted workers—came to the tracks for the last journey of Robert Kennedy. "I seen people running all over!" an electrician exclaimed. "They tried to touch the train as it went by." "The tracks were lined with more people than I've ever seen," another trainman said. "Everyone had a rose or a banner. They were throwing roses at the train." Some of them carried signs saying: "Who Will Be The Next One?" and "We Have Lost Our Last Hope," and simply, "The Gebharts Are Sad." Perhaps these people sensed that they were saying good-bye to more than Robert Kennedy.

The question remains why the murder of the two Kennedys brought forth such an outpouring of public grief. Why did so many who did not particularly admire them in life feel an irreparable sense of loss at their death? Why were the Gebharts sad? Why did a revolutionary like Tom Hayden come to St. Patrick's Cathedral to mourn over the casket of Robert Kennedy? Why, in the homes and shop fronts of every black ghetto do you see photos of Martin Luther King flanked by the Kennedy brothers as a Holy Trinity of martyred saints?

The reason of not simply the manner of their death, for it is inconceivable that the assassination of such conventional politicians as Johnson or Nixon could have evoked a similar response. It is not because they were men who accomplished great deeds, for John F. Kennedy did not live long enough to show that he was more than a mediocre President, while his brother's fame rested almost entirely on the promise that others saw in him. Nor does the reason lie entirely in the Kennedy glamor, although that was surely an important part of it. The Kennedys, for all their overblown rhetoric and cautious performance, conveyed the impression of being something more than power-seeking politicians. For John F. Kennedy that extra element was a true sense of style; for his brother it was compassion and toughness.

To be sure, the Kennedys were glamorous. For many people they became a kind of royal family, and thus satisfied a very real need. Unsurprisingly, many resented this. Resentment came not only from the rejects of society, the pathetic flotsam of the American Dream like Lee Oswald and Sirhan Sirhan, or from business executives who felt they were no longer being accorded the respect they assumed their position merited. It also came from many intellectuals who resented the Kennedys primarily because they were beautiful, rich, and clever. They particularly resented other intellectuals who served in the Kennedy court and thereby basked in reflected glamor. Their resentment, and perhaps even their envy, of the Kennedy court led them to condemn the Kennedys for somehow forcing us to endow them with qualities they did not have. Thus one critic has charged: "What the Kennedy administration wanted, what it sought to do, was to impose an image of itself on American society and American history; an image of itself as the rightful, by virtue of intrinsic superiority, American ruling class."

While there are plenty of political reasons to criticize the Kennedys, such psychological ones seem unconvincing. To hold the Kennedys responsible for what others seek in them is rather like the ancients who in their sorrow struck the bearers of bad news. The Kennedys did not have to *impose* an image of themselves as intrinsically superior, and thus deserving of homage as rulers. We saw them as stylistically superior because in some ways they were. They had money, glamor, and beauty. Which is to say that they were like movie stars. But they also could speak intelligently and sought out the company (or more precisely the willing services) of intellectuals. Naturally there were many who were flattered by this treatment and became acolytes of the Kennedys, just as there were others who found it threatening. But it was not the Kennedys who held themselves up as natural rulers so much as a public that wanted leaders worthy of admiration (and then condemned them, as in the case of Jacqueline Kennedy, when they did something to shatter its fantasies). Kennedyism, like the Beatle-mania of the sixties that was its cultural counterpart, was not a plot foisted on the public, but an audience response—a response that could never have occurred, whatever the public relations effort involved, had there not been a need for it.

While the Kennedys did not impose an image of themselves as a ruling class, Robert Kennedy often behaved as though he had a hereditary right to the Presidency. He scarcely bothered to conceal his contempt for Lyndon Johnson and treated him as a usurper. The Kennedys had their own government-in-exile, with Bobby as the heir presumptive, Jacqueline as the queen, and the old Kennedy staff as courtiers-in-waiting. Kenneth O'Donnell, who served as John F. Kennedy's chief of staff and then stayed on briefly with Johnson, describes, in an excerpt in *Life* from his forthcoming book, an incident in the spring of 1964 that dramatizes Johnson's isolation:

> Everyone was swarming around Jackie Kennedy, who was radiant and happy to be making her first social appearance since her husband's funeral, and nobody was paying much attention to Johnson. I stood in a corner with the President, having a drink with him, and he said to me after a while, "I guess they're all going someplace to a dinner. Are you going with them?" I said I had to go back to work. He said to me, "Would you mind coming back to the White House and having another drink?" He was silent in the car while we were riding to the White House and then he said, "Despite what they think, I am still the President of the United States. But I didn't want it this way."

The Kennedy legend haunted Johnson throughout his Presidency, fed his insecurities, forced him to doubt the loyalty of his subordinates, divided the party of which he was supposed to be leader, and ultimately helped to drive him from office.

Robert Kennedy never forgave Johnson for refusing to name him as his Vice President in 1964, and when he decided to run for senator from New York, it was clear that the Presidency was his ultimate goal. A politician by instinct, he once said that the political life was the only one worth living. That was the way he played it. He would adopt a cause if it seemed useful in attaining his political end, and he did not hesitate to stoop to conquer. He would justify dubious means, such as the play for the white backlash vote in the 1968 California primary, by the righteousness of his cause. This gave him a deserved reputation for ruthlessness. A good many instances of this quality are recounted in *American Journey*. For example, when he was Attorney General in 1961, he asked Ralph Abernathy to call off the Freedom Rides in order not to embarrass his brother, then meeting with Khrushchev in Vienna.

After JFK's assassination he began to evolve a politics of his own that led him away from the conservatism of his youth, when he had worked for Senator Joseph Mc-Carthy, toward something that has been called radicalism. But it was an inconsistent and basically emotional radicalism. It consisted mostly of such "peaceful revolutions" as the Alliance for Progress and the rebuilding of the Bedford-Stuyvesant ghetto. An early champion of counter-insurgency, he looked on General Maxwell Taylor, according to Sorensen, as his "special friend and hero," and he continued to support the Vietnam war long after other senators had come out against it.

Always the politician, he was cautious where he felt public opinion was not behind him. The meeting he arranged in 1963 with a mostly moderate group of black entertainers and intellectuals ended in anger and mutual incomprehension. "Bobby didn't understand what we were trying to tell him," James Baldwin explained. "For him it was a political matter . . . of finding out what's wrong in the twelfth ward and correcting it." Later, however, as Kenneth Clark observed, he gained a greater understanding of the sources of black rage and was able to deal with black activists and young people more effectively than any other white politician. So successful was he in establishing his empathy for black aspirations that today his memory is venerated in the ghettos.

There was never any doubt of his tenacity and physical courage, for he drove himself compulsively to feats of endurance, such as his fifty-mile hike, his ascent of Mt. Kennedy, and his grueling sailing trips, all of which are described in *American Journey* by the participants. He never stopped talking about moral courage, declaring that "only those who dare to fail greatly can ever achieve greatly." Yet even after he finally decided the Vietnam war was a "policy founded on illusion" he refused to challenge Lyndon Johnson for the nomination until Eugene McCarthy had shown it could be done. When he had to back up his noble words with courageous action, and when his action might have made a crucial difference, he remained silent. No wonder that so many who had once urged him to run against Johnson turned away in contempt. The charge of opportunism haunted him to the end. If his emotions were pure, his politics were calculating. His tragedy was that no one could be sure which was the real Bobby.

The enigma of Robert Kennedy ended on a greasy kitchen floor of a Los Angeles hotel, a victim of one of the rootless rejects of that most rootless of all American cities. Today he is mourned as the one figure in American public life who might have been able to bring us together, who could have reconciled rich and poor, black and white, hardhat and hippie. Certainly he was able to stir emotions untouched by any other contemporary politician. He spoke to people who had little in common other than a belief that he cared about them, or that he was different from other politicians. But was the strange conglomeration that formed the Kennedy constituency—white steelworkers and black welfare mothers, fruit pickers and suburban housewives, student activists and Irish cops— an alliance that could have held together? Was it one that could have exercised power, even if Kennedy had been elected? "I never doubted that if he could have gotten the nomination," Tom Wicker said,

> Robert Kennedy would have wished for the support of all the more traditional—even reactionary—elements in the Democratic party. At one and the same time he wanted to have Mayor Daley's support and the support of the college students. The two are incompatible in the long run . . . it isn't a feasible alliance, and it isn't an alliance that's going to hold political power.

Robert Kennedy may have been the people's choice, but in the end he would have disillusioned a good many of those people, for he would have had to choose between incompatible alternatives. His heart cried for the poor and oppressed. But he was a sincere apostle of law-and-order, and the factory workers were no doubt right in assuming that he would not let black militants or white radicals get out of hand. He hated the Vietnam war, yet neither could he accept a unilateral American withdrawal, for he remained a convinced globalist. Right until the end he was talking about America's right to the "moral leadership of this planet," hardly the language of retrenchment. As Tom Hayden commented, Kennedy

> . . . seemed to say that the United States had a legitimate role in Vietnam and that if it were operated correctly, it could have introduced land reform and established a civilian government and brought the people out of their support for communism. He was perpetuating a myth of the cold war. He wouldn't break with that.

Robert Kennedy was never an anti-politician like Eugene McCarthy, who might have wiped the slate clean by getting rid of the old advisers and the old assumptions. As Attorney General, Kennedy was unable even to control J. Edgar Hoover, let alone get rid of him. He was a politician of the old school, with long-standing ties and binding IOUs to the party machines and the pros who ran them.

Perhaps Robert Kennedy would have surmounted everything in his background—his political caution, his ruthlessness, his moral certitude, his compulsion to prove himself, his cold war anti-communism, his opportunism —and emerged as the Messiah who would have led us to the promised land, or at least helped raise us from the muck. Perhaps, but we shall never know. All we know is that Robert Kennedy, like his brother, used a language to which millions could respond. The Kennedys seemed to offer something better than we had, and today we venerate their memory because we know that there has to be something better.

The Kennedy legacy, however, is not a plan of action, and even less is it a "peaceful revolution for the seventies," for the Kennedys were about as revolutionary as Martha Mitchell. Rather it is a romantic nostalgia for a world that might have been different had different people been around and done different things. Not only different things from what others did, but different things from what they themselves did while in office. The Kennedy presidency, whatever its promise of future deeds, was not a record of high accomplishment. In domestic policy John F. Kennedy was a good deal more conservative than Lyndon Johnson. The tragedy of the assassination has made us forget, as I. F. Stone has pointed out, that "Kennedy, when the tinsel was stripped away, was a conventional leader, no more than an enlightened conservative, cautious as an old man for all his youth, with a basic distrust of the people and an astringent view of the evangelical as a tool of leadership."

Like the Wall Street financiers whose advice he sought and whom he beseeched to join his Cabinet, John F. Kennedy was firmly committed to the imperial foreign policy evolved by Acheson and Dulles in the late forties and early fifties. He drew his advisers from the great universities, foundations, and corporate offices and gave them powerful positions in the national security bureaucracy. There they provided him with scenarios for nuclear warfare, "revolutionary development" programs to combat communism, and green beret shock troops to subdue peasant revolutionaries. These advisers considered themselves to be liberals, which indeed they were, as we use that word in the United States. They believed that world peace rested on an ideological balance of power between communists and anti-communists, that economic development would bring political democracy to feudal societies, and that the preservation of an informal empire of client states and dependencies was a vital principle of American foreign policy.

Scarred by the Depression and Munich, honed on the cold war, and eager to demonstrate their "pragmatism," they flocked to Washington to answer the summoning trumpet of the New Frontier. Whether they were Republicans or Democrats, lawyers or professors, they shared one quality: they were fascinated by power. Determined to be tough-minded, they had little interest in showing a "decent respect for the opinions of mankind" which a British foreign secretary had the temerity to seek of them during the bombing of North Vietnam. They shared the opinion of John J. McCloy, uncrowned head of the foreign policy establisment, who in the late summer of 1961 told Kennedy to resume nuclear testing in the atmosphere without worrying about its political effects abroad. "World opinion?" Schlesinger quotes McCloy as saying. "I don't believe in world opinion. The only thing that matters is power."

For the cold war liberals power was the fatal temptation. Equating revolution with communism, they were inherently counter-revolutionary because they feared that changes in the status quo would alter the world power balance. They did not shrink from armed intervention, but they recognized that the old doctrine of massive retaliation had become too dangerous. Instead they evolved a strategy of "flexible response" that was based upon a huge increase in conventional and nuclear arms. This was the foundation for the "2½ wars" theory which required the creation of a military machine that would make it possible simultaneously to conduct not only a major war on two fronts but also a counter-insurgency operation. While such a jump in the arms race was not necessary to contain the Russians—as some of those who planned it now admit—it made possible military interventions such as the one Kennedy inaugurated in Vietnam.

They were eager architects of "nation-building," which they sought to achieve by a combination of foreign aid and the green berets. There was nothing modest in their imperial pretensions, for they believed, as Louis Heren, Washington correspondent of *The Times* of London, has observed, "that Americans could engineer the world and reshape the lives of other peoples to ensure an American peace." Heren's absorbing study of the Johnson years, *No Hail, No Farewell*, shows how the cold war liberals took us into Vietnam and fed LBJ's illusion (which, like his ego, didn't need much feeding) that world peace hinged on which set of authoritarians ran South Vietnam.

Vietnam was a liberal's war. Not a general's war, as professional radicals would like to believe. Not the bureaucracy's war, as Galbraith concludes. Not entirely Kennedy's war, as Heren sometimes implies, nor LBJ's war, as Sorensen would have it. It was a war conceived, promoted, and directed by intellectuals fascinated with power and eager to prove their toughness and resolve. These liberal intellectuals served Kennedy, as they later served Johnson, with single-minded passion, often despite objections from the military. It was no less than General MacArthur, O'Donnell informs us, who told Kennedy to avoid a military buildup in Vietnam, that the domino theory was ridiculous, and that domestic problems should have first priority. Kennedy was reportedly "stunned" by this advice, which was so contrary to that given him by advisers eager to try their counter-insurgency shock troops against the Viet Cong.

But Kennedy was not stunned enough to take Mac-Arthur's advice. He sent American troops to Vietnam and embraced the theories of his hawkish advisers because they corresponded to his own ideas of toughness. It was he who boned up on the manuals of Mao and Che, then ordered the expansion of the Special Forces, and, over the army's objection, reinstated the green beret as the symbol of the elite counter-guerrilla units. Instead of reducing Eisenhower's small aid program to Vietnam, he increased it, and behaved as though the preservation of the Saigon regime were essential to American survival. As early as December 1961, he wrote Diem that the United States "would view any renewal of the aggression in violation of the [Geneva] agreements with grave concern and as seriously threatening international peace and security." Before his assassination (which, ironically, occurred only a few weeks after Diem's) he ordered some 15,000 American "advisers" to Vietnam and prepared the ground for an even larger U.S. intervention by approving plans for the construction of new airfields, ports, and roads to supply a large expeditionary force. U.S. policy was already established when McNamara, a few months after Kennedy's death, declared:

> The survival of an independent government in South Vietnam is so important to the security of all Southeast Asia and to the free world that I can conceive of no alternative other than to take all the necessary measures within our capability to prevent a communist victory.

Sorensen, O'Donnell, and others have argued that JFK would have done better than LBJ in Vietnam. But Heren thinks not, and the record offers little proof. Despite his much quoted statement that it was South Vietnam's war to win, he never gave any indication that he would allow Saigon to lose, and rejected opportunities to withdraw. Instead he committed American forces and evoked American prestige. Both the hawks in his administration and his own instincts as a politician led him to seek victory in Vietnam. Although dedicated to coexistence with the Russians, Kennedy was a romantic imperialist who believed in the old Dulles-Acheson rhetoric of a world split between two incompatible forces. As anointed head of the free world he was determined to prove his mettle to Khrushchev, for the Soviet leader had gained a bad impression of him at Vienna and felt, according to George Kennan, that he was a "tongue-tied young man, not forceful, with no ideas of his own." As Kennedy returned from his meeting with Khrushchev in June 1961, "what worried him," Arthur Schlesinger has written,

> was that Khrushchev might interpret his reluctance to wage nuclear war as a symptom of American loss of nerve. Some day, he said, the time might come when he would have to run the supreme risk to convince Khrushchev that conciliation did not mean humiliation. "If Khrushchev wants to rub my nose in the dirt," he told James Wechsler, "it's all over."

To show Khrushchev that he had to be taken seriously, despite the fiasco of the Bay of Pigs, Kennedy mobilized the reserves in response to the Berlin ultimatum, sent

American troops to Vietnam, and stepped up the arms
race with a dramatic and wholly unjustified increase in
Minuteman missiles and Polaris submarines. Within a
year he was to take the world to the brink of nuclear war
by demanding a Russian capitulation in Cuba, even
though Khrushchev had agreed to accept an exchange for
the obsolete U.S. missiles in Turkey. That eyeball-to-eye-
ball showdown was unnecessary, but Kennedy needed a
victory which was particularly helpful, as Sorensen has
implied in his biography, on the eve of the 1962 Congressional elections. From the euphoria of that victory over
the Kremlin came the decision to teach the communists
another lesson: that "wars of national liberation" could
not be won.

When Lyndon Johnson became President on that fateful day in Dallas he inherited a commitment which he in
turn expanded into a full-scale war. Like Kennedy he believed the old rhetoric about the struggle between freedom
and communism, and like Kennedy he was surrounded by
advisers who favored confrontation. In fact the Vietnam
hawks around Johnson were the same liberal advisers
appointed by Kennedy: Rusk, McNamara, Bundy, Rostow,
Taylor. Years later, when Robert Kennedy came out
against the war and criticized the State Department,
Johnson shot back, "It's *your* State Department!"—which
indeed it was.

Not all of the Kennedy people stayed on. Sorensen left
shortly after the assassination because, in his words, he
found it "hard to walk into the Oval office and find another
man in the President's chair." Later on Roger Hilsman,
James Thomson, George Ball, and a few others followed
because they disagreed with Johnson about the war and
felt it was getting out of hand. But most stayed on, loyally,
like Arthur Goldberg, performing whatever odious tasks
LBJ assigned them, or, like Robert McNamara, hanging
around and talking out of both sides of their mouths until
they were politely kicked out.

Not a single high official resigned in public protest
against the war as a matter of conscience. They remained
loyal to the team, even though they later reversed their

own positions and denounced the war with the same outraged fervor they had earlier used to defend and prosecute
it. But then nothing fails like failure. One of the few
comical elements of the war was watching the green
beret liberals scramble to dissociate themselves from decisions they made while in the administration. What was
politically sound and morally right under Kennedy and,
for some, under Johnson suddenly became, for them,
criminal under Nixon.

The cold war liberals had a formula for every problem
—the polyglot MLF nuclear fleet to resuscitate NATO, the
Alliance for Progress to stave off revolution in Latin America, napalm and green berets to subdue the rebels in
Vietnam. Although they extolled their pragmatism, they
obsessively pursued the programs worked out in their
social science seminars and on their computers, drawing
new conviction from each failure. They engaged in what
Harold Sterns many years ago called the technique of
liberal failure—the practice of being analytical until
further analysis becomes embarrassing, "the method
whereby one hopes to control events by abandoning one-
self to them." The liberals abandoned themselves to the
Vietnam war, and in 1968 the voters, understandably,
abandoned the liberals. Once again they were reminded,
in John Kenneth Galbraith's words, that "wars, just or
unjust, have come with devastating reliability every time
the Democrats have enjoyed power."

The American people were remarkably patient with the
liberals—fighting their imperial wars of intervention in
Korea and Vietnam, paying taxes for a military machine
that grew to gargantuan size under the Democrats, an-
swering their unending summons to sacrifice for goals no
one could explain or justify—until by turning to Richard
Nixon they made it clear that they had had enough. Spiro
Agnew has become a folk hero not by telling lies about
the liberals, but by puncturing their pretensions and their
hypocrisy. Were the Vice President not hitting the mark
with his comments about the networks and effete snobs,
there would be less outraged intimidation. As Galbraith
has said, "a man who can be hushed up by Vice President

Agnew or John Mitchell did not have anything to say worth hearing."

The irrepressible Galbraith has certainly not been hushed up, if such a feat is possible, and his pamphlet, *Who Needs the Democrats?*, is a devastating critique of a party largely devoted to imperial wars abroad and windy platitudes at home. With his customary tone of earnest flippancy, Galbraith recounts a succession of domestic and foreign policy failures that would seem reason enough to disband the party forever. Troglodyte congressmen and faceless bureaucrats suffer the full force of his scornful wrath. But even as he demolishes the record of the party in which he received communion, he cannot quite bring himself to lay blame at the feet of Kennedy or Johnson. One might assume, from reading this book, that the "interventionist bureaucracy" he condemns was secretly carrying on the Vietnam war without either President being aware of it. Like a true believer flailing at dim-witted bishops because he cannot conceive of attacking the Pope, Galbraith remains firmly within the Church by concluding his indictment with a plea to reform the party because "there isn't anything else."

That, unfortunately, is not good enough. While some of his reforms seem eminently reasonable—such as having liberal Democrats vote with the Republicans in order to unseat encrusted Southern Democrats from their Senate committee chairmanships—they only skirt the fringes of the problem. The problem is that American liberalism has exhausted itself. It has no solutions for the ailments of modern society other than even greater infusions of the same bureaucratic ineptitude and military interventionism that it has inflicted upon us for the past quarter century. What has gone wrong is not, as Galbraith and other liberals suggest, that Southerners dominate Senate committees (Fulbright, after all, is a Southerner), or that the New York foreign policy establishment runs the State Department regardless of which party is in power. Rather it is that the liberal formulas—an all-powerful central bureaucracy, an unhindered President, military interventionism—have been tried and found wanting.

The tragedy of American liberalism is that it hasn't worked and no one knows how to make it work. The growing mood of disenchantment in this country is a direct result of the failure of liberal programs that have been put into practice, of liberal wars of intervention whose bills have now come due. The Republicans are enjoying the fruits of that failure not because they have anything new to offer, but simply because they are an alternative.

The transformation of American politics is crucial to the survival of a humane democratic society. But it involves much more than the reform of the Democratic party. It means rejecting what has become self-destructive about American liberalism: the vision of the central government as the savior of the people, and America as the savior of the world. It means evolving a new vision of this society and a new politics to bring it about. Until the liberals realize that, until they stop bemusing themselves with "legacies of hope" based on dreams of a return to Camelot, they will have little to offer that Nixon and Agnew can't do better.

VI. VIETNAM
AND AFTER

Vietnam has made us aware not only that we have an empire, but of the military machine that sustains it, the rhetoric used to justify it, and the imperial politics that maintains it. Facing the truth about the war has been painful, for it has forced us to see ourselves and our society in a new and disturbing light. We are only just beginning to come to terms with who and what we are, and with what our empire means.

Vietnam has been a testing-point. For a variety of reasons—because the war has dragged on endlessly and inconclusively, because we no longer believe in the myth of the communist monolith, because the clients we are protecting seem no better than the adversaries we are fighting, because the war has brought on both inflation and recession in the United States, because it has inspired the revulsion of a whole generation of young Americans against their government, and because it has intensified conflicts that threaten to destroy the fabric of American society and perhaps American democracy—for all these reasons it is now being said that there will be no more Vietnams.

Perhaps not. But this means that the cold war empire will be peacefully dismantled; that repressive client states will be left to fend for themselves; that the Third World will be allowed to have its revolutions; that the American people, through their Congress, gain some control over the imperial foreign policy that is exercised in their name and with their blood; that the self-flatter--

ing dreams of empire be put to rest; that self-assumed moral "obligations" to make the world safe for democracy be exercised at home where some of its most basic values are being threatened; and that the militarization of American society be reversed.

And to make all the rest possible, it means that we have to conquer the deep-seated insecurity that leads the President to declare, and so many of us to agree, that a nation which cannot remake the world in its own image through force of arms, and which imagines that the world even wants to be remade along American lines, thereby becomes "a pitiful helpless giant."

To believe things can be different requires a truly heroic optimism. But perhaps that is all that keeps us going.

Imperial Washington

Two years away, and Washington seems strangely metamorphosed, like a cocoon that instead of giving birth to a butterfly has, in one's absence, produced a frog. In the fall of 1964 it seemed likely that the promises of Kennedy could be redeemed by the energies of Johnson, that the neglected nation might still become a Great Society, and the involvement in Southeast Asia could be quietly liquidated with a vague diplomatic agreement and a few well-chosen words. The long-awaited and long-neglected reform of the American society seemed finally at hand. The interventionist style of the Kennedy administration appeared tempered by the quiet pragmatism of its successor. There was a feeling of renewal and expectation: a belief that although much was difficult, nothing was quite impossible. Washington was on the verge of recognizing that if it had no answers for the world, it at least knew what to do for itself. That optimism has faded. The quest for "excellence" at home has been subsumed by the pursuit of grandeur abroad. The re-building of our cities, the reform of an outdated social structure, the re-cementing of a fractured society—these urgent national needs have once again been pushed into second place by the demands of an ideological war.

Perhaps this was inevitable. Perhaps this war, and the methods used to wage it, were pushed upon us by an uncooperative foe and the demands of an implacable destiny. Perhaps America's role, as Prince Sihanouk of Cambodia has said, is to "spread war and ruin everywhere"—in the name of a higher moral order. If so, we have little choice but to live with the consequences of this role—until we should choose another one for ourselves.

But this was not the role America seemed ready to embark upon only a few years ago. Then, Lyndon Johnson, the voice of compassion and restraint, was blasting the folly of a presidential candidate who sought to win the war in Vietnam by bombing the North and napalming the South. What provocation, what madness, what futility. One could hardly take the Goldwater proposals seriously—until they were adopted a few months after the election by the President himself. Maybe this, too, was inevitable. But a visitor who has been away from the capitol and from the country, between the Presidential campaign of 1964 and the mid-term elections of 1966, cannot help but feel that something rather strange has happened in the interval.

What has happened, of course, is that a minor skirmish in Vietnam involving a few thousand American advisers has turned into a major American war which has preoccupied the administration and is draining energies that might otherwise be employed elsewhere. Washington is a city obsessed by Vietnam. It eats, sleeps, and particularly drinks this war. There is virtually no other subject of conversation worthy of the name, and no social gathering or private discussion that does not inevitably gravitate toward the war. Never, one feels, has a war been so passionately discussed, so minutely examined, so feverishly followed—and so little understood—as the war in Vietnam. People who can rattle off the number of infiltrators who cross the border every week, or the names of village chieftains and Buddhist priests, do not seem to have any clear idea of how we got into this war, or exactly what it is we hope to accomplish.

Constituent assembly—50 million tons—Thich Tri Quang—Can Ramh Bay. This is the face of Vietnam as reflected through the mirror of Washington. A dazzling interplay of names and numbers, of departed politicians and aspiring generals, of anonymous enemies killed and unknown villages "reclaimed," of napalm dropped and harbors built, of bridges destroyed and battalions infiltrating through the jungle. Anonymous enemies indistinguishable, at a bomber's height of 30,000 feet, from our anonymous friends. Anonymous concepts like "voting," "democracy," and "self-determination" which take on—in the metallic offices of the government bureaucracy or in the Danish modern sophistication of a Washington cocktail party—an abstract quality. Vietnam, one feels, has become not so much a place as a way of thinking. "What happens in South Vietnam," an administration official told me rather portentously, "will determine the fate of Asia for the rest of this century. With stakes like that, we can't afford to back out."

A skeptic might be more receptive to the arguments in favor of this war if they were presented with less passion and more reason, if it were possible to feel that beneath the morass of figures and platitudes the administration had a really clear grasp of issues—that it knew exactly where it was going and why it had taken this particular path to get there. But it has not had the time, or the aptitude, or perhaps the understanding to explain this war in terms that could reconcile it with traditional American values. As a result, it has lost the support of much of the nation's intellectual community.

This has bred the crisis of confidence that has been the undoing of governments in other democratic countries and which may yet threaten this one. Anyone who was in France during the long agony of the Algerian war would not be totally out of place in today's Washington. He would find the same impassioned commitment by government officials, the same promise that the fighting was in its "last quarter hour," the same baffled acquiescence by the population, the same revolt of the intellectuals, and the same gradual erosion of confidence by the people in their government. Maybe "it can't happen here"; but it has happened in too many other places for anyone to be sure.

This sense of isolation on the part of the high officials of the administration leads to a good deal of testiness and unwillingness to engage their critics in serious discussion. In the best of times governments do not tolerate criticism easily, but this is an administration which has come to equate dissent with ignorance, or even worse, disloyalty. This is a city of closed minds, where the lines are so tightly drawn that neither side is willing to give the benefit of the doubt, or even at times a modicum of courtesy, to its opponents. There is little about this war that merits sanctimony, but this seems to have become the only emotion left to those who equate opposition with ignorance or evil. Even such favorites of the intellectual Establishment as Walter Lippmann and Senator Fulbright find themselves isolated and reviled by the administration—their arguments automatically discounted for no other reason than that they are in conflict with the current line. "Those people," a State Department official told me, "don't understand what this war is all about."

Maybe the administration is right and all its critics are wrong. Maybe Ho Chi Minh is a new Hitler and the fate of Asia will be determined by what regime rules Saigon. But the argument has tended to be more abusive than enlightening, more concerned with magic formulas and high-sounding phrases than with convincing analyses of what the alternatives really are. The administration would clearly like to extricate itself from a war which is bringing no credit to itself or to the country. Yet it is not willing to accept a settlement which would allow the Vietcong to play a major role in a neutral government. This, in its eyes, would constitute a victory for Peking's doctrine of "wars of national liberation" and would thereby provide the signal for similar guerrilla actions throughout the underdeveloped world. Vietnam is not so much important for itself as for what it symbolizes. With the stakes so high, the administration believes that it has no choice but to fight this war through to the end. Hope-

some of the ideals we're trying to pursue ab
fears are beginning to trouble many people i
ton, nettling the brain like the jets that now
affluent Georgetown and clouding over the here
of the war with nagging questions about the
the American society. The mantle of imper
while it has intrigued some people in the subu
White House, still rides uneasily on the should
day's Washington.

fully, the end would be a negotiated settlement in which the North, in Dean Rusk's memorable phrase, would "stop doing what it knows it's doing," and abandon the Vietcong.

Deeply committed to this war which preoccupies so much of its energies, the administration has not only been exceedingly impatient with its critics, but has shown a disturbing tendency to use its vast powers over public information to convey an impression favorable to its own interpretation of events. "Managed news" first became an issue during the Bay of Pigs landings, when an embarrassed Kennedy administration tried to put a favorable face upon a fiasco. But this administration, involved in something far more serious than a bout with Castro, has shown an even greater willingness to manipulate the news for its own purposes. Some suppression of the news is inevitable during a war, and no government can be expected to tell the whole truth where military security is concerned.

What was troubling about the Johnson administration is not that it kept military secrets from the press, but that the information it gave out was often erroneous and deliberately meant to deceive. In Vietnam the Pentagon's information policy has been under persistent attack by journalists, and there is now a growing belief that the Tonkin Gulf incident—which the President used to obtain a blank check from Congress for waging the war—was, if not entirely fabricated, almost certainly provoked by the U.S. government. Whatever the merits of the war, this is not a policy which can be shrugged off lightly, for it is central to the whole concept of government by consent. An administration which deliberately manipulates the press and the Congress, thereby manipulates the people as well. Whatever this may be, it is not democracy as it is understood by Americans.

Nor is this policy one which is confined to the Pentagon and to military operations. It has now, apparently, been taken over by the State Department and applied to such theoretically academic matters as diplomatic history. Recently a *New York Times* reporter, as a result of some private sleuthing, discovered that the State Department's White Paper on Franco-American relations—and particularly the exchange of memos between de Gaulle, Eisenhower, and Kennedy on the question of France's requests for greater European participation in NATO decision-making—had deliberately omitted key documents in an effort to bolster the U.S. position. Even the archives, it seems, are not safe from news management on the part of an administration overly zealous to prove that it can never be wrong.

Just as Vietnam dominates official, and even unofficial, Washington, so it also dominates any reporting about Washington. This is inevitable, and it is also unfortunate, for it drains away energies that are desperately needed for other, and even more pressing matters. "Were it not for this Vietnam thing," one of the nation's most outspoken journalists said to me, "I'd be able to write about the real crises—about poverty and civil rights and the cities. But as it is I have to—we all have to—write about the war, while everything else collapses around us."

A returning visitor to Washington might not, at first glance, feel that everything else was collapsing. During the past two years this rather patchy, cozy, provincial town has acquired a patina of progress—as we define that abused term. The obligatory Hilton has finally been finished, some handsome new buildings have sprung up along Connecticut Avenue, two quite splendid round structures have erupted in the neo-Roman shadow of the State Department, and the Southwest development project offers an impressive example of the possibilities of urban renewal.

But progress in Washington, like anywhere else, is not measured in tons of concrete poured. While flashy new buildings have gone up for affluent labor unions, giant corporations, and the upper-middle-class federal elite, hundreds of private dwellings have been torn down and thousands of people displaced—most of them the silent poor. The charming row houses of Foggy Bottom have disappeared almost overnight, to be replaced by the ugly scar of a super-highway which speeds commuters out to

the dormitory suburbs of Virginia every night at five. The Washington public school system, at the mercy of a Congressional committee dominated by white Southerners, has virtually broken down, and the students, 90 per cent of whom are Negroes, receive an education which enables them to aspire to the level of gas-station attendant or elevator operator.

In this first American city to have a Negro majority, the problems of the American metropolis can be seen in classic form: a core city of office buildings and department stores, a white enclave of fashionable town houses and high-rise apartments, a mushrooming suburban ring for middle-class white families, and a continually expanding slum area of Negroes alienated from white society and increasingly hostile to a system which keeps them perpetually on the bottom.

This is the other Washington, the Washington that the tourist rarely notices but that every American is coming to see reflected in his own city. This is urban America, where elegant office buildings and apartment houses conceal the breakdown of public services, where expressways speed commuters away from the city problems they help create, where overcrowded and understaffed schools are unable to educate young Americans for the jobs demanded in tomorrow's world, where social disintegration has become the handmaiden of material progress, and where whites and Negroes face each other sullenly over a widening chasm of misunderstanding and fear. Two years ago it was possible to dismiss much of this as growing pains, to believe that the ideals of the Great Society and enormous infusions of federal funds could heal the scars in American life.

Today it is difficult to be so optimistic. A society grown powerful in the belief that all problems are solvable, that such phenomena as defeat and tragedy need never touch this nation, is now finding its assumptions challenged and its institutions put to a terrible test. "I'm not so much worried about Vietnam," a distinguished Senator confessed to me, "as I am about America. I wonder what's going to happen to us if we can't even achieve at home

Topsy's War

Beneath the rival polemics of hawks and doves, the pragmatic justifications of escalation, and the anguished search for a political settlement, lies the greater tragedy of the war in Vietnam: the erosion of the belief by the American people in the virtue of their cause. Within the tragedy of Vietnam, there is an American tragedy as well. Confidence in national leadership has been replaced by doubt, commitment by baffled acquiescence, moderation by a growing impatience with stalemate. This is a war where open dissent has become a matter of course, where draft-dodging is not considered unpatriotic, where the administration has lost the support of its own party in Congress. This is a presidential war, for, as Richard Goodwin observes in *Triumph or Tragedy*, today "the Congressional power to declare war is little more than a ratification of events and acts already past."

For the first time in our history, we do not know why we are fighting, who our enemies are, or even what we mean by victory. Are we trying to contain China, to punish aggression, to show that wars of liberation cannot succeed, to build an anti-communist bastion in South Vietnam, or, as the President said in Omaha, to "determine whether might makes right"? Does anyone really know?

Have the American people ever been honestly told? The President says he seeks a negotiated settlement, yet he pursues a course of military escalation that implies a search for total "victory." He has transformed this confusing struggle among dissident groups of Vietnamese into an American war against the tiny state of North Vietnam. He has tried to force the leaders in Hanoi to negotiate with him by progressively devastating their country, yet he has not been able to break their will. His policy of escalation has been a military monstrosity and a political disaster, yet, as Goodwin observes, "Every step that fails calls forth not an admission of miscalculation but a demand for something more. It is the whole history of this war."

No one can doubt that the President is sick of this war, that he would like to turn American power away from the incineration of pajama-clad peasants to the achievement of his Great Society here at home. Yet he seems to have become obsessed by this war, letting it destroy his sense of proportion and inflate his rhetoric, just as it has swollen our involvement from a few hundred advisers to an army approaching half a million men. He claims that his war aims are modest, yet he is trying to achieve the virtually impossible task of creating a democratic, popularly supported, pro-American government in a land torn by revolution. He speaks of our "moral purpose" in words that sound like the most cruel cynicism. But he has not been able to define what that moral purpose is, or how it can be achieved by the devastation of the two Vietnams, by the mounting sacrifice of American lives for a regime in Saigon which does not even have the allegiance of its own people, and by a continuing escalation that may, as Goodwin warns, provoke the mass intervention of Hanoi's 300,000-man army and quite possibly lead to a war with China.

This is the impasse to which our Vietnam policy has led us, and perhaps no one is better placed to analyze its origins than Goodwin, who was one of the brightest lights of the Kennedy intellectual team and later a special assistant to President Johnson. In this essay he sees a war that happened more by accident than by design, a commitment in which "each individual decision seemed reasonable, carefully limited, even necessary," but where men entrusted with the fate of the nation "looked cautiously ahead while the door closed slowly, ponderously behind us."

"Why should we try to contain China?", asks Goodwin, going to the heart of the question. For it is only on the assumption that we somehow are containing China that the intervention in Vietnam can be justified. The question is direct, but the answer rather fuzzy. China must be contained because her expansion would undermine "the central world purpose of the United States—the creation of an international order of independent states." Further, he adds in a tantalizing, but unexplained, aside, such expansion "would inevitably feed the dark undercurrent of repression and militarism never wholly absent from American life." These are debatable answers at best, and it is unfortunate that Goodwin does not explain an argument which seems to rest on a combination of national purpose and national therapy. Similarly, he argues that we have a vital interest in denying China a sphere of influence in Asia, since "nations have no natural or God-given right to dominate those close to them"—which is perfectly true, yet this is what we grant the Russians in Eastern Europe and demand for ourselves in Latin America.

Yet even though he believes that America's "central world purpose" demands the containment of China, his scale is a relative one. "We are not compelled to fight for every inch of Asian soil or hazard war each time Chinese influence begins to grow," he comments in pointing out that Chinese control of Tibet cannot be measured on the same scale as an assault on India. Switching over from moral purpose to *Realpolitik*, he maintains that the crucial question is not whether Chinese influence is spreading, but *where* it is spreading. America's "central world purpose," it seems, is bounded by cold calculations of geopolitics and strategy.

On this scale, the fate of Vietnam involves no vital

American interest, and Goodwin observes quite correctly that "had the Communists succeeded in taking over the entire country, as they almost did, no sensible American would now be demanding that we go to war to recapture South Vietnam." Demolishing the conventional reasons given for our involvement in Vietnam—the SEATO pact, the belief that this is a testing ground for wars of national liberation, or the beginning of the fall of dominoes—he states with commendable frankness that we are fighting in Vietnam only because we have foolishly committed our prestige. Our only vital interest in this war is "to establish that American military power, once committed to defend another nation, cannot be driven from the field. It is not to guarantee South Vietnam forever against the possibility of a Communist takeover."

Given this interpretation of our stake in Vietnam, Goodwin believes that we must simultaneously follow the road of negotiation and the road of combat: negotiation which will permit the Vietcong to be admitted to a share of power in an ultimately neutral Vietnam; combat to "pacify" the South until negotiations take place. He urges a cessation to the bombing of the North and an honest American initiative for a settlement based on a ceasefire, withdrawal of foreign forces, free elections, and neutralization.

All this is eminently reasonable, and indeed the approach the administration claims it favors. But in trying to limit the stake in Vietnam to one of national prestige, Goodwin does not give adequate weight to arguments which have now become more compelling in Washington. We may be fighting to save our prestige, as he suggests, but why did we commit our prestige in the first place? Was it not for the purpose of preventing a communist, or perhaps even a neutral, South Vietnam? Does anyone really believe that this administration, having committed 400,000 soldiers and the prestige of the United States as a world power to the defense of an anti-communist government in Saigon, will close up its bases and go away once the North has been crushed and the Viet Cong forces dispersed—leaving it to the Vietnamese to set up a neutral government? This is possible, but if it is true, it makes the entire war a colossal fraud. Goodwin is probably correct in his belief that since ritual anti-communism is not a purpose worthy enough to justify American intervention in a strategically unimportant state like Vietnam, our only vital interest is to salvage our prestige. But this is not the administration's position, and in failing to address himself to problems it considers to be vital —such as the containment of China through United States protectorates along her frontiers—he is not really offering an alternative policy.

Goodwin's argument is also blunted by a certain inconsistency. While he believes that the United States has no vital interest in what kind of government rules Vietnam, he argues that "in the South we have no choice but to continue the war," clearing guerrillas from the countryside and pursuing "a long, bloody, inconclusive war of attrition until returning sanity brings a political settlement." But if a communist government in Saigon is no threat to American interests, why should we fight a long, inconclusive war of attrition for a settlement we could have tomorrow? Either we are willing to accept a communist Vietnam—in which case we dump the Ky regime, install a neutralist government which will negotiate with Hanoi, and withdraw to our coastal bases until we can gracefully retire from the scene. Or else we seek a military "victory" that will maintain South Vietnam as an anti-communist bastion—in which case we pursue the policies of pacification outlined by Goodwin. Either America has a vital interest in the political future of Vietnam or it doesn't. If it does, the administration's policy is correct, although its rhetoric is hypocritical. If there is no such vital interest, then we can save our prestige by working out a deal with the Vietcong. What does not make sense, however, is to continue full-scale combat in the South, while allowing the North to supply the Vietcong with men and materials.

Goodwin has written a lucid analysis of the tragedy in Vietnam, but he has not fully come to terms with the contradictions of his own position. Straddling the fence between the role of an administration spokesman ("we are under attack and withdrawal is impossible and unwise") and an uncommitted critic ("a substantial section of the community of power believes that military victory is our principal, perhaps our only, objective"), he compromises his own argument. The architect of our Vietnam policy is not in the State Department or in the Pentagon, where Goodwin has searched for villains, but in the White House. It is here, for reasons best known to him, that this perceptive but unpersuasive prosecutor has refused to look.

Unthinking
the Thinkable

Master storyteller of the unthinkable, Herman Kahn, has penned a just-suppose scenario of what might have happened if President Johnson had not chosen to bomb North Vietnam or send an American army to defend the regime in Saigon. The war effort of our friends in the South, he states, would have collapsed by early 1965, and the two severed parts of Vietnam would have been joined—perhaps under the guise of the elections originally set for 1956. This united Vietnam would, we are told, be prepared to "settle scores" with its neighbors, all of whom would have to "accommodate" to Ho Chi Minh. Laos and Cambodia would accommodate or be absorbed, while Thailand, already faced with insurgency in the northeast, would be forced to call on American troops, or else, being a nation "which throughout its history has not been known for policy consistency at the price of self-destruction, would have changed sides." As the falling dominoes (now apparently back in favor after a long post-Dulles disgrace) gather momentum, Malaysia would be squeezed between communist Vietnam and Sukarno's "fellow-traveling" (an old McCarthy word now revived) Indonesia. Leftists around the world would ask Vietnam and China "how to do it," and even the Russians might be tempted to pursue more extreme tactics.

Thus, for want of Marshal Ky, all of Southeast Asia would follow the unscrupulous Thais and choose self-preservation over policy consistency. The American military foothold on the mainland of Asia would be lost, pro-Western governments would turn to neutralism, or even worse, an accommodation with the communists, and the stage would be set for a tragedy even greater than the one that followed the refusal of Britain and France to oppose Hitler's reoccupation of the Rhineland. The analogy may be far-fetched, but Herman Kahn suggests that Ho Chi Minh can be compared to Hitler (presumably North Vietnam is bent on dominating the world like Nazi Germany), and the determination of the West to prevent the unification of Vietnam is an act of wisdom that will allow us to escape World War III. The road may be long and tough, there may be many who complain of the sacrifices, but our cause is just, and by saving the nations of Southeast Asia from an "accommodation" with a communist Vietnam, we may be sparing the world something even worse.

It is all so very persuasive that one can only marvel that there are those who still do not understand that Ho Chi Minh is Hitler, that South Vietnam and Thailand must remain as American bases, that the neutralization of Southeast Asia would be a tragedy, that the defeat of the Vietcong (or is it North Vietnam?) will mean the disappearance of guerrilla movements everywhere in the world, that the sacrifice of American lives for the regime of Marshal Ky is noble and worthy, and that the steady escalation of the Vietnam war is really a clever way of avoiding a Third World War—even if it should happen to bring one on.

Such a scenario must have been persuasive to President Johnson in late 1964 when—following his election on a promise not to expand the Vietnam war—he promptly did so to save the Saigon regime. But instead of proposing the above scenario of falling dominoes, suppose that Herman Kahn, or someone else of his prestige with access to the White House, had suggested to the President what might happen if he did, in fact, try to prop up the Saigon regime with American soldiers. To those pondering the wisdom of a direct American military intervention, such a scenario might have been sobering, and might even have led them to question the wisdom of a massive American commitment to Saigon. They might have drawn upon the experience of the French in Indochina, and also have been more inclined to make a cold calculation of just how threatening a Vietcong victory might be to American interests.

Such a scenario might run something like this:

The 20,000 American "advisers" in South Vietnam at the end of 1964 would have to be augmented by huge reinforcements of several hundred thousand, or perhaps even half a million, men. Only an effort on the scale of Korea could halt the Vietcong tide before it overwhelmed the indifferent South Vietnamese army. Once such an American army entered the field, however, the National Liberation Front would call on Hanoi for volunteers, who would be infiltrated across the border. The entry of North Vietnamese units into the war would, in turn, require more American troops, and perhaps necessitate the withdrawal of some units from troubled spots such as Germany. Short on manpower, the United States might find itself spread thin in other areas of concern. This could invite new instability in places closer to home than Vietnam.

In Vietnam the American forces, possessing massive fire power and an enormous technological superiority, would try to destroy the communist rebels by air-supported land operations. In addition, the President would be under pressure to expand the air war to North Vietnam. This would be justified as a means of slowing down infiltration, and of persuading Hanoi to withdraw her support of the Vietcong. Air raids against the North would cause considerable hardship, but would not be able to paralyze the war effort of such a technologically unsophisticated society. The bombing might even harden the resistance of the North Vietnamese. The war in the South, fought from both land and air, would inflict grave losses upon the communist rebels, but it would also devastate the countryside and take a heavy toll of the civilian population. This, in turn, would create sympathy for the Vietcong and increased opposition to the Western "invaders."

As American casualties mounted, there would be growing pressure from the military, supported by elements in Congress, and with the acquiescence of a war-weary American public, to extend the bombing to civilian targets. The intensified bombing of North Vietnam would oblige the Russians to step up their aid to Hanoi, particularly of jet fighters and anti-aircraft missiles. But as the devastation of North Vietnam increased, they might feel compelled to supply Hanoi with the means to strike at American bases in the South, such as Pleiku, Danang, and Cam Ranh Bay. This would, in all likelihood, bring about a direct Russo-American confrontation of the kind that could escalate into a total war. Even if the American bases remained untouched, the inability to end the war by increased bombing would eventually lead to calls for an invasion of North Vietnam. While this would not end the guerrilla war in the South, it would provide a temporary relief valve for American frustrations. It might be difficult for a President who had carried the war to this point to resist such expansion, particularly if the climate of stalemate continued the 1968 electoral campaign. In a gamble to end the war he might order an American invasion of North Vietnam, beginning first with a probe into the demilitarized zone in order to establish the "no sanctuary" principle, and then probably an amphibious Inchon-type landing.

In the face of such a desperate situation the North Vietnamese, despite their long-standing fear and distrust of China, would be compelled to call upon their northern neighbor to resist the American invasion. Having lost nearly everything, they would have little more to lose by a Chinese counter-intervention. Even without an appeal from Hanoi, the leaders in Peking would not tolerate an American army on their frontier, and would move south—just as they did in the Korean war when Mac-

Arthur's troops approached the Yalu. This would, of course, be very risky for China, for it would furnish the United States with the pretext to destroy Chinese nuclear installations. But the threat posed by American troops in North Vietnam, and the hope that the Russians, in the final analysis, would be drawn into the conflict and thereby pose a deterrent to an American nuclear attack on China, would probably overcome such Chinese hesitations. At this point one of three things could happen: either the Russians would stand by and allow America to destroy China's industrial and nuclear capacity, in which case Moscow would suffer a serious loss of prestige; or fear of Russian reprisal would deter the United States from attacking China, in which case there would be a Korean-type war in which many thousands of Americans would be killed; or else Washington would call Moscow's hand, and we would be in World War III.

Even if President Johnson were to resist the invasion of North Vietnam, and thereby avoid a dangerous process of escalation, the American aerial devastation of a relatively defenseless communist nation would make it increasingly difficult for Russian leaders to pursue the policy of détente with the United States. Those who ignored the pleas of North Vietnam would likely be replaced by more militant leaders. This, in turn, would help repair the breach between Russia and China and confront the West with something it has not faced for more than a decade: a united communist bloc. A more militant Russian leadership would also be induced to take the pressure off North Vietnam by opening up "second fronts" in various trouble spots throughout the world. Having committed the bulk of its forces to Vietnam, the United States would find it exceedingly difficult to counter such threats, and could suffer a serious loss to its own vital interests.

The Russians would also be induced to aid guerrilla movements in Latin America and Africa, hoping to start miniature Vietnams in such places as Bolivia and Peru, knowing that the United States could not commit its own forces to a half-dozen wars of "national liberation." Even without help from the Russians, such guerrilla movements would draw new encouragement from the lesson of Vietnam. It would prove to these revolutionaries that even the most powerful nation in the world, using the most terrible weapons of modern technology, was incapable of stamping out a determined guerrilla movement against a government which had lost popular support. The awesome power of the United States, once having been brought into operation and found wanting, would no longer serve as a deterrent to Marxist-inspired revolutionaries. The American intervention in Vietnam would, in this sense, stimulate exactly the kind of war it was ostensibly designed to discourage.

Aside from the dangers outlined above, a massive American military intervention in Vietnam would cause grave tensions within the United States itself. It would sharply divide the electorate, many of whom would be incapable of believing that the enforced partition of Vietnam merited the sacrifice of so many American lives. It would alienate much of the intellectual community, which has hitherto generally accepted the ideological assumptions of the cold war. It would lead to a crisis of conscience among young Americans, some of whom would refuse to fight for a cause they considered unjust, and many of whom would become cynical about the purposes of a government which called upon them to die for a foreign military dictatorship in the name of democracy.

Also, as the cost of the war increased, Congress would no longer be willing to provide funds for many of the Great Society programs, and the least privileged members of American society—particularly the Negroes—would suffer and feel themselves to be betrayed. Their bitterness would mount, and be reflected in increased militancy and racial tensions that would further divide Americans from one another. As the war progressed and the elemental emotions of patriotism mounted, opposition would become increasingly impolitic, public officials would be silent, dissent would be equated with treason, and a new round of McCarthyism would be likely. Finally, the democratic consensus which makes possible the remarkable stability of American politics would be threatened by ideological extremism on both Right and Left. Third, and even fourth, parties would spring up, and the United States would be rocked by social, political, and racial tensions that could shred the fabric of American democracy.

While the above scenario might have seemed fanciful in the fall of 1964, we know better today. The cost of defending the regime in Saigon from other Vietnamese has already taken a terible toll of American lives and American prestige, not to mention the lives of Vietnamese who happen to be the pawns in this proxy war with China. To those who believe that Ho Chi Minh is Hitler and Vietnam the Rhineland, there can be no question about the wisdom of such sacrifices. But others, less persuaded by such dubious historical allusions, may wonder—at this half-way point in our hypothetical scenario—whether the defense of Marshal Ky and the prevention of Laos and Cambodia from an "accommodation" with a united Vietnam are causes that justify the expenditure of such blood, and the courting of the even greater dangers that lie ahead.

Why Vietnam?

If South Vietnam goes, the rest of Asia cannot be far behind. Or so we are told. You can almost hear that row of dominoes falling now: Laos, Thailand, Cambodia. Then maybe Malaysia, or Indonesia or Burma. It is a grisly picture, designed to raise goose pimples on the flesh of every red-blooded American. And it does. But what does it really mean?

Let us assume, just for a minute, that the propaganda mill in the Pentagon is right, and all those countries from the China Sea to the Bay of Bengal are waiting to drop into communist hands. Let us assume that only American money and American bayonets keep all of Southeast Asia from "going Communist." Let us assume that the power of nationalism (no point in speaking of democracy where it is only a figure of speech) is so feeble, and the temptations of communist regimentation so overwhelming, that the Asians are panting for the chance to jump on Mao's bandwagon.

If this is the case, what can we do about it? First of all, we can do more of the same. We can keep pouring our soldiers into South Vietnam, where the figure is already creeping up toward a quarter of a million. This is what the French did in Indochina, although they had to give it up after nine years of warfare—despite the fact that they had a stake there, since it was their colony. We can hold on in South Vietnam. There is no longer any serious doubt about that. We can keep our enclaves along the coast and provide a capital for the generals in Saigon.

"Winning," of course, is another matter, if indeed it is anything more than pure fantasy. To subdue the Vietcong probably would require the million-man army that Hanson Baldwin estimated would be necessary. Yet even such a commitment would not end the rebellion, but simply reduce it to the level of sporadic guerrilla warfare. With a million American soldiers occupying the country, South Vietnam could be "saved."

Saved for what? For General Nguyen Cao Ky, that admirer of Adolf Hitler? For the Michelin tire company with its rubber plantations? For the "free world"? Most likely the last, for our economic investment in South Vietnam is insignificant, and the revolving generals in Saigon are merely tools to be used, and endured, for fighting a war which is apparently doomed to continue without end.

We are, it would seem, fighting the war in Vietnam for the sake of democracy. Indeed, any other argument is hardly credible, since the American people could hardly be expected to accept the cremation of Vietnamese villagers by napalm, and the death and maiming of its own soldiers without believing that something more inspiring than power politics was at stake. The President's periodic pronouncements, in their folksy evangelism, are designed to provide just such inspiration. No doubt the President believes them himself. Which is why he, and the lesser lights of his administration have been so outraged by the student demonstrations against the war.

Yet despite all this earnest propaganda and outraged indignation by those who conduct and support the Vietnamese war, it all rings hollow at the core. It rings hollow because it is difficult to believe the official justifications. To accept the official statement that we are fighting in Vietnam to defend the democratic government of those brave freedom-lovers, the Saigon generals, requires a degree of gullibility that a literate population cannot be expected to possess. It simply is not true. And because the administration has tried to justify its policies by deception—revealing a cynicism bordering on contempt for its citizens—it has received a good deal of contempt in return.

So long as this conflict between the official propaganda and the crass realities of South Vietnam continue to exist, there is likely to be disaffection and protest. The students are not being drafted to defend democracy in South Vietnam and they know it. The rest of us know it, too, but being less directly touched, we are also less honest about it. If it is not democracy we are defending in South Vietnam, then what are we doing there? We are, the President and his minions tell us, holding back the tide of communism. This, then, is the real motive for our war against the Vietcong and against North Vietnam, and this is the problem we should be addressing ourselves to: the determination to contain communism.

But even here we are on slippery ground, for the Vietcong, while under communist leadership, has a good many non-communists at its upper levels. Nor is it even certain that the Vietcong, which launched its revolt against Ngo Dinh Diem and followed it through against his successors, has any desire to throw South Vietnam into the arms of Hanoi. According to Jean Lacouture, probably the most reliable of Western observers on Vietnam, the Vietcong prefers the South to remain autonomous, and in the short run, at any rate, seeks a coalition government in Saigon capable of dealing with Hanoi on a basis of friendship and equality.

Thus, it would seem that the Vietcong, while dominated by communists, is not necessarily under the control of the communist regime in North Vietnam. Nor is North Vietnam, although communist, simply the puppet of China that Washington often portrays it as being. Instead of one colossal communist conspiracy organized from Peking, we seem to have a collection of different, and even conflicting, communist groups: the Vietcong which wants to form a coalition government in the South that would bargain with Hanoi; the communist regime in North Vietnam that supports the insurrection in the South, but is desperately trying to avoid Chinese domination; and the clever dialecticians in Peking who are eagerly working to prolong the Vietnamese war as long as possible in hopes of a) dominating Vietnam once it has been laid waste by American bombers, b) undermining American prestige throughout the Third World of emerging states, and c) sabotaging, if possible, the Russo-American détente.

However, by confusing anti-Western nationalism, communism, and Chinese imperialism, and indeed behaving as though they were all more or less the same thing, we have completely lost sight of what is possible—or even desirable—in Vietnam and the rest of Southeast Asia. To deal in realities is to sweep away a good deal of the familiar rhetoric and to accept that communism *per se* is not particularly relevant in the case of Vietnam, or any of the dozen other countries where the same episode could, and may yet well be, repeated.

No matter how much *angst* it may cause us, the nations of Southeast Asia, like most of the poor but aspiring nations of the Third World, will eventually turn to some kind of authoritarian socialism—where they have not done so already. We can call it communism if we like. But it bears about as much relation to real communism as the "people's democracies" bear to real democracy. We would be naive indeed to put much faith in the label under which nations, new and old, justify their policies.

Yugoslavia is nominally communist, Pakistan nominally democratic, and South Africa vaguely fascist—yet we manage to get along with all three quite well without worrying about the fact that their political labels do not realistically describe what really goes on. By the same token, we have even discovered that all communist nations are not alike: that Rumania is not dedicated to our destruction, that Bulgaria is not a menace to anybody, and that Hungary would be delighted to have our friendship. To make matters even more confusing, we have been forced to admit that there is no such thing as a communist monolith masterminded from Moscow, and that the Russians and the Chinese seem to hate each other even more than they hate us.

The labels have somehow all become unhinged. We are now cozy with Russia and are even quietly wooing the states of Eastern Europe. The communism that we find intolerable in Southeast Asia, is neither a menace, nor particularly unendurable where the Soviet satellites are concerned. We can live quite happily with the communist states of Eastern Europe, and we have learned that they are just as eager to avoid Russian domination as we are to have them avoid it.

In Asia, however, we are, mentally, right back where we were with Russia in 1950. We have failed to apply the lesson of Europe, where we learned that nationalism persistently triumphs over ideology, and have instead lumped the communist nations of Asia together. We have declared that the Vietcong are puppets of Hanoi, and Hanoi is a puppet of Peking—and, by our actions, have helped make them so, even against their own will. Where we once saw Russia pulling all the strings in Eastern Europe, we now see China pulling, or ready to pull, all the strings in Southeast Asia, if South Vietnam should ever "go Communist."

But what if it does? Is there any reason to think that a communist South Vietnam would be more amenable to Chinese domination than a communist North Vietnam has been? A crafty nationalist as well as an old-time Communist, Ho Chi Minh has been desperately trying to prevent North Vietnam from falling under Peking's thumb—although he has been given precious little help by the U.S. Air Force. Ho Chi Minh's brand of communism may be a threat to China; it is certainly no threat to us.

We continually proclaim our desire to halt Chinese imperialism in its tracks, and yet we are systematically devastating the country which is best placed to resist Chinese hegemony in Southeast Asia. A strong North Vietnam happens to be communist; what is crucial is that it is Vietnamese. The history of the Vietnamese people has been one of resistance to China. In fact, it is likely that the containment of China could be made easier if Ho Chi Minh did unify the country—as he almost certainly would have done legally if the Geneva Accords had been carried out. Then, shrewd nationalist that he is, he could appeal to both America and Russia for help against the Chinese dragon on his border.

And why shouldn't he get it? Why should we, of all nations, want to prevent Ho from becoming the Tito of Southeast Asia? Under his leadership a unified Vietnam —even if it is nominally communist—would be better able to guard its independence against China than the collapsing regime in Saigon which we are trying to prop up at such staggering human and moral cost. It is not Ho, after all, who threatens our interests, but an expansionist China. And China can only be contained by independent, neutral states on her frontiers.

Does this mean that we should "give up" South Vietnam to the Communists? Perhaps, but the country was never ours to "give" in the first place, and if the government of South Vietnam is incapable of protecting itself against its own people, then it need not be our job to prop it up—least of all at the sacrifice of our own soldiers. We have more than enough client states in the world. What we could use are a few more self-reliant allies who have some basis of support other than American bayonets. If some of those nations want to call themselves Communist, that is their business. But if they can help serve our interests by guarding their independence, then we need not be overly concerned with their labels. This is true of South Vietnam, it is true of Southeast Asia, and for that matter it is true of the rest of the "third world" as well.

The point is not the ideology a regime may profess— we can be as indifferent to the ideals of a good many of our allies as they are to ours—but the policies it follows. In this sense it is hard to see how the military regime in Saigon, even if it can be stabilized, is going to benefit our interests in the long run. South Vietnam may be "saved" from Communism, only to have all of Southeast

Asia fall under Chinese hegemony—even though its governments may be nominally anti-communist.

Thus we are faced with the fact that as far as the interests of the United States are concerned (and, considering what we have done to their country, we can hardly dare speak of the interests of the miserable people of Vietnam), it really does not make very much difference whether South Vietnam "goes Communist" or not. Insofar as a unified Vietnam would be better able to resist Chinese dominance, it might even be better if it did. This means that young Americans are not only being sacrificed for a regime which is the antithesis of America's own democratic ideals, but also for one that is of no benefit to America's political interests.

Small wonder that the administration has had such difficulty explaining its policy. It is doubtful that the administration itself understands what is really at stake. It makes little difference whether the dictatorship in Saigon is communist or fascist, but it matters a great deal what Americans are asked to die for. By refusing to recognize this, the administration has been not only short-sighted and deceitful, it has betrayed a trust.

The Cool Way Out

Moving over from adviser to critic, Arthur Schlesinger, Jr. joins the swelling chorus of those who oppose the Johnson administration's Vietnam policies. In *The Bitter Heritage*, this eminent commuter to the corridors of power makes a notable contribution to the seemingly inexhaustible list of books about the Vietnam war. Trying to stay somewhere near the middle of the road, seeking to placate the doves without alienating the hawks, and attempting to be a dissenter without cutting himself off from those who exercise power, he urges us to "recover our cool" and slow the war down before our rhetoric gains the upper hand over our judgment. A search for a "middle course" that will presumably allow us to emerge with the remnants of our honor and our interests intact, his book is a plea for moderation, detachment, and skepticism.

The Bitter Heritage examines how we got in Vietnam, what we are doing there, why the administration thinks it is important to stay, and how we might be able to disentangle ourselves. As an eminent historian who has both examined and tasted power, Schlesinger probes what went wrong in Vietnam and why "we find ourselves entrapped today in that nightmare of American strategists, a land war in Asia—a war which no President, including President Johnson, desired or intended." As one of the leading intellectual figures of what might be called the government-in-exile, Schlesinger mercilessly probes the weak points of the administration's arguments and policies.

Vietnam, Schlesinger contends, "is a triumph of the politics of inadvertence." We are there not because of a deliberate decision taken with full regard for its impact, but through a series of small steps, each one "reasonably regarded at the time as the last that would be necessary." The fatal steps began when Roosevelt's plan for an independent Indochina was transformed, under the logic of the cold war, into Truman's decision to help the French retain their prize Asian colony; when the Eisenhower administration examined this program of military-economic support and, following the Geneva Agreements of 1954, tried to create an anti-communist bastion in South Vietnam under the mandarin government of Ngo Dinh Diem; when Kennedy increased our troop contingent from 800 advisers to 15,500 men; and finally when President Johnson extended the war to North Vietnam and sent in an American Army now approaching half a million men. A series of steps, which in themselves seemed small at the time, have now led to an involvement from which there is no easy escape, and whose justifications have become so blurred by the accumulation of carnage and rhetoric that they are no longer fully convincing, or perhaps even comprehensible.

Although the roots of the American commitment to South Vietnam are deep and tangled, they are centered, Schlesinger believes, in Eisenhower's 1954 decision to support the Saigon regime of Ngo Dinh Diem, and in the protocol of Dulles' SEATO treaty, which drew a line across Southeast Asia at the 17th parallel in Vietnam. Although that line against communism could have been drawn elsewhere, it was drawn in South Vietnam, and "a vital American interest was thus created where none had existed before." From that self-assumed interest everything else followed step by step in this "tragedy without villains."

Yet if there are no villains, there are certainly actors in this tragedy—actors who at any point along the way could have made different choices, proposed different alternatives, held different assumptions. We did not become involved in Vietnam by accident and we are not remaining there simply because we took a series of seemingly minor steps along the way. The war in Vietnam did not happen to us; we chose to become involved in it. We did not, of course, choose to have it take on such enormous dimensions, nor involve us in actions which many Americans believe to be morally compromising. But this war resulted from decisions deliberately made and firmly carried out. President Eisenhower could not have imagined where his 1954 decision to support Diem would lead us, but today he fully supports the war and even refuses to rule out the use of atomic weapons. President Kennedy might not have expanded the war to the dimensions of another Korea, but it was he—on the advice of General Maxwell Taylor and Walt Rostow—who set the stage for the Americanization of the war by sending in an army of 15,000 men and launching counter-insurgency operations. Above all, President Johnson did not want to sacrifice the Great Society at home to the preservation of Marshal Ky's regime in Saigon. But he chose to do so, even though he could have reversed the tide set in motion by his predecessors and sought a Laos-type settlement for Vietnam.

Having served as an adviser to President Kennedy, Schlesinger is particularly qualified to explain why the American troop contingent in South Vietnam was expanded nearly 100-fold during the Kennedy's administration, why the decision was made to "sink or swim with Diem," and why, in his words, "the projected American solution in 1961-1963 was increasingly framed in military terms." The reasons, according to Schlesinger, were that during those years Vietnam seemed "far less urgent" than such places as Cuba or Berlin, and, perhaps more importantly, that U.S. policy appeared to be working. Virtually unconditional support of the Diem regime, combined with a contingent of military advisers who would train the Vietnamese in such recently-discovered American specialties as the art of guerrilla warfare, would presumably check the rot in South Vietnam. From this policy flowed the "strategic hamlet" program, in which peasants were herded into fortified villages surrounded by barbed wire fences. That this failed to win their allegiance to the Saigon regime was apparently a surprise to no one but President Kennedy's advisers.

Perhaps Kennedy would not have taken such dubious advice had he not himself been infatuated with the idea of "counter-insurgency" warfare as a means of overcoming communist-inspired resistance groups in under-developed countries. What "massive retaliation" was to Dulles, "counter-insurgency" was to Kennedy. The only difference was that Dulles probably never meant it, whereas Kennedy did. Committed to the belief that the United States had an unspoken obligation to build viable nations out of the remnants of Europe's discarded empire, Kennedy saw South Vietnam as a terrain on which communist guerrilla warfare would be challenged at its own level. What he never realized, or perhaps never had time fully to come to terms with, was that this was possible only in countries where the government had large-scale popular support. Otherwise, the only alternative to the insurgents would be an American Army—as President Johnson discovered when the Saigon government began to collapse by late 1964. It is no doubt true, as Schlesinger notes, that President Kennedy "had other matters on his mind" than the disintegrating situation in South Vietnam. Unfortunately this is an inadequate explanation for faulty analysis and decisions wrongly made.

Schlesinger eloquently attacks the ostensible assumptions of the administration's Vietnam policy: that bombing can force the North to negotiate, that Hanoi holds the key to peace in the South, that China is really the instigator of the war, that the risk of Chinese or Soviet intervention is negligible, and that some kind of military "victory" is possible. Yet even though he declares there is "little reason to suppose that bombing will not continue to heighten Hanoi's resolve to fight on," he does not come out for a total halt to the bombings. Instead, he suggests we "taper off the bombing of the north as prudently as we can," and "oppose further widening of the war." This is no doubt less a contradiction in Schlesinger's analysis than it is an example of his circumspection, for in sticking to the "middle course" he is precluded from advocating any radical solutions.

Yet this circumspection has its drawbacks, and it is sometimes difficult to determine exactly what kind of solution Schlesinger really favors. He speaks approvingly, as do many administration officials, of an independent and even neutral South Vietnam. He goes a step further and suggests that this may also be an objective of the Vietcong—and that therefore we should negotiate with them and accept their entry into a Saigon coalition government. At the same time, however, he also states that a unified "communist Vietnam under Ho might be a better instrument of containment [of China] than a shaky Saigon regime." Both of these judgments may well be true, but they are not complementary. Do we want an independent South Vietnam pledged to neutralism, or do we want a unified communist Vietnam under Ho Chi Minh as a barrier to Chinese expansion? Are we fighting for the independence of South Vietnam or are we trying to contain China? Do we want to return to the Geneva Agreements (under which the partition of Vietnam was supposed to be temporary), or should we, as Schlesinger suggests, try to exploit the tension between the Vietcong and Hanoi, a tension which "could help protect the independence of a post-war South Vietnam"?

The administration has never answered this question satisfactorily, nor has Schlesinger really come to terms with it—although he seems to favor the creation of a civilian government in Saigon that will negotiate with the Vietcong, and then an international agreement to neutralize South Vietnam and perhaps to provide for a referendum at some distant date to deal with the problem of reunification. Yet until we decide what it is we are trying to accomplish in Vietnam, how are we going to know whether the stakes are worth it—or how to extricate ourselves?

While all good pragmatists will sympathize with Schlesinger's efforts to keep to the middle of the road, it is fair to wonder whether this will lead to a way out of Vietnam. The policy he suggests does not really meet the objection of the hawks, who see a vital American interest in the preservation of an anti-communist regime in Saigon. Nor does it fully satisfy the doves, who believe we have no business trying to determine what kind of government rules South Vietnam. Either we do or we don't, and if an intelligent policy is to be made, a stand has to be taken on this central issue. The trouble with Schlesinger's middle course is that it may skirt the real problem of what is our stake in Vietnam. Choosing between extreme alternatives is rarely pleasant and most statesmen try to avoid it. Even de Gaulle, who now reminds us of France's magnanimity toward her former colonies, tried a whole bag full of compromises before he finally decided to end the war by turning Algeria over to the rebels.

Perhaps we may be approaching the point where we have to make a similar decision ourselves—a point where we must fish or cut bait: decide whether an anti-communist—or even neutral—South Vietnam is vital to our interests or whether it isn't. If it is, then we must push on with the hawks and pursue this terrible war to its unforeseen, and perhaps unthinkable, conclusion. If it is not, then we may have to let the South Vietnamese settle their own affairs—even if this means a victory for the Vietcong and the reunification of the country under Ho Chi Minh. In either case, the choice is not going to be a pretty one. Which is why, if there is ever to be a negotiated end to hostilities, we have to come to terms with the real alternatives. From this bitter heritage there may be no cool way out.

Nobody's Asia

A respected scholar with a long and intimate experience in Asian affairs, able to speak Japanese and with an attractive Japanese wife, Edwin Reischauer was a perfect choice for Ambassador to Tokyo. Combining intellectual distinction, an unsentimental approach to politics and a deep knowledge and respect for Japanese culture, he was one of John F. Kennedy's more inspired ambassadorial appointments. From 1961 to 1966—from the invigorating optimism of the New Frontier to the deepening morass of the Vietnam war—he was chief representative of the United States to our most important Asian ally. From that vantage point he had a chance to move from the world of scholarship to the world of action. He was one of the most distinguished of those who formed the brain drain that flowed from Cambridge, Mass. to Washington, D.C. and is now working back the other way.

The reflections of such a man upon his experience in government, upon the differences he must have encountered in his switch from the cloister to the embassy, upon the frustrations he obviously felt in trying to get his recommendations translated into policy, and perhaps upon a certain exhilaration in the exercise of power—all this would have made fascinating reading.

Such a book would be fascinating, but it is not the one Reischauer has chosen to write. Instead he has written a short, informative, temperate primer on American policy in Asia. Althought written in an unduly simplistic style, *Beyond Vietnam* is a thought-provoking account of how the United States became involved in a tragic war from which there seems to be no escape, and suggests how we may hope to avoid more of the same in the future. This is a book about what American policy should be in Asia beyond the present preoccupation with Vietnam. Perhaps its greatest utility is in putting the Vietnam war into perspective, in showing how it resulted from a series of mistakes and misjudgments about the realities of contemporary Asia, and how a continued refusal to adjust our policy to these realities could lead to another Vietnam somewhere else.

The basic reality in Asia is the power of nationalism and the unshakable determination of Asians, whatever their political ideology, to forge their own national destinies free from foreign control. Our most grievous mistake has been in trying to impose our own anti-communism upon the Asians at the expense of their nationalism. We have failed to realize that "in Asia, nationalism is the basic driving force and communism the technique sometimes adopted to fulfill it . . . Communism in Asia is but one of nationalism's vehicles." Because of our ideological blinkers, however, we have tended to view any nominally communist movement as necessarily evil, and have indiscriminately aided regimes that declare themselves to be anti-communist. In many cases these self-styled anti-communist regimes prove to be inept and unpopular—incapable of staying in power without American support. Yet the very fact that they are so dependent upon us discredits them to Asian nationalists. Because we are a Western power deeply involved in an area that has only recently shaken off Western domination, "we appear in Asian eyes so much like the colonial masters of the past that we help make those who oppose us seem to be the 'real' nationalists and those whom we support the 'running dogs' of neo-imperialism."

Vietnam Without Tears

There are some subjects about which it is hard to assume an air of enlightened detachment. One is, or at least used to be, religion. Another is sex. And one is surely the Vietnam war. Over the past twenty years (yes, twenty, for it was in May 1950, that Secretary of State Dean Acheson announced that the United States would aid France in its struggle to subdue the communist-led Vietminh) there have been passionate denunciations of America's role in Indochina and (although with increasing rarity) fervent justifications.

The hawks told us we were defending the Free World, holding the line against aggression, protecting a brave people, making the world safe for democracy — you name it. The doves were aghast at our support of self-seeking autocrats and incompetent generals, or our systematic devastation of Vietnam, or the toll wrought on our own society— name it again. The issue long ago became a moral one. The lines have become so tightly drawn and the arguments so familiar that even to launch discussion of the subject seems redundant. Operation Total Victory has now given way to Operation Face-Saving. Nixon's so-called Vietnamization plan, for all its loopholes and booby-traps, is designed to ease us out the back door of a

But if we don't help anti-communist regimes such as those in South Vietnam, won't they "fall" to the communists? In some cases perhaps they might, but Reischauer is not unduly pessimistic on this score, and indeed views communism as a waning force in Asia. However, even if this did happen, he declares, "the loss of Asian countries, either to Chinese or Soviet control or to domestic communists, scarcely weakens us." This is so because, in his words, "we have no vital national interest that can be immediately and directly threatened by Asians." Asia is too weak to pose a military threat to the United States within the foreseeable future, and any communist regime would immediately be faced with the enormous problem of feeding its hungry citizens. Would any Chinese or Russian in his right mind want to assume the responsibility for policing and feeding 400 million Indians or 100 million Indonesians? Not very likely. Even if there should be an aggressive move against a major Asian power by Russia or China, this could be blocked by an American nuclear guarantee. A further reason for being sanguine about the communist "threat" in Asia is that a communist regime is neither permanent, nor permanently hostile to the United States. "A detour into communism today will not necessarily have a decisive influence on what an Asian country is like some decades from now, when its attitudes and role in the world may be far more important to us than they are at present."

If a communist regime is no threat to the United States, what are we doing in Vietnam? We have already lost 14,000 American lives, are spending some $30 billion a year, and are sacrificing grave domestic needs to ensure that a communist-inspired guerrilla movement does not seize power in Saigon. One of Reischauer's most vexing jobs in Tokyo was to defend such policies to the Japanese—policies which are so clearly contrary to his own assessment of American interests in Asia. The puzzle is intensified when he points out that a communist Vietnam would probably have been "highly nationalistic," "free of Chinese domination," and no serious menace to its neighbors or world peace. "Quite possibly a unified

Vietnam under Ho, spared the ravages of war, would have gone at least as far toward the evolution of a stable and reasonably just society as has the divided, war-torn land we know today." Our mistake, he argues compellingly, was to help the French fight their futile colonial war, then to step in ourselves to support an unpopular and corrupt regime which had lost the banner of nationalism to the communist insurgents. Reischauer could hardly be clearer on this point: the United States had no business going into Vietnam in the first place, and would have lost nothing by letting Ho Chi Minh unify the country.

Why prolong the agony if we have no vital interest in who rules South Vietnam? Because we are in so deep that we cannot just pull out, because some of the more unstable South Asian lands "would feel much less secure if the United States, having committed itself to the fight, were forced to admit defeat at the hands of communist insurgents," because our other allies might feel "we would be welching on commitments," and because an abrupt withdrawal could "turn into the worst sort of racist isolationism, which might drastically reduce our usefulness to the less developed parts of the world." In other words, we have to stay because there is no way we can honorably escape—not even through negotiations, which Reischauer justly views as amounting to "virtually a surrender by one side or the other."

Our chief hope, he declares, is for a "slow simmering down of the war" which will "force the other side gradually to reduce the scale of fighting and eventually to accept some sort of reasonable settlement." This is rather puzzling, however, since Reischauer has already defined a negotiated settlement under present circumstances as "virtually a surrender." The simmering down of the fighting doesn't make it any less of a surrender. This would seem to leave him with little alternative than a quest for "victory," however much it may be disguised, as the administration is fond of doing, under the comforting label of "negotiations." This impression is reinforced by Reischauer's prescription for peace, which

includes a barrier across
bombing of the Nort...
the South and incre...
leaves him somewher...
White House. But then,...
leaders in Washington, ...
from mine."

Yet it is not really fair t...
reluctant hawk, standing fir...
which he himself argues are fo...
Despite his lingering loyalty to t...
would clearly like us to get out of ...
any terms we can without seeming ...
commitments," and at one point he eve...
the Saigon regime tries to sabotage our ...
tiate a peace, we could use that as an excus...
His prescription for ending the war, while no...
vincing, is an attempt to bridge the unbridgeable ...
draw without seeming to withdraw, or to "win" ...
paying the terrible price that such a pyrrhic victor...
continue to cost. Like so many other concerned Am...
cans, he would like to seek a "middle way out" that w...
leave our honor intact. But mistakes of the magnitude of
Vietnam are not so easily rectified, and it may well be
that the only alternative to the continuing violence that
is destroying both Vietnams, taking the lives of so many
Americans and Vietnamese, and intensifying the social
crisis within our own society may be a withdrawal which
even such a wise critic as Reischauer still finds hard to
contemplate.

war that cannot be won, that the American people are fed up with, and that no one is quite sure how we ever got into.

We are now in the "I must have been really drunk last night to have done that" stage of the war, the morning-after when it is hard to remember how we ended up where we did, or what possibly could have been on our minds along the way. It is a moment when we want to listen to someone who was there when it happened, but remained sober through it all. It is time to demystify the war, and perhaps no one is better equipped for the task than Chester Cooper, an old Asia hand whose service in government stretches from the 1954 Geneva conference on Indochina right through to the present impasse in Paris. Perched high in the upper strata of the foreign-policy bureaucracy, he was there when the whole thing happened, and like a true professional, he tells it the way he saw it—a foreign policy uncluttered by moral issues, a Vietnam without tears.

Some may find such an approach insensitive, but diplomats are not paid to be indignant. They are profession-als whose job it is to carry out, or occasionally impede, policies made higher up. The policy makers, those who orchestrated our interventions in Vietnam and elsewhere have not been consumed by indignation or carried away by paroxysms of moral fervor. They were sober men con-ducting a foreign policy which, however aberrant it may now seem, was based on very real principles: the division of the world between communists and non-communists, and the determination to preserve existing ideological boundaries—by force of arms where need be. Vietnam was a logical result of that policy. It became important only because that was where the policy finally broke down.

Chester Cooper is an engaging and eloquent guide through the ruins of that failure. With skill, learning, wit and a felicitous literary style he traces our involvement in Vietnam through its various phases, from our aid to the Vietminh during the Japanese occupation, through the decision to aid the French and later prop up Ngo Dinh

Diem, and finally down the slippery slope with LBJ to full-scale war, ending with the interminable talkathon in Paris. His historical reconstruction of American involvement in Vietnam, replete with forgotten statements of various officials over the past twenty years, and rich in personal observation, is an impressive achievement.

What makes *The Lost Crusade* so special, however, is that it shows us the war from inside the national-security bureaucracy.

From this vantage point he deals with the numerous ill-fated peace initiatives, and particularly with the fiasco that occurred during Kosygin's trip to London when Harold Wilson was prepared to serve as intermediary for a peace plan that the White House had no intention of carrying out. It was just one of many such failures. Cooper believes that while some of the administration's peace feelers may have been for real, others, like the bombing pause of January, 1966, "were primarily for the purpose of improving the American image." He offers convincing evidence that the President and his chief advisers—Rostow, Rusk and Taylor—"seemed to have a bombing hang-up," and were continually scheduling raids on North Vietnam just as peace emissaries were arriving in Hanoi, or as intermediaries were tying up delicate negotiations. But probably these would have come to naught anyway, for Cooper admits there was "no great mystery why . . . the North Vietnamese were wary and skeptical . . . [for] many of Washington's plans for a 'political solution' involved, for all practical purposes, a negotiated surrender by the North Vietnamese." That, in fact, is pretty much where we stand today.

One of Cooper's great virtues is that he has no obvious axe to grind. Although sufficiently important to pass on the latest United States word to foreign leaders and to be summoned to midnight briefings, he was not a key policy maker. Vietnam was not his personal disaster. More than an eavesdropper in the corridors of power, he was rather a courier, serving first this President and then that one, carrying out policies that often made little sense in order to secure objectives that seemed dubiously desirable. An intelligent man who kept his ears open, Cooper had a distinguished diplomatic career that led to an important job in quasi-governmental research for the Institute for Defense Analyses.

It is not surprising that *The Lost Crusade* has been hailed by both hawks and doves, for Cooper manages the rare feat of showing us why everything went wrong, without ever questioning the assumptions of those who were responsible for our Vietnam policy. While he criticizes some people for being overzealous, there are few harsh words and no villains. And no attempt to re-examine first principles. At all times Cooper remains above the noise of battle, the supreme bureaucrat amusing himself with word games at the interminable conferences he is obliged to attend, mildly frustrated by the higher-ups who are so intent on picking bombing targets that they have no time to think about policy, and occasionally piqued by those members of the press who seemed "eager to criticize and slow to appreciate the efforts of hard-working, underpaid, sincere officials." Sincere officials do not appreciate public interference in matters of policy.

Cooper reminds us that disasters like Vietnam are rarely one man's fault, that "the Vietnam war was not Lyndon Johnson's invention," but can be traced back to Eisenhower and Kennedy. As early as 1956 John F. Kennedy declared that "Vietnam represents the cornerstone of the free world in Southeast Asia, the keystone to the arch, the finger in the dike." It was Kennedy who first sent troops to Vietnam, who was infatuated with counter-insurgency and wanted to prove that "wars of national liberation" could be defeated by his Green Berets, and who in July 1963, declared, "We are not going to withdraw . . . for us to withdraw . . . would mean a collapse not only of South Vietnam but Southeast Asia."

Cooper is right in pointing out that Lyndon Johnson inherited "more than 'the dirty little war' in Vietnam. He inherited Kennedy's principal advisers on foreign affairs —Rusk, McNamara, Bundy and Taylor; he found himself with a 'commitment' of uncertain specificity and duration." The expansion of that commitment from a colonial operation involving 16,000 American troops to a major war with half a million men was, of course, his own responsibility.

But it is idle to assume that Kennedy, confronted as Johnson was with the imminent collapse of the Saigon regime, would have behaved differently. They were both soldiers in what Cooper calls the "American crusade to save the world from communism," and they both believed that American power had to be used to prevent the post-war ideological boundaries from shifting—even in areas where no threat to American security could be discerned. They were guardians of an informal empire of dependencies and client states.

The war rages on, but the illusions that nurtured it have been shattered. Cooper argues that for our own political tranquility we have to get out of Vietnam "with some semblance of grace"—his formula being an election which the communists may win, but which will at least give the American people the cold comfort that the war was fought for "free choice." Of such camouflages are armistices declared and treaties solemnly signed.

It is possible that the Vietnam war may finally come to a halt through just such a ruse, although it is not easy to see why Hanoi, the Vietcong, or the generals in Saigon should be so obliging. They have concerns more pressing than the sensitivities of the American electorate. But it is the diplomat's job to search for the cool way out, and if Cooper has no answers, he has shown us what the Vietnam war was like from the highest levels of a bureaucracy that never thought to question the logic of intervention until it failed.

Nixon's Inheritance

Richard Nixon inherits a mandate for change and a baleful legacy. Rarely has the need for change been more obvious or more urgent. Rarely has it been felt at so many layers of society: not simply among intellectuals and the tiny minority that concerns itself with foreign affairs, but even among those who normally have been content to leave such matters to professionals. The nation is ready, indeed eager, for a new look at America's involvements —at Vietnam, at NATO and the Alliance for Progress, at the quarantine of China and the old arguments for foreign aid, at the assumptions of nuclear deterrence and the policies of détente, at the relics of cold war and the unexamined premises of America's global role.

The situation is reminiscent of 1952, when Dwight D. Eisenhower was swept into office on a vague promise to end the Korean war and bring the nation back to some semblance of "normalcy." In that election, too, there was the feeling that the Democrats had been in power too long, that they had involved the nation in commitments that could not be honored at a price the people were willing to pay, that deep fissures within the society had grown unmanageable and dangerous. Yet Eisenhower's foreign policy proved to be not much different than Harry S. Truman's. He did, as promised, end the Korean war. But Truman had already begun the negotiations, even though it might have been politically difficult for him to carry them through without incurring the wrath of Republican fundamentalists. The major outlines of Eisenhower's foreign policy—NATO, the Truman Doctrine, foreign aid—were laid down by his predecessor. Eisenhower simply pursued them with a somewhat different style. Still, he did make possible a political truce that finished off Senator Joseph McCarthy, and, for all the sanctimony of Dulles' inflated rhetoric, managed to keep the nation at peace for eight years. His was an administration of consolidation and, in some senses, of retrenchment—precisely what the country needed and wanted in 1952.

By one of the ironies of history, Eisenhower's Vice President finds himself, perhaps somewhat to his own surprise, head of state. And the problems he faces are not unlike those of his former chief. By the same token, his approach to the great issues of foreign policy is as similar to that of Johnson as Eisenhower's was to that of Truman. He inherits a war whose purpose and methods he has never disavowed. Indeed, in 1954 (which, admittedly, was a long time ago when many people felt very differently) he argued in favor of United States military intervention on the side of the French to "save" Indochina. He is a firm supporter of NATO and of "Atlantic interdependence"; a convert to détente, though insisting on "negotiation from strength"; a believer in foreign aid and mutual defense treaties. He offers no new foreign policy, but rather an improved performance of the old one, resting on increased cooperation with allies. "What I call for is not a new isolationism," he said during the campaign. "It is a new internationalism in which America enlists its allies and its friends around the world in those struggles in which their interest is as great as is ours."

There is, at least on the surface, little here to give heart to the apostles of retrenchment and withdrawal. Nixon is a confirmed internationalist, indeed, an interventionist. During his campaign for election, however, he could hardly have failed to catch the popular mood of disenchantment, doubt, and impatience engendered by the Vietnam war—a mood that has spread to much of our foreign policy. Vietnam was not a major debating issue in the campaign. But this meant neither indifference, nor wide-scale public acceptance of the war. Rather it indicated that the war had become as politically undefinable as it has been militarily unwinnable. Hubert H. Humphrey could not attack a war he had spent most of his term as Vice President defending, nor did he make any serious attempt to justify it on grounds of national interest. Nixon, of course, did not defend the war, but neither could he attack it, since it was fought on premises he largely agrees with. The war had become an albatross. Yet the alternatives were so ambiguous and threatening to established positions that none of the major candidates could articulate, let alone propose, any. Nonetheless, these alternatives lurked in the background and everyone was aware of them.

It was assumed by the electorate, and by the candidates themselves, that the war had to be wound up early in the term of the next President. Otherwise he would find himself in Johnson's predicament: neglecting the nation's domestic crisis, incapable of governing effectively, and no doubt unable to run for reelection. Since the war cannot be won militarily, even by destroying North Vietnam, a political settlement, whatever its disguise, will in the long run be little more than a face-saving compromise. What is remarkable is that this has been generally accepted—not because it is desirable, but because it is unavoidable. The crusade in Asia has now come to be viewed, even by such ardent former crusaders as McGeorge Bundy and Robert S. McNamara, as a disastrous misadventure which ought to be concluded as quickly and unobtrusively as possible. Further, Nixon must not only end the war, but, as a corollary, he must conduct his foreign policy in such a way as to insure that there will be no more Vietnams. That is the great lesson of a foreign policy that has been exhausted and must now be entirely rethought.

By force of circumstances, Nixon will have to evolve a diplomacy based upon the supposition that the American people will simply not tolerate another Vietnam. This does not mean, as the Vietnam hawks would have it, that the nation would then be driven into isolationism. Nixon does not believe in it, and relatively few Americans consider it desirable or necessary. The most pacific doves favor some kind of intervention when it involves the survival of Israel or the tragedy of Biafra. The "taste for intervention," in Charles de Gaulle's uncharitable phrase, has become so elemental a part of America's attitude to the outside world during the past quarter-century that it is unlikely any President would—or could —completely reverse it. Certainly Nixon would not want to. For he is an interventionist by conviction, a member of the generation that grew up in World War II, when isolationism became a dirty word, and which in the early years of the cold war discovered how exhilarating and morally satisfying the exercise of international power could be. These are the people who, be they liberal Republicans or liberal Democrats, McGeorge Bundy or Walt Rostow, have held positions of high responsibility under both parties—the people who launched the Bay of Pigs, the occupation of the Dominican Republic, and the Vietnam war.

Thus Nixon is not going to revolutionize the nation's foreign policy because, given his view of the world, he does not think any revolution is necessary. He will be Johnson with a little less arrogance and, hopefully, a little less adventurism. Moreover, his margin for maneuver is not nearly so great as critics of our present diplomacy like to believe. The basic outlines were drawn more than 20 years ago and are not going to be erased overnight. During that time the vast majority of Americans became convinced not only that it was necessary for the United States to intervene throughout the world politically, economically, and when need be, militarily, but also that there was a moral imperative for doing so. The "American Empire," to use an abused but descriptive phrase, rests upon the conviction of most Americans that the world role of the United States is a beneficent one. In fact, without this conviction it would have been extremely difficult, if not virtually impossible, for the last four Presidents to have carried out their interventionist policies.

The mood, to be sure, is changing. While isolationism is not rife in the land, the number of Americans questioning the wisdom, if not the sincerity, of "what America is doing now around the world" has grown to serious proportions. This could not have occurred without the Vietnam war, and particularly if the war had not turned into such a costly stalemate. A good deal of sanctimony went down the drain in Vietnam, and even those who accept the premises of the war are touched by the stigma of its failure. Faith has been shaken, but not destroyed. The nation is ready for a new assessment of its purpose, a new definition of its responsibilities. This can be fairly basic—the McCarthy campaign indicated how willing perfectly average, unradical Americans are to contemplate rather "heretical" ideas about our foreign policy. These ideas simply must not be, or seem to be, revolutionary. That would raise fundamental questions about international responsibility and the morality of the nation-state that few citizens or politicians are willing to contemplate. Foreign policy needs an element of continuity, and the new scaffolding has to stand, unavoidably, on the old foundation.

Nixon inherits, first of all, nearly three-quarters of a million soldiers stationed in 30 countries, four regional defense alliances, mutual defense treaties with 42 nations, membership in 53 international organizations, and military or economic aid programs to nearly 100 nations. Put it all together and it leaves us, in James Reston's words, with "commitments the like of which no sovereign nation ever took on in the history of the world." In addition, of course, the new administration has to cope with a war which the mightiest military machine in the world has been unable to win and which so far has eluded an acceptable political solution.

The war, it goes without saying, is not viable—that is precisely why Johnson was put in a position where he dared not run for reelection, and why Nixon is President of the United States today. Since the Republicans cannot win the war either, they have little alternative but to end it on whatever decent terms they can get, and turn to other pressing, neglected matters. Primary among these, obviously, is the deteriorating condition of the nation's cities and the nation's psyche: the mounting insecurity and disaffection that expresses itself in racial fears, in anxiety over property, in suspicion and hatred of young people who refuse to play the game. Perhaps the Republicans cannot heal this wound, perhaps no one can. But unless it is healed, or at least some effort in that direction is made soon, prospects for the American Dream—what is left of it—are bleak indeed.

The new administration inherits an attitude toward American responsibility and American power that was a necessary corrective to the old excessive isolationism, but now has become encumbering and dangerous itself. It takes over a sense of mission about the uses of American power, the idea that the world would be a better place if it conformed to an American conception of virtue. Many nations succumb to a similar temptation. But the extraordinary power of America has transformed its sense of mission from a vision into a program, although an ill-defined and only half-recognized one. The power of this nation, to a degree not fully realized even by those in whose name it is employed, has been turned into an instrument for the pursuit of an American ideology. That ideology is not merely the defense of the nation, but something far more sweeping: the establishment of a world order on the American model. Its instruments are defense pacts and military bases, foreign aid and defense support, the economic power of the government and American business, and where other measures fail, American combat troops and American bombers.

The new administration inherits, in short, a commitment to intervention as an operative concept of American foreign policy. Within certain limits, intervention is, of course, perfectly proper and necessary. It was right for the United States to intervene in World War II to save

Europe from Nazi domination, just as it was right to intervene after the war to protect and help rebuild the demoralized nations of Western Europe. But this intervention for the military containment of a hostile great power was expanded, in the Truman Doctrine of 1947 and the policies that flowed from it, to a commitment to defend governments everywhere against direct or indirect aggression. In other words, what was a limited responsibility expanded into a global policy that could neither be defined nor restricted in terms of American interests. From the looseness of the Truman Doctrine there emerged a variety of carelessly conceived, dubiously valid pacts and pledges, glossing over the difference between communism as an ideology and communism as an instrument of Soviet power. These came to be treated as though they were virtually identical, thereby confounding the attempt to make a rational assessment of American security interests.

The United States has intervened deeply in the affairs of countries where our national interest was only remotely involved. This has been done in the name of freedom and the struggle against communism. But we have not intervened in a number of countries where freedom is a mockery, such as Saudi Arabia and Haiti; or where it is confined to a privileged few, as in Rhodesia and South Africa; or even where there was open communist aggression, as in Tibet, Hungary, and Czechoslovakia. In some cases we did not intervene because communists were not involved; and where communists were very much involved, as in Central Europe, we did not intervene because we feared the danger of igniting a third world war. In practice what this comes down to is not intervention against injustice, but intervention against communism—where Russian power and national interests are not directly threatened.

That is not a particularly noble policy, especially when one considers the rhetoric in which it is usually framed. But it could be thought of as a necessary or practical one under certain conditions. Unfortunately, those conditions assume that the Communist bloc is a unified conspiracy

directed from the Kremlin and intent upon world domination by, if need be, military means. Whether such assumptions were ever valid (and some, such as George
Kennan, have argued that they were not valid even in
the critical area of Central Europe), they are little more
than a historical anachronism today. The Communist
world has been dramatically split, first by the Russo-
Chinese rivalry, and then by the mounting assertions of
nationalism in Eastern Europe and in the communist
nations of Cuba, North Korea, and North Vietnam. What
is important is not the label a regime chooses to pin on
itself, but the policies it follows. Small communist nations are no threat to the United States nor, as we should
have learned from experience, are they likely to remain
satellites of Moscow or Peking for very long. We coexist
very well with totalitarian governments of the Right. We
can learn to coexist with totalitarian governments of the
Left as well, and let the Russians and the Chinese worry
about the purity of their ideology.

We have defined stability as anti-communism, and
thus we have been drawn into the suppression of progressive forces simply because communists have been
involved. Although it has not been our stated intention
to preserve the status quo, this has been the impact of
our policy. So long as we are mesmerized by communism as an ideology, it will be extremely difficult for us
both to accept the fact that even violent changes in the
status quo need not be hostile to our interests, and to
restrain our urge to suppress violent or even undemocratic movements of social transformation. In some instances violent or undemocratic change is the only way
that the modernization we incessantly advocate is likely
to take place. Regimes which have lost the support of
their own population, which cannot wrench them free
from the bondage of feudalism, which find their *raison
d'être* in the protection of the privileged minority, cannot be saved even by the world's mightiest military power.
That is the lesson of Vietnam, and we have had to learn
it the hard way.

Now that the lesson is painfully being learned, it is up

policy, but a change in direction. This must be so fundamental that it is difficult to see how it can be accomplished without a drastic reform of the nation's social structure and charismatic leadership of the kind few societies ever enjoy or long tolerate. The nation must right the social imbalance that still concentrates power in the hands of the very rich at the expense of the poor, some of whom do not even realize the degree of their exploitation; launch a determined assault on racism that will uproot traditional attitudes and even the structure of our society; find a quality (though not a policy) of leadership similar to that exercised by de Gaulle when he assumed power in a country shaken by revolt; and give conscious recognition of the degree to which much of our foreign policy is rooted in economic and military imperialism. Without recognition there can be no change, and without enlightened leadership there is unlikely to be adequate recognition.

An enlightened foreign policy would require an attitude of tolerance, rather than hostility, toward violent revolutions—even where communists are actively involved or in the vanguard. A few American corporations will suffer, and vestigial attitudes about communism will be shaken. But the national interest of the United States is unlikely to be harmed even if revolutionary governments come to power in much of Latin America—as one did in Mexico more than 50 years ago. Revolution in backward countries is no threat to the United States. The attempt to suppress revolution, however, as we should have learned from the Dominican Republic and Vietnam, involves a threat to the survival of American democracy. The willingness to tolerate progressive-minded revolutionary regimes—however unsympathetic we may find their methods or their political rhetoric—means coming to terms with the whole problem of development in the Third World. It means recognizing that the development process will be nasty, brutish, and long, that democracy may be a political luxury for many such countries, and that the rich nations are going to have to return, in the

to the new administration to apply it with intelligence and dispatch. Intelligence because it must be discriminating, dispatch because it would be exceedingly dangerous to drift along with reflex commitments that are no longer intellectually supportable.

Some elements are worth salvaging: the alliance with Western Europe; the effort, half-hearted though it may be, to aid the underdeveloped world; the limitation on nuclear proliferation; the détente with the Soviet Union. Yet even these worthy objectives are becoming outmoded, or are in a bad state of disrepair. NATO is clearly on its last legs and needs to be succeeded by some less antiquated conception of America's relations with Western Europe. Since neither the United States nor its allies have shown any serious desire to transform NATO into an "Atlantic federation," it has to relinquish some of its more pretentious ambitions and come to terms with the realities of a fragmented, increasingly nationalistic Europe. This means that it must be turned into a more equitable partnership, with the Europeans assuming a continually greater share of the burden of their own defense, or else it must give way to a simple mutual guarantee pact, with the United States pledging itself to defend Western Europe against Soviet attack by whatever methods seem most appropriate.

The latter alternative is not nearly so attractive to the Europeans as the present situation, in which the United States provides both the nuclear deterrent and a powerful land army in West Germany. But American patience is likely to give out even before the balance of payments requires a massive reduction of troop forces in Europe. When that day comes—and it has already been postponed too long—the Europeans will either have to pool their resources in some meaningful way to provide for their own defense, or rely on an American nuclear guarantee that is not supported by American hostages on the Continent. The smaller European countries are not ready to pull out of NATO, for they prefer American leadership to French or German dominance. But the usefulness of the alliance to the United States is diminishing, and now that the Atlantic Treaty is more than 20 years old it is time for the new administration to conduct a long-overdue reassessment.

The Atlantic alliance has been based upon an identity of interests basically limited to the military field. The United States is determined that Western Europe be kept out of Soviet hands. Once that is assured, it is possible to reach various economic, political, and even military agreements that are not necessarily identical with the common interests of the European allies. The Europeans, however, have more than their defense to worry about. They are concerned about the "American challenge" in business and industry, the attempt to achieve economic and political integration, the eventual reunification of the Continent, and Europe's place between two great but unstable empires.

While seeking to maintain the old ties with Western Europe, the new administration is eager to expand the détente with the Soviet Union. Washington's allies have a vested interest in the détente; they also fear that it may be sustained at the price of the indefinite partition of Europe. The superpowers, though, are motivated by the internal mechanics of their own imperial positions, and are learning that cooperation is the price of survival. The hands-off policy toward one another's aggressions (Czechoslovakia, Dominican Republic), the nuclear nonproliferation treaty, the attempt, albeit feeble, to keep the arms race from getting totally out of control—all these are essential if the two relatively satiated superpowers are not to destroy one another. We can expect the new administration to be driven by circumstances into continued cooperation with the Soviet Union.

There is always the danger, naturally, that the Kremlin leadership, which has lately shown signs of instability (as, for that matter, has the entire American political system), will try to upset the present political balance by some sudden act of *force majeure,* that it will provoke reckless moves by its wards in the Middle East or elsewhere, or that there will be a rapprochement with China. Any of these would imperil, if not destroy, the détente

and the whole policy responsible for it. Ye an eventuality, the wiser course, the only vi to proceed on the assumption that cooperatio Soviet Union is possible and desirable.

Just as there is a danger that the Russians n the present balance—whether from an exubei ligerence or from an alarmed defensiveness—the great a danger that the United States may do the If the new administration proves incapable of ke in check what an inspired Eisenhower speech writ ferred to as the "military-industrial complex," if it to press for the kind of absolute military superiority Nixon sometimes referred to in his campaign speech if it falls victim to the same bloated rhetoric and liber self-delusion that haunted the Kennedy and Johnso administrations, if it fails to understand that the cold war with Russia is over and that from here on in even the most advanced industrial societies will be preoccupied with the effort to hold themselves together, then we are in for serious trouble.

It is questionable whether the Nixon administration is up to the task. The foreign policy it carries out, like the policies of its predecessors, will almost certainly be imperialistic. It would be virtually impossible for the United States, with its present economic, political, and social structure, to carry out any other kind of foreign policy. But the Republicans may not delude themselves into believing that their imperialism is necessarily good for everyone it affects. And in this case skepticism may be the first step toward restraint. If the new administration can provide a breathing space between the wars of intervention against communism abroad and the coming guerrilla wars against racism and exploitation within America itself, it will have served a useful function. If it addresses itself to the root causes of the domestic crisis, it could even pave the way for a government, for a concept of community responsibility, that might blunt the edge of domestic guerrilla warfare, and perhaps make it unnecessary.

What is ultimately at stake is not simply a change in

form of development assistance, some of the booty they have extracted from the nonindustrialized ones.

The great problems of foreign policy in the next decade will be those of seeking withdrawal from dangerously overextended positions without succumbing to the mentality of isolationism; of learning to live with revolution in the Third World; of narrowing the dangerous gap between the privileged minority in the Northern Hemisphere and the exploited majority in the underdeveloped nations; of controlling nuclear weapons; of achieving new methods of international cooperation going beyond the war-inducing confines of the nation-state; of accepting a relationship with the Soviet Union and other major powers based on limited cooperation and continued antagonism over a wide range of issues; and of liberating ourselves from the deep-rooted social and political anxieties that are expressed in an emotional hatred of communism and an instinctual fear of revolution.

The hardest, but perhaps the most important, task of the new administration will be to create a climate that will permit a retrenchment from the self-deluding fantasies of global intervention, while making it possible to attack the fundamental causes of disorder and disaffection at home. On the success of this task hangs not only the fate of the Nixon administration, but of the nation itself.

No More Vietnams?

Yesterday's heresy becomes today's cliché. What a few years ago would have been labeled as isolationist, if not vaguely traitorous, is now the new orthodoxy. "We cannot impose ideals on others and still call ourselves men of peace," President Nixon has declared, in outlining a new low posture for the United States and a scaling down of foreign commitments. This is a far cry from John Kennedy's summons to "pay any price, bear any burden, meet any hardship, support any friend, oppose any foe to assure the survival and the success of liberty" anywhere in the world. And it is welcome deflation from Lyndon Johnson's proclamation in the Inaugural Address of January 1965 that "the American covenant called on us to help show the way for the liberation of man."

After Vietnam, the Dominican Republic, and the Greek junta, it is not so easy for an American President to speak with a straight face of the nation's foreign policy being based on the "liberation of man" or the "survival of liberty." The self-glorifying rhetoric of the 1960s has given way to a more studied pragmatism based on the old concepts of self-interest and balance of power. "Our interests," President Nixon has told us, "must shape our commitments, rather than the other way around." Although his actions often belie his words, he recognizes that the nation is fed up with self-assumed obligations to set the world right and with undeclared wars conducted under the tattered banners of a discredited globalism.

No more Vietnams is what the public wants. Yet it is not enough to say that we made a mistake and won't do it again. Most people still believe that the war in Vietnam is some kind of aberration, an event totally without precedent in our national history, and one that will never happen again. But this is to ignore Korea, Lebanon, and Cuba. What is unique about Vietnam is not the fact of our intervention, but its scale. It has already cost some $100 billion, tied down three-quarters of a million men around Southeast Asia, and taken more casualties than the Korean war. Did we stumble into it by accident? Hardly. The war was a result of a succession of conscious political decisions made by three successive American Presidents. Rather than a new departure in our way of looking at the world, it was quite consistent with the unexpressed principles of our foreign policy. Vietnam happened because it was time for it to happen, because we had the military power to make it happen.

Vietnam is precisely the kind of war the American military machine, as perfected in the mid-1960s, was designed to fight. When he came to power, John F. Kennedy inherited a military strategy based on "massive retaliation" with nuclear weapons. Clearly such a strategy was ineffective in dealing with the revolutionary disturbances shaking the Third World and imperiling American influence in such areas as the Caribbean and Southeast Asia. The ability to fight "limited war," Kennedy told Congress in a special defense message in March 1961, should be the "primary mission" of our overseas forces. An avid reader of the manuals of Mao and Che, Kennedy believed that guerrillas had to be met on their own terrain if forces of "national liberation" were to be defeated. Robert McNamara was brought in to reorganize the Pentagon and set up amphibious strike forces. In such cold-war intellectuals as Walt Rostow, Maxwell Taylor, Roger Hilsman, and Richard Bissell, Kennedy found zealous advocates for the new counter-guerrilla warfare. Kennedy ordered the expansion of the Special Forces training center at Fort Bragg, and, over the Army's objections, reinstated the green beret as the symbol of the new counter-guerrilla elite force. In the fall of 1961, General Taylor head of the Counter-Insurgency Committee, went to Vietnam with Walt Rostow and returned urging increased American intervention, including a military task force. In December Kennedy ordered the military build-up to begin.

The arms race took a dramatic jump during the next few years. Billions of dollars flowed into the Pentagon to increase American nuclear superiority and to provide weapons to fight insurrectionary movements in the Third World. The liberals around Kennedy believed they had a mission to bring about an American-style peace based upon political stability and economic development. They saw the underdeveloped nations achieving "take-off" points to economic growth through infusions of foreign aid and technical expertise. And they were convinced that world peace and American security demanded an ideological balance of power. They were ready to intervene wherever necessary to maintain that balance. American military power—both nuclear missiles and conventional forces— had been increased precisely for that purpose. After the Cuban missile crisis of October 1962, when they took the world to the brink of nuclear war and successfully faced down the Russians, they were ready to intervene wherever it seemed necessary.

Vietnam provided the opportunity in the guise of an obligation. Although American intervention in Vietnamese affairs extended back to the early 1950s, Eisenhower had clearly set the limits of American assistance to Saigon. The liberal interventionists, however, were eager to show that wars of national liberation would not pay. Vietnam was their showcase. When Diem failed to live up to their expectations, and when his brother showed signs of political independence verging on talks with the North Vietnamese, the right-wing generals were allowed to get rid of him. With the murder of Diem the legitimacy of the Siagon regime was undermined. This was followed shortly by Kennedy's assassination and the intensified American commitment to an anti-communist government in Saigon.

By the time of Lyndon Johnson's electoral triumph, on a platform of peace and social reform, the Pentagon was ready for the full-scale military intervention that had been engineered in the White House. "McNamara's prodigious labors to strengthen and broaden the U.S. military posture were about completed," according to Townsend Hoopes, a Pentagon official who turned against the war, ". . . U.S. 'general purpose' forces were now organized to intervene swiftly and with modern equipment in conflicts of limited scope, well below the nuclear threshold." In February 1965 Johnson began the bombing of North Vietnam, in June American troops were officially authorized to enter combat, and in July the President ordered an increase in American forces from 75,000 to 125,000. Within four years Kennedy's 15,000 "advisers" had swollen to an American expeditionary force of half a million men, and the Vietnamese civil war became an American war. As the economist Joseph Schumpeter wrote of ancient Egypt's military forces, "created by wars that required it, the machine now created the wars it required."

We intervened from a euphoria of power, generated in part by our success in the Cuban missile crisis and our military superiority over the Russians. The liberals wanted to prove that guerrilla wars were not the wave of the future, and were determined to keep South Vietnam as an anti-communist outpost in Southeast Asia. But they grossly underestimated the price. As the cost of intervention mounted, so the rhetoric rose to meet the occasion. What began as a military-aid program to a harassed neo-colonial outpost that had been abandoned by the French and picked up by Dulles was transformed into a full-scale war. The very scale of our intervention transformed the Vietnamese civil war into a test of American resolve. By our intervention we created the problem that was used to justify our involvement.

As the scale of war increased, so Washington sought various theories to explain why it was worth the cost. First it was to help our friends in the South deal with communist-led insurgents. Then it was to push back an "aggression" from the North, although Hanoi's troops did not enter the war until after the American intervention. We were there, it was said, to honor our treaty commitments, although the SEATO treaty provided only for consultation in case of attack, or to stop that amorphous but virulent force known simply as "Asian communism," or even to prevent the miraculously amphibious Chinese from invading southern California and speeding east along the interstate highway system. Vietnam, we were told, was a test case for wars of national liberation, and if the Vietcong were defeated, guerrillas from the Andes to the Sahara would turn in their rifles and slink home. In a moment of desperation, Lyndon Johnson even evoked the principle of envy, declaring that "what we've got they want" thereby suggesting that we are in Vietnam to defend electric carving knives and remote control TV from the greedy hands of the Vietcong. Later, President Nixon, pursuing Johnson's policies while changing his tactics, again trotted out the balance of power theory, saying that to abandon the Saigon generals "would threaten our long-term hopes for peace in the world."

Nearly a year after assuming office with a promise to end the war, President Nixon presented a plan which called for the gradual withdrawal of American combat troops and their replacement by South Vietnamese soldiers. The plan was tendered as a supplement to the peace talks in Paris between the United States and North Vietnam. Yet it was clearly meant as an alternative to negotiations, since no nation would reduce its military power in the field while conducting negotiations on its own withdrawal.

Vietnamization cleverly defused popular opposition to the war by withdrawing some of the troops while retaining the bases and the commitment to an anti-communist South Vietnam. Its drawback, as Hoopes observed, was that it committed the American people "to the endless support of a group of men in Saigon who represented nobody but themselves, preferred war to the risks of a political settlement, and could not remain in power more than a few months without our large-scale assistance." Yet what could the American people do about it? In the elections of 1964 and 1968 they twice voted for peace, first in rejecting Barry Goldwater and electing a man who said he would not send American boys to die in Vietnam, and then in repudiating the Humphrey-Johnson administration. Both times their wishes were ignored by Presidents who circumvented Constitutional restrictions and pursued the war on their own authority for reasons they declared to be vital to the national interest.

If elections cannot change foreign policy, what is the validity of the political process? If Americans can be sent to die in battle as a result of decisions made by the executive branch, what is the meaning of the Constitutional obligation of Congress to declare acts of war? Traditional politics no longer provides a solution for political ills or implements the popular will. This has led to an increasing emphasis on direct action, on popular participation, on decentralization, and, when all else seems to fail, on violence. Unable to affect the decisions that control their lives—whether they be on the wars they die in, the polluted air they breathe, or the schools where their children fail to receive an education—the American people are driven to strike out against bureaucracy and many of the very principles of government that they have been trained to take for granted.

There has been a crisis of faith in the political process, just as there has been in the realm of science and technology. We have learned that technology destroys even as it creates, and that its gifts, such as DDT and the internal-combustion engine, are bought with our own lives. Our faith in man's future has been shaken as we realize that in the name of progress the very forces that make possible human life on the earth are being tam-

pered with and perhaps inadvertently destroyed. In our
political life, as in our personal lives, we are repelled by
the cult of bigness, and are turning, more in desperation
than in hope, to various forms of decentralization. Those
who once believed that only big government could solve
the problems of a complex society now put an equally
abiding faith in the virtues of the local community.

Both radicals and reactionaries profess to find salvation in local control, the former in flight from the
technology and the war machine that are oppressing
their lives, the latter in an effort to hold on to the old
ways. To both the Right and the Left, government itself
has become a kind of enemy, and faith in political solutions has broken down. The whole society is pervaded by
a deep and destructive sense of powerlessness. Among
conservatives this feeling seeks its outlet against those
who threaten the established order—hippies, dropouts,
militants. These are the people who chant that they love
Mayor Daley and applaud police violence against young
demonstrators. Among radicals this alienation and powerlessness results in desperate attempts to change unresponsive institutions. The universities, of course, are the
obvious targets because there the ideals of community
seem most betrayed by arbitrary and unresponsive ad-
ministrators. This feeling was well expressed by the
student newspaper at the Santa Barbara campus of the
University of California, following rioting, mass arrests,
and destruction: "If we have any community at all, it is
a community based on common frustrations—born of
powerlessness, alienation from one's pre-programmed life,
and contempt for authoritarian institutions." It is a
complaint that even conservatives could share, for it is a
common American condition.

Vietnam intensified, although it did not create, this
sense of powerlessness, of being unable to affect the
decisions that can, literally, mean the difference between
life and death. The war took perfectly decent young
Americans, taught them to use napalm and machine
guns, sent them across the world to a totally alien society
with instructions to kill "communists," and justified this

in the name of freedom. It is not surprising that some of our most sensitive young people, rather than fight a war they consider morally wrong, have preferred to go to jail or seek a saner life in another country. Nor is it even surprising that atrocities like those at Songmy have occurred, for the kind of war we are fighting in Vietnam is a brutalizing experience. It infects everything we do, and comes back to haunt us at home. We were all at Songmy, in one way or another.

There is a great revulsion in this country against the rhetorical globalism of the past two decades. A Harris poll taken early in 1970 showed six out of ten people saying Vietnam was a terrible mistake, with a full one-third volunteering that "we should mind our own business and stop policing the world." In these results the pollsters found "overtones of a new isolationism." No doubt Americans are tired of the violence that has been committed in the name of peace, of the two wars fought since 1950 for objectives that seem increasingly specious and hypocritical, of the unending interventions that are conducted in the tired vocabulary of anti-communism, of the sacrifice of their own social needs to an insatiable war machine that declares itself to be the repository of patriotism. No doubt they see no reason why more money should be spent on MIRVs and ABMs when America and Russia have already stockpiled nuclear weapons with the explosive power of fifteen tons of TNT for every man, woman, and child on earth. But the people have always wanted peace, and they rarely get it—particularly when their leaders believe they have the power to obtain what they want by force of arms.

America is not aggressive by nature. As great powers go, it has been relatively restrained in its use of force. But it has undeniably used its power aggressively, not only in Vietnam, but in the Spanish-American war, and in seizing half of Mexico in the war of 1848. So long as that power is untempered, it will be used whenever military and political leaders think it should be used. So long as we have a military machine anywhere near its present size, it will always find work for itself to do. It will have bases to defend in one or another of the various unstable and revolution-prone countries of the Third World. It will issue solemn assurances, as Air Force generals did in Vietnam early in 1965, that a few well-placed bombs will take care of revolutionaries and communists. And there will be government officials, on loan from corporations and universities, who will tell us that American military intervention is necessary for something noble-sounding like stability or self-determination.

After Korea everyone said there would be no more Koreas. And there weren't. But there was Vietnam. Now it is a cliché to say there will be no more Vietnams. And there probably won't be—in Vietnam. But unless our military power to fight counter-revolutionary wars is reduced, and unless our attitudes change, there might very well be further American military interventions in Asia and the Caribbean. Even while President Nixon asserted that our allies should be able to defend themselves, he declared regarding Asia that "we shall provide a shield if a nuclear power threatens the freedom of a nation allied with us, or of a nation whose security we consider vital to our security and the security of the region as a whole." We are allied with forty-two nations and, judging from past behavior, consider virtually every non-communist country in the world as being vital to our security. Does that mean we are supposed to go to war whenever the President considers it "vital"? Who gave him the authority to provide nuclear shields for whatever Asian nations he desires? Even while saying there must be no more Vietnams, the administration conducted a covert war in Laos and invaded Cambodia without bothering to inform its government or the American Congress.

The legacy of globalism still weighs heavily on American foreign policy. Having intervened actively for thirty years, it has become almost a reflex action. Whenever there is talk of retrenching commitments, the global interventionists raise the specter of isolationism. They say that the experience of Vietnam may induce us to turn inward and ignore our responsibilities to the rest of the world. The danger is exaggerated. With the world's most powerful economy and mightiest military force, the United States could never again be isolationist. Regardless of how many Americans might desire it, the nation's economic and political interests make it impossible.

Yet it might not be a bad thing if we did ignore some of our self-assumed "responsibilities" for building democratic, capitalistic nations out of feudal societies. The results of isolationism could, in most cases, hardly be much worse than the results of our interventionism, which, except for Europe, have ranged from the stupid, as in Lebanon, Cuba, and the Dominican Republic, to the tragic, as in Vietnam. They have brought no credit on us, nor have they appreciably advanced the causes of freedom and self-determination we are ostensibly promoting. It long ago became obvious, even before Tet and Songmy, that the best thing we could have done for the Vietnamese was to have left them alone.

By now it is a truism to say that we ought to set our own house in order before we declare ourselves responsible for the welfare of the entire world. It might even be said that we don't have any idea of what the welfare of other societies might be, and not very much understanding of how to improve our own. The emphasis is now on national priorities and on saving this country from drowning in its own pollution, or turning into a police state, or descending into the savagery of a race war. But powerful voices like President Nixon's still cling to the old rhetoric and warn us of the disasters that would occur "If America were to become a dropout in assuming the responsibility for defending peace and freedom in the world."

It is questionable that such disasters would occur, since outside of Western Europe (and in such countries as Greece and Portugal, not even there) the United States has not been occupied in defending peace and freedom. It has simply sought to maintain the status quo and prevent revolutionary groups, particularly those led or thought to be led by communists, from coming to power. The moral imperatives of our foreign policy, our interventions in support of self-serving oligarchies and military strongmen, have never fooled anyone but ourselves. America is not going to be a dropout in defending her own interests. No nation is, if it has the strength to do otherwise. But America would do well to cease the hypocrisy which seeks to justify its interventions in the name of a higher morality. Then it might be easier for our officials, not to mention the public they are supposed to be serving, to distinguish between interventions necessary to defend the United States and its most intimate allies, and those which spring from a euphoria of power.

No more Vietnams? It would be unwise to take any bets on it. The heady rhetoric of the 1960s has been deflated, but great power still provides an irresistible temptation. There will be a danger of more Vietnams until there is a world power balance that will make such unilateral interventions far more hazardous. Only then are we likely truly to have "our interests . . . shape our commitments, rather than the other way around." Undeniably we have learned something from Vietnam. But it may be simply that we should never again intervene in Vietnam.

Vietnam has not caused our troubles, but it has clearly intensified them and made Americans aware of their severity. It is not only the ideals of the nation that are being tested, but its very survival as a free society. Our power has not brought us security, any more than our wealth has brought us tranquility. Nor have the noble ideals on which this nation was founded insured social justice for the millions of Americans who, because of race, or poverty, or misfortune, have been excluded from the system and the benefits it is supposed to provide. The dispossessed are now finding a voice, and their cause is being taken up by young idealists on campuses and elsewhere who, despite the hostility of their elders and mounting repression by the authorities, maintain a persistent belief that the promise of American life can be made real to all Americans.

For more than three decades this country has been absorbed in foreign affairs, foreign aid, and foreign wars.

We may not have very many more years to preserve our own divided society and help create with others a tolerable international order free from the fear of instant obliteration. Having failed to reform the world, we can now turn to the more important task of saving this nation from betraying its ideals, and insuring that "man's last, best hope," survives the elusive quest for empire.

Index

About the Author

RONALD STEEL was born in Morris, Illinois, and has degrees from Northwestern University and Harvard. As a foreign service officer, he served in Washington and the Middle East. Mr. Steel has lived in Europe and has traveled extensively on the Continent and in North Africa. He was a Congressional Fellow of the American Political Science Association. In 1964 he published *The End of Alliance*, a study of America's relations with Europe, and in 1967, the highly acclaimed *Pax Americana*, which Henry Steele Commager called, "the most thorough, the most ardent, and to my mind, the most persuasive critique of American foreign policy over the last twenty years that has yet appeared." *Pax Americana* won the 1967 Sidney Hillman award for nonfiction. In 1970–1971 Ronald Steel was Paskus Fellow at Jonathan Edwards College at Yale University. He is currently ingaged in writing the biography of Walter Lippmann.